For Martin,
With much respect
and appreciation for
educating & entertaining
us. I hope you enjoy
this book.
Best wishes –
JOHN TCHEN
10.01

John Kuo Wei Tchen

New York before Chinatown

Orientalism and
the Shaping of
American Culture
1776–1882

The Johns Hopkins University Press

Baltimore & London

Frontispiece:
"A Night Scene in the Bowery,
New York," *Harper's Weekly,* Feb. 26, 1881.
(Wong Ching Foo Collection)

© 1999 The Johns Hopkins University Press
All rights reserved. Published 1999
Printed in the United States of America
on acid-free paper

2 4 6 8 9 7 5 3 1

The Johns Hopkins University Press
2715 North Charles Street
Baltimore, Maryland 21218-4363
www.press.jhu.edu

Library of Congress Cataloging-in-
Publication Data will be found at the
end of this book.
A catalog record for this book is available
from the British Library.

ISBN 0-8018-6006-7

Go back; look at the baby in his mother's arms; see how the outside world is first reflected in the still hazy mirror of his mind. . . . Only then will you understand the origin of the prejudices, habits, and passions which are to dominate his life.

—Alexis de Tocqueville

If I am not what I've been told I am, then it means that *you're* not what you thought *you* were *either!*

—James Baldwin

CONTENTS

ILLUSTRATIONS

I was born of a twisted fate. If it were not for racism, I would not be alive right now. My parents said they took the last boat out of Shanghai as the Red Army was entering the city. My four older brothers and sisters were already studying at midwestern universities, and after a brief sojourn in Hong Kong and Taiwan, my parents were able to obtain visitors' visas for the United States. With the exclusion of Chinese still in effect, they decided to secure their permanent-resident status by having me. This story, while an intensely personal one, is actually prototypic of the Asian American experience. What unites otherwise extremely diverse individuals, groups, and sensibilities is a shared legacy of racially defined foreignness. The history of Chinese in the Americas and of Chinese Americans takes its shape from permutations in the construction of this "alien" status.

This history is made up from discarded fragments—a census entry here, a drawing there, a suggestive hand-written letter somewhere else—that do not fit into any established narratives yet give us the potential to see American history with fresh insight. Walter Benjamin, the German Jewish analyst of modernity, described the surviving shards of the past as "fragments of true historical experience which have been scattered by an explosion." These "fossils" of the past, when scrupulously studied, become "a flashing image" that can bring critical insights to the linkages between the past and the present.[1]

Can such pieces of detritus be sorted out and fashioned into a history? It is necessary work, for as Fei Xiaotong, the University of Chicago–trained Chinese sociologist, once observed, this nation is "a land without ghosts," a place where people are so busy with promises of progress that they have forgotten where they come from and who their ancestors were.[2] I write this book with the faith that we, as citizens of the United States, the Americas, and the world, can live with and learn from our ghosts in order to work together for a more just and democratic future.

The pioneering writer and community builder Louis Chu said that he wrote *Eat a Bowl of Tea* on the subway. Relying on my trusty computer, I cannot claim such a distinction. However, this book was very much written in transit between different parts of my life. And the true pleasure of working on such a manuscript is the people one meets along the way.

This book was initially conceived while I was still on staff at the New York Chinatown History Project, now called the Museum of Chinese in the Americas. It was researched and written as a Ph.D. dissertation while my parents' health was slipping away, while my partner Judy was pregnant and our Sara came into the world, and while I was working at the Asian/American Center and the Department of Urban Studies of Queens College, City University of New York. And it was completed at Asian/Pacific/American Studies at New York University. This book, therefore, was squeezed into my life while I was working as a cultural activist and public historian, mourning the passing of my parents, and delighting in the ebullient spirit of my daughter.

In transit, I've accumulated countless debts too numerous to acknowledge fully here. Thanks go to my former collaborators at the Museum of Chinese in the Americas, especially Fay Chew, Steve Chin, Paul Calhoun, Adrienne Cooper, Jim Dao, Bud Glick, Yuet-fung Ho, Charlie Lai, Lamgen Leon, Mary Lui, Judith Luk, and Dorothy Fujita Rony; my former colleagues at the Asian/American Center of Queens College, who include Roger Sanjek, Ruby Danta, Joe Doyle, Madhulika Khandelwal, Margo Machida, and Wu Hong; and my current colleagues at A/P/A Studies at NYU, who include Tomo Geron, Swati Khurana, Risa Morimoto, and many other faculty and students. In addition to all the support above, a Professional Staff Congress–City University of New York grant and financial support from Dean Philip Furmanski at NYU have made the research and completion of this manuscript possible.

I would like to thank the following library and archival staff for helping me with good cheer and patience: the Research Division of the New York Public Library, the Billy Rose Theater Collection of the New York Public Library at Lincoln Center, the Music Division of the Library of Congress, the North Carolina State Archives, the Rare Books and Manuscripts Collection of the University of North Carolina at Chapel Hill, the Stewart Culin Papers at the Brooklyn Museum of Art, the New York City Municipal Archives, the Barnum Museum in Bridgeport, Conn., the Ronald G. Becker Collection at Syracuse University, the Library of the Peabody Museum of Salem, the New York Society Library, the Library Company of Philadelphia, and the Theater Collection of the Museum of the City of New York.

My appreciation also goes to all the following individuals who have gone out of their way to help me find valuable research materials: Bruce Abrams and Joe Van Nostrand at the Office of New York County Clerk were wonderfully generous with their time and nonbureaucratic in their demeanor; Deborah Gardner, while working on her own project, helped identify and provide me with materials from the New-York Historical Society; Roy Goodman of the American Philosophical Society in Philadelphia was very generous with his time and was good company to have a lager with; Norman Brouwer of the South Street Seaport Museum Library shared his files on the *Keying* with me; Ralph Sessions located a pair of male and female shop figures for a tea store; Mary Witkowski of the Bridgeport Public Library kindly took time out to show me her impressive collection of posters; William Sherman of the National Archives helped me find crew lists for the port of New York; Donna Lamb and Stephan Haimowitz of the New York State Office of Mental Health made it possible for me to look at the records of Quimbo Appo with a minimum of red tape; Jonathan Goldstein shared information about Nathan Dunn's Chinese Museum; Arthur Bonner generously shared his exhaustive newspaper clipping research for his book *Alas! What Brought Thee Hither? The Chinese in New York, 1800–1950*; Julia Sharpe of the Mount Airy County Library introduced me to descendants of the Bunker families; Gretchen Worden of the fabulous Mütter Museum gave me a personal tour of nineteenth-century medical practices as they related to the Bunker twins; and Mary Gallagher and Elizabeth Nuxoll of the Papers of Robert Morris, Queens College, have been an ongoing source of insights and information about the American China trade. Finally, my thanks go to some wonderful people in Mount Airy, North Carolina: Tanya Reese, Dorothy Haymore, and Ruth Minnick provided me, in their stories and their hospitality, with insights as to why Chang and Eng found this part of the world so inviting.

I have benefited in many different ways from the suggestions and comments of the faculty of New York University, especially Patricia Bonomi, Barbara Kirshenblatt-Gimblett, Karen Kupperman, Carl Prince, Dave Reimers, Danny Walkowitz, Susan Ware, Annette Weiner, and Marilyn Young. I also want to thank Dan Czitrom, Evelyn Hu-DeHart, Timothy Gilfoyle, Ron Grele, Gene Lebovics, Ben Lee, Larry Levine, Lisa Lowe, Sucheta Mazumdar, Gary Okihiro, Michael O'Malley, Dave Roediger, Nayan Shah, K. Scott Wong, and Renqiu Yu. I've had the privilege of working with Henry Tom of Johns Hopkins University Press, who has provided precise and always helpful editorial suggestions. Thanks to Mary Yates for her fine job of copyediting and to James O'Brien for indexing. My special thanks go to Tom Bender for reading countless drafts of the manuscript and always offering valuable ideas on how to improve and sharpen what and how I write.

I would also like to express my thanks for the support of good friends and colleagues who have helped my work in ways probably unknown to them. Lung "Pop" Chin (who has since passed away), Fay Chiang, Him Mark Lai, Charlie Lai, William "Charlie" Chin, and Ruthanne Lum McCunn have each provided very useful background insights on the Chinatown experience in the United States. Yoshio Kishi has provided invaluable bibliographic support over the years. Richard Drezen made it possible for me to have the physical space to write. Jeanne Houck provided me with regular pep talks, research assistance, and very useful suggestions. Henry Sapoznik, as well as supplying me with sheet music and other valuable historical documents, always had interesting and wonderful insights about American commercial culture. Madeline Hsu, Gloria Lee, and Doris Lee were of great help in locating and reproducing documents for me. Jeffrey Escoffier, Sumiko Higashi, and Robert Snyder made many useful content and editorial suggestions. But most of all, Judy Susman and Thuy Linh Nguyen Tu provided immeasurable intellectual, editorial, and research support to complete the manuscript.

This book is dedicated to Lin-sie Chao Tchen (1906-93), Judy Susman, and Sara Zhi Hua Zhao Tchen-Susman. Without them, none of this would have been possible, or worth pursuing.

INTRODUCTION

The use of Chinese things, ideas, and people in the United States, in various imagined and real forms, has been instrumental in forming this nation's cultural identity. The beginning and end dates of this study mark two contrasting uses. The American Revolutionary War left a loose confederation of former colonies in debt and facing the challenge of what to do with political and economic independence. A distant and exoticized empire somewhere in the "East Indies," referred to variously as Ophir, Sinae, Cathay, and finally as China, figured prominently in the imaginations of some of the founders. For them China was an imagined place of fabulous luxuries, an advanced civilization that the founding fathers and mothers sought to emulate. By the end of the nineteenth century, Chinese laborers were no longer needed to build the economic infrastructure of the Pacific coast states, and anti-Chinese riots forced industrialists and railroad moguls to hire whites.[1] The Chinese Exclusion Act was passed, and the United States sought to gain economic and political mastery over a tottering Qing Dynasty. The formulation of a nationalist identity, of an America imbued with a "manifest destiny" perched on the westernmost shores ready to expand across the Pacific, marked the long transition to a global dominance rivaling that of the British Empire and the dawning of what publishing mogul Henry Luce dubbed the "American Century."[2]

It would be easy (and tempting) to make the claim that the transplanted British and other European forms of stereotyping changed from a "positive" image during the colonial and new-nation period, in which the passionate desire for "oriental" luxuries abounded, to a "negative" image marked by Chinese exclusion.[3] Though roughly accurate, this characterization hides a more complicated set of dynamics. The representation of Chinese things, ideas, and people shifted dramatically from 1776 to 1882, in a manner that coincided with shifts in the political, economic, and social institutions of the United States. Moreover, both representations—the positive and the negative—played a role in the formation of a modern "white" identity. This study seeks to tease out more subtle patterns in U.S. history. For this purpose it is useful to borrow and refashion an interpretive tool developed in literary and cultural analysis.

Critic Edward W. Said was the first to formulate the critique of "orientalism" in his analysis of how Western European literary and university elites define their own civilization in juxtaposition to their perceived and imagined Middle East—a world of opulence, harems, and all-powerful patriarchs.[4] To adapt Said's concept to the United States requires an understanding of how this phenomenon of orientalism was transplanted and took root in the Americas. In the Anglo-American world it was commonly believed that human civilizations originally arose, like the sun, in the farthest reaches of the East and advanced progressively westward. Hence, the ancient civilizations of China, India, and the Arab world represented cultures that were past their glory. Following the arc of the sun, ardent nationalists proclaimed Europeanized America the next great occidental civilization; manifest destiny was in this sense not only a colonizing vision of the frontier but also an occidentalist view of extending European American Protestant civilization into the Pacific.[5] The formulators of U.S. identity, while greatly influenced by European ideas, sought to advance a unique form of American nationalism that often used China and the Chinese symbolically and materially to advance a revolutionary way of life—to make a culture infused with this faith in individualism and progress. Orientalism, therefore, became a cultural phenomenon intrinsic to American social, economic, and political life. The criteria for defining the basis of this nationalist narrative, however, need to be contextualized before we can understand how this orientalist other played against the American occidentalist self.

Rooted in Western European Enlightenment and mercantile capitalism, the great possibilities of a new revolutionary "man" and society—and the limits thereof—were born in 1776.[6] The American Revolution heralded the creation of a freer social order independent from the monarchies of Europe, but it also left the European American founding fathers with the daunting task of formulating a new national identity suited to the world's first postcolonial nation. Across this threshold of Western modernity circulated Chinese things, ideas, and people.[7]

Beginning in the 1780s, three revolutionary processes were in motion. First, English merchants, bankers, and industrialists reorganized cotton cloth production into a factory system drawing upon colonial plantations and slave labor. Lancashire factories inaugurated a machine era of "constant, rapid and up to the present limitless multiplication of men, goods and services."[8] Second, this economic "takeoff" was paralleled by the political activism of French revolutionaries. The seizing of the Bastille represented the popular demands of liberty, equality, and fraternity for all male subjects; sans-culottes wanted more political participation, equal justice before the law, and fuller powers to citizens.[9] Third, these "dual revolutions" were accompanied by the creation of a "middle-class order" of upwardly mobile strivers. American radicalism especially embodied a social revolutionary spirit in which the ethic for individual self-improvement unleashed the pursuit of individual desires and the cultivation of one's own abilities.[10]

The beginnings of U.S. modernity in these decades after the revolution, therefore, were characterized by the rise of self-made men and radical changes in everyday economic, political, and social life. Individual career opportunities were progressively opened to talent, "or at any rate to energy, shrewdness, hard work and greed." Visible increases in facts, knowledge, and techniques promoted the idea of enlightened men able to create civilizational wealth and progress.[11] By the 1800 presidential election, liberal capitalism in the United States would emerge triumphant.[12]

This age of revolution "ushered in new relationships between the individual and society, relationships articulated as ones involving greater freedom of action, self-possession, and autonomy of self in relation to others." Freedom increasingly implied that "the basic building block of society was no longer the family, the clan, the tribe, but the individual self."[13] The U.S. Declaration of Independence and the Constitution embodied a specific cultural matrix of political, economic, and social values. Here Locke's philosophy of individual life, liberty, and property (transmuted into happiness) was codified at the actual founding of this new society.[14] The Constitution defined white propertied males, those believed to be rational and capable of self-determination, as the standard-bearers of U.S. citizenship.[15]

Freed from the will of aristocratic superiors, relationships between individuals were to be voluntary and ideally released from external coercion. Hence, one's own labor would be exchanged in contractual agreements with an employer—each party pursuing its own private, rational self-interest. Increasingly, budding capitalists were able to pursue individual wealth in the marketplace, unfettered by the customary obligations to lord or monarch. Possessing luxuries from "the Orient" was one means by which well-being came to be measured. Hence, the pursuit of "life, liberty, and happiness" in this middle-class nation also became the pursuit of consumable luxuries.

In practice, this transformation of everyday life produced many anxieties. Under capitalist relationships the propertyless were condemned to hire themselves out; freedom, indeed, had a dark edge. Although certain individuals were now technically "free of [the] means to evade the obligation to work for another," not all benefited.[16] Life, liberty, and luxuries were proclaimed "inalienable," universal rights, but they were enjoyed only by those who had succeeded in the rising new culture and were deemed part of "we the people." This specifically Anglo-American Protestant notion of citizenship was defined by a person's "industry" and "rational" use of natural resources for individual benefit. The new culture of progress not only appealed to basic human desires for abundance and security but also created an unprecedented form of human identity: that of the propertied individual apart from the group. Society would now be made up of detached individuals not necessarily belonging to anything other than themselves. Progress and freedom also implied social alienation.[17]

The unleashing of individual passions had to be harnessed into socially constructive interests.[18] Yet it was not always possible to reconcile the competing freedoms promised by individually oriented material self-improvement with the broader principles of political equality. The freedom to pursue profits in the marketplace also aggravated divides between the wealthy and the poor. Such economic freedoms weighed in precarious balance to political freedoms. A society premised on equality and democracy necessarily conflicted with an economic system that generated economic disparities.[19] As the American variant of bourgeois culture developed, increasingly straining republican traditions of hierarchy, interdependency, and social virtue, strivers for upward mobility came to desire and expect the unlimited freedoms of both wealth and equality. As the quest for wealth and equality accelerated with more citizens, territorial expansion became imperative. Americans also began to tie westward expansion to a sense of civilizational greatness and historical destiny.[20]

This "age of revolution," consequently, bore the seeds of the "age of empire" to come.[21] Layered on top of the ongoing expropriation of native peoples' national lands and the enslavement of Africans to work the land, further territorial expansion westward brought European Americans into contact with longstanding Hispanic settlements and prompted the recruitment of Chinese labor. In addition to being categorized as a racial type, or racialized, these non-European others were measured by the emergent norms of bourgeois individualism and found lacking in varying ways. Core cultural standards of industry and rationality generated varying judgments of being lazy, childlike, superstitious, backward, pagan, uncivilized, and effeminate.[22]

White supremacy, however, did not define all relationships at all times. In the process of urbanization and westward expansion, Americanness came to mean a pluralistic contact with cultural others. Boundaries were delineated and intercultural zones created. These border zones embodied various configurations of cultural mixing and hierarchy. In this manner local community building across the frontier, or in cities, articulated the interaction of white, Protestant, European American selves with various peoples of profoundly different cultures.[23] Alongside racism, the contact with non-Western peoples wrought mixed port cultures and frontier settlements in which were forged new hybrid human identities and cultures. Rough forms of social intermingling and acceptance seemed to prevail. Furthermore, rural trading outposts and urban commercial streetscapes seemed to negotiate culturally different needs and desires effectively. Such marketplaces became important initial openings for more mixed cultural interactions to develop. These zones were not only and not always defined by hostility and exploitation, but also by friendships, interminglings, and the birth of new multicultural peoples. European Americans therefore came to articulate the nation's contradictory mix of not being like Europe: individualist egalitarianism, pluralist consumerism, white supremacy, and cultural intermixture became defining qualities of an exceptional "Americanness."[24]

New York City will be the site for this historical interpretation. That port city was a zone of intercultural contact, translation, and interaction; for the sake of this study I have called this time and place New York before Chinatown. The generative site of the nation's economic activity, New York City became the nexus for the exchange of commodities, ideas, and people. Not only was this seaport key to the burgeoning international economy, it was also the communications hub, brokering representations of self and otherness for the emergent American culture. The traffic in goods, ideas, and representations of China and Chinese people changed over the decades. New York was at the heart of these exchanges of judgments and values. It was a contact zone negotiating the manifold intermingling, integration, segregation, and exclusion of numerous cultures of European and non-European descent.[25] Decade by decade, Americans of British, Dutch, German, Protestant, Irish Catholic, and other heritages devised a sense of their own selves in relation to various cultural others. Most prominent among these others were African Americans and Native Americans. However, perhaps the least acknowledged and least understood aspect of non-European influence in the Americas has been Chinese things, ideas, and people. Measuring oneself against the exoticized and the alien became a means toward stabilizing, and destabilizing, a sense of belonging and normalcy with a sense of freedom and individuality.

Chinese migrants and travelers, looking for adventure, wealth, and better lives, wandered into these American dynamics and unwittingly participated in successive and peculiarly American forms of orientalism—each layered on top of the other, sometimes displacing but most often complicating existing attitudes and lived realities. This New York before Chinatown, as a place and an era, is examined in terms of three overlapping cultural formations of orientalism.[26] Each formation configured social, economic, and political processes that changed over time. The first part of the study explores how British and Continental varieties of occidentalism and orientalism were transplanted onto American soil. The second part explores how this form of identification was Americanized in the commercial milieu of New York, and the third part explores how orientalism became ingrained in the politics of the nation. Each form of orientalism operated according to its own internal logic and sense of time. These patterns were animated by the faith in civilization, progress, and destiny that prevailed during this era of U.S. social, economic, and political development. Each formation of orientalism began with some admiration or fascination for an actual Chinese thing, idea, or person, then went through a phase of emulation and mimesis, and ended with European American mastery and dominance.[27]

Part 1, "A Culture of Distinction," examines the phenomenon of patrician orientalism and the manner in which European forms of orientalism were adapted in the founding decades of the nation. Anglo-American desires for luxuries, trade, and an independent political identity structured the context in which China and the Chinese were understood by the elite and the striving elite of New York. This patrician orientalism can be characterized as primarily social, conferring status on those who possessed Chinese things and ideas.

This founding generation already held specific attitudes, fanciful and otherwise, about China. Some, guided by European Enlightenment perceptions, idealized Confucian court culture. Most, particularly those within the patrician culture, however, simply exchanged and collected rare consumer goods as a badge of taste and distinction and a means to sociability. The revolutionary fathers, from George Washington to Gouverneur Morris to Thomas Jefferson, embodied such core practices.

Desires to emulate and trade with China sent the first ship of the new nation to establish diplomatic and economic relations with the distant empire. New York would become the major port of the nation largely because of the profits of the early China trade. The transportation revolution of faster, larger ships and canals linking port cities and their rivers to interior markets organized the life of Manhattan Island by its rhythms. The city prospered the more it was able to create a chain of interlinked individuals trading for goods made in China, unloaded by longshoremen from the docks of New York, transacted in the countinghouses, and transported by itinerant merchants into the hinterlands of the Mohawk Valley and destinations beyond for barter and sale. The experiences of the few first Chinese entering New York City (and the nation) were defined by this preestablished intersection of commercial, cultural, and political interests. Chinese were viewed as friendly, nonthreatening, and pleasing to the dominant culture—in brief, Chinese merchants were viewed as procapitalist, Protestant-like "mandarins."

Some members of the founding generation echoed the concerns of the European philosophes. "Oriental" wealth, in their view, was derived from a civilization ruled by despots. In contrast to this image of decadent oriental opulence and despotism was the occidental ideal of a rational, self-regulating, free society of individuals as envisioned by John Locke. The perceived excesses of "the Orient" were condemned, but they were also a source of fascination and guilty pleasure.[28]

As New York merchants became self-made men of wealth, admiration of China turned into ambition to control the China market. In classic colonial fashion, an occidental port that was nurtured by the wealth of the China trade helped to undermine that empire's sovereignty. Under the banner of "free trade rights," New York merchants shipped opium into China and transported indentured "coolie" laborers to South America and the Caribbean. The British-initiated Opium Wars forced China to open its ports to Western trade, the profits from which helped to underwrite the myriad cultural and civic institutions of New York's much vaunted public culture.

Part 2, "Port Exchanges," turns to the period of commercial orientalism, a time between the completion of the Erie Canal and the end of the Civil War when some New Yorkers came to order part of the chaos and alienation of rapid urbanization with what they saw and read about China and the Chinese. This form of orientalism can be primarily characterized as a response to the era's populist marketplace economics. The earlier form of luxury-trade orientalism still thrived for elites and the nouveau riche, but a commercial marketplace of eager consumers was generating other representations of Chinese things, ideas, and people. Breakthroughs in print technology created a newly aware and accessible urban public. The penny press, combined with the Bowery culture of theaters, dime museums, lectures, merchandising, and public spectacles, popularized the idea of experiencing for oneself, of reading daily newspapers, and visiting urban "sights."

Real, living individuals from China and the Chinese diaspora responded to the patrician and commercial forms of orientalism in various adaptive ways: becoming tea merchants, behaving as "mandarins," intermarrying with neighboring Irishwomen, forming mutual aid organizations, appealing to the general public's good will, using the courts to protest mistreatment, and returning to China. Early Chinese New Yorkers intermingled with other citizens of lower Manhattan's port culture, forming a highly creolized community. Various Chinese performers, including the "Siamese twins," Chang and Eng Bunker, and cultural entrepreneurs, such as Phineas T. Barnum, will be examined within this commercial milieu. What was it about these Chinese performers and objects that so fascinated the American public? How did this fascination shape what was presented? And what can this tell us about the formation of American cultural identity?

This pastiche of commercial orientalisms was subject to a marketplace that catered to consumers who would buy only certain products and representations about Chinese things, people, and ideas. Actual Chinese and European Americans in yellowface performing on New York stages and in museums were presented in ways that further elaborated and reinforced attitudes transplanted from England, among other European influences, but also invoked new competing views in response to reading and viewing publics. Their performances became a means for the New York public to sort out some of the great and mundane questions of the day. With whom could one find friendship and form social ties in a chaotic metropolis filled with strangers? How could differences among peoples of the world be explained? How had peoples' appearances become deceiving?

In part 3, "The Chinese Question," I focus on what happened during Reconstruction and its aftermath. During this period Chinese laborers and Chinese civilization became the center of a national political debate. Political orientalism dominated in an era in which patrician orientalism and marketplace orientalism continued to exist. Selected images of Chinese people and things became part of highly charged debates about who constituted "free labor" and "assimilability"—speaking to the very definition of who an American citizen could and should be. As the U.S. territories expanded westward in the nineteenth century, New York City became preeminent as a modernizing commercial hub, and China was no longer essential for furthering the port's commercial wealth.

By the late 1800s the fascination with Chinese goods and values had been eclipsed by attitudes of fear and loathing. New York merchants had made fortunes off the port and created an elite civic culture. Their culture of distinction had also served to aggravate conflicts between labor and capital. And the anxieties of such conflicts were increasingly vented toward Chinese labor. Chinese New Yorkers were increasingly represented as abject opium-smoking, rat-eating criminals who threatened public virtue. From 1870 onward, "Chinese" and "China" became useful as broadly symbolic reference points in public discussions about the meaning of servility and freedom, progress and stagnation. Monopolists and industrialists used Chinese immigrants as a ready source of wage labor and as a way to discipline rebellious wage workers. Independent artisans and striving immigrants responded by shutting Chinese out of a range of producer industries over which they still had some control. While the actual numbers of Chinese in America were still small during this time, their very presence sparked growing anti-Chinese sentiment. This political orientalism recast desire-imbued and ambiguous representations into an exclusionary and segregationist discourse.

The Chinese Exclusion Act, passed in 1882, kept Chinese laborers from freely immigrating into the United States. Various Chinese New Yorkers responded differently to these increasingly hostile circumstances, but their cumulative actions laid the foundation for the development of multilayered, transnational identities: those who maintained their sense of themselves as overseas Chinese, as diasporic migrants, and as settlers in the Americas. The later development of New York's Chinatown reflected this experience: Chinese migrating to New York were increasingly limited to cleaning the clothing or houses of the middle class or segregated into businesses serving fellow Chinese. Chinatown embodied both a residential and a commercial ghetto.

As new frontier Pacific cities such as San Francisco were built, northeastern cultural geographies mapping districts of light and shadow, self and "otherness," were transplanted westward. Each of these new cities encountered its own mix of peoples, yet the underlying racialized, hierarchical, moral dynamics of the good and the evil remained basically the same. In this sense the violent anti-Chinese movements of the Pacific coast were intimately linked to the port-culture dynamics of New York. Chinese things, ideas, and people continued to cross into the metropolis, but they were less and less free to flourish in the life of New York City. A highly intermingled culture was pushed underground, and Chinamen became ghettoized in a Chinatown. In one hundred years, a revolutionary republic pursuing life, liberty, and luxuries became a largely segregated, white, consumer nation pursuing an empire of "free trade."

PART 1

A Culture of Distinction

Can it have been merely by coincidence that the future was to belong to the societies fickle enough to care about changing the colors, materials and shapes of costume, as well as the social order and the map of the world—societies, that is, which were ready to break with their traditions?

—Ferdnand Braudel

CHAPTER 1

Porcelain, Tea, and Revolution

O<small>N THE EVENING OF</small> J<small>ULY</small> 9, 1776, impassioned New York citizens and Continental soldiers pulled down the two-thousand-pound gilded statue of King George III on Bowling Green, breaking off its head and mutilating its nose.[1] In the months to come, Manhattan, a half-evacuated trading port, would be the scene of the next battle of the Revolutionary War.

British general Sir William Howe's disciplined force, some thirty-two thousand militia, ten thousand sailors, and fifty-two warships, descended the coastline from Boston. Ragtag volunteers began arriving in all types of transports, many still dressed in their hunting shirts and leggings—nineteen thousand in all. These rebels slept on the floorboards of empty houses or in simple tents. As one observer recorded, "Hardship, exposure, unwholesome food, bad drinking water, improper sanitary arrangements, insufficient hospitals, a dearth of physicians, the general ignorance of the nature of diseases and the proper treatments, sent hundreds of poor fellows to the grave." Women and children were ordered to evacuate, as reports circulated that the city was to be burned if defeated.[2]

In the midst of this scene of chaos and deprivation, General George Washington made plans for New York City's defense. At the same time, under Washington's customarily close personal supervision, his New York City housekeeper, Mrs. Mary Smith, proceeded to furnish his New York home. Carefully kept accounts and receipts reveal the purchase of mahogany knife cases, a carpet, a damask tablecloth, a feather bed, pillows, a tureen, eight porcelain mugs, two dozen plates, and other miscellany. Pro-British Burling Slip merchants Frederick and Philip Rhinelander supplied numerous imported creamware dishes, sauceboats, plates, and fluted bowls, including three, more costly, "china" bowls. And the Bayard Street retailer George Ball sold "burnt china cups & saucers" and other tea service items to the household.[3] During this time the general and Mrs. Washington kept up "a high level of comfort in dining and furnishings," maintaining a "tolerably genteel" table.[4] By September, major miscalculations had forced Washington's inexperienced troops to retreat. At great expense and trouble, the general's household was packed up and reestablished at the Morris-Jumel Mansion in Haerlem Heights.[5]

What explains this desire for luxury in the midst of war? It would be easy to ridicule General Washington's extraordinary attention to material wants at this moment of hardship. This enigmatic anecdote, however, offers fresh insights into this founding generation's efforts to formulate a cultural identity. While these details may appear trivial to traditional interpretations of early American history, they pose a question fundamental to this study: Why were tea, porcelains, and other representations of China so desired by the founding fathers and mothers of the United States?

"To Fix the Taste of Our Country Properly"

In 1777 a cache of tea was found concealed in some woods, and Brigadier General Nathaniel Heard wrote asking the commander-in-chief how to dispose of it. Washington personally wrote back ordering it "to be sent to the Quarter Master General for the use of the Army." When available, valued supplies were distributed to officers in a hierarchical manner. While based in West Point in 1779, Washington gave detailed instructions as to which officers, staff, and surgeons should be issued which supplies. Tea was to be distributed as follows: "Fifty pounds of the best quality for future disposal: one pound of the best kind to each General Officer; half a pound of the same to each field officer and head of a staff department and a quarter of a pound pr. man of the remainder to any other officer of the army who shall apply."[6] The general's careful deliberations on the apportioning of tea exemplified his proper role as a patriarch rewarding his officers. In addition, his insistence on having Chinese tea sets, or Wedgwood queensware, certainly reminded him and his officers, in the heat of battle, of his status and authority. Such luxury items were particularly scarce during war, and their rarity made Washington's role in distributing tea all the more significant: it was a means of reinforcing the symbolic identity befitting a gentleman of his position and authority.[7]

Not of prosperous parentage, Washington was well aware of the divide between the haves and the have-nots of Virginia. Before the war he had witnessed firsthand the conditions of the poor in the frontier settlements he visited while working as a surveyor.[8] Common people on the frontier still ate meals from a communal family bowl, often using their hands to scoop out the food. In more settled areas the poor were more likely to eat their porridge with spoons. Wealth was measured throughout the century by the number of chairs one owned, or by whether one had a frame bed or lived in a dwelling having more than one room.[9] For those aspiring to differentiate themselves from the majority of Americans, it became important to recondition one's behavior and learn the proper use of such "instruments" as knives, forks, and spoons that signified luxury and elegance.

Described by historian Gordon Wood as an "autodidact," Washington too worked tirelessly at uplifting himself from his humble origins to the status of landed gentry (as distinct from farmers, whom he called the "grazing multitude").[10] He constantly sought to emulate British elite culture. At the age of fifteen he wrote down a collection of maxims that he called "Rules of Civility and Decent Behaviour in Company and Conversation." Drawn from a seventeenth-century etiquette book, they reveal a young man self-conscious about modifying his appearance and behavior in the company of his betters. "Loll not out the tongue," he reminded himself, nor "keep the Lips too open or too Close." And "in speaking to men of Quality do not lean nor Look them full in the Face."[11] Washington was not alone in his endeavors to remake the self; he was eminently representative of the outstanding offspring of this new nation, disciplining body, mind, and manners so as to become a gentleman. His tea-drinking and porcelain-collecting habits embodied these efforts. They further embodied the contradictory crosscurrents of the emergent Anglo-American revolutionary culture: they show Washington striving to be both a proper British gentleman and an American revolutionary.[12]

In 1755 Washington placed his first order for Chinese porcelains. Sending three hogsheads of tobacco, he prevailed upon London "chinaman" Richard Washington to choose a set of goods "agre[e]able to the present taste" and "good of their kind." (Eighteenth-century British porcelain merchants, male and female, were called "chinaman" or "chinawoman" and their goods "china" being sold in "china shops.") Introduced by a fellow planter, Washington had to place his trust in this unknown merchant. Desperately hoping to be treated fairly, he emphasized their shared surname: "I should be glad to cultivate the most intimate corrispondance with you, not only for names-sake but as a friend, and shall endeavour in all things to approve myself worthy your Regard."[13] Such was the nature of the British Empire that a Virginia planter was at the mercy of a British shopkeeper.

Washington's material desires derived from European aristocratic culture as filtered to the middling class. Having gained a taste for the "baubles of Britain," many Americans would not be denied the pursuit of these luxuries. First coveted by European courts, furs from North America, sugar from the plantations of the West Indies, coffee and spices from Java, chocolate from the cacao plant in South America, and teas *ad infinitum* became available in domestic markets at more affordable prices. In eighteenth-century Europeanized America, less costly teas, nankeens, and inexpensive blue and white porcelains (often used as ballast on ships) began appearing in more homes. These once exotic consumables became attainable in everyday life.[14]

When they couldn't get the authentic goods, Europeans and some Americans made copies "after the Chinese taste." The French term *chinoiserie* referred to the seventeenth- and eighteenth-century fashion for European-made imitations of Chinese goods. These were the creations of craftsmen who had no firsthand experience of a distant and highly romanticized "Cathay." Gold-embroidered tapestries of small people living in a willow-patterned world, elaborate gardens with "gossamer pavilions," architecture with pagoda-style roofs, faux porcelains, fantastic latticework, fanciful stage sets, lacquered furniture, and various other decorative notions formed the material expression of this European orientalism.[15]

Once elected president, George Washington moved to the first presidential "palace" at Pearl and Cherry Streets. Lady Kitty Duer remarked that it was appointed with the "best of furniture in every room, and the greatest quantity of plate and China that I ever saw before. The whole of the first and second Story is papered, and the floor covered with the richest kind of Turkey and Wilton Carpets."[16] Included in the inventory of purchases were "Japan'd Tea trays," queensware, and a large order of "China."[17] A Mrs. Robinson wrote, "There is scarcely anything talked of now but General Washington and the Palace." Dressed in the latest fashions from Europe, many made of Chinese silks, this "republican court" excited all (with the notable exception of what Robinson called "those styled Anti-Federalists").[18]

Washington wrote to New York merchant Gouverneur Morris, who was negotiating tobacco sales in Paris, asking him to shop for stylish porcelains. Morris wrote back, "You will perhaps exclaim that I have not complied with your Directions as to Economy, but you will be of a different Opinion when you see the Articles. I could have sent you a Number of pretty Trifles for very little Cost, but . . . your Table would have been in the Style of a petite Maitresse of this City, which most assuredly is not the Style you wish." The gender and class implications of Morris's phrase "the Style of a petite Maitresse" must have persuaded Washington to accept a grander role. "I think it of very great importance to fix the taste of our Country properly," Morris continued, "and I think your Example will go so very far in that respect. It is therefore my Wish that every Thing about you should be substantially good and majestically plain; made to endure."[19]

A year later the Washingtons moved to even larger quarters at 29 Broadway, formerly occupied by the French legation, where more elegant and much larger teas, state dinners, and receptions were to be held. Belonging to the departing Count de Moustier, the legation sold to Washington a large service of fine, fashionable white Sèvres porcelain with simple gold decorative borders. Sèvres porcelain, like the Meissen ware of Germany and Wedgwood of England, represented France's most advanced efforts at emulating Chinese porcelain wares.[20]

For a new nation in which dwellings were generally still humble and material belongings only modest, Chinese commodities signified what sociologist Pierre Bourdieu has termed "distinction." French émigré La Rochefoucauld-Liancourt observed as late as 1797 "some good brick houses," but "in general" most dwellings were "mean, small and low, [and] built of wood." In New York, families engaged in certain trades worked and lived in sheds, shanties, and cellars along the East River, often sharing living quarters with boarders. Grant Thornburn, for example, rented a modest one-level wooden building at 22 Nassau Street that served both for setting up "housekeeping" and as a nail-making workshop. With his wife, he divided the six- by twelve-foot space into "a store, kitchen and bedroom which also served for our parlour." The living space was furnished with "a bed and bedstead, pine table (value fifty cents), three Windsor chairs, a soup pot, tea kettle, six cups and saucers, a griddle, frying pan, and brander." Notice that even in such a modest abode, Thornburn had a space he could call a parlor, equipped with six teacups and saucers. His status may have been that of a workingman, but his aspiration was clearly higher.[21]

Upwardly striving Americans not only wanted tea sets, porcelains, and tea. As historian Richard Bushman has illustrated, such desires also created a demand for housing that could show off the owners' wealth and accommodate more and more personal belongings. Multistoried houses with hall-way stair entry areas and separate rooms for entertaining, dining, cooking, and living came to set a new standard for genteel living.[22] The tasteful display of passionately coveted things from the "Orient" and the "Indies" (and elsewhere in the non-European world) distinguished one moneyed space from the other.

Corrupting Virtues and Revolutionary Passions

While George Washington coveted Chinese luxuries, other revolutionaries argued that the consumption of luxuries corrupted virtue. While many New Yorkers envied, and emulated, the wealth and refinement of Chinese court culture, some radicals urged a complete boycott of foreign luxuries. They argued, with little support, that Americans could make their own tea from local flora. The love of luxuries from the China and Indies trade came to represent the antithesis of Anglo-American republican virtue; such things were deemed addictive and corrupting.

Earnest moralists read—and took to heart—the advice of the English radical Catharine Macaulay. In the New York edition of her 1775 address to the people of Britain, Macaulay observed that after a "long succession of abused prosperity" the British Empire had been lured into a "ruinous operation by the Riches and Luxuries of the East." Popular British novelist Tobias Smollet wrote that the "Roman Commonwealth of old" and other civilizations had been ruined because "Luxury and Profuseness" from the Orient "led the Way to Indigence and Effeminacy; which prepared the Minds of the People for Corruption; and Corruption for Subjection; as they have constantly succeeded one another, and will do so again, in the same Circumstances, in all Countries, and in all Ages." In America, Benjamin Franklin worried about new dependencies. In the *Columbia Magazine* he stated, "One is astonished to think of the number of vessels and men who are daily exposed in going to bring tea from China, coffee from Arabia, and sugar and tobacco from America: all commodities which our ancestors lived very well without."[23] Apparently, many believed that the East India Company and the new financial order were ruining "old England."[24]

Procommerce political philosopher David Hume, among others, disagreed with such positions. Hume acknowledged that "all the Latin classics . . . we peruse in our infancy . . . universally ascribe the ruin of their state to the arts and riches imported from the East." However, such sentiments regarding the corrupting effect of "Grecian and Asiatic luxury," Hume maintained, "mistook the cause of the disorders," which really proceeded from an "ill model'd government" and the "unlimited extent of conquests." In his view, luxuries refined the arts and the arts promoted liberty.[25] Yet the desire for "oriental" goods was stronger than the threat of "oriental despotism."

Indeed, the right to easy access to desired Chinese consumer goods threatened to overwhelm radical boycott positions. In England the freedom to consume such foreign items as tea, to wear what one wanted, or to set one's table with porcelains had long been subject to a tradition of social controls. To varying degrees of success, highly elaborated "consumption by estates" laws fixed standards of conduct and comfort according to social rank. British monarchs and the aristocracy sought to limit commoners' access to luxury goods and the display of wealth beyond their fixed status. Pride of apparel was deemed "an exemplarie of evill [which] induceth the whole man to wickednesse and sinne."[26] Luxury-targeted tax codes especially imposed upon middling peasants further proscribed the popular consumption of foreign goods.

The Stamp Act of 1765 and the Townshend Act of 1767, levying a duty upon imported glass, paper, tea, lead, and paint, extended such sumptuary sanctions to the American colonies. These actions led to the organization of a popular revolt, or as T. H. Breen has noted, created a unifying issue for private consumers to rally around.[27] Boston merchants urged customers not to buy British goods, sloganing, "Save your money and you can save your country." The New York Sons of Liberty resolved an even more dramatic position during the tea boycott: tea drinkers threatened "the liberties of America."[28] In the end, of course, boycotters and consumers both attained their goals, for the smuggling of tea continued unabated. Average Americans chafed at any sumptuary limits on consumables deemed foreign and therefore taboo. British East India Company tea may not have been acceptable to consume, but tea smuggled by Americans was.

As the Sons of Liberty learned, the popular desire for consumer goods could be used as a driving force for political independence. "Freedom," in part, was defined as unfettered access to the "baubles of Britain." After all, it was the British Crown's augmentation of the East India Company's power to control the consumption of Chinese goods that precipitated the various tea boycotts. During the New York Tea Party, held months after the Boston protest, Alexander McDougall, a leader of the Sons of Liberty, addressed his "Fellow Citizens" under the pen name "Hampden" in self-consciously Lockean terms: "The chief end of all free government, is the protection of

Property, from Injuries without it." McDougall explained that he used the term *property* "in the large sense, in which Mr. Locke uses it, as comprehending Life, Liberty, and Estate."[29] The letter spoke of propertied male citizens' "natural liberty" and their right to "defend themselves" against "the control and Tyranny of others"—ergo, their right to rebel against King George's despotic authority as wielded by the East India Company.

A letter signed "Scevola," published in the same newspaper as that by "Hampden" and addressed to the commissioners of the East India Company, defined what being "a free, independent, and determined people" in radical American terms meant. Americans would not allow "parliamentary despotism" or the East India Company to root itself in their country, nor would they be forced to swallow "the loathsome pills of slavery and oppression." The desire for Chinese goods was subject to the same rationale. As long as Americans worked hard for the material objects of their desire, why shouldn't they have the unfettered right to trade and consume such luxuries?[30]

Elite Community Building

Chinese goods were not used simply to satisfy materialist desires, however. For Gouverneur Morris's fellow New Yorkers, the culture of consuming and giving luxury objects became intrinsic to the formation of a merchant-led patrician elite. Rituals of using, giving, and passing on Chinese objects were a means of community building.

As the elite practice of separating the workplace from the house became more commonplace in late-eighteenth-century America, women became responsible for "raising the standards of the quality of domestic life in the household, raising the standards for rearing and educating children, and assuming the moral guardianship of all family members and even of society as a whole."[31] With the assistance of servants and slaves, the home became a vehicle for cultivating genteel moral virtue. Among other things of value, Chinese objects of distinction were critical to this process. Most notably, tea time and the family dinner were turned into secular rituals for social interactions between family, friends, and guests to take place.

The social practice of paying calls to private residences and having tea was a highly refined means of establishing one's worthiness and credibility, as well as a primary means of social mixing (including mixing across gender lines). Of a visit through North America in 1781, Abbé Robin noted, "The greatest mark of civility and welcome they can show you, is to invite you to drink [tea] with them." Performed according to British and Continental standards, the serving of tea required the proper "Tea Geer": teapot, cups, saucers, tea table, tea caddy, caddy spoon, and other items. The more stylishly elaborate the "equipage," the more refined the server. The tea table, a specialized piece of furniture either imported from China or made in Europe "in the Chinese style," certainly augmented prestige. Ultimately one's true character was measured as much by one's refined possessions as by one's conduct and conversation.[32]

Historian Thomas Bender has pointed out that eighteenth-century patrician life was highly community-oriented, constantly reinforced through personal and social ties. British guides of this period described verbal discourse as "the Cement and Soul of Society" or—the language of the marketplace beginning to transform all—"the greatest commerce of our lives."[33] Tea time was one way of pursuing this "commerce," of reinforcing these social ties. In sharp contrast to the time ordinary folk spent in common taverns—"the eternal haunt of loose disorderly Peoples," as John Adams called them—tea time represented a social space wherein one could demonstrate one's skills in the art of "Conversation" with others (particularly women) who displayed "Wit," good "Sense," and "Virtue." In his diary Adams described a gathering at which a woman talked about the awkward behavior some "People" had once displayed at one of her teas; her story, Adams reported, embarrassed some other members of the gathering, some "shoe string fellows that never use Tea." While he deplored the woman's indiscretion, Adams did not challenge the firmly entrenched notion that one's skills at having tea revealed one's sophistication and pedigree.[34]

Indeed, in this Anglo-American world the lack of such refinement invited derision. A 1777 British cartoon of "The Old Maid" illustrates a dour, unsophisticated figure sipping tea from a dish along with her cat.[35] The social norms of the time were such that any well-acculturated patrician could appreciate the satire of the illustration and the humor of the ignorant error (taking "have a dish of tea" to mean literally to sip from a dish). Patriarchal disapproval sanctioned those who did not conform. Displays of refinement, by contrast, merited praise and reinforced chains of acceptable social relationships.[36] This core activity—the refined social interaction of tea time—generated collateral patrician activities such as reading and collecting, and the objects collected in turn afforded guests as well as hosts the opportunity to display their knowledge and etiquette.[37]

Figure 1. The tea ritual, painted by Susanna Truax, 1730. The ritual of drinking tea was associated with elite status and material well-being. This stylishly dressed Hudson River valley woman is holding a sugar cube in a spoon, ready to plunk it into her teacup. (Gift of Edgar William and Bernice Chrysler Garbisch © 1988 Board of Trustees, National Gallery of Art, Washington)

Figure 2. Great American Tea Company poster, mid-1800s. Manhattan businesses expanded as strivers to the middling class sought to cultivate genteel consumer behaviors. (New-York Historical Society)

In a comparable, but less public, manner the family dinner also became a highly ritualized activity. Coinciding with the separation of the workplace from the home, evening meals became the only time of the day at which all family members were guaranteed to be together: "This ritual was used for reinforcing family ties and inculcating family members, particularly children, with moral values."[38] And as already evidenced by George Washington's lavish table settings, fancier porcelains were used for the more prestigious gatherings.

General sociability, far more than specialized erudition, was prized; "things" Chinese had become one of the forms of currency for gaining cultural "distinction." Adapting the European elite's craze for Chinese export items and European chinoiserie, New Yorkers cultivated a taste for Chinese and Chinese-style luxuries. The rituals that surrounded these things and the constellation of meanings associated with them created a powerful field of distinction and power.[39] In this Dutch-British island of strivers and self-improvers, desired luxuries played a critical role in expressing bonds of intimacy, friendship, identity, and power. As the demands of economic self-interest were increasingly framed in opposition to the more familiar social norms of love, family, trust, honor, and civic duty, and as old status hierarchies were destabilized by individual mobility, socializing and gifts became even more important in establishing and reestablishing personal ties.

Women had a more intimate, memory-keeping relationship to these Chinese things than did men. They were largely responsible for developing and maintaining bonds of sentiment.[40] The giving of valued gifts became an important means by which networks of sentiment were woven. The giving of gifts created a shared sphere of meanings, power, and hierarchy. In the process, sentimental values were consolidated between the givers and the receivers. In effect, the process of giving helped to reinforce the authority of certain traditional core values.[41] This paradox of "keeping-while-giving" can be amply demonstrated by the manner in which New York patricians used their most prized porcelains. Important life-cycle events were marked by the giving of gifts to bring those with established wealth and the nouveau riche together into a shared civic society.

A Chinese enameled punch bowl given to Alexander Hamilton and Elizabeth Schuyler by her parents in 1780 to commemorate their marriage, for example, signified the Schuylers' acceptance of Hamilton into their family and social circles. The Schuylers' closet friends, associates, and often kin were the Hudson Valley Knickerbocker elite: the Delanceys, Livingstons, Van Rensselaers, and Van Cortlandts. The marriage (and the bowl) thus marked Hamilton's rise in New York society. A year later General Washington offered him command of a battalion, and the following year he was appointed Continental receiver of taxes and admitted to the New York bar.[42]

Perhaps the most important role of such valued gifts was their intergenerational effect. In elite families of this era, children had a familial obligation to learn and practice a world of behaviors and knowledge that would perpetuate their family's wealth and status. To this end, specially inscribed objects and toys, miniaturized from adult scale, were given to help acculturate children. Chinese objects such as toy porcelain sets would be passed down from generation to generation, and children were quickly socialized into the ritualistic behavior associated with the objects. For example, Mary

Clinton, the daughter of De Witt Clinton's brother, owned a blue and white tea set with her initials monogrammed into the design. And Martha Hicks, the daughter of Thomas and Martha Buchanan Hicks, prominent New York Quakers, had "MH" inscribed on each of her cups and saucers. Young girls playing with miniature tea sets learned how to emulate the behavior of their mothers at tea parties. Indeed, Chinese porcelains were so much a part of the adult world that one handmade dollhouse dating back to 1834 prominently displayed a tiny Chinese blue and white platter and tea set in the dining room. The set was given by New York's Governor and Mrs. Joseph C. Yates to their granddaughter Susan Daniel Watkins.[43]

The governor and Mrs. Yates's gift expressed their love and their wish that Susan should carry on their legacy. Through the medium of the dollhouse and the tiny play porcelains, they were communicating their desire that their grandchild be properly cultured. If the patrician boy's obligation to his family was to master the constantly destabilizing world of commodities and the symbolic knowledge necessary for that work, the patrician girl's obligation was to master the conversion of things into a world of stable and meaningful human relationships that would provide the family with a sense of secure identity.[44] In this way Chinese export porcelains became Americanized by family crests, designs, and added sentimental meanings.

For this Anglo-American society the range of objects reflecting the social self became quite broad. For George Washington it certainly included his land, slaves, house, and the material embodiment of his service as a general and president. For Hamilton it included his achieved ambitions. And for Susan Watkins it probably included her dollhouse and her relationship to her grandparents. These possessions became so inalienable to one's personal sense of self, William James pointed out in another context, that their loss represented far more than the actual material object, for "there remains, over and above this, a sense of the shrinkage of our personality, a partial conversion of ourselves to nothingness."[45] By implication, the loss of access to such sentimentalized things, from the Orient and elsewhere, was an important concern.

Teas, porcelains, and other such luxury goods played a key role in the formation of this hybridizing Anglo-American identity. The founding fathers were socialized in a universe of British symbolic meanings. Freedom, happiness, property, individuality, rational self-interest, corruption, tyranny, despotism, and so many other concepts were part of ongoing debates about

Figure 3. Miniature blue and white porcelains and dollhouse of Susan Daniel Watkins, 1834. Play was one way in which sons and daughters were socialized in the values of their parents. (John P. Papp, photographer, courtesy of the Schenectady County Historical Society)

how one tamed wild passions, harnessed them via self-cultivation, and became a gentleman without overindulging in luxuries and becoming "effeminate" and corrupt.

How Did China Become Wealthy?

The founding generation of European Americans sought to abstract lessons from what had been written about China's Confucian-based civilization. They were fascinated by extant translations of the great sage's linkage of personal virtue with the affairs of the state. The maxim that the morality of a civilization's patriarch-leader was responsible for the general well-being and wealth of his nation appealed to revolutionists and republicans alike. Jesuit priest Jean Baptiste Du Halde's influential book *The General History of China* credited such centralized moral and civil authority with the creation of the Grand Canal, the Great Wall, the civil service system, and national taxation, and with the benevolent management of natural resources in balance with national trade. In addition, the well-regarded writings of

Voltaire, Quesnay, and associated political economists (now referred to as physiocrats) celebrated China as a stable and prosperous agricultural civilization that should be emulated in the West.[46]

Such books and thinkers had a significant influence on the ways in which Benjamin Franklin and Thomas Jefferson, both of whom had spent time in Paris, thought about how to make the new nation prosper. Franklin, for example, regularly noted a wide range of "useful" Chinese flora, fauna, crafts, inventions, and practices adoptable in America, such as windmills, mulberry trees and silk production, rhubarb, rice cultivation, papermaking, and central heating.[47] The printer-philosopher-inventor's penchant for parables also illustrated his transcultural uses of Chinese knowledge. He attributed to "a certain Chinese Emperor" a saying that effectively reinforced the Puritan Protestant values of collective hard work: "I wil, if posible, have no Idlenes in my Dominions; for if there be one Man idle, some other Man must sufer Cold and hunger." Indeed, an indicative passage appears in the introduction to the first volume of Franklin's American Philosophical Society journal: "Could we be so fortunate as to introduce the industry of the Chinese, their arts of living and improvements in husbandry . . . America might become in time as populous as China."[48]

Jefferson, meanwhile, owned a copy of Du Halde's book (which he later sold with the rest of his collection to form the Library of Congress), spoke authoritatively about a Chinese play, and planned on having a miniaturized Chinese pavilion (modeled after one in Kew Gardens) and Chinese temple built for his treasured garden at Monticello. More significantly, however, Jefferson translated Count Destutt de Tracy's *Treatise on Political Economy,* a work that extended the physiocrats' interest in Confucian moral statecraft. A central argument of this book, which Jefferson believed "should be . . . in the hands of every American citizen," was an exposition of the connection between virtuous individual will and its salubrious social effects. Destutt de Tracy linked utilitarian moral virtue with individual will and individual will with "happiness," defined as the possession of property. French thinkers had transformed translations of Confucian philosophic ideals into a pragmatic Lockean theory for generating individual and national wealth, and Jefferson became the school's major U.S. advocate.[49]

In contrast to George Washington's love of porcelains, Franklin's practical curiosity, and Jefferson's sociophilosophical bent, Alexander Hamilton thought about China primarily as part of the global exchange of resources and goods. He paid careful attention to Malachy Postlethwayt's *The Uni-*

versal Dictionary of Trade and Commerce. The following entry was typical of Hamilton's notes:

> Asia.
> Productions; all those in Europe with the adition of many either in greater abundance than there or not produced there at all—
> There is a great abundance of diamons pearl coral gold silver copper, iron, sulphur red earth, salt-petre, allum quicksilver, potter's earth (of which is made the porcelain) raw silk cotton, tea, sage, coffee, nutmegs, mace cloves cinnamon pepper, indigo china-root, aquila-wood, rhubarb, musk, vermilion, sticklack borax, *lapis laxuli,* Dragon's blood, cubebs frankincense, saffron myrrh, manna, ambergrease and many other of the valuable drugs and gums.

Such notations not only marked what any given nation produced but also indicated what access that nation had to the Indies market and what made it wealthy. Rates of exchange and equivalencies, what Hamilton called "political arithmetic," fascinated the man. He wrote notes on the relative values of gold to silver in Europe and China, the labor needed to maintain a "hundred in all the necessities of life," and what America as the newcomer to global trade might offer to these markets.[50]

These were some of the ways in which European thought about China came to be used in the new nation's quest for wealth and civilization.

Murphy's *Orphan of China*

In addition to the circulation of goods and books, cultural productions, such as plays, spectacles, and events, became important vehicles for the formulation of political concepts of American nationalism and foreign "others." The New York performances of *The Orphan of China* offer an unusual opportunity to gain insights into how this process worked.

The Orphan of China, a tragic play by British playwright Arthur Murphy, was based on earlier adaptations of a Chinese opera. Murphy's version appeared in 1759, receiving good critical reviews in England and periodic revivals. The play premiered in colonial New York in 1768; it was performed by British military actors in 1779, then again in 1787. In the next century the play was staged in 1842 and, according to theater chronicler George Odell, "remained popular the rest of the century."[51]

In 1787 the play was staged at New York's John Street Theatre, one of the nation's first and most important stages.[52] The following lines opened the production:

> Enough of Greece and Rome. The exhausted store
> Of either nation now can charm no more. . . .
> On eagle wings the poet of to-night
> Soars for fresh virtues to the source of light,
> To China's eastern realms; and boldly bears
> Confucius' morals to Britannia's ears.[53]

The fact that *Orphan* played at the John Street Theatre in New York before, during, and after the Revolution is significant. Despite the political divides between colonial Tories, British soldiers, and revolutionary patriots, the piece commanded continuing interest on the part of all. Indeed, they shared many cultural values.

The original play, *Zhaoshiguer*, is considered by Chinese scholars to be a "minor operetta" that was penned around 1330 by the Yuan Dynasty writer Chi Chun-hsiang.[54] Nevertheless, its translation by the French Jesuit Father Premare gave it significant visibility in the West. Thomas Jefferson confidently recommended the work to his brother-in-law as one of the classics of Chinese literature.[55] Though accepted as an "authentic" Chinese work, the Chinese opera was effectively transformed by Premare into a European tragedy. As this minor Chinese opera entered European intellectual circles, it was regularly retranslated, reinterpreted, and rewritten, with each version introducing significant changes to the characters, their names, and the story line.

The original was based on a historical event occurring in the middle of the Yuan Dynasty (fourteenth century). In five scenes, militarist Tu-ngan-cu plots to kill the entire clan of Minister Chao-tun, some three hundred people. A faithful family doctor, Ching-yng, saves the life of an orphaned male heir by concealing him and then sacrificing his own son, passing the heir off as his own. Through twists of the plot, the villain comes to believe that the family doctor has aided him in killing the orphan (actually the doctor's son), and he takes the real orphan under his protection. The boy is brought up without any knowledge of his real lineage until he reaches manhood some twenty years later. Ching-yng eventually reveals the orphan's true family identity. In the meantime, the emperor becomes wary of the military leader's growing power. Upon learning of the real parentage of the orphan, he commands the orphan to seize the villain, enabling the orphan to take revenge on behalf of his decimated family. The play ends with the orphan and Ching-yng kneeling before the emperor, listening to the decree that rights the wrongs and rewards their Confucian virtue.[56]

Intellectuals used various versions of *Orphan* to support different European concerns, ranging from the attempt to articulate formal universal principles of successful drama to more political matters.[57] Bishop Richard Hurd, for example, thought that he found in Premare's translation of *Zhaoshiguer* conclusive evidence of universal "common sense." Surely, Hurd argued, if such an isolated and ancient culture as China could recognize the rules of common sense, "what effects must it not have in more enlightened countries and times, where the discipline of long experience, and criticism (which is improved common sense) come in to the assistance of the poet?"[58]

Voltaire used his version of the play, *Orphelin de Chine*, to respond to Jean Jacques Rousseau's pessimistic argument that art and science could not transcend moral corruption. He rewrote the piece to emphasize the victory of morality over barbarism. Revenge was deemphasized and philosophy foregrounded. Moral culture, Voltaire insisted, could triumph over politics.[59]

Murphy greatly admired Voltaire, but unlike the French philosopher's Gengis-kan, who assimilated Chinese court culture, Murphy's tyrant Timurkan was an unrepentant Mongol to the end. His victims died, but Timurkan also fell to the sword of the triumphant orphan Hamet. Instead of keeping his orphan an infant, Murphy focused on Hamet as an adult, an individual "moral agent" capable of "revenging himself on the destroyers of his family."[60] In contrast to Voltaire's debate with Rousseau, Murphy was more concerned about the public responsibilities of the king. By further consolidating the dramatic action and filling his stage with a great deal of explicit violence and emotion, Murphy created a popular, liberal British play.[61]

The 1797 published version of Arthur Murphy's play reveals his attitudes toward China in a prologue and epilogue. While emphasizing the radical Whig preoccupation with the enlightened responsibilities of governance, he told his public to "set your hearts at rest," for British government and people were far superior to the Chinese.[62] In British cosmopolitan culture, China was steadily losing its luster as "an exotic land of wonder" and wisdom and was taking on the new cast of a "provincial empire eager to clasp the British constitution to its breast."[63] As the British Empire expanded and became more self-confident during this era, other empires began to look less impressive and novel, and more arrogant attitudes gained currency.

In late-eighteenth-century New York City, in contrast, China had not yet lost its attraction. As a minor and peripheral city of the British Empire, New York still welcomed what London perceived to be out of fashion. This context explains the success of Murphy's play. The play's periodic staging nevertheless warrants a deeper explanation. How could it please both British soldiers of an occupation army and American revolutionaries?

The rewriting, critical appraisal, staging, and restaging of the play in New York, via England and the Continent, help us understand the ways in which New Yorkers, while proclaiming their independence from England, continued to identify strongly with broader, deeply held European orientalist values. When audiences bought tickets to attend what they believed was an authentic Chinese play, what were they transacting? And whom were they buying this from?

Orphan simultaneously allowed for a critique of the British monarchy, gaining the legitimacy of Chinese civilizational precedent for American values, while also reconnecting U.S. cultural perspectives to an Anglo-Saxon cultural tradition. In a prorevolutionary New York context, *Orphan* could easily be received as a play that justified the War of Independence. As China had been tyrannized by a foreign despot, so had the colonies. The restoration of harmony and order meant not simply that Chinese once again ruled Chinese, but that the "public weal"—the popular mandate given by the people to the ruler—had been reestablished. In the American context, this interpretation easily justified and reinforced the rebellion of republicans over monarchists. Revolutionaries could enjoy *Orphan* as a play about the universal striving for "republican virtue." Self-sacrifice for one common good was not simply an American invention, nor simply part of the claimed Greco-Roman heritage of good Anglo-Saxons; it was also a universal truth, demonstrated by this play from a culture so different from the United States.

While aligning China on the side of Western notions of republican virtue, a damaging and countervailing message was emerging, echoing radical tea boycotters on the dangers of "oriental" goods bringing corruption. As long as China represented Confucian antiquity, it could be extolled as one with Western Enlightenment traditions. But as the British Empire's fortunes and power rose, the China of contemporary geopolitics came to be viewed as outdated, again subject to foreign rule. "Overzealous" monarchs in China were despotic, whereas "people's hearts" supported British monarchs. However, debt-ridden Americans could ill afford to take on such an imperious British attitude. For them China was still a place to be admired and envied, a source of luxuries and the hoped-for savior of the American economy. At the same time, growing familiarity would soon breed contempt. European and Anglo-American theater both appropriated and subjugated Chinese difference into a realm of exoticized contrasts—for now, an orientalist "otherness" to be idealized and emulated. Murphy's epilogue articulated what would become an American refrain about China: "They all are crippled in the tiny shoe."[64] The gentry practice of binding women's feet, thought to be ultra-feminine and erotic (and clearly a means of patriarchal control), was used to symbolize all of China. In this view, Chinese monarchs, and by inference all Chinese men, were de facto tyrants.

Patrician Orientalism

In this founding generation, different individuals with their different dispositions used Chinese and Chinese-style goods and ideas in various ways. George Washington sought distinction through his export porcelains and queensware. Alexander McDougall created a more radical, democratic America in revolt against tea and despotism. Alexander Hamilton sought wealth through his marriage and political arithmetic. Generations of Schuyler women gave valued gifts to forge bonds of sentimentality. Generations of John Street Theatre–goers used *Orphan* to sort out their feelings toward mother England, monarchy, and/or revolution. While each use of orientalism differed, such various practices wove together an everyday life that helped to define an independent occidental identity emulating China and drawing upon British patrician culture, but not tied too tightly to either. This patrician orientalism both helped to formulate order and hierarchy for a commonweal elite and was sometimes used to challenge the status quo. This varied generation of founders shared and shaped an elite, patrician-oriented culture. This elite culture embodied an underlying consensus that the trade of goods and ideas with the empire of China would be beneficial to the building of distinction, independence, development, and wealth, and to the governing of the new nation.

Perhaps this complex patrician orientalism was best embodied by New York merchant Gouverneur Morris. In addition to promoting a proper exemplary taste for the national elite, he helped to formulate and realize the nation's early policy toward China. In 1783 Gouverneur Morris wrote a letter to the secretary of Congress supporting a trade scheme of Robert Morris, his friend and business partner. "Exchange for the superfluities of the East" should be promoted, he wrote, to "prevent the Europ Powers from draining us as they now do of our Specie."[65] The establishment of the China trade was presented as an act of patriotism, a part of nation building.

In late-eighteenth-century usage the term *exchange* was part of the lexicon of terms associated with the rise of capitalism and international trade. The word originally implied the reciprocal bartering of goods for goods, as distinct from the giving of money for goods, which constituted a "sale." The ability to trade goods freely, in barter or with specie, denoted calculated mutual self-interest at work—assumed to be "fair bargains struck between . . . free individuals."[66] Fundamentally different things had to be made equivalent in the negotiation process. And as evidenced by George Washington's constant anxieties about his London china merchant, "unequal exchange is intrinsic to the exchange process itself."[67]

For the process of exchange to work, it was believed that the natural and man-made resources of the Orient should, as a matter of "natural rights," be freely open to exchange. The term *superfluities* connoted excess from what was necessary, a superabundance. Merchant and national wealth, therefore, was contingent on either the taking over of established trade routes to the richest Asian lands and empires from European rivals, or the finding of new routes. Adam Smith proposed that a rising nation's surpluses must then be "sent abroad and exchanged for something of which there is a demand at home."[68] Demand drove exploration, wars, and the establishment of trade ports. By 1776 the British East India Company's trade with Canton, only one port in glorious China, was surpassing all the trade of all the Indian ports on the Arabian and China seas combined. The rapacious quest for trade advantages and the taste for tea and other refinements became ways of measuring a nation's greatness and a people's cultural sense of entitlement.[69]

Gouverneur Morris's words carried meanings that were fundamental to the way in which patrician Americans understood and assessed themselves, their propertyless brethren, and all people, ideas, and things related to China, the "Indies," and other parts of Asia. In actuality, Morris was articulating a complex set of socioeconomic exchanges. The foreign exchange of goods between individuals, peoples, and nations was understood within the daily domestic negotiation of social relationships. Those wanting upward mobility and more access to the "baubles of Britain" and the luxuries of China pressed for a loosening of prior elite controls. At the same time, revolutionaries sought to reestablish a society of order and deference. Both those in favor of and critical of the republican court and those in favor of and critical of republican simplicity implicated Chinese goods and ideas in some way or another. Desired Chinese and Chinese-style luxury goods and ideas, imbued with symbolic meanings, were integral to the formulation of a new American individual and nation—an identity to be further reconstituted in the process of exchange itself. Before the Revolution, these beloved things became part of the driving force for social, political, and economic change. After the Revolution, such expectations propelled the consumer republic to seek its own trade routes. The solution to postwar malaise would be to trade directly with China.

The question of what China wanted was a key to early American wealth. The question of how China became wealthy was a key to how cultural nationalists formed their mythos of American destiny. Modernity was born of this new civilization, rising phoenixlike from the ashes of "old" despotic civilizations.

CHAPTER 2

What Does
China Want?

WRITING AT THE Revolutionary War's end in 1783, Samuel Shaw, the secretary of the Society of the Cincinnati, lamented the national plight: "Is America prepared for the reception of the long wished for blessing? What system has she adequate to the government and prosperity of her rising empire?"[1] The scramble of individual self-interest severely tested republican virtue.

The nation confronted enormous challenges. As historian William A. Williams has pointed out, "Suddenly outside the British Empire, the thirteen free American states faced fundamental problems and clashing alternatives. Each could go their own way . . . [or] join close neighbors in a largely independent regional federation, compromise to form a stronger confederation, or create a new imperial system."[2] How could a poor nation, victorious in defeating a great empire, now develop its own vision of wealth and destiny? Such was the challenge of the toast proffered on the eve of the British evacuation: "May an uninterrupted commerce soon repair the ravages of war!" Largely in response to these questions, the voyage of the *Empress of China*—America's first ship to trade with China—signaled the nation's confidence in international trade as the key to prosperity. This voyage, this "landmark in the history of American commerce," initiated the rise of New York City as the major port of the nation, and the rise of the nation as a global maritime power.[3]

Once direct trade and its accompanying interactions had begun, unexpected paradoxes emerged. The closer Americans got to real Chinese, dispelling their imagined "Orient," the more their respect for and emulation of Chinese civilization diminished. Americans believed that the creed of life, liberty, and happiness justified demands for "free" trade, and having overcome British controls, they decried China's regulation of its trade and ports as "despotism." The confident revolutionary nation and the power it had broken with found a common antagonist in an "oriental" empire resisting the "Occident." Directly engaging China and the Chinese forever complicated America's occidental identity.

The Scramble

John Ledyard, celebrated by maritime historian P. C. F. Smith as a sort of Johnny Appleseed of oriental trade goods, believed that he had all the answers to the nation's questions.[4] Ledyard traveled through the Pacific and learned what goods Chinese merchants wanted to trade and how to use that knowledge to the advantage of U.S. merchants.

Ledyard was one of two Americans who served with British captain James Cook during his explorations from 1776 to 1779. Searching for a quicker passage to Asia, Cook and his crew sailed the uncharted stretches of the Alaska–Pacific Northwest–California coastline, encountering Indians and "Asiatics," Russians and "Equismauxs," who were engaged in the trade of otter and other skins. Ledyard was part of the "discovery" of what were to be called the Sandwich Islands (Hawai'i). Upon arriving in the Portuguese colony of Macao, the crew caught glimpses of the vast emporium of coveted goods Chinese artisans produced for the world market and discovered firsthand that Chinese merchants were willing to pay twice as much for furs as buyers in Kamchatka.[5]

In 1783 Ledyard rushed to rewrite and publish his journal of the voyage, *A Journal of Captain Cook's Last Voyage to the Pacific Ocean, and in Quest of a North-West Passage between Asia and America, Performed in the Years 1776, 1777, 1778, and 1779* (1783). It was the first book published in the United States to describe the people, places, and resources of the Pacific, thus marking the Americanization of direct Western knowledge of the Pacific world. Besides documenting the potential for the Pacific Northwest–China fur trade, Ledyard also expressed an unabashed sense of occidental destiny, his preface confidently asserting, "The following voyage among many others it is presumed will frame the praises of the civilized and enlightened world; the object was noble, it was gloriously concluded, and terminated happily."[6] The book, however, was just the beginning of Ledyard's designs; he planned to fit out a suitable vessel to the Pacific Northwest coast from the Atlantic Northeast to purchase fur pelts for trade with China.[7]

Ledyard's vision interested a number of men associated with the Revolution, notably Robert Morris. Morris, in association with Daniel Parker and Company—comprised of the transplanted New England speculator Daniel Parker, the French entrepreneur John Holker, the influential New Yorker William Duer, and other "sundry merchants of Boston"—formed what one interested investor immodestly called "the American India Company": a privately owned version of the European East Indies companies.[8] The "mad, romantic, dreaming Ledyard" thought he had found his financier, but he would soon discover, at great personal expense, the ruthless ethics that would become typical of the emergent trade.[9] Morris used Ledyard's ideas for the China trade but backed off promises he had made regarding Ledyard's involvement. Ledyard left for France, hoping to find a backer there. Proud, persistent, and a failure, he later walked across Siberia, forever searching for his quick route to China, and exited from the historical stage.[10]

For Robert Morris, Ledyard's scheme coincided with the idea proposed by a close associate two years before. John Holker, who had key connections to such individuals as the French foreign minister, urged his sometime partner and boss Morris to form an American-style East Indies company. Seeking an alliance with the French in their intensifying rivalry with the British Empire, Holker believed that their mutual antipathy to England would make them a powerful challenger.[11] William Duer, John Holker, Daniel Parker, and Robert Morris would become the savvy merchant group behind the *Empress*. Robert Morris was the most important of the group. By 1781 he was acknowledged as the preeminent businessman in America, and as such he was appointed to the position of superintendent of finance in the federal government. By 1783 Morris was growing increasingly weary of his public position; the China trade represented a chance to reenter private business. He made this move with great caution and secrecy.[12] Given Morris's heavy governmental responsibilities and public criticism of profiteering, he had to be extremely careful in his business dealings.

Holker had come to the United States in 1778. His British émigré father ran a textile mill in Rouen, and several important French companies commissioned Holker to represent them. In Philadelphia he became the official buying agent of the Royal French Marine and the French consul-general of Pennsylvania, Delaware, New Jersey, and New York. Because of conflicting government and private interests, he was removed from both these positions. He had also entered into partnership with Morris on commodity speculation. Historian Clarence Ver Steeg has estimated that Holker's extensive activities in shipping, privateering, commission business, lands, and speculation in securities made him one of the leading business figures of the time.[13]

William Duer—English-born and married to Lady Kitty Duer—had inherited a share of his father's extensive plantations in Antigua and Dominica. He also served as Lord Clive's aide-de-camp in colonized India and had been a delegate from New York to the Continental Congress. New York and national businessmen perceived Duer to be a leading light, even after he became embroiled in scandal. His pecuniary interests extended from New England to Pennsylvania; he owned a distillery, equipped the troops, speculated on land, and bought up New York State securities.[14]

The "American India company" plan was to have as many as six ships: two would trade with Europe, two would sail directly for Canton via the tried-and-true European route eastward around the Cape of Good Hope, and the last two would follow the more treacherous westward Ledyard route around Cape Horn, one traveling to the Pacific Northwest coast and the other to French Polynesia. Those ships would then go on to China with their cargo of pelts and other tradable goods. The men had to scale back their grand plans within a matter of months, however, and the fleet was reduced to two ships. Vaingloriously, one ship was christened the *Empress of China* and the other, the *Emperor of China*.[15]

Robert Morris invested his profits from the last days of the war in the China venture.[16] Already involved in a business relationship with Holker while superintendent of finance, Morris appointed his French partner agent of marine. Holker later had to resign because of direct conflicts of interest.[17] William Duer was to serve as the supercargo on the westbound ship. But Duer was wary of Parker. Writing to John Holker, Duer confided, "I must, my dear Freind, Confess to you that the Treatment I have received from some of the Parties makes me Undertake the Voyage with rather a heavy heart." Holker counseled him "to Sacrifice [his] Interests"—advice of classic republican proportions.[18] Duer, claiming poor health, withdrew as supercargo.

Parker was unable to produce the promised Boston investors and, claiming that he had to advance large sums of his own money, asked all partners to invest more. Duer questioned Parker's honesty. Holker risked drawing bills from one of his prestigious French merchant-banking firm connections, who refused to market and insure the bills. Morris appears to have transferred U.S. government funds into his private account to cover his share of the investment.[19] Without consulting his partners, Parker hired Society of the Cincinnati secretary Samuel Shaw to serve as supercargo and further sweetened the deal by suggesting that once they were in Canton, Shaw could load a second ship for his private gain. Shaw agreed to serve, providing he could hire his friend and fellow society member Thomas Randall to serve as second supercargo. Over Parker's objections, the others hired John Green as captain.[20]

The question arose, What does China want? Deciding not to undertake the risky Pacific Northwest venture proposed by Ledyard, the partners had to come up with a prized commodity other than furs for the China trade. The young nation had yet to manufacture anything the Chinese gentry would find desirable. Having plentiful natural resources and foodstuff industries of its own to draw upon, China had no need for American trade staples like salt fish, rum, flour, barrel staves, or lumber. Silver and gold specie were always valued by Chinese merchants but were scarce in postwar America. But to the wonderment and pecuniary delight of the French, Dutch, British, and now the American traders in North America, the Chinese wanted ginseng *(rensheng)* enough to trade their finest teas, spices, porcelains, silks, and other manufactured goods for it. Why the Chinese placed so much value on these fleshy tubers was not evident to European Americans. Its curative powers were unknown to the British and Continental medical traditions. Ginseng was an exchange item par excellence. It was a rare and highly valued medicinal food in China but in the United States was considered to be useless. Even though the Iroquois had used the root, it was never adopted by Anglo-Dutch-American medical or folk medical practice. The root grew in China but was subject, like salt and other items, to imperial monopoly, thus making the item prohibitively expensive. As part of a folk medicine and philosophic tradition of nutritional and spiritual well-being, it was a highly sought after preventive and restorative medicine, believed capable of treating cancers, rheumatism, diabetes, sexual dysfunction, and aging.[21]

The plant grew wild up and down the Atlantic coast, in the foothills of the Adirondacks down through the Appalachians. Father Joseph Francis Lafitau, a French missionary among the Iroquois, was in 1717 the first European to note its presence. Heeding the information that the Chinese valued this root, he searched for it in North America. After several months he came upon the plant, pulled it out of the ground, and showed it to an Iroquois he had hired to help him look. She confirmed it as a known medicinal plant. In three years' time a company was established to gather, clean, and dry the root and ship it through France for trade with China.[22] For European Americans and Indians living and operating in these foothill regions, ginseng became a reliable commodity to exchange with itinerant traders for needed goods. Once the China market opened up, male and female "sang diggers" of all ages and groups began digging for the root.

The extant letter and logbook of a Major Jelles Fonda, a self-described "Indian trader," offers an example of how the ginseng trade operated in New York. Writing from Caughnawaga in September 1774, Fonda told of being asked to buy ten thousand pounds of the root at two shillings a pound. His "Indian Book" log, covering 1762–76, recorded the receipt of ginseng for large quantities of rum and, interestingly enough, quantities of Chinese tea and porcelains for Indian and Dutch gatherers. "Christie Drunken Waries Daughter" (a name that reflected Fonda's biases) traded for a teapot in 1769. "Lydia, White Mouthed Brant's Wife," traded for a half-pound of tea and four cups and saucers later that same year, and more in the following months. Similarly, in 1800 Barent Sanders, his brother, and "a negro man named Jack" (a driver who was presumably a slave) traveled the Mohawk Valley near Albany to buy the root. Sanders's journal was grandly titled "Memorandum of the Proceedings of Barent Sanders respecting a journey and abode among the Indians to manufacture Ginseng Roots." In it he describes purchasing the roots by bushel measurements and hiring "squaws" to clean and brush the roots till they "began to shiny."[23] These examples suggest that the desire for tea and a proper cup reached far beyond the striving middle class of the metropolis.

The partners recruited Dr. Robert Johnston of Philadelphia to trade for the root in Pennsylvania. Johnston had served as a surgeon during the war and was a trusted member of the Society of the Cincinnati. He would also eventually sail on the *Empress* as the ship's surgeon. On August 28, 1783, while Ledyard was still negotiating with Robert Morris, Parker had placed an order with Philadelphia merchants Turnbull, Marmie, and Company for a huge amount, eventually numbering some two million roots. On September 3 Johnston received an advance to begin his search in the Appalachian hinterlands of western Pennsylvania and Virginia. After months of a grueling traveling schedule and constant problems with receiving sufficient cash to pay for his commitments, Johnston gathered more than thirty tons of the root that Turnbull, Marmie, and Company had shipped to New York. He paid anywhere from three shillings to five shillings per pound. Daniel Parker optimistically predicted that the *Empress* would arrive to "a great market" well before the European ships and garner $15 a pound. According to the *Chinese Repository*, traders made as much as 500–600 percent profit on the ginseng.[24]

The *Empress of China*

The black hull of a 360-ton Boston-made ship sat low in its berth, creaking and rolling as the sea pulled at its hemp moorings. Its forty-two-man crew had been ready to cast off and unfurl the ship's three sails for the last month. The cargo hold was packed with Spanish silver coins and barrels containing 57,687 pounds of ginseng. In all, a fortune was invested in this speculative venture. It had cost the partners $120,000, an amount that would have purchased twenty-four thousand acres of prime land.[25]

After months of planning for the maiden voyage, everything and everyone was finally prepared—all, that is, except whatever passed under the aegis of providence. It was the coldest winter in living memory; New York Harbor, chosen because of its deep all-weather egress, was frozen solid.[26] Further delay would mean financial disaster. In a detailed letter of instructions to Captain Green, the owners of the *Empress* expressed their concern: "It being of very great Consequence to arrive in Canton before any other Vessel which can go from Europe with fresh Ginseng, every attention has been paid, as you know, to procure a Ship particularly calculated, both for fast sailing and to encounter rough Weather."[27] This ship was now competing with those of powerful European empires. Yet the severity of the winter made even revolutionaries who had defeated the might of King George wait anxiously. Major Shaw knew from his artillery command in the Continental Army that timing was essential for the well-being of this impoverished fledgling republic. Battles with the king's banditti had been lost through inattention to duty and uncontrollable circumstances. And now, only a year after he had put away his officer's uniform, sword, and laced hat, a month, a week, a day, could still make all the difference between success and failure for his employers.

Shaw's journal entries provide some insight into the pressures experienced by these gentleman revolutionaries and the significance of their venture. Having reached maturity with the expectation of pecuniary rewards and success in business, Shaw was left feeling impoverished by his eight years of service in the Continental Army. His letters regularly lamented his inability to keep up the necessities and appearances of his office. At one point he asked that half a dozen shirts and "cravats" be sent to him. On another date he expressed his worries over losing his horse in battle. The loss of a horse would diminish his authority, and it would take two years of military pay to replace the creature. While lamenting the "decay of public virtue" and increase in "avarice," he confided his innermost frustrations to a close friend: "If it did not look too much like self-applause, I might say that I engaged in the cause of my country from the purest motives. However, be this as it may, my continuance in it has brought me to poverty and rags; and, had I fortune of my own, I should glory in persevering, though it should occasion a sacrifice of the last penny."[28] Shaw was hardly impoverished compared with the majority of Americans with lesser family means, but his memory of wealth produced an acute sense of loss.

Shaw, like so many others of the revolutionary generation, had high hopes for the China trade. In a letter to his brother he wrote, "I shall sail for China by the 15th of January, from New York. The terms on which I go promise something clever, and I hope to shake you by the hand in two years. . . . If Heaven prospers my present undertaking, it will be in my power to help you [financially]."[29] The voyage was seen as the means of raising Shaw and his family to their rightful societal status.

But the American venture into the China trade was riven by corruption and competing self-interests. Upon inspecting Parker's cargo just before the *Empress* set sail, Shaw discovered that $2,300 worth of the declared $20,000 silver specie was mysteriously missing. He was responsible, as the business agent, for the missing bullion. He confronted Parker with the problem, and Parker promised that he would supply the money before sailing, never amending the bill of lading. However, once the *Empress* was headed to China, Shaw discovered that Parker had never restored the missing silver specie. At the same time, Parker's partners were pressing him to pay a growing number of creditors large and small, American and French. Their honor impugned, Duer took action. He filed suit for $150,000 and sought Parker's arrest with $20,000 bail. After dissolving Daniel Parker and Company, his partners pressed him to open his account books, whereupon they discovered that he had consistently falsified his entries; he had diverted nearly $200,000 to his personal accounts. In July 1784 Parker fled to London, Amsterdam, and Paris, not to be seen again.[30]

Upon learning of Parker's deceptions, Holker attempted to sell his share of the cargo's profits even before the ship's return. This action precipitated a serious breach in his longstanding friendship with William Duer. Holker reported, bitterly, "I have mortgaged my personal Estate: & all these misfortunes happen me through your introducing to me D.P. as a worthy Caracter." The fractured relationship between Holker and Duer revealed the strains placed upon personal and collegial bonds by the market society. Holker continued, "In this situation you'll talk of engagements of honour, when I am honorably pledging every farthing in the world for the Company's debts, which I did not Contract, at the very time that you are so very largely in debt to me Personally, for heavy sums." Holker warned Duer that he needed some financial support, "if you sincerely wish to have any claim to my Esteem or friendship."[31]

Captain Green had his own challenges. British navigation restrictions had made it illegal for colonial subjects to engage in international trade, and few colonials had yet had the opportunity to visit the fantastic "Cathay" Marco Polo had written about. Many were not certain what to call the distant civilization. The generic term *Indies* had been in use among Westerners since the fifteenth century and loosely denoted "a region or place yielding great wealth or to which profitable voyages may be made." In 1776 Abbé Raynal defined the East Indies as including "all regions beyond the Arabian Sea and the kingdom of Persia." Mixing names and places, Captain Green labeled the flyleaf of his seagoing logbook "A Jurnal of An Intended Voyage on Board the Ship Empress of Chinea Bound from New York to Canton In India."[32]

For a sea captain who had never ventured beyond the Anglo-American corridor, Green's sailing directions were typically nonspecific. They were to arrive in Canton, with the aid of only a roughly drawn map, navigational instruments, and the following instructions: "You will make all expedition from New York to the Cape de Verde Islands . . . thence Eastward & Northward to the Island of Clote, thence to the Island of Java . . . thence thro' the Straights of Sunda to Macao, the Charts off that Coast with Dunns directions, herewith delivered to you, will afford usefull matter of instruction on the Subject."[33] With no previous direct experience, the venture moved ahead on desire and hope.

Finally, after fortnights of delays, the temperature gradually rose. The ice clogging the Narrows through which all ships sailed in and out of New York Harbor began to break. On February 22, 1784, as the ship *Edward* cleared New York for London with the ratification of the Treaty of Paris and as George Washington celebrated his fifty-second birthday, the *Empress of China* sailed out of the port of New York. The ship enjoyed a rousing salute at Fort George and sailed past Sandy Hook into the Atlantic Ocean.

Oblivious to all the internal intrigue of the investors and the crew, commercial newspapers of the northern Atlantic ports were brimming with hope. The adjectives *youthfulness, intelligence, optimism,* and *vigor* that were used to describe the crew also clearly expressed the way in which journalists wanted to imagine the new nation. Besides any diplomatic activity the *Empress* would be engaging in, metaphorically the ship and its crew became closely identified with the fragile hopes of and for the country and its people. The *New York Packet,* published by a fervent supporter of Hamilton-style Federalism, cheerily reported:

> Yesterday morning several vessels left the Wharves. . . . Among others was the *Empress of China.* The morning being pleasant drew a large party of gentlemen to the Battery. . . . All hearts seemed glad, contemplating the new source of riches that may arise to this city, from a trade to the East-Indies; and all joined their wishes for the success of the *Empress of China,* with thanks to the concerned who thus early and nobly stood forth the friends of commerce and their country.[34]

Like Samuel Shaw and Robert Morris, the spectators hoped for an outcome that would combine what was good for the nation and what was good for their private interests as gentrified merchants.

Philip Freneau, patriotic poet and journalist, celebrated the departure of the *Empress* with an ode to "eastern gems":

> With clearance from BELLONA won
> She spread her wings to meet the Sun,
> Those golden regions to explore
> Where George forbade to sail before. . . .
>
> To countries plac'd in burning climes
> And islands of remotest times
> She now her eager course explores,
> And soon shall greet Chinesian shores,
>
> From thence their fragrant TEAS to bring
> Without the leave of Britain's king;
> And PORCELAIN WARE, enchas'd in gold,
> The product of that finer mould.

> Thus commerce to our world conveys
> All that the varying taste can please:
> For us, the Indian looms are free,
> And JAVA strips her spicy TREE.[35]

A sense of liberation animates this poem. The desire to trade "where [King] George forbade" represented a type of maritime right many Americans had fought for. Further, the freedom to trade enabled Americans to indulge their taste for luxuries. American liberation became integrally tied to free trade and the possession of Chinese goods.

Transacting Cultures

The American foray into the China trade also produced a series of unanticipated consequences. In New York the business venture launched by members of the Society of the Cincinnati was plagued from the start by corruption and self-interest. In this new nation, relationships of deference and reciprocal responsibility were in constant flux. In Canton, by contrast, as Shaw discovered, American traders and missionaries found common cause with their former enemy Great Britain, among other European counterparts. Commercial desires united them. The exchange chains of the China trade linked people who were totally foreign to one another, making partners of former enemies and enemies of former partners. Having established the fact of political independence, patrician Americans' postcolonial experience in China was to remind them just how British and how European they truly were. Ultimately driven by the pursuit of luxuries and gain, these Americans located their allegiances with an occidental identity now increasingly juxtaposed against and not emulating the Orient.

Upon the *Empress*'s arrival in the Portuguese colony of Macao, Samuel Shaw discovered a sociable community of European "gentleman" traders and military who welcomed the Americans. He specifically noted how cordial even the British merchants were. Indeed, one British officer visited "to welcome your flag to this part of the world." This camaraderie between Europeans and Americans arose, in part, from their common challenge of maximizing their trade interests with Chinese hong merchants. Just as significant, however, a European cosmopolitan patrician culture pervaded the settlement, bringing cultural harmony to trade rivals. Europeans and Americans exchanged dinners, visits, gifts. Henceforth, Americans became members of a convivial, albeit competitive, club.[36]

American and Chinese merchants necessarily established barter rates and gift exchanges to conduct business. In this bargaining process Shaw found common sentiment with his competitors. Shaw echoed other European traders on the shrewd "knavery of the Chinese," pointing out how "the small dealers, almost universally, are rogues" who "will not scruple to offer one third of what is demanded for merchandise."[37] By nature the bartering of very different goods required a process of balancing subjective and uneven desires. Shaw regaled readers of his memoirs with one bargaining session in which the Chinese merchant communicated in what Shaw clearly cast as a childish, "pidgin" English, foreshadowing comic routines that would later appear on the New York stage:

> One of them offered me for an article less than one half the price at which I valued it, and would come day after day and make the same offer. I treated him politely every time, and adhered to my first demand, which he finally complied. After the bargain was settled,—"you are not Englishman?" said he. "No." "But you speak English word, and when you first come, I no can tell difference; but now I understand very well. When I speak Englishman his price, he say, 'So much,—take it,—let alone.' I tell him, 'No, my friend, I give you so much.' He look at me,—'Go to hell, you damned rascal; what! you come here,—set a price my goods?' Truly, Massa Typan, I see very well you no hap Englishman. All China-man very much love your country."

These lowly comical "rogues" were sharply differentiated from the elite "merchants of the co-haong" who Shaw and others believed were "as respectable a set of men as are commonly found in other parts of the world."[38] In the Anglo-American storytelling imagination of extreme characterizations, Shaw found two types of Chinese merchants: the lowly trickster Chinaman and the refined merchant gentleman, whom he called a "mandarin," adept at Western ways.[39]

As was true with the European traders, a certain amount of socializing existed between the hong merchants and the Europeans; they exchanged niceties and gifts. Given the frequent episodes of indebtedness and bankruptcy experienced by Chinese and European merchants alike, some genuine acts of friendship did occur. For example, the editor of the New York–based *Merchant's Magazine*, Freeman Hunt, featured the story of a Chinese merchant helping his European brethren. Extraordinarily, the merchant forgave an English trader an $870,000 debt! Furthermore, upon learning of the trader's death, he donated money to the man's two surviving children.[40]

The voyage of the *Empress of China* did not simply represent the exchange of material goods; it also initiated the establishment of relationships between peoples of starkly contrasting cultures and sociohistorical systems. The tea pickers in China traded their teas to river traders, who transported the processed leaves to urban-based merchant middlemen, who sold their selected teas to one of a few hong merchants in Canton designated by the emperor to trade with Westerners. Likewise, the trading of ginseng linked thousands of people living on the peripheries of the Atlantic Northeast coast to the ports in which these processed roots were traded. In this sense, the roots were more than a simple object for trade; they came to embody a series of human relations and hidden labor in the "manufacturing" of the root. As with porcelains and teas, the value of this good, though fixed during any given transaction, was highly subjective and variable. Indians and "frontier" European American settlers harvested it, processed it, and sold it; itinerant peddlers traded it for goods and sold it to port-based merchants who bought it wholesale and then sold it for often spectacular profits. Each exchange in this chain brokered very different expectations and desires. American sang diggers and Chinese tea pickers now depended on this international process of exchange for subsistence.

However, any transactions between one individual at one end of the chain and another person at the other end were brokered by port-city merchants. These translocal social relationships offered the possibility of cross-cultural contact, communication, and understanding. Yet such interactions were necessarily limited by capitalist trade relations. Merchant traders in Canton and now New York controlled these global interactions and played a critical role in negotiating cross-cultural desires into commodifiable exchanges. Items seemed rarer when they assumed a new identity as long-distance trade goods. Prolonging the appearance of rarity depended on the ability of the exporting party to maintain a monopoly of knowledge about the item; in this period, control was held at the port of trade.

With the voyage of the *Empress,* what had been a peripheral colonial outpost became a hub of mercantile commercial capitalism. The ambitions of New York's port merchants necessarily implicated the people and development of the valleys and frontiers of the Hudson River. Ginseng, for the moment, became a cash crop for the China trade. Though powerful in the new nation, American port-city traders were still relatively powerless in Canton. The *Empress* partners had to pull their limited resources together and find common cause in this vulnerable first venture. Paradoxically, once the *Empress* had been launched, the cherished bonds that had made the revolution possible frayed to a breaking point. The voyage of the *Empress* initiated direct U.S. involvement with China, a continuous cross-cultural process of interaction against which Western social, economic, and political values were constantly measured and contrasted.

American merchants came to form two parallel sets of allegiances, split along class and cultural lines, one bonding elite Chinese and American merchants, and the other bonding eager and often frustrated Western traders negotiating the Chinese system. Despite the camaraderie, power divided along a West-East axis of the balance of trade. The Chinese government constantly thwarted Western traders by limiting access to the goods they desired. Western traders felt manipulated and subject to tyrannical control and wanted more flexibility. Chinese officials confined Westerners to an international trading area and insisted on their adherence to Chinese customs and laws.[41]

Disdain and Deception

From the inaugural voyage of the *Empress*, returning American traders began to communicate a dramatically different representation of China from that of Jefferson. The emperor's control of all foreign trade infuriated merchants wanting access to the China market. The patrician orientalism of admiration began to shift toward disdain. "Their government is admirably well adapted to make them hypocrites and knaves," declaimed Erasmus Doolittle, a colonial merchant. Amasa Delano, another merchant and perhaps the one most sympathetic to the Chinese government, reported that there was "only one law in China, which will be condemned by the people of countries where there is more freedom enjoyed." According to historian Stuart Creighton Miller, who studied scores of traders' logbooks, "In the eyes of these traders, China was a huge pecking order in which each official terrorized those under him, which resulted in cowardice, corruption, venality, and deceit." "Despotism" was an "impure source from whence the black stream of vice flows to infect the whole nation."[42]

In the American context "despotism" came to represent the opposite of the bourgeois individual ideal as articulated by Locke and Adam Smith. Slavish behavior, attributed to any outside limits imposed upon one's freedom in the liberal marketplace, was automatically thought to be a sign of despotism. Any sense of social responsibility was thought to be voluntary and to emanate from the free, rational, male individual. Locke emphasized how different people from different environments and ways of life were made lazy: "Some . . . misemploy their power of Assent, by lazily enslaving their Minds, to the Dictates and Dominion of others, in Doctrines, which it is their duty to carefully examine; and not blindly, with an implicit faith, to swallow."[43] Despots were de facto the enslavers who controlled their subjects, happy or unhappy, whether by tradition, sacred tests, or the raw exercise of violence. Male despotic rule over women was perceived to be tolerated "without resentment."[44] And it remained an open question whether those who had been enslaved were capable of becoming free and self-possessed.[45] Shaw's first encounter with real Chinese in 1784 foreshadowed the contradictory but ultimately dehumanized way in which Chinese immigrants would be adjudged in New York and the nation in the following century.

Fifteen months after the *Empress* left the Narrows of New York Harbor, the ship and crew returned to their home port to a thirteen-gun salute. New York newspapers wrote jubilantly about the ship's full cargo of highly prized goods. Teas, silks, nankeens, porcelains, fans, and other items were unloaded. Besides bringing fanciers of Chinese goods what they desired, the successful voyage swelled nationalist pride and optimism. Indeed, the one voyage out begot two shiploads in. Second supercargo Thomas Randall stayed behind to hire and load a second ship of Shaw's and Randall's private "privilege" goods, the *Pallas,* in which he would soon return.[46] The *Empress's* cargo made a modest (though satisfactory) 25–30 percent profit to its investors, but it immediately took on a broader significance. A May 1785 issue of the *New York News Dispatch* predicted that the *Empress's* return

> presages a future happy period in our being able to dispense with that burdensome and unnecessary traffick, which hitherto we have carried on with Europe—to the great prejudice of our rising empire, and future happy prospects of solid greatness; And . . . whether or not, the ship's cargo be productive of those advantages to the owners . . . it will promote the welfare of the United States in general, by inspiring their citizens with emulation to equal, if not excell their mercantile rivals.[47]

This trade represented a chance to compete on a global scale and an independent means to distinguish Anglo-Americans from their former colonizing motherland.

While the press heralded the *Empress's* return, Shaw immediately went about seeking a resolution to the problem of the missing specie. The acids of economic individualism had already eaten away the bonds of republican solidarity, and now Shaw was to find himself doubly disgraced in the eyes of the remaining partners. Besides being angry at his passive complicity in Parker's deception, they were shocked to discover the agreement that had enabled Thomas Randall to return from China in a second ship, the *Pallas*, carrying an additional $50,000 of private merchandise. Having hoped to corner the market with their own Chinese goods, they couldn't believe that their own supercargoes had undercut their monopoly. They filed suit against Shaw and Randall. Shaw filed suit against Holker for his 10 percent of the cargo. Years of legal and court battles postponed any resolution. Finally, in 1791, Shaw managed to have Parker sign a letter admitting his deception. Parker also agreed to pay back Holker and the other partners, but as late as 1813, Parker had still not paid his debt.[48]

The hoped-for solidarity of the postwar republican aristocracy, embodied by the Society of the Cincinnati, was not easily convertible to peacetime joint ventures. In contrast to a European aristocratic past of hierarchical, customary social relationships and government-sponsored trading companies, human relations in postrevolutionary America were, at core, quite brittle and were increasingly mediated by market-driven advantage and power. Parker's deceptive sincerity enabled him to operate in the guise of an honorable man who could massively profit from the partnership. His faked ledger book had the power to mobilize scores of people, dissolve partnerships, and ruin friendships. In this commercial marketplace, power exercised under false pretenses could result in far-reaching effects. Parker's warning to Captain Green that "the Chinese are very great Rogues" begins to assume an ironic aspect. A comment that would later become a widely circulated stereotype about the Chinese was in fact a truer description of Daniel Parker himself.[49]

Contact with the realities of Chinese society, economic policy, and politics had soured the Jeffersonian and Franklinesque admiration for China, but the passionate coveting of refined Chinese things continued unabated. American traders were unable to understand and accept Chinese differences or suspend their ethnocentric judgments. Their notions of a proper universal human being were defined by behavioral norms that disdained the cultural differences they encountered. And as these exemplars of the rising U.S. culture distanced themselves from these foreign "others," so too they differentiated themselves from the not so distant Anglo-American republican heritage of a strong governmental hand regulating economic activity.

CHAPTER 3

The Port's Rise

Despite the embargo of all American trading vessels imposed by President Jefferson on August 12, 1808, John Jacob Astor was able to gain special clearance for his five-hundred-ton ship, the *Beaver*, to leave New York Harbor. Astor managed to convince Jefferson that the *Beaver* was carrying an important "mandarin," a Mr. "Pun Hua Wing Chong," who had to be immediately returned to China. Otherwise, according to Astor, the United States would risk straining diplomatic relations. The next day, scandal broke out: New York's *Commercial Advertiser* claimed that the "mandarin" was in fact a "dock loafer" who had arrived from China on a recent ship. Merchants in New York officially protested to Jefferson, and Astor wrote a public letter offering to prove that he had not deceived the president.[1]

Despite the public embarrassment, President Jefferson stood by his approval. Weeks earlier he had sent Albert Gallatin, the secretary of the treasury, a blank passport for the vessel that indicated his rationale for exempting this man from the shipping embargo: "The departure of this individual with good disposition may be the means of making our nation known advantageously as the source of power in China, to which it is otherwise difficult to convey information." On August 15 he wrote another letter to Gallatin expressing his ongoing concern: "The opportunity hoped from that, of making known through one of its own characters of note, our nation, our circumstances and character, and of letting the government understand at length the difference between us and the English, and separate us in its policy, rendered that measure a diplomatic one, in my view, and likely to bring lasting advantage to our merchants and commerce with that country."[2] For Jefferson, the risk of being hoaxed by the German-born Astor was of less concern than the benefit of seizing whatever opportunities he could to establish favorable relations with China.

Various biographers of Astor have since claimed that his story was pure fabrication and that Mr. Chong was either the *Advertiser's* "dock loafer," the merchant's personal servant, someone picked up in a New York park, or "just an American Indian" dressed for the part. Speculation also lingered that this entire incident was a ruse fabricated by Astor to challenge Jefferson's political authority and right to impose the embargo. Whether or not Astor intended the incident to provoke a political showdown, he had gained the upper hand. The *Beaver* sailed out of New York Harbor with Astor's supposed diplomat and $45,000 worth of goods, proceeded to pick up a cargo of furs on the Northwest coast, sold them in Canton, and returned with a load of Chinese tea to make $200,000 in the embargoed market.[3]

A private letter dated August 11, 1808, signed by "Columbus" and sent to Secretary of State James Madison, provides a more plausible explanation of Mr. Chong's identity. "Mr. Winchong," the writer claimed, who is represented as "a china mandarin[,] I know well and [knew] him before he left Canton. He is no more a mandarin than one of our shopkeepers is for that is his occupation." Apparently this Chinese merchant had come to the United States expressly to collect money owed him by Samuel Shaw and Thomas Randall, the business agents of the *Empress* and the *Pallas*. Merchant Chong arrived to discover that "Shaw is since dead [having died in 1794] and Randall with hard labor can scarcely support his indigent family therefore not a cent has been collected from Him." Indicating that "Mr. Winchong" was not alone, Columbus pleaded, "It would be cruel to the highest degree for any person to object to Mr. Winchong and the other Chinese having permission to return to their native country."[4] With this historical fragment, we gain some glimpse of Shaw's business dealings. It is somehow fitting, and ironic, that in this era in which republican virtue was being challenged by emergent capitalism, the first documented visit of a Chinese person to New York City was undertaken in order to collect an errant, and irretrievable, bill.[5]

As the fortunes of the *Empress's* crew and investors withered, those of John Jacob Astor rose. This anecdote marks the beginning of two significant shifts of power, the first in regard to U.S. political policy in Asia and the second in regard to the decline of the port of Canton and the rise of New York. Astor's unbridled self-interest, in this case, shifted the fulcrum in the balance between the wealth of China and the aspirations of the United States.

His aggressive pursuit of personal profit was tacitly approved by President Jefferson.[6] Furthermore, in the decades to come the United States joined European nations in prying open China's economy for "free trade." The sovereignty of China would decline as the economic power of the United States rose. In effect, Astor's rise in the nineteenth century was in direct relation to the rise of the port of New York and the decline of the empire of China. Once Astor made his wealth, he turned his attention to the New York real estate market and also secured his position within the ruling civic culture of this rising port city. Indeed, Astor epitomized the rise of the bourgeois individual, and this rise shifted the uses of Chinese things, people, and ideas by New York elites.

Wealth Becomes Manifest

Merchant Chong arrived in New York at a telling geopolitical moment. During the first half of the Napoleonic Wars, 1793–1807, U.S. commerce flourished. Both France and England turned to American shipowners as a neutral party to supply their foodstuffs and trade their goods. With French and British West Indian and other goods passing through American ports, exports swelled from $20.2 million in 1790 to $108.3 million in 1807. Shipowners' profits jumped from $5.9 million to $42.1 million. In the same year both the Bank of the United States and the Stock Exchange were established in lower Manhattan.[7] This increased wealth stimulated domestic consumption fourfold. The commercial windfall ended abruptly with the British blockade of American reexport trade in 1807. To the protest of port merchants, President Jefferson responded with the embargo of all American overseas trade. His vision of building the nation would focus on cultivating alternative trading partners and on obtaining enough land for a republic of small landowning farmers.[8]

Throughout the late 1700s and early 1800s, northern Atlantic port cities grew rapidly. Farsighted politicians and investors were able to capitalize on a revolution in transportation technology. Responding to the demand for faster and more reliable water transport, Robert Fulton was able to promote his steamship in 1807. The Hudson River to Albany became a major interior market for the city. Influenced in part by the widely admired Grand Canal in China, former mayor (now governor) De Witt Clinton was able to persuade a Republican New York state legislature to finance the Erie Canal.[9] Completed in 1825, the waterway spurred the port's rise. Through New York

Harbor, exterior markets of the Atlantic and Pacific worlds were increasingly linked to the western interior of North America. By the end of the 1820s some fifty steamboats and five hundred to seven hundred ships were based in New York harbor, with some fourteen hundred ships bringing goods and peoples from foreign ports annually. By the 1840s even the proud seafaring merchants of Boston and Salem were shipping all their cargo from New York. During the Napoleonic Wars the port of New York aggressively brokered the purchase of slave plantation cotton, bought in Charleston, Savannah, Mobile, and New Orleans, and shipped it to Europe via New York. The city's exports already constituted one-third of the nation's total, and imports amounted to one-half.[10]

The unprecedented growth of economic opportunities in the northeastern ports attracted aspiring immigrants from Europe. New York City had become the largest city of the nation, surpassing Philadelphia by the 1810 census. The port's population tripled from under one hundred thousand people in 1810 to over three hundred thousand in 1840.[11] Two such immigrants, Stephen Girard of Philadelphia and John Jacob Astor of New York, were able to enter the China trade to make vast fortunes.[12] Astor was a German immigrant who had the freedom simply to focus on making a fortune, seeking the quickest and most profitable trade opportunities. In contrast to the partners and crew of the *Empress*, he did not self-consciously carry the social or political future of the nation upon his shoulders. He was unfettered by their larger philosophical and political concerns of nation building.

Opium and "Coolies"

Astor and his fellow New York merchants devised a series of short-term solutions to obtain what China was willing to barter. For Americans, the supply of good-quality ginseng soon dwindled. By the 1790s Astor and others had realized John Ledyard's vision of a fur trade. Astor bartered with Indians for sea otter pelts, seals found around the Falkland Islands, and pelts gathered by North American fur-trading companies to be sold principally to New York merchants.[13] The bonanza ended with a mass slaughter that brought about the near extinction of these fur-bearing animals. Moreover, by the War of 1812 the Canton market had become overstocked.

Until the discovery of gold in California decades later, the United States had no precious-metal mines of any significance. Still, from 1805 to 1827 the U.S. treasury recorded far more specie exported to Canton than mer-

Figure 4. South Street from Maiden Lane, 1828. Manhattan's trade
increased greatly after the completion of the Erie Canal.
(Collection of the New-York Historical Society)

chandise. In 1816, for example, traders shipped out $1.9 million of specie
while only exporting $0.6 million worth of merchandise. The following year
they exported $4.5 million of specie in contrast to $1.1 million worth of
merchandise. The future of the American trade with China depended on
reversing the disadvantageous balance of payments. Those vested in the
trade economy sought to devise new strategies to do this, with entrepreneurs
in the port of New York leading the way.

Through his trade with the Pacific Northwest and Canton, John Jacob
Astor had built up a general-merchandise firm in lower Manhattan. Astor's
American Fur Company had invested in a ship to Canton in 1802 and continued to send at least one or two ships a year up until the War of 1812. In
return, he built up a huge inventory of teas, silk goods, nankeens, porcelains,
and other miscellaneous items. Because of the continual wars in Europe,
American ships carried many China goods directly for trade with Bordeaux,

Hamburg, and Mediterranean ports. Wealthy enough to warehouse his goods and auction them at the most advantageous moments, Astor was able to profit greatly from the war years. Sometimes three fleets would be operating simultaneously, one between Europe and New York, another between New York and China, and the third in the Pacific Ocean.[14]

Astor, like other merchants, regularly sought new commodities that China wanted—items that would not require the relinquishing of silver specie. One solution was quite obvious, though only temporary. He, along with many other American shippers, began to emulate the British practice of trading opium. In 1816 Astor picked up forty piculs—more than five thousand pounds—of Levantine opium from the port of Smyrna, a port not controlled by the British, and smuggled it directly into Canton. Records in 1817 show Astor shipping ninety-five piculs. The Turkish opium was of a grade inferior to the British product from Bengal, but it still provided an opening wedge for American entrée into the trade. Biographer Kenneth Porter hypothesized that Astor traded opium for several years but may have decided that it was not profitable enough and withdrew from trafficking after 1818. However, J. P. Cushing of Boston—cousin of Caleb Cushing, who later became the Chinese consul—reported in 1819 that Astor purchased 100 of the total 180 piculs of opium Cushing brought in.[15]

Given the periodic crackdown on the drug by Chinese officials, opium was not so easy to sell. Officials had to be bribed and pirates evaded, and even then moneys made from a lesser-quality drug were often considered too risky for smaller, less powerful merchants. James and Thomas Perkins, principals of a prominent Boston trading firm, considered Astor their main—indeed, only—competitor. In a letter to their agent the Perkinses wrote, "From the intention of the Chinese to be very strict about Opium, the competitions you fear we think will not exist. We know of no one but Astor we fear. It is our intention to push it as far as we can."[16]

The extent of Astor's involvement in the continued smuggling of opium into China has yet to be documented. However, we do know that Astor continued to bring the drug into the port of New York, a few cases at a time. Indeed, the April 29, 1825, issue of the *New-York Gazette and General Advertiser* carried a paid advertisement offering three cases of Turkish opium for sale. Astor did withdraw from the China trade later that year, funneling his investments into Manhattan real estate, which consumed more and more of the firm's time. At his death in 1848, Astor's estate was valued at $20 million—New York's largest private fortune to that date.[17] The exchange of furs, and not opium, was the basis of Astor's fortune. However, his shift from catering to what China wanted to trafficking in the illicit drug represented an attitudinal sea change. From this viewpoint, another victory over tyranny had been won.

Historian Michael Greenberg has calculated that during the first four decades of the nineteenth century, opium became the single largest commodity of international trade. By the 1830s, the drug accounted for two-thirds of the value of all British imports into China, becoming the chief trade item exchanged for tea. A British pamphleteer in 1839 argued the significance of the trade in stark terms:

> The turn of the balance of trade between Great Britain and China in favour of the former has enabled India to increase tenfold her consumption of British manufacture, contributed directly to support the vast fabric of British dominion in the East, to defray the expenses of His Majesty's establishment in India, and by the operation of exchanges and remittances in teas, to pour an abundant revenue into the British Exchequer and benefit the nation to an extent of 6 million Pounds yearly without impoverishing India.[18]

In contrast to the four thousand chests of opium trafficked annually by the British before 1821, American involvement in the trade was fairly modest. After the War of 1812, for example, opium accounted for 6–15 percent of the American China trade. Yet once silver coins are taken out of the calculation, opium accounted for at least 20–30 percent of the goods bartered. After an 1821 crackdown on smuggling in Canton, the illicit drug trade moved to Lintin, an island outside the control of the Chinese government. A new system was established wherein Chinese smugglers paid silver for the drug, an arrangement far more profitable than the sluggish and covert operations in Canton. The smugglers would then take care of all the bribes and assume the risk of the trade. This system became what one historian has called "a model of efficiency, security, and profit" that took advantage of superior Western ship speed and firepower. With this reduction of risk, the opium trade doubled in the 1820s and doubled again in the 1830s.[19]

By 1838–39, the year Commissioner Lin Zexu (Lin Tse-hsu) sought to stamp out the trade, China had been inflicted with forty thousand chests of opium, or some 5.3 million pounds. For much of the 1820s, opium was the only part of the China trade making profits. The aggressive increase in Americans' opium purchases from India compelled the British East India Company to expand its cultivation of poppies in the Bengal.[20] Historian

Jacques Down has argued persuasively that the increased American involvement in the trade—from developing new sources of supply to expanding the market—forced the British to expand further and protect their own trade, and ultimately led to the Chinese government's increased efforts to stop the importation of the drug, climaxing in the Anglo-Chinese Opium Wars (1840–42, 1856–60).[21]

Trade interests also drove the development of new technologies that could improve the United States' position in the world of international trade. American aggressiveness stimulated the development of a design for faster clipper ships, which rapidly spread the smuggling operation along the China coast. By 1847 these larger clippers carried as much as seven hundred tons at unprecedented speeds. The fastest ships could make it to China and back in a fraction of the time of the *Empress's* voyage.[22]

During these early decades of the nineteenth century, New York–based China trade houses battled to dominate local and regional markets. Rivaling Astor was Thomas H. Smith. Smith also traded opium but entered the tea trade in the 1820s after having gained an incredible $3 million of government-deferred import tax credits. He reinvested the funds in more tea and consequently had glutted the market by 1826. The price of tea dropped, and Smith went bankrupt. In Smith's place six firms emerged over the years to become the major China trade houses of the city: N. L. and G. Griswold, Goodhue and Company, Grinnell, Minturn, and Company, Howland and Aspinall, Talbot Olyphant and Company, and A. A. Low and Brothers. These houses arranged sailings, ordered shipments from their agents in Canton, and sold their goods wholesale at New York auction houses. All these trading firms, with the notable exception of Olyphant and Company, engaged in the opium trade. At least one agent, William Law of a later reorganized Minturn and Champlin, tried to extricate himself from an unpaid debt to a Chinese merchant by illegally trading the drug.[23]

Two decades later William Law's nephew, Abiel Abbot Low, would demonstrate more sophistication in handling the politics of the illicit trade. A. A. Low was born "of a pure New England stock" in 1811 to Seth and Mary (Porter) Low of Salem. His father was an importer of "drugs and India wares," who resettled the family in Brooklyn. After working for his father for a number of years, Abiel joined his uncle, William Low, to become a clerk in what was the largest American house in the China trade, the Boston firm of Russell and Company. Founded in 1824 by Samuel Russell and Philip Ammidon, the firm specialized in opium and by 1827 had become the largest

American seller of the drug, acquiring Perkins and Company in 1829. Abiel Low learned the workings of the firm from the ground up, beginning as a junior clerk. After four years he became a partner. He then spent seven years in Canton and Macao before returning to New York in 1840 to establish his own firm. Taking advantage of clipper ship technology, A. A. Low and Brothers concentrated on trading opium for tea.[24]

As American trade proliferated, the ways of profiting from China also multiplied. The luxuries and opium trades were not the only ways to wealth. New York shippers, for example, were also prominent in the coolie and guano trades, thereby further involving Chinese laborers in the daily life of the port city.[25] The metropolitan consumer demands of the European and North American elite and middle classes precipitated the expansion of colonial plantations into tobacco, sugar, cacao, coffee, spices, and other luxury foods turned necessities. The profitable demand for sugar and the British banning of slavery in 1807 prompted the revival of indentured contracts to keep the exploitative plantation system in the colonies alive. As the British pressured the French, Spanish, and Portuguese to follow the ban, colonial powers created the coolie labor market. From 1838 to 1870 over half a million Chinese and South Asian men were shipped—in conditions often compared with the notorious "middle passage" of the African slave trade—to Cuba, Peru, Mauritius, Demerara (British Guiana), Brazil, Trinidad, Jamaica, Natal, Reunion, and other colonies.[26]

Although the research has been fragmentary, we know that Americans were involved in this trade system in several ways. American shipbuilders led the fabrication of the "slaver" ships, "renowned the world over for their beauty and speed." American shippers were also intimately engaged in the coolie trade, especially after the early-1850s gold-rush booms in California and Australia had subsided.[27] Furthermore, they actively traded for the goods produced from such indentured labor. Notably, shippers such as William Russell Grace, future mayor of New York City, transported nitrogen-rich bird droppings, guano, from Peru to replenish overworked American soil.

The detailed involvement of New York shippers in the transport of Chinese contract laborers still needs to be researched, but anecdotal information indicates great activity. *Hunt's Merchant Magazine* reported in 1856 that most of the ships engaged in the trade were from the ports of New York and Boston. The *New York Journal of Commerce* published a letter of a crew member stating that his ship had seven hundred "coolies" on board and was expecting to load another two hundred. Many "crimps" (Chinese henchmen) tricked or kidnapped men on board. Shippers paid $15 to $20 per man and sold them for $250. Over thirty-two American vessels traded coolies. One writer has estimated that from 1852 to 1858, American ships transported forty thousand laborers.[28]

In 1861 *Harper's New Monthly Magazine* featured a detailed report of one 1857 voyage from Macao to Havana. The three-thousand-ton *Norway* sailed from New York carrying coal for the U.S. naval squadron patrolling the China Seas. On the return voyage 1,037 Chinese men were packed into two lower decks rigged with "tier on tier of berths, or rather shelves—for they were without sides or dividing partitions." Rebellion ensued, a fire below deck started, and "coolies" were flogged and shot. Upon the ship's arrival in Havana, it was reported that seventy had been killed outright or had died of untreated gunshot wounds, and up to sixty had died of dysentery.[29]

As early as 1844, guano from the Chincha Islands off the Peruvian coast was used to fertilize the worn topsoil of Maryland tobacco plantations.[30] At the height of this trade, four hundred thousand tons were loaded on ships a year. Purchased at $15 per ton, the extraordinary fertilizer sold in the United States for $50. At any given day of the year, 100 to 150 American and European ships were docked waiting to be loaded.[31]

The harvesting of these domed mountains of accumulated droppings was noxious, dangerous work. The scorching heat and intense ammonia fumes caused eyes and skin to burn, noses and ears to bleed.[32] Chinese laborers, often tricked into signing eight-year indentured contracts, were shipped to Peru to perform this brutal labor. Writing to the U.S. secretary of state, the consul, D. J. Williamson, reported the conditions he observed. Each worker had to dig and cart one hundred wheelbarrow loads a day. "They are indifferently fed and clothed," Williamson reported, "and as a consequence one fourth of their number become sick, but are not admitted to the Hospital while they retain strength enough to stand." Guards were employed "to prevent them from committing suicide by drowning, to which end the Coolie rushes in his moments of despair."[33]

It was in the midst of the guano trade that nineteen-year-old Irish entrepreneur William Russell Grace arrived in Callao with his father. At fourteen, William had already worked odd jobs in New York City; at eighteen, he had formed William Russell Grace and Company in Liverpool, England, brokering passage for Irish émigrés. In 1851 William's father, James Grace, organized 180 Irish men, women, and children to work at a sugar plantation in Peru. This plan, and others recruiting European families, was later aborted, to be replaced by one involving Chinese contract laborers. In 1854 Grace became a full partner of James Bryce and Company. They chartered guano shipments to New York and San Francisco and made a fortune. By 1865 Grace was able to open up a New York provisions and shipping company, becoming a notable part of New York City civic, political, and corporate history.[34]

An Ideal Port of Exchange

With historical hindsight it has become clear that the *Empress of China* not only signaled the beginning of the rise of the port of New York but also inaugurated the diverse ways in which merchant shippers came to profit from Chinese labor, directly and indirectly. In turn, the flow of international and domestic trade reshaped the contours of Manhattan's streetscape, ultimately creating the neighborhoods and political culture in which migrating Chinese would live.

The wealth accumulated through the China trade was inscribed onto the physical form of the city. The Revolutionary War had left entire sections of lower Manhattan in charred rubble. Decade by decade, lower Manhattan would be reconfigured to maximize the efficiency of trade. Docks extended all around lower Manhattan, with shipyards extending along the East River to Corlear's Hook.[35]

Historian Elizabeth Blackmar has carefully documented how the shipping industry ran vertically through all occupational groups, from merchants, clerks, and shopkeepers to shipbuilders, dock workers, and mariners. The shipping industry controlled the most visible wealth of the town, the slips, piers, and storehouses that formed the port's center. The British practice of dumping cheap goods in New York during the colonial era regularly flooded the city with items bought and sold at auction. Such activities undercut the prices of American-made goods and kept foreign goods streaming through the port. Wholesale dry goods were carried along Pearl Street. Retail dry goods were located more inland along William Street. By the 1830s, hatters, fur merchants, and stove dealers were centered on Water Street between Pearl and South Street, wholesale grocers along Front Street, and silk dealers around Hanover Square. The Beekman swamp further north featured leather goods tanned locally.[36]

Colonial merchants had built their households, which often combined houses and offices, on Wall, Broad, Whitehall, State, and Water Streets, adjacent to or in sight of their wharves and warehouses. The ground level featured the office and counting room. The most substantial merchant houses boasted public and domestic space above: suitably decorated drawing rooms, parlors, and spacious halls. Often their clerks, bookkeepers, or junior partners boarded in these combination office-homes. These merchants' houses were among the largest work establishments in the city and relied on slave, wage, and family labor to serve both the transit of commodities and household maintenance. Wholesale and retail stores, such as Frederick Rhinelander's china shop, were found on streets immediately in from the wharves.[37]

New York's city directory showed that in 1795 one-twelfth of the city's men were merchant-importers, factors, and wholesalers. Another twelfth were grocers or tavern or boardinghouse keepers. Just over two-fifths of listed New Yorkers were artisans, the people who produced goods, and under one-fifth were cartmen and laborers, the people who transported those commodities through city streets or supplied manual labor. The women listed in the directory were widows, boardinghouse keepers, mantua makers, or milliners.[38]

Mercantile dominance of land use pushed many artisan-owner households out of the shoreline wards and northward into less desirable parts of the island. "The expansion of opportunity for some New Yorkers rested on the constriction of opportunity for others."[39] The deep, protected harbor gave merchants a clear advantage, and they proceeded to develop the shoreline wharf districts. Yet another form of generating wealth became quickly evident. Large landholders took advantage of the growing population of the port and speculated on the buying, selling, and renting of real estate and buildings. In the course of the eighteenth century large landed estates and farms were often subdivided and sold again. Such speculation increased property values by over 700 percent between 1795 and 1815, squeezing out the city's artisans, laborers, and new arrivals.[40]

Prominent in this landscape dominated by the shipping trades were the coffeehouses where the merchants conducted their business. "Before the building of the Exchange (opened in 1827), New York merchants maintained regular exchange hours, boards of directors held weekly meetings, and brokers and auctioneers conducted scheduled auctions at the coffeehouses of Wall Street."[41] In effect, coffeehouses were the hubs of the economic exchange chains linking individuals inland and overseas. These coffeehouses formed one of the central arteries of a patrician life through which Chinese things and people circulated.

John Jacob Astor's investments offer a concrete example of the ways fur, luxury, and opium profits were parlayed into Manhattan land and buildings. His 1845 last will and testament, enacted upon his death three years later, offers some details of the real estate portion of his estimated $20 million fortune. The following is a sample of what he left his children and grandchildren: Lafayette Street properties from the Bowery to Broadway, between present-day Astor Place and West Third Street; the land between Charlton Street, Morton Street, Greenwich Street, and the Hudson River, constituting one hundred lots; the westerly side of Broadway between Broome and Spring Streets and the land on the easterly side between Spring and Prince; four houses and lots on the westerly side of Broadway between Prince and Houston Streets, extending to the rear on Mercer Street; the lot and house on 585 Broadway, backing onto Mercer Street; nine lots on Eighth Avenue and Twenty-sixth Street; forty-three lots fronting on Seventh Avenue, Bloomingdale Road, Thirty-seventh Street, and Fortieth Street; eight lots on Avenue A, between Sixth and Seventh Streets; twenty-two lots on the block of Hamersley, Varick, Bedford, and Downing Streets; and the land between Bloomingdale Road, the Hudson River, Forty-second Street, and Fifty-first Street. Other properties included a country estate and thirteen acres at Hellgate plus lands and estates in the canton of Geneva, Switzerland.[42] Astor's holdings show how wealth was mapped onto Manhattan's street grid. Astor's profits from the China trade enabled him to become a major landlord of the Manhattan streetscape. The alchemy of trade transmuted pelts and opium in Canton into prime real estate in New York.

This cursory discussion of the impact of the China trade does not sufficiently illustrate the ways in which a hierarchy of money and power was being formulated on this island. Entrepreneurial merchants took advantage of consumer desires to organize the many different exchange chains. As already discussed, the elite habit of drinking tea out of tea services drove both George Washington and the various sang-digging Indians of the foothills to exchange the goods they possessed. But Washington had sufficient money and power to exert a genteel discipline over himself and over his own property. He was personally insulated from the actual labor necessary to tend, harvest, and cure his tobacco; his slaves did that work. "Christie Drunken Waries Daughter," on the other hand, to the degree that she wanted tea and teacups, had to spend hours each day digging and curing the ginseng root herself. She could be disciplined by the account ledger hundreds of miles away. A single entry by a pen in the port of New York could produce an entire chain of effects: the callusing of hands in the Adirondacks, the procuring of more Chincha Island guano, or the requisitioning of another load of coolies.[43]

Merchant Philanthropy and Elite Virtue

Having built their wealth from the China trade and other commercial activities, New York's merchants began promoting a distinctive, refined civic culture of arts organizations, historical societies, and educational institutions. The marketplace values of self-interested individualism came to infuse the institutions these merchants created. Enlightenment-inflected, marketplace-driven, and class-specific interests formulated the missions of this network of civic organizations, as well as the particular notions of social welfare, useful knowledge, history, health, aesthetics, and normality that came to be promoted. Ironically, as will be shown in part 2 of this book, China-trade surpluses were reinvested in a civic culture that severely limited the ways in which Chinese New Yorkers would be represented and the ways in which a Chinese quarter would emerge. These merchants formulated their own moral economy, one that enriched those who conformed and diminished those who didn't.[44]

In 1788 Noah Webster, a staunch defender of his beloved city, admitted that New York was yet lacking in those "societies for the encouragement of science, arts, manufactures, etc." characteristic of progressive Enlightenment cities. Elihu Hubbard Smith, a physician of distinction who was a cofounder of the private intellectual coterie the Friendly Club and editor of its publication, *New York Magazine,* complained in his 1795 diary about the pecuniary bent of local lawyers: "The history of the City of New York is the history of the eager cultivation & rapid increase of the arts of gain, & the neglect of elegant & useful science, the art of genius, taste, & society." Indeed, one magazine essayist publicly decried "the love of gain" that was so "very prevalent" before the Revolutionary War and that was fast turning the entire city into a "theater for *speculation.*" Dominated by Knickerbocker lawyers, physicians, and businessmen, the city's moral and cultural improvements were driven by its economic development.[45]

Like so many other New Englanders who migrated to New York in the early decades of the nineteenth century, painter Samuel F. B. Morse sensed a sea change after the War of 1812. Having considered the relative merits of Philadelphia, Boston, and New York, Morse chose New York. In 1823 he wrote to his wife, "New York does not yet feel the influx of wealth from the

Western canal, but in a year or two she will feel it, and it will be advantageous to me to be identified among her citizens as a painter." Morse keenly understood that cultural patronage would follow commercial success; the nouveau riche would want to emulate the culture of distinction.[46]

Prominent among the urban boosters who comprised the culture of distinction were hundreds of New York men and women involved in the China trade from 1784 to the Civil War. John Pintard, East India trader and cultural activist; Robert Minturn, partner of China traders Grinnell, Minturn, and Company; John Jacob Astor; Philip Hone, auctioneer, onetime mayor, and diarist; Abiel Abbot Low—these were but a few of the many entrepreneurs who would forever shape the civic culture of what was to become the preeminent city of the nation. A second generation of postrevolutionary New York merchants became the philanthropists who made this process possible. Their cosmopolitan civic culture formulated both a non-European American self and a European-derived conviction of oriental otherness.

John Pintard, for example, was born of French Huguenot parents and raised by his prosperous merchant uncle. In the late 1780s Pintard profited handsomely from the China trade and quickly moved into the arena of city politics, becoming an alderman at this time and later, in 1791, a representative in the state assembly. Pintard was an investor with speculator William Duer, Daniel Parker's former partner in the *Empress* venture. After sharing a financial disaster with Duer and then going to jail for improprieties of his own, Pintard returned to New York and became an influential politician. Acting as an officer or trustee, he helped to found key elite institutions that included the New-York Historical Society, the New York Institution of Learned and Scientific Establishments, the American Academy of Fine Arts, the New York Society Library, the Literary and Philosophical Society, the Chamber of Commerce, the Free School Society, the Society for the Prevention of Pauperism, the Society for the Encouragement of Faithful Domestic Servants, the General Theological Seminary, the French Protestant Church, the House of Refuge, and the Erie Canal Celebration Committee. Like Charles Willson Peale of Philadelphia, Pintard was also the prime mover behind efforts to create a museum to "form a school of useful knowledge" that would "diffuse it to every class." He transferred the museum he established under Tammany Hall's auspices to John Scudder and subsequently it went to Phineas T. Barnum.[47]

As for John Jacob Astor, the impact of his fortune has continued to this day, but it first became visible with the establishment of the Astor library in

1849. Other fortunes and careers rode on Astor's back. Philip and John Hone, for example, operated a successful auction business from 1800 to 1821. It prospered by serving John Jacob Astor's trading activities. After Astor's death Hone reflected, "My brother and I found Mr. Astor a valuable customer. We sold many of his cargoes, and had no reason to complain of a want of liberality or confidence."[48] Hone was elected mayor in 1834, and he became a fixture in New York's elite culture.

Over the decades A. A. Low came to epitomize the New York philanthropist-businessman. From 1856 to 1866 he was the president of the New York Chamber of Commerce and later was highly respected as a civic leader, important to the Packer Institute, the Brooklyn Library, the Long Island Historical Society, the Society for Improving the Condition of the Poor, the Union for Christian Work, and the City Hospital, among other institutions. His son, Seth Low, was to distinguish himself as mayor of Brooklyn, president of Columbia College, mayor of Greater New York, and president of the powerful National Civic Association.[49]

In sum, a network of organizations and merchants, fostered by their relationship to the market, distinguished New York City as the rising cultural center of the nation. This ensemble of Protestant institutions would set the standards of proper conduct for the hundreds of thousands of new residents flooding the city.

The enrichment of merchants such as John Jacob Astor by the China trade and other ventures marked the gentrification of New York City. Grand mansions were built showcasing luxury goods from the Orient and elsewhere in a manner of taste that George Washington and Gouverneur Morris would have envied. These nouveaux riches further augmented their claims to distinction by creating a bourgeois civic culture in the fine arts, history, and education. Although contemporary Chinese government and society were no longer admired and emulated as they had been in the time of Hamilton, Jefferson, and Franklin, China's opulent legacy of court culture, embodied in such coveted objects as Ming vases and embroidered silk robes, still reigned as a baseline of elite cultural distinction. This bourgeois culture was deeply inflected with European patrician orientalism, yet in the age of U.S. liberal capitalism no aristocratic titles were conferred to mark social arrival. Patronage and philanthropy, however, helped to transform the merely wealthy into cultured guardians of the civic culture. The imagined luxuries of China were now reproduced in private homes of the elite. This ability to emulate such a court culture signaled not only arrival for these parvenus but also the symbolic cultural mastery of China itself.

A culminating moment in U.S. patrician orientalism came in 1876, with the display of the porcelain work of Karl Müller at that year's Philadelphia Centennial Exposition, a fair celebrating the rise of American industry and material culture. This tête-á-tête tea service by Müller, of the Union Porcelain Works of Greenpoint, Long Island, is an important, fascinating, and disquieting piece. One critic described the service in detail, praising it for "the delicacy of the ware and the shape, and for beauty of design":

> On the top of the tea-pot to form the handle for the lid we have a China-man's head, an appropriate idea for a teapot, while on the sugar-bowl the head is that of a spruce-looking negro, suggestive of the workers on a sugar plantation in the South. The handles of the cream-pitcher and teapot are copies of our charming pitcher plant, out of which two squirrels are peeping; while the feet of the set are rabbit's heads, and the spouts are supported by winged imps. The coloring of one set is an odd-shade of salmon.[50]

In many ways this is a typical work of chinoiserie. Indeed, Müller and the Union Porcelain Works are credited by pottery historians as being the first in the United States to master porcelain production techniques. By Chinese or European standards, the tea set was by no means special, yet for the embryonic American porcelain community it was a landmark accomplishment. What makes the set particularly memorable, however, is the placing of the "Chinaman's" head on the teapot finial and the "spruce-looking negro" man's head on the sugar bowl. For most Americans at this time, it was perfectly acceptable to have exoticized people represent desirable consumables. Africans, Indians, and people of other racial types had long been identified with various desirable consumables, and the consumption of such items was often memorialized in representational objects such as carved wooden figures: the wooden American Indian used to sell cigars, or the wooden "Chinaman" that commonly stood in front of nineteenth-century tea stores.[51]

Müller's porcelain marked the rise of American culture from impoverished minor-nation status. In this masterful work, the patina of eighteenth-century romantic aspiration had been painted over with a brash, industrializing confidence. Müller, a German immigrant artisan, could win fame and acceptance in the United States by giving aesthetic expression to a rising American imperial vision. Jenny Young, a late-nineteenth-century critic and

Figure 5. Karl Müller's tête-à-tête tea service, Union Porcelain Works, Greenpoint, Long Island, 1876. This tea set, displayed at the 1876 Philadelphia Centennial Exhibition, exemplified the sense of mastery Americans felt in the arts of civilization. (Brooklyn Museum. Lent by Franklin Chace)

promoter of American pottery, provides a clue to the politics of this style: "The rule appears to be to study the antique, but instead of copying or reproducing the works of the ancients, [American artists] follow their example in choosing subjects from everyday life of the artists own time." Rapid industrialization, the aggressive expansion into the "frontier," and the influx of skilled artisans from Europe gave American potters their own sense of "manifest destiny." Young elaborates: "With a limitless wealth of materials at his command, and gifted with enterprise, originality, and taste, the American artist can look confidently forward to taking his place beside the best the world has produced."[52]

By 1876 this proud, rising New York civic culture presided over the faith in the U.S. mastery of Chinese material culture, people, and civilization. Patrician orientalism was a developing phenomenon that responded to the changing uses elites and strivers had for an imagined China. The culture of bourgeois liberalism was able to define itself in numerous ways in relation to this other. Fundamental questions of community formation were raised and resolved in the interaction with Chinese goods, ideas, and people. The gnawing issues of capitalist modernity, such as individualism and distinction, sociability and sentimentality, civilizational advance and progress, were broached, worked through, and resolved. In this culture of patrician orientalism, admiration shifted first to emulation and then again to a sense of civilizational mastery.

The European and U.S. military's prying open of China's ports to free trade combined with a sense of political victory over despotism to formulate a triumphant, patrician-inflected, elite culture in New York; an insular world of cultural confidence, refinement, and exclusivity was created. U.S. elite community identity formation used China in a double sense: America drew upon China as a means of distancing itself from Europe, and it symbolically sought to dominate China as proof of destined civilizational progress.

Elite culture, however, did not define the whole of U.S. culture. The Sons of Liberty certainly learned that they could not control the popular desire to consume tea. The expanding capitalist economy and new urban populations offered new frontiers for other ways of making money besides trade and real estate. An elite society founded on the radical individualism of the white male citizen would soon encounter the myriad challenges posed by a demand-driven commercial culture responding to the exploding population of new urban dwellers and consumers.

PART 2

Port Exchanges

Commerce is King.

—*De Bow's Review,* 1859

CHAPTER 4

A Pioneer
Settlement

O{N THE NOON OF JULY 14, 1847}, New Yorkers
were treated to a spectacular sight: a 160-foot Chinese vessel called the *Key-ing*. A *New York Herald* reporter narrated the event as a fairy tale:

> In the dreams of opium land, they had fancied that they were still in the land
> of Mandarins and Hanging Gardens, and that they were being attacked by
> the ferocious outside barbarians, and reduced to powder as fine as their best
> gunpowder tea. Happily, however, they found that it was but a dream. They
> awoke, and found that the only castle they were to storm was Messrs.
> French and Heiser's Castle Garden.

Another reporter thought it "a queer looking concern," reminding him of
an immense "snail shell set upon edge, with three sticks stuck perpendicu-
larly through it." The ship was towed into New York Harbor and docked at
Castle Garden, the public hall for cultural events located at the Battery. Because of advance newspaper publicity, the ship's arrival was anticipated by
thousands of New Yorkers. People began "to flock towards the Battery" at
ten-thirty in the morning, and by eleven o'clock "respectable" individuals
had assembled in numbers second only to those mustering upon "the President's arrival."[1]

In the port of New York, perceptions of China and the Chinese were shifting dramatically. Seven decades after the sailing of the *Empress of China*,
the burgeoning commercial culture of New York would play a pivotal role
in promoting representations of China and the Chinese that would be highly
consequential to the destiny of Chinese New Yorkers. The penny press targeted all urban dwellers as potential consumers. Newspapers and inexpensive
books written in a popular style not only reported news and advertised goods

but promoted viewpoints and marketed spectacles.[2] Print capitalism in effect transformed a streetscape of diverse individuals into a public that increasingly viewed itself as living a shared New York City experience.[3] The visually driven marketplace of "sights" fostered a distinctive form of orientalism in which images and beliefs were sold and bought by a public eager to make sense of its own place in this heterogeneous urban environment and of its nation's place in the world. This was the New York in which Chinese were beginning to settle.

A Public Spectacle

The *Keying's* captain, Australian British Charles A. Kellett, was well prepared for the interest the ship would attract. Beginning the next day, the ship could be boarded for twenty-five cents from 6:00 A.M. until 6:30 P.M. daily. "Tickets can be had at the entrance of Castle Garden," advertised the *Herald*. On July 16 the Common Council tendered to the captain and officers of the *Keying* "the usual hospitalities of the City," optimistically declaring that "a new era in our commercial intercourse . . . with the Celestial Empire [has been opened] by the arrival within our harbor of the first Chinese vessel." This outdoor public event was carefully staged.[4]

The *Keying* was a coastal trader that Charles Kellett had reportedly purchased for exhibition at the Crystal Palace exhibition in London. He carried a crew of some twenty Europeans and thirty to forty Chinese. All but one of the Chinese were "common people." Clearly distinguishable from the others was "Eesing," identified as "a specimen of the second class of Mandarins." A reporter remarked that "he seems to be well-bred, intelligent and polite," much like a British earl. "He can talk a little English, is quick of apprehension and came out simply as a traveler, anxious to explore this Western world and carry back an account of it to the Emperor."[5]

Kellett had the walls and ceilings of the main cabin, some thirty-two feet long by twenty-eight feet wide, painted yellow and covered with birds, monkeys, flowers, and landscapes. In the words of one incredulous New York reporter, the room was filled with glass cases displaying "specimens of almost everything produced or used in the Chinese empire." Framed Chinese paintings hung on the walls, and lanterns "wrought in the most elaborate and curious art" hung from the ceilings. A "cupboard-like" shrine stood at one end of the room, and a grand, round inlaid table with chairs occupied the center space. Crowds were to continue visiting the *Keying* into

September, and there was so much to fascinate that visitors could "search and scrutinize every hole and corner and each find something that excites remarks and wonderment." But the most telling change Captain Kellett may have made to the Chinese vessel was the display of five flags at the stern, each flag representing one of the treaty ports that the British had created with their victory in the Opium Wars.[6]

The inveterate diarist and former mayor Philip Hone paid his twenty-five cents to view these "Chinese Visitors." On July 29, 1847, he noted, "A Chinese Junk is moored off Castle Garden to the great delight of the curious New Yorkers. . . . She is said to be the real thing. Her model and equipment such as we never saw, and her long-tailed crew objects of infinite amusement." Estimates of visitors varied from up to four thousand per day to fifty thousand visitors overall. At twenty-five cents a visitor, Kellett stood to make a tidy fortune. But matters were not so simple. Entrepreneurs Charles Heiser and Philip French had leased the Castle Garden docking to Kellett in exchange for as much as a "four-fifth part of proceeds" of the daily receipts, which on August 7 amounted to $274.24.[7]

The *New York Herald*'s coverage of the *Keying* offers an unusual example of how one daily news publication helped to create a sustained and marketable spectacle. Day after day for two months the *Herald*'s "City Intelligence" column featured the latest on the "Chinese Junk." Nestled amid reports of the latest fires, suicides, bank defaults, and runaway slaves, the coverage of the *Keying* blurred the contemporary journalistic distinctions between "news" and "advertisement."

The *Herald*'s almost daily coverage was light, promotional, and folksy in nature. "The English seem to have much trouble in gaining permission to visit the city of Canton, but this more favored country," quipped the journalist, "has had a sample of China itself brought to its door, and shown them for the small sum of a quarter." The next article gushed in closing, "No, our friends with the unpronounceable names and astonishment proof countenances, must not be allowed to go, at least until we have all seen and appreciated them." In August, Southern tourists, "who are now thronging to our hotels," and merchants from the South and West, "who may be here making their fall purchases," were told that "there is no exhibition in the States so attractive as this one." Indeed, the exhibition is "the wonder of a wonderful age."[8]

From week to week "City Intelligence" featured different aspects of the exhibition as well as daily activities. On July 28 the column reported that

Figure 6. The *Keying* (*center*) anchored in New York Harbor in 1847. Samuel B. Waugh, "The Bay and Harbor of New York," ca. 1855. (Museum of the City of New York. Gift of Mrs. Robert M. Littlejohn)

"the citizens of New York will have an opportunity to day of witnessing Chinese idol worship with all its concomitants of kneeling, sacrificing and offering up gifts. . . . There will be dancing, singing, &c., &c., . . . the strains of which will no doubt sound very strange to persons who never hear[d] such music before." Three days later the paper stated, in the tone of an advocate, "We understand that a number of our citizens are desirous of seeing the religious ceremonies of the Chinese, not being able to avail themselves of the former opportunity. We trust the captain will have them repeated." And sure enough, on August 4 the once-in-a-lifetime opportunity to witness "some grand religious festival" was repeated. On another day the *Herald* insightfully described what would soon become the standard manner in which New Yorkers learned about China. The *Keying*, the writer observed, "conveys to us a better idea of the natives of China than all we could gather by reading a score of books on the subject." Commerce, not scholarship, would be New Yorkers' access to the larger world: "They can see all that they could see in the great city of Pekin or Canton, for the sum of two shillings."[9]

On August 28 the usually upbeat promotional coverage took a dramatic negative turn. Perhaps intended as a final and cynically calculated effort to increase the number of visitors, the daily "Chinese Junk" title was changed to "Opium Smoking." "Such of our citizens as desire to witness the effects of opium smoking," stated the *Herald* rather clinically, "can do so by visiting the Chinamen of the junk. . . . Every one of them indulge in the practice." "The Mandarin Kesing," the reporter testified, "cannot give up his opium which he indulges in to excess. The effect which the smoking of this pernicious drug has on the human system can be seen by visiting that vessel."[10] The last-minute publicity ploy succeeded in keeping the ship open for an additional three days.

The humorous and lighthearted character of the *Herald*'s coverage effectively exemplifies the contours of a packaged "otherness." The coverage represented the Chinese of the *Keying*—with their mistaken dreams of "opium land," their "unpronounceable names," their "astonishment proof countenances," and their "idol worship"—as terribly backward and rather quaint. In the first article about the *Keying*, the *Herald* reporter focused on the reputedly unchanging nature of Chinese civilization: "She presents to the sight what was the favorite model of Chinese shipbuilders 9,000 years ago, for this model is the same as they used at that time. A junk of 1847, and a junk built in 100 B.C. would if they could be seen together, present about the same appearance." This fallacious conviction is revisited in another article: "[The

Chinese] are peculiarly attached to old notions, and will not permit the slightest innovation in anything."[11]

While the *Herald* prodded its readers each day to go see the junk and regaled them with anecdotes and chatter, a serious labor conflict was brewing between the Chinese crew and Captain Kellett. *Herald* readers, however, were not privy to this information until the final days of the *Keying*'s stay. On August 31 the piece on the mandarin smoking opium appeared, but in a separate article directly under it was "Row on Board the Chinese Junk." Taking the side of authority and order, the article claimed that opium smoking had induced some of the Chinese crew to attack the captain:

> At about five o'clock yesterday afternoon, Captain Killet [*sic*] went on board the junk with money to pay the crew their monthly wages; when some dispute arising amongst the Chinese, who were under the effects of opium, the long tails turned their combined force against the captain, who was only able to restore quiet by calling in a police force. Seven of the mutineers were locked up and the rest preferring comfortable quarters on board the junk, desisted further insubordination.

Authorities held the seven Chinese at the Tombs and charged them with assault and battery. They were to appear in front of Justice Osborne in the Court of Special Sessions three days later. Unfortunately, the transcript from the trial no longer exists, but the *Herald* did devote considerable space to this last article about the *Keying* in New York. In contrast to the *Herald*'s presumption of poppy-induced antisocial behavior among the Chinese, the court found in favor of the crew members and "severely reprimanded" Captain Kellett "for the manner in which the foreigners had been treated."[12]

The Chinese crew members testified through a translator that in China they had been tricked into thinking they were to accompany Captain Kellett and the British crew on a trading voyage to the island of Java, at which point they would have the option to disembark or to continue on to the next port. They were to be paid $8 per month for up to eight months, at which time they would be returned to Canton. Once they had embarked, however, the captain and the British crew "punished [them] into obedience" by making "free use of the rope." Upon arriving at the island of St. Helena, the much-touted mandarin was said to have come on board and told them that if they did not cooperate quietly, "they would all be shot." One of the crew was in such despair that he attempted to commit suicide by jumping overboard, but he was rescued and held on board. At this point the crew pro-

duced a contract written in Chinese and translated by S. Wells Williams, a
lawyer and author of books on China. The contract verified the claims of the
arrested crew, adding that after eight months the captain was required to return them to China.[13]

The crew members further testified that upon hearing of the departure
for another port (on September 5 they would have served ten months), they
approached Captain Kellett with their concerns. Their contract had expired,
and they wanted to be compensated for back wages. As they approached the
captain, he left the room, delegating Edward Revett, the mate, to force them
into signing a receipt for money they had never received. They tried to take
hold of Captain Kellett and make him listen. At that point the scuffle broke
out, and the ship's officers called in the New York police.[14]

What happened to the crew was again presented (and distorted) by the
media. According to a November 1847 article in the *American Magazine*,
Christian "benevolence" saved twenty-six of them. A Captain and Mrs.
Richardson took them into their Sailor's Home on Cherry Street for three
weeks' lodging. A Mr. Lin-King-Chew, described as a "devoted Christian"
and a "Chinese gentleman of education, and of distinction and property in
his own country," attended to their "spiritual welfare." He gave them each
a translation of the Bible and read portions of it to them daily during their
stay at the Sailor's Home. On October 4 they prepared for their return trip
to China by attending "divine service" on the Floating Church, at which
time they were presented with two "beautiful" woodcuts and a sermon: an
interior and exterior view of the Floating Church accompanied by an exposition on the efforts of the Episcopal Church throughout America to increase the "spiritual benefit of seamen."[15]

In the fall the twenty-six Chinese boarded the *Candace* for their voyage
home. After another round of religious rituals invoking "God's protection,
in the beautiful prayer of the Liturgy for persons going to sea, concluding
with the Lord's prayer and the benediction," the sailors were "in tears at
parting with their kind friends, Capt. and Mrs. Richardson, and their beloved
countryman, Lin-King-Chew, whom they almost worshipped for his many
acts of generosity, sympathy and friendship." The final parting scene was
described by the *American Magazine* as "truly worthy of an artists pen":

> The whole rail on the starboard side was lined with the swarthy figures of
> these bare-headed Mongolians, shaking their hands in the air, and looking
> towards the steamboat. The caps of the crew were flourishing aloft behind

them, as they gave their three cheers, which were answered by the ladies waving their handkerchiefs, and the response of the gentlemen. When these had ceased, the Chinese sailors struck up their farewell song, which continued, in their harsh, cracked voices, till both vessels were so far separated that the sound died on the air.[16]

If we are to believe the story as written in this magazine, Christian charity triumphed over the excesses of British commerce. The Chinese crew were portrayed as completely passive: their actions in their own behalf were conveniently left out of the narrative.

To maintain public curiosity in an urban visual and print culture, journalists and promoters sought control of the exotic foreignness of the crew. The once-in-a-lifetime chance of seeing something authentically Chinese appeared to be eroding before their very eyes. The crew, the *Herald* claimed, were acculturating to Western ways: "The Chinamen of the Junk are rapidly adopting the manners and customs of our citizens. They use knives and forks at their meals instead of chopsticks [and] they smoke cigars from morning till night."[17] Rather than seeing these sailors as in fact quite open to trying out new experiences, the journalists' anecdotal judgments about unbridgeable Chinese differences built on essential notions of racial otherness. These visitors were cast as burlesque caricatures who could never acculturate to American culture. Indeed, the harder they tried, the funnier they appeared. The unspoken attitudes embedded in these nineteenth-century racial/ethnic jokes were expressions of shared popular prejudice—assumptions mainstream Anglo-American culture held about the superiority of its own way of life and biologically defined difference.[18]

The *Herald*'s proclivity for entertainment was counterbalanced by the *American Magazine*'s all-consuming focus on demonstrations of Christian benevolence, and neither discourse paid much attention to the Chinese sailors' actual experiences. In both cases, the coverage served mainly to promote in a popular format a particular set of moral values and a particular point of view. Whether sensational or moralistic, the journalistic coverage of the ship and the exhibition within was a characteristic expression of the commercially driven form of orientalism. Captain Kellett, the promoters, and the Chinese crew members were players in a larger geopolitical struggle over material and symbolic control of what China and the Chinese signified.[19]

The Australian British captain left with his profits, and a largely new crew, and sailed for Boston, Providence, and eventually on to England. In London the war trophy was put on display for many months. Her teak planking was eventually used to build two ferries and many small souvenir sewing kits.[20]

An International Port Culture

When the *Keying* and its crew docked at Castle Garden, they set foot in a geocultural landscape that had been transformed by a hierarchy of class, ethnicity, and race etched onto Manhattan Island. The propertied elite were moving to fancier addresses uptown, and Chinese New Yorkers were already part of a lower Manhattan international port culture—a mixing and shifting amalgam of individuals and groups from many places, staying, leaving, and always on the move.

In 1807 the Board of Alderman appointed, and the Jeffersonian governor approved, three large Federalist landholders—Washington confidant and former New York senator Gouverneur Morris, state surveyor Simeon De Witt, and former New Jersey senator and Trinity Church member John Rutherford—to determine the layout of the city above Chambers Street. They were given the "exclusive power to lay out streets, roads, and public squares" and "to shut up or direct to be shut up any streets or parts thereof which have been heretofore laid out." By 1811 the street commissioners had prescribed the grid of wide avenues running north and south and streets east and west that exists today. Low waterlogged areas, such as the now polluted Collect Pond and the surrounding swamps, were filled in, and rocky, hilly vistas were leveled to maximize productivity and orderliness.[21]

This vision of "republican simplicity" writ onto Manhattan's landscape embodied all the unresolved ambiguity of elite distinction and popular democracy. On paper the plan was fair, but the quality of built structures, restrictive covenants, and occupational and residential clustering quickly defined the hierarchical cultural geography of the grid. Private parks and the prohibition of "offensive establishments" in certain upscale neighborhoods, for example, kept certain blocks free of breweries, bakeries, and stables.[22]

In effect, the docking of ships, the port trades of the lower, eastern shoreline of Manhattan and the swamp district, came to define the trading, manufacturing, and poorer area of the city. Despite the increased traffic and affluence of the island, brought on by the Erie Canal and the entry of huge numbers of German, Scotch, and Irish immigrants, the lower wards of Manhattan were being passed over by the burgeoning gentry for new housing construction further up on the island while immigrants and the working poor remained behind in the still sunken and swampy Fifth and Sixth Wards.[23]

Massive immigration of Irish Catholic men and women packed the Sixth Ward, where people rented out cellars and garrets. One-family houses were being subdivided into many crowded makeshift rooms. In one Baxter Street alley house, shelflike bunks served as beds, and in another lodging not a "chair, table, or any other article of furniture save a cooking utensil . . . [and a few] beds were found."[24] The Irish, often called the "niggers of Europe" and tyrannized by British and other European Protestants, were subject to intolerance, racial scorn, and limited opportunities. They made a home of the polluted, diseased manufacturing district that patricians avoided on the move uptown.

The incoming Irish encountered a community of African Americans settling in what Frederick Douglass referred to as "Stagg Town." In addition to African American mariners, many freed blacks worked in a variety of skilled artisanal occupations. Timothy Weeks and William Johnson, for example, were shoemakers, and Peter Williams was a tobacconist. In 1801 African American Solomon Bell owned a saloon serving blacks and whites in the area. And by midcentury Pete Williams owned Dickens Place, the best-known dance hall in the Five Points. Many denizens of the Sixth Ward, in a legacy of slavery, were of mixed European and African blood. It was here that self-described "citizens of color" founded such pioneer community-building institutions as the African Methodist Episcopal Church and the African Free School.[25]

This relatively free cultural zone lay beyond the control of patrician Protestants, and it cultivated its own commercial culture. The Bowery became the grand boulevard of these polyglot New Yorkers. Here denizens of the tiny lodgings of the district could intermingle on the sidewalks and in cellar taverns, dime museums, dance halls, oyster bars, tattoo parlors, and bordellos. "This was a world of street gangs, masculine bravado, and noisome entertainments—where Melville's mariners, renegades, and castaways mingled with the workingmen, where the young Whitman could loiter to watch the butcher boy–dandy exchange his killing clothes for his 'duds' and launch into his repartee, his shuffle and breakdown."[26] While never explicitly developing the notion of a distinct port culture, various historians have delineated segments of this hybridizing lower Manhattan as different from, and often challenging, authority, wealth, and Protestant patrician normalcy.[27] Though this world was far from egalitarian and hardly without conflict, various prac-

Figure 7. "The Old Brewery and Its Neighborhood, at the Five Points, New York," ca. 1840s. Drawn from a highly moralistic perspective, this depiction of the Five Points as lowly and disorderly substantiated popular perceptions of this immigrant, working-class, and mixed port culture.
(Collection of the New-York Historical Society)

tices of food, language, dance, performance, and everyday life intermingled, forming a unique popular culture.

In cellar dance halls, African Americans would be joined by Irish, Chinese, and anyone else looking for a good time. Indeed, the Reverend Samuel Prime was shocked by the "motley multitude of men and women, yellow and white, black and dingy, old and young . . . a set of male and female Bacchanals dancing to the tambourines and fiddle; giggling and laughing." Out of this mingling of cultures came such popular performance styles as tap dance, combining the lower leg movements of clog dancing with the upper body movements of African dance. Various pidgin Englishes, mixed with "flash talk" and other swapped phrases, were spoken to facilitate communication across linguistic groups. Country dialects of Chinese mixed French, Creole, Gaelic, and Spanish with various African and other trading-port-pidgin utterances.[28]

Figure 8. "Along the New York Docks—An Unaristocratic International Restaurant,"
Harper's Weekly, Oct. 21, 1871. This lithograph is a rare illustration of the cultural
intermingling in the everyday life of the port culture. In it, artist Sol Eytinge Jr.
expressed his disdain for lower-class dock workers. (Wong Ching Foo Collection)

The northward-bound patrician culture would come to abhor the lower
Manhattan port culture as violent, uncontrollable, polyglot, and contrary
to refined civic culture. New York elites judged entering Chinese by this
moral accounting. Measured against the proper occidental self, some Chinese evoked charity, others pity, and a few praise. Those who caught a glimpse
of this culture were confronted with differences they could not bridge without interlocutors. Instead, producers and journalists, looking out for their
own interests, sensationalized the differences.

A Diasporic Settlement

In 1854 the Reverend Edward Syle conducted an informal survey of lower
Manhattan, searching for the whereabouts of a troupe of Chinese opera performers who had arrived two years earlier. Syle first spoke to the Reverend
Lewis Pease, the founder of the Five Points House of Industry, located just
below present-day Worth and Baxter Streets. Pease stated confidently, but

inaccurately, that there were some forty Chinese in the entire city, some living off the public charities provided on Ward's Island and others living in boardinghouses on Cherry Street below Chatham Square. Pease also pointed out, more accurately, that "some others had been a long time in this country, and had married here; and others yet were to be found serving behind the counters in tea stores." One Chinese man they called Okkeo had been a servant at the Five Points Mission. He was described in rather patronizing terms as "proving remarkably reliable and trustworthy."[29]

Syle proceeded to the Fourth Ward, below Chatham Square. In this largely Irish immigrant neighborhood he found several boardinghouses with Chinese occupants. He was appalled by their living conditions, and he framed his reaction in the context of a missionary perspective: "I must remember that I am writing about the heathen, the Chinese heathen, I mean." In one place, he said, "I found some thirty or more of them stowed away, like steerage passengers in an immigrant ship, in two small rooms the wretched and filthy conditions of which I will not stop to describe." He found eight sailors from Ningpo and Shanghai playing card and dice games with a layout for smoking opium nearby. He then visited a nearby building that housed members of the now defunct opera company. Christian pity and a chance for proselytizing punctuated Syle's written observations. He noted that the actors did not trust him:

> With the exception of Okkeo . . . I have not heard of one of these poor heathen who has been taken by the hand, in a spirit of compassion. . . . Is it any wonder that I found them distrustful and shy of me, as though I was concocting some fresh scheme by which they were to be victimized. . . . Even the white cravat did me no service in their eyes, for they seemed not to know anything about Clergymen, or Missionaries or Christians as such. I looked in on one boarder of their little apartment and saw a shrine, with their little idols in it, before the ever burning lamp and the smoking incense. Need I say that I left that room with a heavy heart.

An "old Canton man" told Syle that thirty-three actors were still living in New York. In three other houses he found a total of thirty cooks and stewards working on nearby ships. One of these houses was operated by a Chinese man who had married an Irishwoman. They had been running the boardinghouse since 1840. Syle completed his survey with a description of the much-pitied troupe of Cantonese opera performers now living destitute on Ward's Island. Of the fourteen there, some were making cigarettes. He also noted "opium smoking apparatus to be seen here." In all, he located more than seventy Chinese.[30]

Syle's moralistic accounts can be supplemented by state and federal census records. Mandated by the Constitution, the federal census served to enumerate citizens, primarily for the purpose of congressional representation. An 1805 city census was taken to locate "able and sufficient jurors." In addition, census figures were sought to measure the impact of yellow-fever epidemics.[31] The Anglo-American cultural propensity for ordering and categorizing propelled these accounts also to solicit empirical data about occupation, country of birth, children in school, and personal savings. These new data were used in various ways by the growing government bureaucracies to regulate and allocate social resources. Then as now, such surveys were neither a comprehensive nor a faithful representation of who lived where and for how long. However, they do provide some evidence of a Chinese presence in lower Manhattan since the merchant Chong's 1808 visit.

Months after Syle's survey, in 1855, New York State census takers walked the streets of the Third, Fourth, and Fifth Wards of lower New York and found some thirty-nine Chinese men in their apartments. One census man found the ship *Andrew Foster*, docked off lower west side piers, renting berths by the week. Of the forty-two boarders on this ship, three were Chinese: John Napoo, twenty-four, born in China, working as a cook and living in New York since 1849; John Assam, twenty-three, born in China, also a cook, living in the city for two years; and William Assam, twenty-four, a seaman from China, in New York since 1849. About this same time another census official found John Huston and his wife Margaret at home with their two young daughters. Huston was a common enough Anglo-American name; however, this man had been born in China, was twenty-eight years old, and had come to New York in 1829, when he was two years old. He was a seaman and a naturalized U.S. citizen, possibly distinguishing him as the first Chinese to become a citizen in New York. His Irish wife was a couple of years younger and had been in New York for only two years. Their girls, Kate and Mary, were two and one, respectively, and both had been born in Manhattan.

Of the thirty-nine Chinese men the census takers reported, thirty-four were located in the Fourth Ward, the heart of the vast and newly arriving Irish tenement community. Their households varied from boardinghouses to small apartments with married couples (and possibly children) to apartments with boarders. William Longford, for example, was a twenty-two-year-old Chinese cigar maker who had arrived in New York the previous year. He rented beds in his apartment to two older, and also recently arrived, cigar workers in their thirties, a clerk, and a tea store worker. In contrast, Zi Ting and Jo Palty, both peddlers, boarded in Patrick and Ellen Toohy's apartment. Patrick was a musician from Ireland, Ellen had found a job as a garter fitter, and with their two-year-old son, Joseph, they had come to New York via England in 1854. Conversely, John and Almira Lewis sublet their home to two Italians. John, a forty-eight-year-old Chinese sailor, had been living in New York for twenty years. This meant that he had been in New York since 1835.

Ar Yeep ran a boardinghouse for peddlers. Aw Hone, Aw Yan, A. Yung, A. Row, An Ow, An Fow, An Ew, An Son, An Too, and George Smith were all recent arrivals.[32] In one building the census taker found five apartments each of which was occupied by a Chinese man married to an Irishwoman. Among these couples were John and Louisa Atchen, who ran a "Chinese boarding house," and William Brown, a Chinese ship steward in New York since 1825, married to Rebecca Brown, an Irishwoman who had come to New York at seven and had lived in the city for twenty years. Their six-year-old son, William, was a native New Yorker. Singmer Dosia offers a final sample of the diversity of this early community. He is categorized as a "mulatto" sailor born in China. His name suggests an uncharacteristic U.S. transliteration of a Chinese name. Could he have come from China by way of Macao and the Caribbean or Latin America? Clearly he and his name had been through some cross-cultural changes.

In all, the census takers recorded eleven Chinese peddlers, three "segar" makers, twelve sailors, three cooks, five stewards (one deceased), three boardinghouse operators, one clerk, and one teahouse worker. As an indication of the necessarily superficial nature of the census, no specific mention was made of the opera performers, although they may have been counted among the peddlers. Given that Atchen's and other sailors' boardinghouses each reported only a single boarder, many more sailors, cooks, or stewards could easily have been added to this list of thirty-nine. This figure would bring us closer to Syle's impromptu findings of over seventy Chinese. A Chinese man, interviewed by the New-York Times, estimated 150 Chinese in New York.[33]

Eleven of the men found by the census takers were married (in all cases, to Irishwomen). Among those married were two of the three boardinghouse operators and eight of the eighteen merchant mariners. None of the peddlers

Figure 9. "The Result of the Immigration from China," *Yankee Notions,* Mar. 1858.
Chinese men partnering with Irishwomen had become common enough by the
1850s that the phenomenon was satirized on this magazine cover.
(Wong Ching Foo Collection)

was married, nor was any of the men who kept some version of a full Chinese name, whereas five of the thirteen men with Anglo first and last names were married, and six of the thirteen men with Anglo first names were married. Indeed, this pattern was evident enough that in 1858 *Yankee Notions* portrayed this phenomenon with an ostensibly humorous caricature.[34]

These records indicate conclusively that Chinese sailors were entering, leaving, and sometimes staying in East Coast ports years before Yerba Buena was renamed San Francisco in 1847. Indeed, at least one Chinese seaman, named Williams, felt that New York was home enough that in 1836 he had an account at the Seamen's Bank for Savings. The bank's identification records had a note stating that the depositor "speaks good English for a Chinese."[35] Hence, earlier anecdotal stories about Chinese and other Asian mariners can be placed within a broader historical context. Historian Kenneth Scott Latourette, for example, stated that "Atit, a Cantonese who had resided in Boston for 8 years, became a citizen of the United States" in 1845. And, as discussed in chapter 2, the *Pallas* arrived in the port of Baltimore in 1785 with a crew of "Chinese, Malays, Japanese and Moors, with a few Europeans." Similarly, Van Braam Houckgeest's eight house servants, as early as 1796, were most likely the very first Chinese service workers in the United States. A survey of crew records of ships entering and leaving the port of New York confirms this early presence. In 1835, for example, a Lesing Newman was serving aboard the ship *John Taylor* of New York, bound for Liverpool. Newman was reported to be twenty-three years old and a Chinese-born naturalized citizen residing in New York. A forty-year-old John Islee who lived in New York was serving on board the Salem-based ship *Mason*, preparing to set sail from New York for Liverpool on July 4, 1847. That same year the ship *Adelaide* of New York carried Ben Sanchez of China, twenty-eight years old, leaving for Havana.[36]

The presence of Chinese in Atlantic world ports before the influx of Chinese into San Francisco should not be a surprise. The centuries-long seafaring tradition of diasporic Chinese traders and adventurers, the European penetration into Asian markets, and the Western fascination with export luxury goods all brought Chinese seamen into Spanish, Portuguese, British, and U.S. shipping lanes. As early as the late sixteenth century, Manila galleons brought Chinese craftsmen and servants to Mexico and, later, Filipinos who migrated to the Gulf of Mexico to form eighteenth-century fishing villages.[37] Ben Sanchez may very well have been a part of this longstanding Chino-Latino trade tradition.

With the rise of the port of New York in the early decades of the nineteenth century, Chinese were moving between New York Harbor and points throughout the colonized world: Manila, Calcutta, Lima, Havana, the West Indies, Antwerp, Liverpool, London, Batavia, and elsewhere. Yet as shown by the small New York settlement, it was not until the aftermath of the British attack against China over opium, when Chinese ports were forced open to Western and Japanese penetration in 1842, that large enough numbers stayed in European and New World ports to form a community. The creation of additional treaty ports, in Guangzhou, Amoy, Fuzhou, Ningpo, and Shanghai, in which Western nations had extraterritorial powers had the unanticipated effect of providing more opportunities for Chinese to ship out on Western vessels. Though the topic has yet to be researched, Chinese sailors, cooks, and stewards probably served on American clipper ships that participated in the nefarious drug trade.[38]

According to an 1856 *New-York Times* article, "a great many" of the Chinese walking the streets of New York had escaped from the "brutal taskmasters" of the Peruvian Chincha Islands. Evidently some indentured workers escaped or completed their contracts and made it onto ships frequenting Peru–New York trade routes. Perhaps Singmer Dosia, the seventeen-year-old "mulatto" sailor from China, survived such a horrible journey and lived to tell about it. It is important to note that these early reports about Chinese in New York were intertwined with a public discourse on Chinese and Indian "coolies." Such reports of unwitting and voluntary semislavery, as coolie labor came to be characterized, reinforced prior European ideas of "oriental despotism" and slavish behavior. On the eve of the Civil War a long, probing article in *De Bow's Review,* for example, asked a central question: "What is the plain English of the whole system? Is it not just this?—that the civilized and powerful races of the earth have discovered that the degraded, barbarous, and weak races, may be induced *voluntarily* to reduce themselves to a slavery more cruel than any that has yet disgraced the earth, and that humanity may compound with its conscience, by pleading that the act is one of *free will?*"[39] New York editors and writers were clearly conscious of the global labor and capital context of their local coverage.[40] Irrespective of such debates, however, this mixing of peoples in port cultures in everyday life continued unabated. Trade and profit-making drove this creolizing process, thereby creating these cross-cultural interactions in plantations and port-culture zones throughout the Atlantic world, the Indian Ocean, and, increasingly, the Pacific.

The interport nature of Western maritime trade, ever drawing "peripheral" countries into a global division of labor, inadvertently allowed for multinational crews and the formation of multicultural districts in international port cities. The constant turnover of European and American crew members left shipmasters searching desperately for experienced mariners, of whatever skin hue. Master George Bradbury's 1856 voyage to "Hong Kong and elsewhere" attested to this perennial problem. Upon arriving in that port, he personally appeared before the Hong Kong consul James Keenan and complained that a goodly portion of his American sailors had left the ship: "It was impossible for him to procure a crew of American seamen who were able and willing enough to perform the duties of seamen and . . . in consequence thereof [he] was compelled to ship a crew of Manilla men." That same year the *Samuel Russel* of New York arrived in Hong Kong with no Chinese among its twenty-three-member crew, but eight Chinese signed up for $13 per month for ports in China and Europe.[41]

The fact that Chinese sailors, cooks, and stewards regularly served on U.S. ships originating from New York well before San Francisco was considered a significant port of call makes the individuals noted in Syle's survey and the census of particular interest and importance. These reconstructions of what may have been the very first Chinese community in the United States enable us to see the crucial role New York has played in the lives and cultural representations of Chinese in the United States.

An 1856 *New-York Times* article, "Chinamen in New-York," estimated that there were 150 Chinese, "mostly employed as sailors," in lower Manhattan. A few years later another *Times* reporter visited two sailors' boardinghouses located at 78 James Street and 61 Cherry Street. He reported that the two houses were similar in layout. At the James Street house the first room on the second floor was a dining room, dormitory, and lounge area. Along the walls of the room were "fixed berths," three deep as on a ship, where two "Chin-Chins" were sleeping. While a group of sailors, "some of them dandies ashore," puffed on cigars and played cards, the reporter spoke to a man called "Pasching" who politely answered questions in broken English while his Irish wife and five-year-old boy looked on. A cook was in an adjoining room preparing soup. At Cherry Street the boardinghouse operator's wife was a German woman, visiting with the Irish widow of a Chinese man. There the reporter believed he saw a man "dead drunk in his berth" with an opium pipe.[42]

Ah Sue, a travel-weary cook and steward on a Hong Kong–New York packet route, is credited by an 1885 *Tribune* reporter with being the first Chinese to settle in New York. He landed at 62 Cherry Street in 1847 and opened a very modest tobacco-candy store, likely the first Chinese-run store in New York, and operated a small boardinghouse for Asian sailors. In a year's time he reportedly met and married an Irishwoman named Murphy.[43] Although he was not the first to settle—John Huston, John Lewis, John Atchen, William Brown, and others were already living in the area and married to Irishwomen years earlier—he may have been the first to open a boardinghouse. It is possible that, prior to his doing so, longtime Chinese New Yorkers took transient seamen into their own apartments. These arrangements may have proved a problem with any increase in seamen, however, because the apartments could accommodate only so many cots. Given the apparent increase in mariners in the 1840s, it was only a matter of time before the more entrepreneurial among these Chinese decided to try earning a safer and potentially more lucrative living on land by renting a large space and providing room and board.

Packet ship cook and steward Ko Lo Chee, who took over Ah Sue's sailors' boardinghouse at 62 Cherry in 1867, actively recruited Chinese to settle in New York. He wrote to countrymen in California and China about the city's business advantages. Ko was also an early advocate of sailors' rights, a well-paid activity. He aggressively called on incoming ships to inquire about the condition and treatment of Chinese sailors aboard. In instances of unpaid wages, cruelty, or duress inflicted upon Chinese crew members, he "made war upon the vessel or its master." In one case he compelled a captain to pay $2,000 to a Chinese cook for unpaid back wages and for assault and battery. Of this sum the obliging cook paid Ko 60 percent. Years later Ko reportedly returned to China with $50,000 in savings. As of 1885 his house was still in business under his name and doing quite well.[44] Apparently such boardinghouses as Ko's tended only to sailors, the largest segment of the community, nonsailors having to create their own habitats.

The census data indicate that those individuals who decided to stay, at least for a while, in New York City often engaged in the cigar- and cigarette-making and peddling trades. The first Chinese settler in Alvin Harlow's often cited *Old Bowery Days* was such a "cigar man." Ah Ken, who reportedly arrived in 1858, was "probably one of those Chinese mentioned in gossip of the sixties as peddling 'awful' cigars at three cents apiece from little stands along the City Hall Park fence—offering a paper spill and a tiny oil lamp as a lighter." These cigar vendors may have been recently arrived immigrants who could only find work peddling or carrying billboard signs. Ah Ken later opened a little cigar store on Chatham Street and lived on Mott.[45] William Longford, John Occoo, and John Ava may have been the first Chinese to break into the skilled craft of cigar making in New York. The tight control cigar makers kept over their trade suggests that these men had some prior experience in the craft.[46]

Chinese cigar peddlers, on the other hand, probably had no such advantages. Like many other immigrant peddlers, they simply could not get better jobs. The satiric *Yankee Notions* noted the entry of some of the opera actors into the cigar-peddling trade with a mischievous wink at their plight. "Celestial Occupation in New York" showed a peddler, his hand out, with a tear rolling down one cheek. Another drawing humorously depicted what was a daily problem for Chinese walking in public: their queues were constantly the target of pranks by white boys and men. *Ballou's* reported "overgrown boys and rowdies" who, adopting the "latest style" and behaving like the Bowery stage character "Mose," walk up to one of the Chinese stands, "coolly select a cigar," and then "walk off."[47]

A *New-York Times* reporter visited a cigar peddler's boardinghouse in the rear basement of 391 Pearl Street in 1856. (Given the address, this may have been the same place listed in the 1855 census as being operated by Ar Yeep.) Rented by a Mr. Akkbo since 1851, who also cooked meals and cleaned, it was apparently similar in layout to the sailors' boardinghouses. Bunks lined the walls, and there was a long table for eating and lounging. "On the dingy colored walls were sundry Chinese ornaments." Each of Akkbo's fourteen or so boarders paid $3 per week, grossing him a handsome $168 per month. Even after expenses are deducted, boardinghouse keepers did quite well compared with the $15 to $25 of a sailor's monthly salary.[48] Assuming similar rates at the other boardinghouses, those Chinese who opened such small businesses stood to make substantially more than by sailing, and certainly more than by selling cigars. It is difficult to estimate how long these cigar vendors stayed with Akkbo and how steady his income actually was.

A cooperative spirit prevailed among the boarders, indicating some early forms of mutual aid. The *Times* reporter witnessed four boarders sick in their beds: "They have been unable for a long time to do anything for their own living, and are supported by their countrymen—each from his own small earnings contributing to their comfort. Four have died in that room within the last three years, and the expenses of their funerals were paid by contributions from among themselves."[49]

Figure 10. A Chinese cigar peddler and a Chinese beggar, *Ballou's Pictorial*, May 19, 1855. (Wong Ching Foo Collection)

The Chinese who settled in the lower wards of Manhattan Island added complexity to the mix of ethnicities, trades, and languages of this region. This mixing of Chinese with non-Chinese makes one detail from the census data and crew lists doubly intriguing: the pattern of taking on Western names. In many such instances, the names were Anglo-Christian ones, which suggests that they were acquired within some British-dominated zone of influence. The practice may have begun with British and/or U.S. missionary incursions into China as early as the nineteenth century, but it was especially prevalent after Hong Kong became a British colony in 1842. Occasionally near-familial affectional bonds developed between British employers and their Chinese house servants, to the degree that the servant would adopt his boss's last name. Or perhaps these names originated at sea with British or American shipmasters giving their Chinese crew "proper" names. Among the Chinese sailors found in 1857 crew lists leaving New York were Joseph Achoy, William King, Thomas Taylor, John Young, John Williams, John Asine, John Francis, George Crof, John Charles, and Taysona Alconda— all claiming New York as their home residence. Those Chinese who signed on to American ships in Hong Kong were still registered with informal Chinese first names such as Aty, Ah Sing, Ah Sam, Ah Moy, and Ah Sen. They may have been given English names on their way to the Americas or Europe. A third possible source of Anglo-American names was Bible and English-language classes held in overseas Chinese communities. The Chinese Mission established by the Fourth Avenue Presbyterian Church claimed to have 156 young Chinese men passing through its classes by 1871, a substantial portion of the Chinese settlement.[50]

The more assimilated these men appeared—equipped with a Western name and some knowledge of standard English—the more access to the dominant culture they could gain. They often served as translator-interlocutors, interpreting both language and meaning between less adept Chinese New Yorkers and officials. Despite the English adaptations, however, Chinese individuals clearly understood that Anglo-American culture was not their own. In fact, the adoption of a Western name did not mean that the Chinese name had been forsworn, nor did it necessarily mean that the individual had embraced Christianity. The Chinese name would continue to be used among compatriots and the European American name among non-Chinese. Indeed, it was a traditional Chinese practice to take on various names throughout one's life: a childhood family name, a school name, a formal business name, and so on. This naming strategy continued in New York for many decades, especially, it seems, with those individuals who frequently dealt with non-Chinese. For example, the missionary, court interpreter, and farm owner J. M. Singleton, living in New York from 1882 on, used only his Chinese name—Chu Mon Sing—in the Chinese community. Loo Kay Sog, a San Francisco–born, China-schooled New York businessman, from 1911 onward was better known by his "Americanized" name of Harry C. Law.[51]

This adaptive naming practice was not so different from the voluntary Anglicization of their names by many eastern and southern European immigrants. It was another element of the pattern of Chinese involvement in a creolizing downtown culture. The adoption of Anglo-American names—like the marriages to Irishwomen and the establishment of families—signaled that many of these Chinese intended to stay.

The Tong Hook Tong Dramatic Company

Alas, we come now upon the subjects of Edward Syle's search: the Tong Hook Tong Dramatic Company. In contrast to the prepackaged *Keying* display and the Anglicized performance of *The Orphan of China*, the Tong Hook Tong offered a fully staged, elaborately costumed, authentic Chinese opera. Yet the manner in which this troupe was received clearly tested the limits of New Yorkers' taste and the nature of philanthropy in the elite civic culture.

In 1852, Likoon, a prominent elderly merchant in San Francisco's burgeoning "Chinese Quarters," along with Norman Assing and Tong Chick, formed a bold investment plan. Months before, they had made arrangements with a "wealthy impresario" in Guangzhou by the name of Amoo to bring the acclaimed forty-two-member opera troupe, the Tong Hook Tong Dramatic Company, to San Francisco. Although documentation on the opera group is thin, we do have the reported testimony of Leong Mun Ahgeu, the group's translator.[52]

The Tong Hook Tong Dramatic Company was a Cantonese opera organization that, according to Leong, had achieved a substantial reputation in Guangdong Province. Leong stated that the troupe's trip to Gaam Shaan (Jingshan), the newly coined name for San Francisco and the region, had been "induced by the wide spread reports of the fabulous wealth of California" and was expected to "make independent fortunes for every member of the corps." Their sponsor, Amoo, stayed in Guangzhou, Likoon managing the troupe on his behalf while in the United States. After a successful run in

San Francisco, Likoon signed a contract with a New York promoter, and by April 1 they were on the *Cortes*, bound via Panama for New York.[53]

The recent success of a number of plays set in China, with European American actors playing in yellowface makeup, encouraged New York theatrical agents to try to book what was at first perceived as a highly desirable property. A George N. Beach, purportedly representing a wealthy and responsible syndicate, negotiated the contract. His investors, or so he said, included a Captain Agnew, John Friston, D. S. Dimon, Mr. R. H. Collyer, and, among others, the master impresario of New York himself, Phineas T. Barnum. The company would be featured at the event of the year, the Crystal Palace exhibition. Beach agreed to pay Likoon and the company a tidy $6,000 a month for a ten-month renewable contract, with a $10,000 advance and all travel expenses, room, and board. Depending on their skill and prominence, members of the company would earn $1,200 to $5,000 a year, and the translator $150 per month. The company had every reason to believe that their success in New York was guaranteed. Beach had agreed to pay the steamship agents $6,000 for the travel expenses.[54]

Likoon and a partner named Min Chu were lodged comfortably in cabin class, while the interpreter, two cooks, and thirty-six performers languished in steerage. The opera troupe arrived in May to find the promoters disorganized and refusing to honor their contract. When steamship agents presented the $6,000 bill, Beach declared insolvency, claiming that Barnum had backed out and that other members of the syndicate could not cover the amount. Barnum denied any involvement.[55]

The company was stuck. Unaware of the full implications of the action, Likoon took responsibility for the debt by signing a lien agreement on the costumes with the steamship agents. The fabulous wardrobe was extensive, irreplaceable, and, according to one advertisement, worth $100,000. The new owners estimated the worth of the costumes at $40,000 to $60,000. In the meantime, the inauguration of the Crystal Palace exhibition had been delayed until July. So Beach booked the company into Niblo's Garden beginning on May 20 for fifty cents a ticket, a steep drop from the $6 box seats sold at the opening night in San Francisco.[56]

The *New York Herald* column featuring musicals and theater performances described the opera company in a grandiose manner reminiscent of the fanciful and elaborate festival spectaculars staged by Garrick for British audiences. "The great Canton Histrionic Chinese company," as the *Herald* dubbed the troupe, comprising fifty performers, male and female, celebrated as the most distinguished artists in China, will give their third representation of the ceremonies, festivals, games and amusements of China to-morrow evening. They will also play several airs peculiar to their country. They will exhibit the military exercises of their soldiers, and the Japanese tumblers and Chinese Tartars will display feats peculiar to their nations, which taken as a whole, forms a very interesting entertainment.[57]

Contrary to what the reporter believed, there were no women in the troupe. In Chinese opera tradition, female roles were always played by men.

The *New York Evening Post* announcement was not much different. It inaccurately spoke of "religious rites, peculiar ceremonies, extraordinary amusements and wondrous feats of the inhabitants of China, Tartary, Siam and Japan." The article greatly exaggerated the nature of the costumes. Instead of representing them as outfits made for operas, which were nonetheless valuable, the reporter claimed that they were the type actually worn by nobility: "Their wardrobe contains the exact dresses worn by the Emperors and Mandarins of every dynasty during four thousands years."[58] In an obvious effort to encourage attendance, the journalists were presenting the troupe in the stereotypic mode as people from a fixed and changeless civilization.

Newspaper critics immersed in Western traditions had a difficult time grasping the Cantonese opera form. This was something very different from the highly Westernized staging of *The Orphan of China*. A *Tribune* reviewer tried, without much success, to evaluate what he was seeing. The program he saw began with a religious ritual that included "benediction and blessings for the future welfare of the United States," followed by a "presentation of the Gods and Goddesses of the Beasts, Birds, and Fishes from the Throne of the Imperial Dragon," and ended with a "Grand Marriage Ceremony" featuring the entrance of the emperor and the unveiling of the bride. Limited by Anglo-American society's scant exposure to Chinese culture, the reviewer was looking through the prism of the material and trade culture he knew. "The whole [drama] reminded us of splendid gilded tea boxes galvanized into motion—the figures are so grotesque, pompous and [of] that indescribable compound of cultivation and barbarism which distinguishes the great Empire." After attempting to describe the parade of characters who "came with glorious pomposity and ching-changed or cumfee-hoed in front of the platform and then ascended the platform," he described the singing and music as "a compound of distressed cats, an old pump handle, ungreased cart wheels, a poke on a tin kitchen, and the spiritual rappers in communion with the infernal regions." He responded very positively to the costumes, "gorgeous to the last degree, all that silk, crepe, gold-tissue—the cumulated splendors of Chinese taste." He also liked the tumbling: the acrobats were "sufficiently active and the somersaults, doubtless revolving from the remotest antiquity, would do credit to modern performers." But in all, the minimalist staging, the highly stylized movements of the actors, the unfamiliar music, and the epic nature of the play proved to be a combination too alien for New York audiences to appreciate, however much they might respond to the costuming and the acrobatics. The reviewer concluded with a backhanded compliment: "It certainly is a privilege to be brought into communion with the distant and the past by such attractive means."[59]

The Niblo's Garden performance ended within the week, the last night being for the "benefit of the company." The agent, George Beach, disappeared with the moneys and made no arrangements for additional appearances. In the meantime, the troupe's bill at the Shakespeare Hotel had mounted up. After two months the syndicate had only paid some $300 and still owed around $700. Taking up many rooms at the height of the tourist season, the members of the company offered to leave. But the proprietor of the hotel, Eugene Lievre, carried them for the time being, hoping that the situation would soon change.[60]

On June 29 the New York Herald devoted almost a third of its front page to an article about their plight. Titled "The Celestials in New York, Desertion and Destitution of the Tong-Hook-Tong Dramatic Company—A Case for Philanthropists, &c.," the article recounted the entire story of the company, including all details of their contract with Beach. This verbatim reprint of their contract was used to make the irrefutable case that they had been cheated and abandoned. If it were not for philanthropists like "the benevolent" hotel proprietor Lievre, "the poor Chinese would now be recipients of public alms at Ward's Island." The article was clearly intended to solicit sympathy for them as a cause célèbre. Was another source of generosity to appear?[61]

Unfortunately, while entrepreneurs and well-wishers made several offers to the company, none had sufficient capital. Meanwhile, the opera group sought to resume performances in order to raise money for their fares to San Francisco. They finally managed to arrange a single performance on July 4 at Castle Garden. All seemed hopeful. They had arranged for the temporary use of their mortgaged costumes and counted on the Independence Day crowds.

A fireworks display and a "grand ball" punctuated the evening. But the proceeds were disappointing. A number of days later an "American and German" committee of "wealthy and highly respectable gentlemen" negotiated another benefit at Castle Garden to "aid the Chinese who were betrayed, defrauded and then deserted and left to beg, steal or starve." The event was a limited success. After expenses, they were given a check for $680.50, which was turned over to pay some of their back bills. Six days later the *Herald* reprinted as "A Card to the Public" a note of thanks from Leong and Likoon. The English- and German-language presses were thanked for free advertisements, as were the committee, the performers, and a Madame Anna Thilion, who had donated $50. Likoon lamented, "We did not come to this country as beggars. Honest ourselves, we were deceived by putting too much confidence in those persons who brought us into the miserable situation we are in now; therefore we really think we do not deserve our unfortunate fate." Still without costumes, or much hope of returning to California, Leong and Likoon asked, "What shall become of us now? We do not know."[62]

After brief appearances of their "Tumblers and Combatants" at Burton's Theater, an appearance at a theater in Brooklyn, and an unsuccessful donation drive, the group lost all hope. Lievre could no longer afford to keep them on. Some were taken to a workhouse on Blackwell's Island (later renamed Roosevelt Island), where one member of the troupe attempted suicide. Others drifted through the streets, "looking forlorn and neglected," selling cigars and fabrics from their personal belongings.[63] They were to join the ranks of a small but growing community of Chinese living in lower Manhattan.

An "Exemplary Chinaman"

Norms of patrician philanthropy formed the backbone of the ways in which newspapers such as the *New-York Times* would report on and measure Chinese as either upstanding merchants or pitiable beggars, proto-Christian or "heathen." These early representations, based on eyewitness accounts and firsthand knowledge, provided a believable public narrative defining who Chinese people truly were. The depictions, however, failed to engage seriously with the numbers of Chinese already living in parts of the city.

In his earlier efforts to locate the destitute and disbanded Tong Hook Tong performers, Edward Syle had been directed to Quimbo Appo, an English-speaking tea seller who seems to have been the single best-known Chinese person in New York. Syle was favorably impressed with Appo and his business acumen: "I saw a veritable Chinaman," Syle wrote in a somewhat surprised tone, "playing his part as a salesman with an alacrity of movement and flourish of manner that was quite exemplary." In contrast to the opera troupe beggars on Broadway, Appo was presented as one who knew how to operate in the commercial environs of New York and as an independent, rational individual. From Syle's admiring individualistic vantage point, Appo "wanted nobody to take care of him but was abundantly able to be the guardian of his own interests."[64]

Appo told Syle that he had been born in Zhusan, an island off the mouth of the Yangtze River, at the midcoast of China, in 1825 and had lived through the British shelling of Shanghai during the Opium Wars. How much of this biography can be trusted is difficult to say. Appo does, however, appear to have been one of the Chinese who took to the trade routes to the West—somehow gaining his atypical name. He claimed to have traveled with Prussian missionary Karl Gutzlaff, who went into forbidden interior sections of China with the faulty belief that Chinese needed only to be exposed to Christianity to be converted.[65] Living on an island under constant battles for control by the West, Appo was likely, since Zhusan was a strategic island for British and American opium traders, to have been among those Chinese nationals who gained access to Western ships after the 1842 Treaty of Nanjing. Appo told Syle that he then sailed to Yerba Buena in 1844, well before the United States claimed the territory and years before other Chinese were known to have been in that Mexican trading post. In that same year he sailed to Boston as a cook and steward on the *Vandalia*. Later, in New Haven, he married an Irishwoman named Catherine Fitzpatrick. They eventually moved to New York, where he found work in a tea store. They had a daughter and a son.[66]

Appo functioned well in English and was a shrewd shopkeeper. While in the store, Syle was impressed by a particular incident. A customer wanted to use a dollar note to pay for a small quantity of coffee. Appo told the customer, "You want to change this note, [you] must buy half a pound, then can do." The surprised customer did what was asked of him.[67]

An 1856 *New-York Times* reporter called upon "Crimpo" Appo months later to gain access to cigar peddlers. Appo was willing to talk to the reporter about his countrymen, for he hoped that "public attention could be directed to the condition of some of them—particularly those who sold cigars in the street—for the cold of Winter would soon debar them from this mode of

Figure 11. "Scene in Fulton Market, New York City," *Ballou's Pictorial*,
June 28, 1856. Chinese peddlers were an everyday part of the port culture.
(Wong Ching Foo Collection)

obtaining a sustenance." Appo used the *Times* article as an opportunity to
advertise the desperate plight of the vendors: "Being totally unacquainted
with the language and customs of this country, they are unfitted for almost
any City work, but they are anxious to be employed, and would like situations on farms."[68]

Appo lived and worked at a tea store located at 50 Spring Street, well
above the relative poverty of the Fourth and Sixth Wards. He did not own
the store but apparently earned a decent wage. Tea was a major import item
for the port of New York. By 1860, $8.3 million of a national total of $8.9
million of imported tea was handled by tea merchants in New York. Retail-
ing tea promised opportunities for Chinese in the city. (Indeed, Syle helped
three of the opera performers open a tea shop in the Gowanus section of
Brooklyn, close to the Greenwood Cemetery, helping the remainder to find
day-laborer jobs near the tea store. Syle also noted that at this time Chinese
could be found tending tea emporiums in Boston, Albany, Cincinnati, Day-
ton, Indianapolis, and other eastern cities.)[69]

Four fellow tea dealers were visiting Appo when the *Times* reporter arrived to meet him. "One young fellow," as the reporter described him, "quite dandyish in his appearance, wearing a shawl, and all that, announced his intention of learning to read and write the language, to become an American citizen, and to marry an American girl."[70] For this aspiring tea dealer, Appo must have been a successful role model. Not having much of a Chinese constituency from which to draw customers, these merchants would not have found it a viable option to operate in a Chinese dialect. Being able to effectively communicate with English-speaking New Yorkers was a prerequisite to doing well. The young man's attitude, combined with the pattern of intermarriage evident among many early Chinese, clearly indicated Chinese willingness to intermix with non-Chinese neighbors.

Even within such a small community, however, class tensions were evident. Individuals such as Appo presumed to speak on behalf of those who did not have the English or the education to communicate effectively with Americans. Other Chinese sought to distance themselves from their poorer countrymen. English-speaking Chinese were among those who drafted and signed a petition disassociating themselves from the Chinese beggars found on the streets of New York. In 1856 a petition was sent to the editor of the *Tribune* with thirty-seven Chinese signatures. Titled "Protest against Chinese Beggars," the petition charged that these wayward men were "spurious Chinese, who are impostors, and who are utterly unworthy [of the] sympathy of the citizens of New York." The petitioners claimed that these beggars in actuality "spend their money in drunkenness and among the vile dens of Water Street." That "they are from Shanghae," noted the petitioners, was reason enough to doubt their veracity.[71]

Thus, class and regional differences divided this community as surely as racist attitudes, pranks, and violence committed against them bound them together. The impoverished, unmarried, and unsettled peddlers and beggars contrasted strikingly with the petition signers or the tea-merchant dandy who attended a Methodist church. Class, job, language skills, and knowledge about American culture varied dramatically among early community residents. And such differences implied a variety of personal and collective survival, accommodation, and advancement strategies.[72]

From "Mandarin" Merchants to Street Beggars

In a matter of decades New York had risen from obscurity to become a major international port city. While merchant Chong had visited in 1808 to collect a trading debt, former opera troupe performers now roamed lower Manhattan begging for spare change. As power had shifted from Canton to New York, New Yorkers' perceptions had become more layered, complex, and convoluted. The orientalism of elite cultural distinction now commingled with staged spectacles and real Chinese beggars. This shift in the New York culture of representations corresponded to a shift in American diplomatic attitudes toward China.

In June 1859 American representative John E. Ward waited on an armed frigate prepared to cruise up the Peiho (Beihe) to Peking to deliver a letter to the emperor from President Buchanan. Induced to go to Peking by land, Ward arrived at the Forbidden City and was told that he would have to deliver Buchanan's letter in person. Ward would have the distinction of being the first American to have an audience with any Chinese emperor. Of course, he was expected to perform the proper traditional rituals before the emperor. Ward, echoing British refusals of earlier decades, defiantly stated that America was a republic and that he would not bend his knee even to his own president. He knelt, he said, "only to God and woman!" The audience with the emperor did not occur, and the treaty was ratified in another city.[73]

Ward's defiance of Chinese custom indicated America's rising confidence. Five years earlier Commodore Matthew Perry and his "black ships" had forced open Japanese trade.[74] Now, following the gains of British gunboat diplomacy, the United States broke its nominal "neutrality." Premised on notions of proud individualism and the protection of colonial interests, Ward's behavior echoed that of Lord Macartney in 1793. Americans, like the British before them, would refuse to "kowtow" to any Chinese "despot" or to recognize any nation's right to regulate its own trade. If not voluntarily offered, "free trade" would be imposed by force. Protestant missionaries were now free to bring the word of Jesus Christ to all heathens; God and capitalism could now liberate a "half-civilized" China. Resistance abroad to "foreign devils," of course, would continue to escalate, ultimately bringing about revolution and fervent antiforeigner movements.[75]

The praising of Appo and the charity extended toward the crew of the *Keying* should be understood against this backdrop. The era of admiration for China was waning. Anglo-Americans felt increasingly confident that they were not only not British and not European but also not emulating China any longer. In New York, respect and admiration for China shifted toward missionary charity, pity, and eventual disdain. In the popular media, China was increasingly represented as an eclipsed civilization, and Chinese were increasingly cast as beggars. Indeed, Chinese and begging had become a pervasive association in the city's public culture. The city's newspapers incorporated this image into their portrayals of everyday street life, bolstered by testimonials of what New Yorkers were seeing for themselves. An 1857 book reviewer in the prestigious journal *Putnam's Monthly* remembered "a scamp on the lowest step of the Astor House" who was "cunningly playing on that harp of a thousand strings, the sympathies of a Broadway crowd. . . . 'Please buy something from this poor Chinaman!' . . . Begging considered as one of the Fine Arts." We have already considered the 1857 *Yankee Notions* cartoon satirizing the tearful Chinese cigar peddler; another *Yankee Notions* cartoon portrayed a job-seeking Irishman impersonating a "Chaney man." Titled "A Promising Applicant," this anti-Irish cartoon portrayed the "Hibernian Celestial" appealing to the charity of the good storekeeper with a mock Irish dialect: "Would ye be afther 'imploytn a pore craythur ov a Chaney man, as is fur away from home an country?"[76]

By the 1850s Chinese beggars had become a commonplace, and much discussed, fixture of the city. Their existence took on metaphorical value above and beyond their specific circumstances.[77] The 1855 poem "On a Chinaman in Broadway," published in the *United States Democratic Review,* probably best exemplifies this metaphorical turn. The "poor native of Cathay," begging "by the dusty footway" and "transfixed as in a dream," effectively shatters the "curious childhood" images patrician New Yorkers had formed from their "heir-loom China." While the beggar dreams, "the world's great heart," New York, "pants round [him]." While the "long grass" of China's plains waves "untrodden," here "a rushing progress sweeps." Again, the Chinese and China are represented as a changeless people and landscape, in contrast to the vibrancy and movement of the United States. "We, the vanguard of the nations, we poise our wings for flight," whereas China merely kindles "up the smouldering ashes of dead primeval lands."[78]

The 1850s New York emphasis on Chinese beggars had clearly taken on a larger resonance. Their presence attracted the kind of attention that had been accorded to the departure of the *Empress of China* seven decades before. Unlike Freneau's *Empress* poem of romantic respect, "On a Chinaman in Broadway" noted the end of the United States' early relations with China. In these intervening decades New York had become a continental power in its own right, and China now appeared an object of pity. The *Putnam's Monthly* reviewer probably expressed what his readers were already sensing: "Decidedly it is hard to imagine a grave, great and glorious Chinaman.

There is something essentially ridiculous in all their pertainings of the outlandish creature." This was a dramatic change from the strong positive identification with Chinese people and culture that the *Empress* and the *Orphan* had evoked: "For myself, I think I could with less embarrassment, with a more successful air of indifference to the grins of the crowd, stand shaking hands, on Broadway, with a veritably tailed gentleman from the interior of Africa . . . than I could do the very same, by any impouse [*sic*] of cosmopolitan affability, with Chu-Jin-Seng."[79]

Any chance for the revival of the Tong Hook Tong Dramatic Company ended when their invaluable and impounded costumes, instruments, stage sets, and other items were sold at auction. Representing what one reporter described as the "cumulated splendors of Chinese taste," sixty lots valued at from $40,000 to $100,000 sold for a little over $1,000.[80] With its performers dispersed and properties gone, this unique opportunity for actual cross-cultural exchange between Chinese and U.S. theatrical cultures was lost.

The patrician admiration for Chinese luxuries remained fundamental to the culture of distinction. However, the rise of American political and economic power fostered a self-serving attitude toward the Chinese. When wronged by an Australian British sea captain, Chinese sailors were treated with Christian charity; when seen to be an adaptive and shrewd businessman, Quimbo Appo was praised as "exemplary"; when exploited by an unscrupulous New York producer, the opera performers evoked much newspaper coverage and some charity, but they ultimately ended up with pity. All such Chinese became newsworthy spectacles, attracting great public interest. This interest, it was discovered, could sell newspapers and tickets. Thus, a commercial culture of the marketing of public spectacles created a distinctly New York form of orientalism that shaped and limited the possibilities of Chinese Americans' everyday life. Members of the pioneer Chinese settlement had to negotiate their lives within this powerful market-driven society. Different individuals with different language, trade, and social skills would devise their personal strategies in this intercultural zone. Amid the hustle and bustle of ships coming and leaving, a handful of Chinese managed to find a home in the port culture that enabled them to survive, set down roots, and become polyglot New Yorkers. Some, such as Quimbo Appo, could build their careers within the class-bound perceptions of patrician orientalism. For others, opportunities opened up in the port's stage and dime-museum culture.

CHAPTER 5

"Edifying Curiosities"

I N 1841 A "Yan Zoo—Chinese juggler" appeared in New York; the "Feejee Mermaid" (a monkey head and torso joined to the lower half of a large fish) and the purported "Coffin of Mahomet" were displayed at the same time. In 1843 the "Mysterious Boy Hajah from Persia" and the "Tartar Cavalry" made their appearances on New York stages. In contrast to the *Keying* exhibition and the Tong Hook Tong Dramatic Company, performances such as the "Chinese necromancers," Chinese "tumblers and combatants," and the "double-jointed Chinese dwarf Chin Gan" were explicitly packaged and promoted for New York audiences.[1] Over the decades, dozens of other "oriental" acts performed on stages small and large. Many of these performances were hoaxes. "Ursa the Bear Lady," for example, featured a midget from Calcutta, India, whose lower body was costumed in a bearlike outfit, claws and all; she posed on all fours. And "Gondio and Apexia, Famous Sweeka-Sere People of Lower Burmah, B.E. India," were two small men with pointed heads (or, in medical parlance, microcephalics) further exoticized in Asian ethnic costume. The "Wild Men of Borneo" were actually two dwarfs, Ohio brothers Hiram and Barney Davis, listed by one court record as "imbeciles."[2] Shorn of the sticky difficulties of real cross-cultural differences posed by the crew of the *Keying* and the Chinese opera troupe, these acts were designed to cater to what audiences could most quickly assimilate and respond to. Putting on display people from the imagined faraway land of coveted oriental luxuries proved to be a successful money-making scheme.

Throughout the nineteenth century various Chinese and other Asian and Pacific peoples journeying on Western trade routes sought to make a living performing as "edifying curiosities" in the many dime-museum, the-

Figure 12. Ursa the Bear Lady, ca. 1850s. Stage and dime-museum performers had *cartes de visite* made to sell after their performances. This photograph is by Charles Eisenman, who had a studio on the Bowery.
(Syracuse University, Ronald G. Becker Collection)

ater, and performance spaces of the city. If the performance was well presented, citizens would be willing to pay some curator entrepreneur to see, question, and experience a different culture. We do not know much about these early performers, but the little we can glean provides important insights about how their "otherness" was exoticized in a commercial culture. The Chinese on display necessarily had their bodies, clothing, and cultural differences commodified and simulated to compare and contrast with prevailing notions of European American normality. This array of "sights" constituted a veritable showcase for the new mass audiences of an ever more populous New York.

According to historian Donald Lowe, visual perception was central to Victorian culture, driving the rise of visual metaphors even in poetry and fiction. The ability to simulate likenesses improved greatly during this era of mechanical, technical, and theatrical reproduction, raising public consternation about what was real and what was fake. Visual discernment and believability became a primary means for gaining some mastery over urban disorder.[3] Furthermore, the mobility afforded by quicker forms of transportation (the locomotive) and communication (telegraphs and daily newspapers) collapsed older, more fixed notions of seasonal time and staying in one's place.

The preoccupation with visuality helped individuated selves moving within the urban landscape to gain some bearings in their relation to the hectic urban scene. Before he invented the photographic daguerreotype in the 1820s, Louis Jacques Mandé Daguerre invented the stationary panorama. Viewers sat in a room while a panoramic scene rotated around them. Dioramas, stereographs, mechanical figures, photographs, and a host of other objects that transported the imagination and tricked the eye were invented during this period. Magicians thrived in this era in which seeing was believing but the hand was "quicker than the eye." The fascination with racial others, "monstrosities," and stereotypes was personally experienced through these various visual media.[4] Much in the way aristocrats and patricians engaged in travel writing, the urban middle classes could now consume a visual array of commercial "edifying curiosities" to discover their own personal relationship to other cultures, peoples, and parts of the world. To survey a panorama of China, a miniature of a primitive village, or a living animal or exoticized human on display or to witness an "oriental conjuror" all evoked a sense of wonderment and situated one's place in the world.[5]

The word *curiosity* has specific orientalist roots. The *Oxford English Dictionary* defines *curio* as "an object of art, piece of bric-a-brac, etc. valued as a curiosity or rarity"; the term is "more particularly applied to articles of this kind from China, Japan, and the far East."[6] *Curiosities* defined objects that could be owned, collected, and taken away from their original environment. It was an acquisitive and possessive word that, not coincidentally, grew in usage in proportion to the global expansion of the British Empire. Transglobal trade made possible the transglobal process of collecting from "remote" cultures. Curiosities, then, were often objects or subjects brought back from colonial hinterlands to the metropoles for possession, collection, and display. Curiosity could, in this era of print and staged culture, become a profitable enterprise. With urbanization and the intermingling of peoples from all parts of the world, exhibitions created a controllable forum in which scholar-scientists, everyday people, and performers could engage the public in addressing public questions about natural and human diversity.

Marketing *Homo Monstrosus*

Not receiving subsidies or patronage, New York exhibitors offered programs they believed the public would be willing to pay to see. The popular belief in human monsters from distant lands became a bankable curiosity.

In 1755, Linnaeus distinguished *homo sapiens* from *homo monstrosus* from *homo ferus* (wild man). Although his earlier classifications did not explicitly rank indigenous Americans, Europeans, Asians, and Africans in any hierarchy, the value-laden descriptions did suggest a clear and predictable pecking order, from those governed by "habit" and "caprice," to those governed by "opinion," to those governed by "customs." In this view of the world, the "monster man" became the "wild man" who multiplied into different-hued "sapiens"—all linked in "one chain of universal being." One of Linnaeus's students, Fabricus, tried to explain Africans as the product of cross-breeding between humans and simians. By the end of the eighteenth century such explanations were circulating within European intellectual circles as "the great chain of being."[7]

Clearly, the 1859 publication of Charles Darwin's *Origin of Species* further problematized the relationship of men to other species. Aristotle's still influential idea of *lusus naturae* ("joke of nature") mixed with the idea of *homo monstrosus* to produce a biological science infused with distorting racialized explanations. Chinese people, consequently, were typed as "long-headed" and "conic," that is, resembling the microcephalic individuals in sideshows. Such a judgment was represented in descriptions and drawings of Chinese men with shaved foreheads wearing queues, which gave the exaggerated appearance of a sloping and pointed head. The notion of deformed heads being related in some way to Chineseness continued well into the twentieth century, with the use of the term *Mongoloidism* or *Mongoloid idiots* to describe those with Down's syndrome.[8]

The stage became the public site to play out general ignorance and to test systems of knowledge. Science and commercial entertainment, in this sense, developed hand in hand. Good business logic made clear that the fearsomeness of the human monsters could not be so exaggerated in advance promotion that the mass of potential customers would be scared away. Questions about the "races of mankind" intermingled with notions of "manifest destiny" and progress further spurred Americans to query their place in the world. Early "dime museums," as places for the collections of artifacts, displays of real people, and performances of magic and new technologies, played a central role in this civic discourse. The disdain for such places expressed by Henry Tappan, future president of the University of Michigan, also serves to confirm the dime museum's central role in New York City. After returning from the British Museum in 1851, Tappan bemoaned that New York's museums were but "a place for some stuffed birds and animals, for the exhibition of monsters, and for vulgar dramatic performances—a mere place of popular amusement."[9]

As the preeminent site for the production and reproduction of culture, the port of New York largely determined where a performance would be seen, what would be seen, and how it would be seen. By midcentury the metropolis boasted the nation's largest potential public audience. The many Bowery and Broadway theaters, exhibition halls, and newspapers created a variety of venues in which performances could be tested out, refined, and promoted. The sheer numbers of performance stages and their proximity to one another created a hothouse atmosphere in which successful acts could be quickly copied the next day on another stage.

The most important role of New York City in developing a national commercial culture was enacted behind the scenes, in the establishment of an infrastructure committed to the business of culture. With a strong base in trade having spawned the communications, publishing, and banking industries, Manhattan became an ideal environment from which European and European American cultural productions could circulate. New York City served as a generative base for museums and performances. The production of exhibits, the bookings of performances, and their banking, accounting, transportation, and promotional operations were all centered in Manhattan.[10]

"The Chinese Lady"

An engraving of Afong Moy from the 1830s, reproduced as figure 13, shows how Chinese women were pictorially transmuted from a distant time and place into contemporary Manhattan. The border frames her habitat like a period room in the Metropolitan Museum of Art. She sits, quietly self-contained, with hands clasped, and she stares at the viewer. She is wearing a Qing Dynasty silk gown, loose-fitting for comfort and easy mobility, with matching trousers. Her hair is pulled back in a bun held in place and decorated by two chopsticklike hairpins sticking out in a manner typical of married women of her era. Her feet, bound with small, pointy slippers, are in-

Figure 13. "Afong Moy: The Chinese Lady," 1835.
Lithograph by Russo Browne (Museum of the City of New York, Print Archives)

discreetly featured on a two-step wooden pedestal. In fact, the entire parlor serves as a pedestal for this exhibition. An elaborate canopy of drapery frames the space above her head. A decorative Middle Eastern latticed dome crowns her. Despite the flatness of the rear wall, all the flanking furniture and carpet lines have been carefully angled toward an imaginary point behind her, thus drawing the viewer's eyes to her. She is not only technically at the center of the image, she is meant to be the center of attraction.

And yet the graphic is not simply a conventional nineteenth-century portrait of her. The viewer's eye is drawn to the material environment surrounding her, to two engravings featuring Western representations of a Chinese man and a Chinese woman. An eight-sided lantern with translucent panels, decorated with small human figures, an octagonal taboret table, and a teapot with a single cup and saucer signal Chinese authenticity.

This parlorlike setting is not quite a true parlor. Either the artist or the actual designer of the interior has angled the walls of the room to serve as a stage. Moy appears to be fifteen to twenty feet away, situating the viewer at a point comparable to where viewers from the pit might have been in a standard Manhattan theater. But instead of angling upward from the pit, the artist has privileged the viewer by presenting the scene from a higher vantage point looking downward. This angle of vision implies the class distinctions of more expensive gallery and balcony seats.

From a purely formal descriptive level, this image is enigmatic and difficult to understand. Moy appears lonely and a bit anxious. The orientalesque bric-a-brac, latticework chair, and settee at stage left are conspicuously empty. And the furnishings are invitingly angled toward us, as if it would be a favor to her if we were to join her. Who was this Chinese woman? Where was she? And what story did this print tell?

Afong Moy was most likely the very first Chinese woman to appear in the United States.[11] However, we do not really know her name. The spelling of her family name, Moy, indicates that she was probably Cantonese. And the "A" (or more commonly "Ah") prefix indicates a familiar form of address, hence "Afong" was not her formal given name. Apparently, for her producers and her audience, her actual name did not matter. She was promoted as "the Chinese Lady." Newspaper clippings indicate that she came to appear on New York City stages in 1834. In June the *Commercial Advertiser* reported that the American Museum was having "a party of Indians [who were] to dance and hold council, and the Chinese Lady was there 'as usual.'" Five days later she was featured with "Schweighoffer, the magician," and "Finn, the blower of glass."[12]

By November, according to the chronicler of early American theater, George T. Odell, she was appearing on a stage at 8 Park Place: "Afong-Moy, in native costume, showed Manhattan belles how different ladies could look in widely separated regions." The *New-York Times* reported that her "monstrous small" feet, four inches long, attracted audiences: "Her beauty is of a soft and sleepy cast, as all Chinese beauty should be. Her dress is what a critic would call 'indigenous,' that is to say, emphatically Chinese in all its points and attributes, and her feet would scarcely fill an infant's first slipper." This was probably the first Chinese woman this reporter had seen, yet he was already a critic confidently making judgments about what a Chinese beauty "should" look like![13]

In the next two years Afong Moy appeared at the City Saloon, with "Harrington, the magician and four dioramas depicting the village and battle of Waterloo"; Niblo's Gardens, the popular theater where the Tong Hook Tong Dramatic Company first appeared; Peale's Museum, where she was followed by the Siamese Twins; and the Marble Buildings on Broadway, while she "was waiting for a ship to China." She appeared in a "concert" at the Brooklyn Institute along with the Canderbecks, who performed "songs and recitations in German," S. W. Bassford, a "professor at the Piano-Forte," and "Hanington's Hydro-Oxygen Microscope." Whether or not she ever actually left for China is unclear, but in 1845 a "Chinese Lady" reappeared in advertisements for the Temple of the Muses. She apparently talked and counted in Chinese and ate with chopsticks, thus "render[ing] the exhibition highly interesting to lovers of curiosities."[14]

These references seem to be the extent to which Afong Moy's life was recorded. Her own voice does not speak to us; we have only fragments of commentary. What can be gleaned, however, are the circumstances of her staged appearances. Indeed, once we have the date of her performances, the artist's rendering can be reexamined. In addition to a formalist description of the visual image, we can now begin to place it in a historical context.

Her cultural difference—exemplified by "monstrous" bound feet—made her a profitable "curiosity" for New Yorkers who knew about China and the Chinese only through literature, newspapers, and imported commercial objects. The British missionaries and their publications, who reported to the empire and the Anglo-American world about how China was despotically "patriarchal," were virtually fixated on Chinese women's bound feet. Missionaries had been leaving New York City for China since 1809 and occasionally returned to the United States to lecture and raise funds.[15] Protestant missionaries intentionally appealed to the curiosity that middle-class audiences had about China. One means of appealing for aid was to emphasize the most exotic aspects of Chinese culture. This legacy of exoticism may well explain the enigma of the engraving, the parlor with the formal qualities of a stage. For early-nineteenth-century American Victorians, the parlor and the stage were not entirely distinct. Families would frequently entertain each other in the parlor. This is evident in the artist's decision to portray the room in ways that make it both a stage and a parlor. The display of potentially threatening "exotic" and abnormal people, therefore, was in effect made safe.

In the context of traditional Chinese culture, this parlor scene is strange in other ways as well. The Western imitation and interpretation of Chinese and Middle Eastern design, the highly elaborate layering of fabric and carpeting on wood, the very notion of a parlor sitting room—all make this stage distinctly less Chinese than Anglo-American. Yet to the Anglo-American eye the setting appeared to be in the "Chinese taste."[16] Moy's dress was authentic enough, but she was surrounded by oriental-type objects that symbolized the patrician culture of distinction. Although the critic-journalist of the New-York Times thought he knew that Moy looked the way a Chinese beauty "should be" and that her dress was "emphatically Chinese," he did not comment on the inauthenticity of the setting. In fact, probably unbeknownst to him, the setting was far more Victorian than anything else. But these cultural conventions were such common emblems of middle-class definition by this date that they may have appeared "naturally" Chinese.

Moy was presented and re-presented graphically in what later would have been considered an anthropological setting. She was a live person, placed as an extension of her culture amid objects supposedly Chinese, almost as if she were part of a natural-history-museum environment or a display of zoological specimens. Afong Moy's stage appearance was an easily accessible, domesticated, and contained means for Anglo-Americans to gaze at and try to understand cultural, and what was increasingly defined as racial, difference.[17]

Judging from her dress and hair style, Afong Moy was most likely married. Judging from the few Chinese women who ventured beyond China at this time, she was likely to have been of humble origins—from the countryside or laboring segments of the port cities.[18] What makes her particularly fascinating and significant is that she somehow managed, at least for a few years, to earn a livelihood by sitting and performing simple demonstrations. It is important to point out that who she was in actual life was largely irrelevant to how she was represented on stage and iconographically. In terms of the emerging commercial culture, consonant with the conventions of Western theatrical performance, it simply did not matter.

The artist's engraving and the way the newspaper reporters wrote about Moy offer significant insights into the popular commercial culture of New York City. Even with sparse documentation, however, we can venture an appraisal of her relation to the culture of New York. Judging from her many appearances in a short amount of time, she had moderate theatrical success. Yet without English-language skills, she evidently had little power to manage her own situation. She was marketable as a curiosity, trapped within the American taste for consuming visual display.

The United Siamese Brothers

> Susan,
> I have two Chinese Boys 17 years old, grown together. They enjoy extraordinary health. I hope these will prove profitable as a curiosity.
> Captain Abel Coffin

In this casual manner the soon-to-be-renowned "Siamese Twins" Chang ("Chun") and Eng ("In") were introduced by sea captain and "exhibit" shareholder Abel Coffin to his devoted wife in Boston.[19] The boys were perfectly formed, "normal" identical twins except that they were joined by a ligature at midtorso. The year was 1829. In decades to come Chang and Eng would negotiate the rewards and perils of being on tour through every state in the Union and much of Europe, Panama, Cuba, and southern Canada. In sheer market terms the twins were to prove "curiosities" of unusually lasting value. Not only were they were viewed as "exotics" from an undifferentiated Asia, in the manner of Afong Moy and the Tong Hook Tong Dramatic Company, but they were clearly *lusus naturae*, or a "joke of nature," which multiplied their commercial value. It was this combination of racially and biologically framed qualities that made them such highly bankable performers.[20]

Although a great deal was written about Chang and Eng while they were alive, and even more has been penned since their deaths, we know remark-

Figure 14. Chang and Eng Bunker, 1839. The twins represented themselves as refined patricians, as evidenced in this souvenir poster sold after their performances. (Wong Ching Foo Collection)

ably little about their actual identities and viewpoints. As with Afong Moy, reporters did not bother asking the most basic biographical questions about them. Their original family name is unknown. Nor have any published accounts explored what languages they spoke, how literate they may have been, or what their impressions of the United States were. Such basic gaps in knowledge should be contrasted with the surplus of anecdotal stories about train trips, fights with customers, and fights between them, as well as speculation on how they managed to perform sexually. We know that their managers and longtime friends James Hale and Charles Harris, and Chang's son-in-law Zacharias Haynes, among others, staunchly stood up for them to correct the plethora of wild stories and rumors.[21] Unfortunately, except for what their descendants have told reporters, their own stories were never documented. The twins never endeavored, nor apparently were they ever offered the chance, to write their own autobiography.

The American public first gazed at these Asian "Double Boys" upon their arrival in Boston, where they proved an immediate sensation. The *Boston Patriot* supplied the best advance publicity the promoters could have hoped for: "We have seen and examined this strange freak of nature. It is one of the greatest living curiosities we have ever saw. . . . They will probably be exhibited to the public when proper arrangements have been made. They will be objects of great curiosity, particularly to the medical faculty." The second week in Boston, fellow investor Robert Hunter and Coffin rented a tremendous tent that held several thousand people, bombarded the city with posters, and charged fifty cents admission to see the "Siamese Double Boys." They played to large gatherings and toured Providence, New York, and Philadelphia for eight weeks thereafter. Hunter and Coffin immediately made back their initial investment, plus sizable profits.[22]

Predictably, descriptions of the twins rested on the quick impressions gained from seeing them perform or from interviewing their managers Coffin, Hunter, or Hale. The great majority of journalists represented the twins with such phrases as "strong and active," "good-natured" and of "pleasant countenances," or "happy and gay" and "quite contented with their lot." They were observed to be loving brothers who were "affectionate" with one another, "their arms round each other's necks."[23] The brothers' happiness was ascribed, in part, to their considerate managers, who were depicted as loving patriarchs performing a service to humanity. As one Dr. George Buckley Bolton told his colleagues at the Royal College of Surgeons:

I cannot here deny myself the pleasure of stating the kindness which has at all times been evinced towards these youths by Captain Coffin, Mr. Hunter and Mr. Hale: The unwearied anxiety manifested by these gentlemen for their welfare and happiness, and the liberal manner in which they have uniformly afforded the means of investigating so curious an object of philosophical inquiry, entitle them equally to the thanks of the philanthropist and the lover of science.[24]

In marked contrast, the twins were described as helpless creatures to be pitied, needing the custody of a kind guardian. A Dr. Felix Pasclair published an open letter in the *New York Courier and Enquirer* stating:

Among the subjects of natural curiosity which are derived from the animated creation . . . none could excite more really painful feelings of pity than the contemplation of these ill-fated fellow creatures. We are however much relieved by hearing that they were not abandoned by their parents— that an American navigator had received them in trust from their mother, to be returned under contract with such a stipulated fund as to be sufficient for their maintenance and future comfort; also to have them as far as possible instructed in our language.[25]

Whether "happy and gay" or "ill-fated" and pitiful, the twins were not represented as having a voice of their own, let alone independence of will or intelligence. Despite the fact that they were now eighteen-year-old men, vigorous and quick-witted, they were constructed a priori as helpless and witless creatures who needed white male guardianship.

As Chang and Eng toured, their performance was crafted to appeal to the curiosity of their audiences while at the same time staying within the bounds of conventional respectability. Although they were first displayed in a large tent, the twins were most frequently featured in halls or theaters. Their performances were presented in "rooms" in a high-toned manner for more intimate groupings. Their early touring broadsides, printed by J. M. Elliott of New York, read, "The United Brothers, Chang-Eng, very respectfully acquaint the Ladies and Gentlemen of ——— that they will be in that place on ——— and will receive visitors at the ———." The 1839 lithograph they sold during their performances pictured them in elegant suits, confidently standing arm in arm in a parlor with a patterned floor covering, chair, checkerboard, and table. Their audiences were most often modest in size, about twenty people a performance, who sat with them and visited, almost as if for afternoon tea. In fact, the twins did not think of themselves as putting on "a show."[26] Like the parlor of Afong Moy, their performance space was made to look like a Victorian parlor recreated on a commercial stage.

Large advertisements heralded the arrival of Chang and Eng in New York in 1829. The *Evening Post* article headlined "Wonderful Natural Curiosity— The Siamese Twin Brothers" noted their appearance at the Grand Saloon of the Masonic Hall on Broadway from nine in the morning until two in the afternoon and again from six to nine in the evening. They were on stage eight hours a day. Their three-week booking was regularly attended by over-flow audiences.[27] The brothers had by this time developed an act in which they appeared in Chinese costume with their queues. Their uncanny physical coordination was demonstrated by routines highlighting their athleticism. They performed somersaults and backflips. They sometimes displayed their not inconsiderable strength by carrying the heaviest member of the audience around the room, in one instance a 280-pound man. Lithographs show them playing draughts, thus demonstrating their dexterity and swiftness. If the audience was particularly responsive, they would challenge members to a game of checkers or chess to demonstrate their intelligence. And they had learned enough English on their voyage to Boston to answer basic questions.[28]

Audience members regularly sought to examine the brothers' linking tissue for themselves, which quickly became a source of anger, sometimes resulting in fights with their patrons. Capitalizing on the suspicion of hoax and the paying audience's understandable curiosity, Coffin regularly invited locally prominent doctors to examine and certify the authenticity of the brothers. Such actions inevitably brought about free extra publicity in local newspapers. With the permission of Captain Coffin, puzzled doctors regularly performed cursory physiological and neurological experiments on Chang and Eng, followed by a public disclosure of their findings. Dr. Felix Pasclair, the "special correspondent of the medical society of Paris," for example, underscored the unique opportunity in the twins' display. He wrote an open letter to the *New York Courier and Enquirer* that proved to be perfectly suited for publicity: "One hundred and twenty-eight years have elapsed since the occurrence of the formation of a double human being. . . . The rarity of preceding similar cases in Europe or elsewhere, has induced me to communicate the recent occurrence of two male children now offered to our observation in the city of New York." A binder of doctors' testimonials was on display as part of the exhibition.[29] Promoters in this commercial arena cleverly flirted with both commonsense ideas of normalcy and scientific knowledge.

After a week in Philadelphia the twins returned to Manhattan to depart for a grand tour of Great Britain. Captain and Mrs. Coffin, Robert Hunter, and their future manager, James Hale, as well as some others traveled first class, while Chang and Eng were placed in steerage, a fact the twins would note and about which they would later express great bitterness. In case the twins were to die in transit, embalming chemicals were brought along with the idea that Chang and Eng could be preserved and exhibited in England even after death. Hunter and Coffin also took out a $10,000 life insurance policy on the brothers, an amount so large that three insurers had to underwrite the policy. The Concern would profit from them alive or dead.[30]

The twins appeared at the Egyptian Hall in Piccadilly in November and remained in London for seven months. They were visited by Queen Adelaide, others of the royal family, foreign ambassadors, nobility, and "most of the philosophers and scientific men of the age." The stay went so well that they toured the British Isles for another eight months, traveling some twenty-five hundred miles, some three hundred thousand visitors paying to see them.[31] Their plans, however, were not fully realized. It was thought that viewing Chang and Eng would cause pregnant women to give birth to joined twins, the result being that their Continental tour was canceled.[32]

The constant scrutiny caused great personal strain, and as Chang and Eng became more aware of American customs, they became sensitized to instances in which they were treated with disrespect. While they were in Exeter, Massachusetts, a local doctor told Chang he would like to stick a pin in his shoulder to see if Eng would notice. Chang retorted, "If you stick a pin in me, my brother Eng might knock you down." In Athens, Alabama, a local doctor accused them of being a hoax; they struck him and were arrested for assault. The *Salem (Mass.) Mercury* reported that a local colonel had called them liars and provoked one of them to hit him with the butt of a rifle. The brothers were fined $200.[33]

As was typical of performances of this era, Chang and Eng concluded their act by selling and autographing engravings and pamphlets (sold for twelve and a half cents) as souvenirs of the visit. These printed representations reveal the careful ways in which the twins' public image was managed.[34] When they were first introduced to the public in exhibit, Captain Coffin had their manager, James Hale, assemble a sixteen-page pamphlet "for sale only at the exhibition room." The frontispiece engraving showed the young brothers arm in arm, with their playthings, a racket and chess pieces (which emphasized their childlike image), a sketch of a palm tree in the background.[35] They were dressed in Chinese garb with their queues wrapped around their crowns. Their eyes gazed out at an angle to the viewer, almost as if they did not notice that they were being looked at, all of which conveyed a friendly and exotic impression. And despite their being adults, the Concern deliberately marketed them as youths. In what was likely an 1830 lithographic print of the twins, they were again illustrated as children, drawn much shorter than their actual height of five feet two inches. In proportion to a fatherly, mature man standing next to them, they seem to be the height of young adolescents (or else the adults are nearly seven feet tall).[36]

Their brochures had a standard format. The pamphlet James Hale wrote in 1831 was prototypical. In addition to several pages of doctors' testimonials, which included a signed statement by eminent British physicians placed prominently at the beginning, Hale wrote an "Account of the Siamese Twin Brothers" that can best be understood as Coffin's version of Chang and Eng's lives. Hale began his story by describing the location of Siam and emphasizing how backward a nation it was. Offering examples of punishments witnessed by Captain Coffin, Hale wrote, "The government of Siam is probably one of the most despotic and cruel in the world." He then inaccurately described the brothers as being "of the poorer class"; their description of themselves as "merchants" he characterized as "facetious," because they merely engaged in "the duck and egg trade." Hale then claimed that Coffin had essentially rescued the youths from a grim life by bringing them to the United States. "The mother and children were equally pleased with the voyage," Hale wrote, "as a sufficiency was left for her support, and all were aware of the respectability of those in whose charge they were placed." As further proof of Coffin's heroism, Hale stated, "The youths never express[ed] any desire to return to their native country" and hoped to "pass the remainder of their lives in Europe or America." Furthermore, they were eager to acculturate into American society, as evidenced by their keenness to learn the "manners and customs of our country."[37] In all, Hale represented Chang and Eng as being upstanding, if sometimes quaint and infantilized, characters. The affection expressed toward them fell within a language of dominance and domestication, which ultimately reinforced a smug American sense of well-being and enlightenment.[38]

The motif of the mock-Victorian parlor set upon a commercial stage captures the way in which commercial orientalism surrounded and greatly complicated patrician orientalism. The sense of a private visitation was staged to provide public audiences a feeling of vicarious intimacy. The parlor represented a private place for entertaining guests, safely removed from the chaos of the streetscape. Like fine Chinese porcelains, Chang and Eng were presented as live, interactive collectibles, and their display was "edifying" within a culture of distinction. Yet they were packaged for a marketplace that exploited their rarity to gratify larger societal curiosity.

Peters's Chinese Museum

On January 1, 1849, John Peters Jr. opened "The Great Chinese Museum" at Broadway and Prince Street. While its advertisement of "Ten Thousand Things on China and the Chinese" was a bit exaggerated, it was a huge and magnificent assemblage of "curiosities" from China. During its public exhibition the collection was arguably the largest outside of Asia, in sheer size exceeding Philadelphia Quaker merchant Nathan Dunn's collection.[39] John Peters was apparently one of the "young men . . . encouraged to go at their own expense" on diplomat Caleb Cushing's 1844 mission to China—"to add dignity" to the endeavor. On the heels of Britain's military invasion of China over its "right" to the "free trade" of selling opium there, the Treaty of Nanking was negotiated, making Britain "a most favored nation" in trade.[40] The United States dispatched Cushing to attain most-favored-nation trading status as well.

Peters, twenty-two years old, was listed as a merchant on Wall Street and living with his father, John R. Peters Sr., in the upwardly mobile Chelsea section of Manhattan at Twenty-second Street near Eighth Avenue. By 1850–51 he seems to have been working and residing at 539 Broadway, the address of the Chinese Museum. He identified himself to a federal census taker as a "gentleman." Perhaps the museum management business enabled him to enjoy a life of greater leisure. Working probably as a civil engineer, he continued to operate his business out of 539 Broadway until 1856.[41] Nothing beyond this is known about the man.

In his catalogue, *Ten Thousand Things on China and the Chinese: Being a Picture of the Genius, Government, History, Literature, Agriculture, Arts, Trade, Manners, Customs, and Social Life of the People of the Celestial Empire, as Illustrated by the Chinese Collection,* Peters asserted that "the collection was formed without reference to labor or expense, with the aid of

Chinese, and the American Missionaries, who have resided a long time in the country, and are well acquainted with the language, manners and customs of this curious people."[42] It seems likely, therefore, that the missionaries referred to were those attached to Cushing's mission, namely the Reverend E. C. Bridgman, the Reverend Peter Parker, and, later, S. Wells Williams, who was the translator of the *Keying* crew's contract.[43] Once assembled, the exhibition was originally intended to reside in New York City but, with "no suitable place for its exhibition," was first taken to Boston and Philadelphia before it finally opened at 539 Broadway.

The exhibition itself must have been a singular visual experience. The entrance featured Chinese calligraphy flanking richly carved gold leaf and lacquered panels, as if the visitor were entering a Chinese temple. The couplet was translated "Words may deceive, but eyes cannot play the rogue." Inside, massive rectangular glass cases were situated in a neat Victorian aesthetic of evenly spaced, numerically ordered design elements. The largest cases contained groups of full-size Chinese figures peopling a range of scenes that included the chambers of the emperor and empress, a Canton merchant's store, a woman's private living quarters, and an opium smoker's den. Smaller cases displayed models of public works and lots of manufactured goods, foods, crafts, and the like. Some four hundred paintings, all executed by Chinese artists, hung on the walls. And hundreds of lanterns of various geometrical and animal shapes were suspended from the high ceiling. A full-size "Tanka" houseboat of the type encountered by Westerners when first approaching the ports of Hong Kong and Macao was featured as well. At face value the exhibition celebrated the admired luxuries of China and attempted to contextualize them spatially with three-dimensional recreations. The presentation was formal and restrained.[44]

Exhibition cabinets were coordinated with interpretive catalogue text. Peters, hardly an expert on Chinese culture, drew heavily upon the writings of primarily British and American diplomats and missionaries for his descriptions. Sir George Staunton, Sir John Barrow, and John F. Davis, for example, were all members of British diplomatic missions and had authored widely read volumes after their travels. Besides being a missionary and adviser, Elijah Bridgman also edited the highly influential and Protestant-financed *Chinese Repository*, a major English-language source of information on China published in Hong Kong. Historian Stuart Creighton Miller has described these individuals as "gatekeepers" of American public opinion.[45] It was through their eyes that interested segments of the American public viewed the material arts of China.

Who was this audience likely to have been? Presumably, any resident of or visitor to New York City (or Boston or Philadelphia) with a quarter to spare could have visited the Chinese Museum. A closer reading of journalists' descriptions of the exhibit clearly indicates who they thought the primary target audience was. The *Herald,* for example, wrote on the second day of the exhibition's opening, "We recommend the public . . . pay a visit to what we consider an highly intellectual and rational scene of amusement." *Hunt's Merchant Magazine* evaluated the exhibit in Boston, pointing out which cases would be "of great interest to the mercantile portion of the visiters." Moreover, the *Hunt's* reporter observed that "whatever might have been the merits" of the Opium War, it had "placed the commerce of China with foreign nations upon a more permanent and solid basis," and, additionally, "the morals of the nation, which appear to be extremely debased, will receive an improved tone, not from an idolatrous philosophy, but from the spirit of a genuine and enlightened Christianity."[46] From the fact that this collection had been gathered as part of Caleb Cushing's delegation, and from the comments about the "highly intellectual and rational scene" and the "great interest" the show would have for "the mercantile portion" of the audience, it is clear that Peters's exhibition embodied the material and pecuniary interests of merchants and businessmen.

It is useful to consider the evocative qualities of an exhibition featuring material objects presented in situ. Besides making a foreign culture more tangible and real in an era of tiny daguerreotype photographic reproductions, for its mid-nineteenth-century visitors the life-size sets evoked a vicarious tourist experience. Peters promoted the idea; journalists picked it up. Echoing the catalogue introduction, a *New York Herald* writer stated, "A visit to this collection is as instructive as a voyage to Canton[,] more so, indeed as we question much of voyagers to Canton only ever see so much of Chinese life as is displayed here."[47] For Peters's self-interested mercantile audience the exhibit conveyed a sense of intimacy and privilege, as if they were invited guests of the Chinese court.

In nineteenth-century Anglo-American culture, artifacts and material objects were thought to contain self-evident lessons on the morality and civilization of any given culture; in the United States the proper display of such objects would promulgate the virtues of the materialist-driven Protestant work ethic. George Brown Goode, early curator of the Smithsonian Museum, for example, adopted a Linnaean system of categorizing and displaying his collections. Intending to create a three-dimensional "encyclopedia of civilization," he organized his display cases of comparable objects to begin with the most "primitive" (invariably non-Western) and progress to "the most perfect and elaborate object of the same class" (inevitably Western). Goode felt that such great-chain-of-being displays would give the museum visitor a concrete lesson on the racial superiority of Anglo-Saxon high culture, the logic being that superior cultures produced superior things.[48]

Peters's collection represented a kind of personal compulsion, typical of a historically specific and culturally encouraged Western "possessive individualism." Like George Washington decades earlier, this upwardly striving man was "creating himself" by purchasing and surrounding himself with objects both cultured and primitive.[49] Hence, Peters, a young and ambitious man, can be understood as seeking to gain social status by collecting and curating. On the larger social level the collection also represented an effort at the domination of a culture. With the ability to possess and organize, to give nomenclature and categorize, books and exhibits became powerful analytical tools for gaining control and mastery over things and ideas Chinese. Peters, as collector, can be understood as a man of his social class of merchants, missionaries, diplomats, and journalists. In this sense Peters's exhibition was produced by and intended for those who had direct interests in the China trade, whether as merchants, missionaries, or diplomats, while also attracting those of the upper and middle classes as well as the general public who were simply curious.

If the structure of the exhibit provided a foundation for superiority over the other, we must also look toward the particularities of content to more fully understand the social meaning of the Chinese Museum. It embodied a shift in the representation of China and the Chinese, which I discussed in the previous chapter. The Enlightenment view, held by many of the founding fathers, saw China as a wise, enduring, ordered, rational, and civilized culture that had much to teach a young nation. Peters's catalogue echoed such sentiments. He praised the civil service for its emphasis on talent over wealth and influence. He praised the cultural emphasis on learning and, in general, commented that the Chinese were a "happy, contented, and industrious population" with a government "well administered," "on the whole."[50]

At the same time, more critical comments about China are evident in the catalogue narrative. Peters's praise of a happy, contented, and industrious people was couched within a critical discussion of the absolute patriarchal power of the emperor of China. Additionally, Peters found that the Chinese legal system sanctioned torture to elicit confessions and punished those found guilty of crimes in seemingly cruel and unusual ways. Among other examples of "peculiarity," their religions were fraught with superstition and rituals "similar to those of the Roman Catholics." Peters concludes with a statement embodying his seemingly contradictory (and proto-cultural-relativist) position: "The Chinese have been ridiculed for assuming to be the only civilized nation in the world. This assumption is probably owing to their peculiar institutions. They live in the past, we in the future, and consequently they are not to be judged by our standard."[51]

The tensions embodied in this statement are reflective of the criticisms of prevailing eighteenth-century Enlightenment-influenced views by more immediate trade, diplomatic, and missionary interests. While remarkable for its relativist respect, Peters's statement was less nonjudgmental than it purported to be. To live in the past was not a prized value. In an era of fiercely competitive mercantile interests, China resisted opening its doors to Christian missionaries and capitalist "free" trade. Judged by the standards of a Protestant, materialist-driven culture, China seemed to stagnate; its hoary government and strange cultural ways seemed to stand in the way of material progress.

The exhibition articulated what engaged citizens of the United States needed to know about China for their cultural and economic self-interests. Such self-interests inevitably shaped what was considered worth knowing about China and how China and the Chinese were to be judged.[52] By materializing American trade interests, Peters effectively made otherwise seemingly irrelevant government treaties and policies tangible and compelling for a genteel public. This instrumental vision was exclusive by design. It had limited popular appeal. In contrast to dime museums and live performances promoted with sensationalistic claims, these objects required more serious effort to comprehend. Peters's base of patrician support was by nature clubby, private, and class-bound. A popularizer's hand, however, would soon revivify public attention to this Chinese collection.

Barnum's "Chinese Family"

Phineas T. Barnum is commonly remembered for his shaping of the American circus (1871–91), but his real passion—and his pioneering work, pursued in his earlier years (1841–68)—was the American Museum on Broadway and Ann Street. The brilliant cultural producer played a key role in articulating a particularly American style of packaging orientalist ideas and people for general consumption.[53] Even tired acts were miraculously reworked and made popular and profitable by his marketing genius.

While his famed American Museum was undergoing six weeks of major renovations, Barnum appears to have rented Peters's Chinese Museum. On April 22, 1850, Barnum's Chinese Museum opened at 539 Broadway. Barnum's only contribution in re-presenting the Great Chinese Museum to the public seems to have been the replacement of Peters's name on the catalogue cover with his own (deleting any sign of Peters's authority) and the coupling of the exhibition ("for two weeks only") with "the unparalleled wonder, the most extraordinary curiosity yet—a real Chinese beauty, with FEET 2½ inches long," accompanied by her "Living Chinese Family." On June 17 the American Museum reopened to full-column newspaper ads.[54]

Barnum's ploy was immediately successful. The *New York Express* enthused:

> Barnum's enterprise stops short of nothing that is strange or wonderful. How he could tempt a Chinese lady of unquestionable character and position to travel among the "outside barbarians," and how he could smuggle her out of that mysterious country, no one can imagine; yet he has done both. Miss Pwan-Yekoo, the Chinese belle, with her Chinese suite of attendants, is drawing all Broadway to the Chinese collection. She is so pretty, so arch, so lively, and so graceful, while her minute feet are wondrous! She only remains in the city a couple of weeks, having been engaged to go to England.[55]

Barnum claimed that in six days twenty thousand people came to see this new sensation.[56] Although portrayed as just one member of "The Living Chinese Family" in an 1850 Currier's advertising print, "Miss Pwan-Ye-Koo" herself was overwhelmingly Barnum's main attraction. From the very first day Barnum gave her top billing. Miss Pwan, and not her "family" and not the Chinese collection, was promoted in paid newspaper ads.[57] The others were extras.

The entrepreneur promoted his addition of live Chinese to the exhibit in characteristically modest fashion: "With such striking additions, it will at once be perceived that this Museum can not have its equal in the world. It is complete in every respect." Even more tangibly than Peters's collection of costumed mannequins, crafts, and objects of industry, "it transports us to China itself; and furnishes to the eye and ear a perfect and lasting impression of the Chinese as a nation, their habits, their customs, and their singularities."[58] With this bold move Barnum could simultaneously become more respectable by virtue of possessing a patrician collection while continuing to make money in the commercial market.

Once again, we know little about Miss Pwan or her "family." She left no diaries, gave no interviews, and wrote no memoirs. Her personal papers, if she had any, have not been collected in a historical society. We don't even know the Chinese characters for her name. The Currier print tells us that she was seventeen years old, dressed in holiday finery as a "lady," purportedly had two-and-one-half-inch feet, and played the Chinese lute. Barnum offered only his tantalizing showman's pitch about Miss Pwan:

> Miss Pwan-ye-koo will be pronounced peculiarly prepossessing. She is young and handsome, vivacious, artless, refined in her manners, and delicate in her deportment. She is well known to belong to a family of high standing in the Celestial empire, and possesses all the accomplishments of mind and person so eloquently enlarged upon by the poets of that mysterious country. She is the first Chinese *lady* that has yet visited Christendom; the only other female ever known to have left the "Central Flowery Nation" in order to visit the "outside barbarians" having been one of apocryphal reputation and position in her own country.

Barnum's talents lay in turning this Chinese woman with bound feet into an entertainment people would pay to see. Without offering any real biographical specifics, he made her seem to be of the Chinese "upper ten"; to see her was a once-in-a-lifetime opportunity. She was an "eloquent," intelligent, and morally upstanding "lady," soon to be wed to a high Chinese official. By stressing the "watchful jealousy" of Chinese men, Barnum made visitors feel that they were gazing upon "a rare curiosity" that even Europeans living for years in China could "not secure." Central to the sight were Miss Pwan's tiny feet. Her bound extremities were of special interest in journalistic accounts and to the public. Nine of the sixteen "opinions of the press" quoted in the *Barnum's Chinese Museum* catalogue made a point of mentioning her "fairy feet."[59]

Her "suite"—the accompanying members of her "Chinese family"— were not blood relatives at all. Miss "Lum-Akun" was said to be Miss Pwan's maidservant. Aged twenty-three, she was described by Barnum as "a fair

Figure 15. Pwan Ye Koo and her entourage, represented in "Barnum's Chinese Family," Currier and Ives, 1850. (Wong Ching Foo Collection)

specimen of the Chinese women of her class. She is comely and agreeable." Dressed in everyday wear, probably deemed more appropriate by Barnum for a woman of a lower station, she did not have bound feet. Thirty-two-year-old Mr. "Soo-Chune" was described as a professor of music. Said to be an "*artiste* of reputation," he was shown by Currier as playing the *erh hu*, a two-stringed violin. He was accompanied by his two children: "Amoon," his seven-year-old daughter, and "Mun-Chung," his five-year-old son. The children were also robed in holiday dress and were presented as "perfect novelties, as types of Chinese juvenility." Barnum asserted, in a tone reminiscent of Peters's, that "unlike the notions many of us have formed of the rising generation among the odd people, we are compelled to admit that these specimens of 'young China' are really pretty, graceful, and intelligent. They can not but please, with their bright eyes, light-hearted smiles, lively tongues, and modest behavior." An eighteen-year-old Mr. "Aleet-Mong" served as their interpreter and was shown standing behind the sofa. The translator

probably served as the group's liaison with Barnum and helped them negotiate New York City.[60]

We have no way of knowing how Miss Pwan and her suite were displayed
in the museum. If the better-documented presentation style of Chang and
Eng offers any clues, Pwan and her family were probably seated in a room
with a certain set repertoire that offered plenty of opportunities for audience interaction. As often as once an hour Soo-Chune would play an instrument, and the group would occasionally sing, "conveying an accurate idea
of Chinese harmony."[61] Barnum's description of Amoon and Mun-Chung
indicated that the children added life and spontaneity to the overall performance. The translator would field questions from members of the audience and relate to them whatever the performers said. Judging from what
appears to be a proscenium curtain in the background, it is possible that the
family was displayed on a stage in the museum building. Since concerts were
regularly given in the "assembly rooms," some sort of credible performance
space must have been housed in the 539 building.[62] Onlookers could easily
compare their own lives with that of this Chinese "family."

When Miss Pwan and her Chinese family were first advertised, Barnum
emphasized that their stay was to be "for two weeks only." By May the ads
were claiming that they would only be in town for "re-engagement for a
short time longer," and no more ads appeared for the family after June 16.[63]
Barnum displayed them for a total of eight weeks. It was advertised that Miss
Pwan was to go with her entourage to England, where the "nobility [were]
dying to see her." On June 19 Barnum wrote a letter to his good friend and
fellow showman in Boston, Moses Kimball, requesting his aid to an "M. Wil-
mot, who visits Boston to make arrangements for the Chinese Family who
will exhibit there soon."[64]

In an August letter to Kimball, Barnum revealed much more about the
actual relationship and the contractual agreement he had made with Miss
Pwan and her associates. He asked Kimball to contact

> a Chinaman at Redding's tea-store in Boston who wants to travel with our
> Chinese Family as interpreter &c. He asked me $20 per month and his board.
> I wish you would go and see him and tell him that if he will come and man-
> age them properly so that they behave themselves I will have him for one
> year at $20 per month and his board, and I shall no doubt be glad to have
> him continue at the same rate for six years that being the time the Chinese
> are to remain with me.

Apparently their New York City interpreter Mr. Aleet-Mong did not travel with them. Perhaps he was not able to "manage them properly" enough to get them to "behave," or perhaps the successful Manhattan run had provoked a contract dispute that the young interpreter/manager could not handle. Whatever the case may have been, the six-year contract makes very clear that the "Chinese belle" and her suite were not passing through on their way to meet British royalty; they were simply another of the showman's business deals. Miss Pwan was not an aristocrat about to marry a high Chinese official. Barnum's representation of her was all a part of what Robert Bogdan has termed the "aggrandized" and "exotic" modes of a showman constructing an exhibit for public consumption.[65]

The contrast between John Peters and Barnum is useful to consider here. Even though Peters's mannequins greatly improved the accessibility of his vast inventory of Chinese objects, Barnum understood the superior value of live acts and how to promote his entire package to the press. Just as the popular press had misrepresented the crew of the *Keying*, Barnum cared more about what would pique public curiosity than the messy details of real people and cultures. In effect, Barnum's mass-marketed stories had no necessary relationship to his museum objects and displays; his signifiers did not have any necessary connection to the signified. What was important was that the public bought the story, or at least paid to come and question it.

What was Barnum's reward for his efforts? His expenses were relatively low. We know that a newly retained interpreter could make $20 a month with no promise of a raise in six years. We also know that, in 1843, Barnum was offering Kimball's well-established act "Yan Zoo," the Chinese juggler, $15 a week for two weeks.[66] Assume that Barnum did contract members of the "family" from China and that, like the twins, they were naive about Western money matters and contracts (with the possible exception of the interpreter). Assume that they were given a six-year no-raise contract, like the one being offered to their interpreter. And assume that they made less than Yan Zoo, the Chinese juggler, who was a known moneymaker. We can guess that Miss Pwan earned $40 a month, Mr. Soo-Chune (along with his two children) $30 or possibly $40 a month, Miss Lum Akum $20 or $30 a month, and Mr. Aleet-Mong $20 a month. This made for a group paycheck of $110 to $130 a month, or as much as $260 for their New York engagement.

In contrast, Barnum's profits were substantial. With a conservative estimate that his figure of twenty thousand visitors in the first six days was doubled through the entire stay, Barnum would have grossed $10,000. Although this figure may not have been much compared with the amounts brought in by Jenny Lind, whose receipts began later that year (and who was paid $1,000 per concert times 150 concerts), or by General Tom Thumb during his 1848 New York tour ($16,000 for four weeks), or by a "giantess" appearing during a run of unusually good weather in 1848 (approximately $7,840 per month), it kept Barnum in the public eye until he reopened his American Museum.[67] The diminishing returns on a less profitable Chinese Museum are likely to have accounted for Barnum's pulling the Chinese family the week of June 17 and closing the museum a month later. What became of the collection is unknown.

Simulations

Just as porcelains and goods manufactured in China prompted European pottery makers and designers to copy and make their own versions, so real Chinese performers and Chinese living in lower Manhattan prompted New York's cultural producers to mimicry. Much like chinoiserie or Murphy's *Orphan*, these copies were often viewed as being superior to the Chinese originals.

Visual, mechanical, and staged representations of faux Chinese had several advantages. As exemplified by the failure of the Tong Hook Tong opera troupe, authentic Chinese culture was too strange for New Yorkers' tastes. The sensibility of the Chinese opera was quite different from European American traditions. Language was also a problem with authentic Chinese performers; translators were necessary and an added expense. And the performers did not always conform to the way they were being packaged. One British magazine complained, for example, that Pwan Ye Koo had picked up a "low vulgar Yankee slang" ill befitting someone from the courts of China. Similarly, a *New York Evening Express* reporter expressed regret that the *Keying's* Chinese crew were losing their exoticism. He noted "the astonishing velocity with which they initiate themselves into the mysteries of modern refinements."[68] The independence demonstrated by the crew of the *Keying*, the Bunkers, and Pwan Ye Koo exemplified just how difficult it was to control and profit from living human beings. If real cross-cultural interchange was not important, then real Chinese were not necessary. Simulated Chinese were a much more manageable and far less expensive solution.

After the *Orphan of China*, New York cultural entrepreneurs built on the

British and French traditions of orientalist theater and made them American. Such plays as *The Yankees in China* (1839), *Irishman in China* (1842), *The Cockney in China* (1848), and *Mose in China* (1850) not only situated various serious and comic American types as naturally belonging in this foreign land but also Americanized the European yellowface tradition.[69] Chinese names were consistently mocked. For example, *China, or Tricks upon Travelers,* performed at Mitchell's Olympic Extravaganza in 1841, featured a Mr. Graham as "Ching Chong Chow" and a Mrs. Watts as "Fouchafee." More than forty years before Gilbert and Sullivan's *Mikado* we have names such as Prince Pretty Pill, Pig-Taili, Skidamalink, Bumble Bee, Cupid, and Glowworm. And in 1856 Ephram Horn of Charley White's Serenaders sang and acted in a distinctly American performance of *The Chinese Wash Man* in the "Chinese Rooms" at 539 Broadway.[70]

References to these "Chinese Rooms" appear just around the time of Peters's Chinese Museum, suggesting some connection to his enterprise. We can surmise that they were called "Chinese" because of some interior oriental architectural elements. However, the space was used as a general public space and did not feature specifically Chinese entertainment. In addition to opera, classical music, giraffes, dogs, monkeys, and evenings of magic, a December 1849 program featured Gliddon's moving panoramic canvas of Egypt and Nubia; a November 1852 showing featured thirty-two "moving pictures" of the American Revolution; and an April 1853 comedic lecture featured John E. Owens describing his recent ascent of Mount Blanc with "gigantic scenery" and "musical illustrations."[71] In the early nineteenth century, empirical sciences were illustrating how easily the human eye could be tricked into thinking it was seeing something real. Magicians regularly used new optical and mechanical inventions to create such simulations in their acts. Furthermore, panoramas, dioramas, the camera obscura, zeotropes, magic-lantern slides, stereopticons, and a host of other inventions tested the boundaries between what was real and what was illusion.[72] The aura of magic, wonder, and technology gave this hall exoticized commercialized associations befitting the imagined China of P. T. Barnum. In the same way that clipper ships gave American sea trade a decisive advantage, New York entrepreneurs' readiness to apply technological advances to cultural productions characterized a sense of civilizational progress defined as the marriage of technology and commerce.

Another technological breakthrough that was used in the practice of commercial orientalism had to do with visual imagery. In 1798 the French printer

Didot announced his invention of what he called the stereotyped plate for reproducing images on the printing press. This technological development foreshadowed the lithographic and photographic template processes that would be developed in the decades to come. As a rising commercial city, New York quickly adopted this among other technologies for the commercial arts. In addition to the theatrical stage, the printing industry was now able to reproduce, commercialize, and provide unprecedented distribution for images and symbols of the popular culture. As Walter Benjamin pointed out in his classic study "The Work of Art in the Age of Mechanical Reproduction," lithography "permitted graphic art for the first time to put its products on the market, not only in large numbers as hitherto, but also in daily changing forms." This responsive technology was ideally suited for a fickle culture of ever expanding consumer choices and styles—perfect for daily newspapers, posters of changing theatrical venues, and trade cards responding to the dizzying trends of business transactions.[73]

Chinese people quickly came to be exploited in this way. They were mechanically reproduced by this aggressive commercial culture—on stage, in lithographic prints and photographs, and in other media. And each time real Chinese were mimicked, simulated, and reproduced, their port-culture experience was abruptly altered, reduced, and/or simplified. Visual images abstracted from real people were also disengaged from the real complexities of their lives, from the layered creolized cultural practices of Chinese New Yorkers. The resulting abstractions—narrow racialized types—were easily recognizable, and therefore highly salable. These images elicited different emotions—provoking laughter, assuaging fear, and forging solidarity between members of a paying audience by formulating a pan-European occidental identity in juxtaposition to the stereotype of a yellow face. Particularly popular images were pirated into endless chains of visual reproductions bearing virtually no trace of the original quality, taking on new, stereotyped auras of their own. Such images, however, had a powerful effect on the real, everyday options of real, everyday Chinese; the representation became the real thing. In New York's commercialized marketplace, this magic was authentic.

One such endlessly reproduced image was that of the Chinese man partnered with the Irishwoman. The small settlement of Chinese men having relationships with Irishwomen was probably first captured by the crude visual representation of the March 1858 cover cartoon of *Yankee Notions,* reproduced as figure 9 in the previous chapter. The apple-selling Irish-

Figure 16. "A man's a man for all o' that," ca. 1870s–80s. The New York phenomenon of Chinese men having relationships with Irishwomen became a standard comedy routine in the popular culture of lower Manhattan. Here an actor in yellowface appears in a routine with a caricature of a lowly Irishwoman. (Wong Ching Foo Collection)

woman is marked by her shabby dress, scarf, and coarse features. The Chinese man in the background is signified by his conical hat and queue. Their children embody a visual mix of the two but are most improbably represented as having shaved foreheads and queues. The visual stereotype is considerably strengthened, moreover, by the lengthy burlesque dialogue captioned underneath. Mrs. Chang-Fee-Chow-Chy and Mr. Chang-Honey are engaged in an exchange of virtually incomprehensible mock-Irish dialect and mock-Chinese pidgin:

> *Mrs. Chang-Fee-Chow-Chy* (the better half of the Celestial over the way)—
> Now, then, Chang-Mike, run home and take Pat-Chow and Rooney-Sing wid ye, and bring the last of the puppy pie for yer daddy. And, do ye mind? bring some praties of yer mother, ye spalpeens.
>
> (*To her husband*)—How be's ye, Chang Honey?
>
> *Chang-Honey*—Sky we po kee bang too, mucho puck ti, rum foo, toodie skee sicke.[74]

Real people were being satirized in newsprint drawings, such drawings further proliferated popular stereotypes, performers and playwrights further promoted such images, and toy manufacturers believed that such images were sufficiently broad for general public consumption in the form of mechanical toys marketed nationally.

The image reproduced in figure 16, "A man's a man for all o' that," shows two actors playing out a comic routine between a mock-Irishwoman and a man in yellowface. The image, dating from the 1870s or 1880s, may be a souvenir from a well-known theatrical performance such as Charley White's *The Chinese Wash Man* or one of Edward Harrigan's plays portraying the washerwoman Mrs. Dublin and the laundryman Hog-Eye.[75]

The staging of the mock–Chinese man's body was carefully calculated to the conventions of the time. One playwright articulated his costume directions for local productions: "Jing (as a Chinaman)" should be outfitted with a ludicrous combination of "blue blouse, loose yellow pants fastened at the ankles, white stockings, [and] heavy brogans." The shaved forehead would be simulated by a "flesh colored skull-cap," which if unavailable to purchase "can be made of unbleached cotton like a night-cap, made to fit close to the head; color with flesh ball, cut holes on each side for the ears to appear, and it will be tight." Finally, Chinese men were prescribed to have a "very red face" with "black about the chin and over the lip to have the appearance of being unshaved."[76] In years to come the art of yellowface prosthetics and

Figure 17. "Trouble Ahead," Show Window Publishing Company, ca. 1870s.
This advertisement for a mechanical store-window display of the Chinese male/Irish
female mix-up is an example of how deeply such stereotypes penetrated the
commercial culture and everyday life. (Wong Ching Foo Collection)

makeup became standardized and the materials readily available from catalogues.

Not only could one laugh at the comic stereotype of these Irish-Chinese
"mix-ups" on stage, in print, and in photographs, but mechanical toy simulations could also be purchased in catalogues. In figure 17 we have the imagined racialized Chinaman and Irishwoman abstracted from real life and staged
yellowface and now relegated to the status of a three-dimensional me-

chanical reproduction, dating from the 1870s. This simulation of the stereo-type would later be fully realized, marrying film technology with established stage conventions, in such films as *Broken Blossoms* and *The Hatchetman*. But for now these mechanical productions were quite compelling. Indeed, they came to represent and echo actual events in the downtown interna-tional district.[77] Real Chinese-Irish intermixtures in lower Manhattan were represented on stage and made into comic, broadly marketed routines seen and laughed at by audiences across the nation.

During this period of American history, as technological breakthroughs made it possible to circulate visual images disentangled from books and news-paper illustrations, a commercialized visual culture came increasingly to sup-plant written and oral/aural narratives, becoming a highly potent popular symbolic language. Racialized stereotypes took on a life of their own as part of the standard vocabulary of a visual culture. An image of a real Chinese person, for example, could quickly be displaced by semblances and symbol-ically sufficient caricatures. These uneven exchanges automatically degraded actual people and disempowered them from being able to represent them-selves.

The audience for the "edifying curiosities" of a market-driven culture prized the simulations as much as, if not more than, the real—that is, until, the real themselves had become so confounded with the stereotype that most people could no longer tell them apart. Displays and simulations abstracted what was seen and performed from the live, human contexts and progres-sively reproduced commercial representations to the point of grotesque, indiscriminate stereotypes. At this point the visual language of yellowface came to signify a universe of meanings having far more to do with the host culture than with who and what were originally being represented. And who, ultimately, were the victims? Afong Moy, Chang and Eng, and Pwan Ye Koo, among many others, were captured and trapped in this culture of mechani-cal reproductions—but, it must be added, so were the buyers and sellers of these circulating images. Viewers who believed these representations be-came imprisoned in a world of racial caricatures and power relations.

By midcentury, living and breathing Chinese people passing through and residing in New York were being displayed, mimicked, and mechanically simulated by the commercial culture ad nauseam. Some of these tropes were admiring and benevolent, others hostile and dehumanizing, some ambigu-ous and mixed. Despite the dissonance of perspectives, all were accommo-dated as part of the universe of representations produced, circulated, and consumed by a market-driven visual culture of mechanically reproduced stereotyping. At the beginning of the century chinoiserie, tea, clipper ships, and other benefits of the China trade still financed national salvation. By the middle of the nineteenth century a commodifying culture had arisen that was both adoring and hostile, while also being nothing more than a swirling selection of racialized symbols circulating and ready to be produced and reproduced as profitable "edifying curiosities" in a "free" marketplace. In this process both Chinese and Americans were being defined—one as the other and one as the self. The real lives and needs of Chinese people in New York and the commodifying stereotypic forces of the market created an even more powerful chain of exchange than that of the early countinghouse.

To become a self-made man in this commercial orientalist marketplace meant different things to Chinese and non-Chinese. A further exploration of the performances of the Siamese Twins and P. T. Barnum will help us gain insight into this dynamic. The experience of Chang and Eng illustrates that what was salable greatly defined what kind of individuals they could become. The extant documentation of their celebrated and much scrutinized lives sheds light on the cultural forces impacting on lesser known and marginally referenced Chinese and non-Chinese New Yorkers.

CHAPTER 6

Self-Possessed
Men

P HINEAS T. BARNUM and Chang and Eng Bunker were New York City–based cultural entrepreneurs *extraordinaires*. For much of the nineteenth century they promoted and performed a range of acts, sometimes contradictory in nature, that dominated New Yorkers' and the nation's real and imagined understanding of China and the Chinese. They responded to and helped reformulate public interest by crafting and recrafting their performances to stay in the public eye over many decades. In contrast to patrician cultural activities, which were supported by a narrow and restricted base, broader popular cultural productions depended on what the general public was willing to buy. Barnum and the Bunkers shaped commercial orientalism, and this marketplace shaped them. Just as the port of New York depended on the China trade to become the economic hub of the nation, the commercial culture of New York depended on a constellation of racialized performers. In this sense, personal life choices were inextricably interlinked with the possibilities and limits of the cultural production of salable performances. The personification of social success, therefore, meant one type of success for Barnum and something different for the Bunkers.[1]

Contrary to current popular belief, Chang and Eng in fact had few dealings with Barnum and assuredly did not owe their careers to him.[2] The brothers managed themselves, and their reputations were firmly established by the time they met Barnum. Indeed, commentators noted that they were better regarded than the president of the United States and even more famous than heavyweight boxing champion John L. Sullivan. Rather than dwelling on the twins' conjoinedness or on Barnum's cleverness, however, it is far more revealing to examine how their careers as self-made men constituted and were in turn constituted by a process of commercial orientalism. Just as different members of the founding generation made different uses of Chinese goods, ideas, and people, so too did the twins and Barnum. Barnum packaged and repackaged his acts, whereas the twins packaged and repackaged themselves.

The Connecticut Yankee

Barnum's life spanned a time of rapid urbanization in Connecticut. He was born in 1810. Finding the chores on the family farm disagreeable, young Barnum became a clerk in a country store. By the age of twelve he had already learned the requisite skills to become successful: "Swapping stories with the local wits who gathered at the store, exploiting his employers as well as his customers, Barnum mastered the art of sharp practices." According to biographer Neil Harris, he embodied a feisty, aggressive Jacksonian spirit. He was "always willing to fight for the right of fighting itself, to compete against competitors, audiences, or self-styled experts. But the terms had to be fair."[3] This combination of shrewdness and fair play was supposed to define true Yankee character.

In an era of change in which the agriculturally rooted verities of an "honest day's work" and an "honest day's pay" had eroded, the Protestant work ethic was being redefined in a more urban market context. Barnum's statement that he "never really liked to work" should be understood in this light.[4] Like George Washington and Samuel Shaw, Barnum believed in the self-made man who, by dint of character, could overcome any God-given limitations and triumph. The Protestant notion of work as a form of prayer, "ascetic exercise," was being redefined by entrepreneurs in more self-serving materialist terms.[5] Work, for Barnum, became a form of self-discovery, character building, and moral rebirth—the individual testing and proving himself against the world. Barnum labored at providing leisure and escape for urban masses. Managing entertainment that people would be eager to consume became his life's passion and mission. And at this he was a genius.

Brought up in a fire-and-brimstone Congregationalist tradition, Barnum was a self-converted Unitarian Universalist. He deplored the bleakness of the Congregationalist doctrine of a preordained "elect" chosen from above regardless of earthly good works, greatly preferring the notion of a universal god of love "who will finally restore the whole family of mankind to holiness and happiness."[6] Barnum's religious conversion came about as a result of a personal crisis, one that led him to undertake his first European grand tour and, tellingly, also marked the beginning of his fascination with the Orient.

Barnum's problems became evident by 1844. His clever American Museum exhibitions had earned him great acclaim, but his profits were sagging, and so was his enthusiasm. As he put it in his 1869 autobiography, "I myself relished a higher grade of amusement."[7] Craving patrician respectability, his confidence shaken, he left the United States for a European sojourn that would offer him time to reflect. From 1844 to 1847 Barnum accompanied two-foot one-inch, fifteen-pound Charles Stratton on what would be remembered as their triumphant General Tom Thumb tour of Europe. They were greeted with great excitement and reaped large profits.[8]

While in England, Barnum had occasion to visit the seaside resort of Brighton. There stood the Royal Pavilion, a complex of horse stables and residential mansions with spired domes and minarets. Like the ornamentation of London's famed Egyptian Hall, it was an expression of the British fascination with things oriental.[9] Evidently Barnum's imagination was sparked by what might be described as Brighton's royal colonial-fantasy architecture. Upon returning to the United States in 1847, he commissioned architects to build an "Oriental villa" in Fairfield, Connecticut, which he dubbed Iranistan. The design mixed Moorish, Byzantine, Chinese, and Turkish palace styles.

Situated on seventeen acres, Iranistan was a filigreed and fanciful creation measuring 124 feet on its longest axis and 90 feet to the tip of its highest onion-shaped dome. It took some five hundred artisans to make and cost $150,000. Barnum used renderings of the mansion on his stationery, and he promoted it widely. Like many typical expressions of European orientalist interest, it casually jumbled together styles and symbols from several different cultures. Barnum's "Chinese library," now reproduced at the Barnum Museum, filled with bookcases and furniture, was described as "truly 'celestial,'" its walls "covered with Chinese landscapes in oil . . . by one of the best artists in Paris."[10] It would have been more accurate to call this room a "chinoiserie" library, but such was the carefree confusion of the time.

The ornate mansion with its exaggerated Asian-style ornamentation embodied Barnum's attempt to substantiate his outsized desire for status within the patrician culture of distinction. His version of patrician arrival remained consistent with that of past strivers: the possession of Chinese things still signified arrival, even though the wealth had been acquired in a very different way. A nineteenth-century striver like Barnum could profit from

Figure 18. P. T. Barnum's Iranistan, *Gleason's Pictorial Drawing Room Companion,* ca. 1847. Barnum built his eclectic orientalesque home upon returning from a successful tour in England and an inspirational vacation at Brighton. (Wong Ching Foo Collection)

the expanding urban economy and cultivate a market of eager customers by toying with preconceived myths and ideas. Tellingly, Barnum's display of conspicuous consumption in the form of Iranistan was made possible by his exploitation of public orientalist curiosity and stereotypes. In this era of magical stage transformations, Barnum's American success story can be measured, in part, by his ability to parlay one form of orientalism into access to a more prestigious form.

From Siam to New York

Born in 1811 in Siam, a year after Barnum, Chang and Eng were the sons of Nok and Ti-eye. Their father was believed to be a Chinese fisherman and their mother at least half Chinese, part Malaysian. Neighbors reportedly called the brothers the "Chinese Twins." Having lost their father and many brothers and sisters to cholera, they worked, as all young people did, to help their family make a living. Chang and Eng first became fishermen and then, between the ages of ten and thirteen, peddlers, hawking wares on the river. After being summoned by the emperor to visit the court in Bangkok, they were able to sell their royal gifts to local merchants to invest in ducks. This enabled them to enter the business of selling preserved duck eggs, and in a single year the twins sold twelve thousand eggs at a good profit. At the age of fourteen Chang and Eng were supporting their family and prospering. Except for occasionally being summoned by the emperor, they were not viewed as persons who should be displayed or segregated from everyday life.[11]

Chang and Eng were very protective of each other and their joined twin-ness. When they were first being displayed, any suggestion of their separa-tion caused great anxiety. As one New York doctor commented about them at age eighteen, "They are so satisfied with their condition, that nothing renders them so unhappy as the fear of a separation by any surgical opera-tion: the very mention of it causes immediate weeping."[12] It is evident that cross-cultural attitudes about physical differences were sharply divergent, and the brothers had to quickly learn about and defend against these con-trasting encounters.

Chang and Eng took pride in being Chinese. Besides being known to their neighbors as the "Chinese Twins," they thought of themselves as Chinese. In their 1836 pamphlet, the publication of which they personally super-vised, there is much emphasis on the "immense number of Chinese emi-grants," how "they had many more privileges than the natives," and how (even though their mother was only part Chinese) they were born of "Chi-nese parents."[13] They evidenced a certain amount of Chinese ethnocentrism quite typical of many overseas Chinese in the Nanhai, or Southern Seas set-tlements. The term *huaqiao,* or overseas Chinese, embodies this historical sensibility. Even those Chinese who had settled in the Nanhai and lived there for generations were thought to remain Chinese at heart. The nature of seg-regated Siamese ethnic politics kept Chinese and Siamese identities sepa-rate. There was no promotion of a plural cultural sensibility, no such thing as a hyphenated Chinese-Siamese. Ever sensitive to the class hierarchy of the United States, the twins may also have wanted to emphasize their more privileged ethnic background.[14]

Despite their strong sense of Chinese identity, the twins did adopt the name Bunker, and much lore is associated with how this came about. The most common story is repeated uncritically by Kay Hunter: While in New

York, they decided to go to the Naturalization Office to become citizens. After waiting in a "long line of applicants," they finally spoke to the man at the desk. He asked their names and soon ascertained that they had no last name. "It was explained to them that they could not become American citizens unless they had a Christian name and a surname." While the brothers were talking over their dilemma, a man named Fred Bunker said, "I'd consider it a real honor if you two gentlemen would care to use my name." Hence their surname.[15] In fact, the twins became U.S. citizens in 1839 in North Carolina and were not required to take on a surname. They were legally naturalized under the names "Chang Eng (commonly known as the Siamese twins)." And, in fact, they adopted the last name Bunker in honor of their friendship with the Bunker family in New York City. Their personal friend and unpublished biographer, Judge Graves, stated that sometime around 1832 the twins met three brothers, Fred, William, and Barthuel Bunker, who were wine and tea merchants at 13 Maiden Lane. Chang took a great liking to one of their daughters, Catherine, and later even willed his estate to her. They then began frequently using the Bunker name, although it was not made legal until 1839.[16]

Contrary to the perception of the brothers as having arrived from a superstitious and backward country, they had more entrepreneurial skills than the great majority of other immigrants to the United States. In Siam the early death of their father had prompted them to go out and develop sophisticated business skills, learning to calculate figures and negotiate prices. The twins were not naive country bumpkins. Boston and New York were actually smaller than Bangkok.[17] Still, there is no denying that Chang and Eng had left their mother, family, and culture, were at the mercy of men they hardly knew, and were being stared at and prodded by strangers. They had crossed an immense ocean, which delineated an even more immense cultural boundary.

In their audience with the emperor, they had been accorded respect, but in their display in the commercial marketplace, they were viewed as objects. Indeed, evidence confirms that they very quickly came to resent the way the public and their managers were treating them. While in London they were annoyed that visitors would not stop staring at them during meals. The response they devised was to catch the eye of the onlooker and cease eating until the staring stopped, then continue to eat as if nothing had happened. As one sympathetic reporter observed, "They evidently longed for a release from the exhibition; for asking the time, and being shown a watch, their attendant said that they complained of its being 'too slow.'" By the time they returned to New York from the British tour in 1831, they spoke "English tolerably well" and "were fond of talking."[18] They had begun to gain a sense of their rights in this new world and would start fistfights with especially rude customers. They may not have yet been able to articulate what they found wrong in the attitude of their patrons, but the seeds of what they would soon express were clearly planted during this early period. Their performances had become a form of servitude and the clock their enemy.

Declaring Independence

In contrast to Barnum's fairly straightforward strivings to be an independent Yankee peddler, the Bunkers had to fight for separation from their contract with Captain and Mrs. Coffin. On April 11, 1832, their manager and friend Charles Harris wrote about how the tour was progressing. An incident in Virginia had revealed the deep rage the twins were feeling but had not yet articulated. Harris reported that

> a medical man drew up a memorandum concerning C & E for one of the Norfolk papers which was a very well drawn up paper & calculated to do us much good were it not for one sentence which stated that they (the Twins) were sold by their Mother to Mr. Hunter & Captain Coffin. On hearing this CE's rage knew no bounds & they made me go immediately to the young Doctor who drew out the memorandum & ask him how he came to state such a thing.

Upon hearing that the information was from a medical book in "every medical man's hands," Chang and Eng were deeply upset.[19]

Harris expressed his surprise that such a statement would be made about their mother. The twins replied "that they were not at all surprised for it was not the 1st or 2nd time that they were questioned on the subject of matters which ought to have been kept quite private & never ought to have been made the subject of idle conversations." Their sense of propriety had obviously been violated. Moreover, the charges were false, and "this mixture of truth and fiction [was] doubly provoking to them." The incident stirred "almost daily conversation" between Chang and Eng. The "idea of persons looking on them as children who had so hard-hearted a mother has sunk but too deeply in their minds."[20] They were two perfectly aware and capable men who had willingly signed a contract. Further, they were very protective of their mother's reputation, which had now been publicly maligned—in Chinese culture, the height of personal insult.

By May 11, 1832, the brothers had decided that they had had enough, and they declared that they would leave the Coffins at the end of the month. May 11 was their twenty-first birthday, and they believed that their obligations to the good captain had been fulfilled. Mrs. Coffin reacted immediately and reminded the twins of how much she had done "for their comfort" and how much she "loved them." She would not allow them to go.[21]

In a letter they dictated to Harris, as was their practice when communicating with the Coffins, the twins responded point by point, firmly and with barely disguised anger. As to a supposed "promise" they had made to wait for Captain Coffin's return before quitting, they replied, "There must be a great mistake"; they understood that he was to be back several months prior and that "of course when they attained the age of 21—they were 'Their Own Men.'" With regard to attending to their comfort, the twins snapped back that they "have no doubt that the number of thousands of hard shining dollars which they have enabled [Mrs. Coffin] to spend have made her like them." They sincerely hoped she would "look into her own heart & they feel confident she will discover that the great loving & liking was not for their own sakes—but for the sake of the said Dollars." In closing, Harris wrote, "They have asked to affix their signature to it to stamp it as their deed, their sentiments & their feelings, concerning the transactions." They signed, in bold script, "Chang Eng Siamese Twins."[22]

In the three subsequent letters to Captain and Mrs. Coffin, the twins expressed their views and values directly. They had taken over their own management and no longer spoke through Harris. For the first time, Chang and Eng began actively to refer to themselves as "we" and "I" and to use the possessive "my." The use of such direct phrases as "we have asked Mr. Harris," "I wanted," and "[it] has come to my knowledge" all declared their de facto independence and self-management. In these letters they delineated an inventory of grievances that reflected what they thought was egregious wrongdoing.

The issue of their having been "purchased" from their mother was still very much on their minds. In a letter written "¼ past 12 at night" on July 4, they likened their treatment by the Coffins to the plight of an "Old Merchant Ship"—an unintendedly apt historical metaphor for the China trade—that had once brought "rich freights to its owners" but, now weatherbeaten, was left "lying in the mud & waiting to be sold for firewood." But, they declared "I am more fortunate than the poor old unserviceable ship, for altho' *'I have been bought'* (as has been said to many of me) yet *'I cannot be sold.'"*[23] They had come to believe that Captain Coffin did not really care about them or about keeping his word. "If I were to go home *immediately* It would be almost 48 months instead of 18 months from the time I left till the time of my return home, but if I remained quietly for *48 years* in the same situation of *servitude* . . . the promise of sending me home would not have been once thought of." Moreover, "As to Captain Coffin's promise of giving my mother $500 more (& which promise I was witness to) I very much fear that as, [quoting Mrs. Coffin's letter] *'Captn. C will be a loser by the concern as it now stands'*!!!! so my mother has a slim chance of seeing 500 cents much less Dollars."[24]

In October 1832 Captain Abel Coffin finally returned and sought to meet with Chang and Eng. He was surprised by how much they had matured. Coffin maintained that the brothers were breaking their contract; his arrangement with the government of Siam had been for a period of seven years, although he conceded that he had told their mother that they would be gone for only two and a half years, simply to calm her fears. Chang and Eng stood their ground: "This kind of double dealing was but badly calculated to induce us to remain with him any longer."[25] They believed that the agreement had been that their mother would receive $1,000, and that they would be gone for a maximum of eighteen months and be paid $10 per month. They also believed that once they turned twenty-one, they had fulfilled all their contractual obligations. And, as they made abundantly clear, Coffin still owed their mother $500. They told Judge Graves that they had long suspected Coffin of pocketing money that should have been sent to her, but that they had agreed to remain with him until they were legal adults because the "same strict and rigid compliance with all their promises and engagements which characterized them all through life induced them to remain with the man who they regarded as unfaithful, until their full term should be completed lest they should prove as faithless as he had been."[26]

Whatever had been agreed upon verbally was not fully detailed in their contract.[27] Written in classic Lockean terms emphasizing free will and consent, the contract made no reference to an eighteen-month period or to a precise amount due the twins' mother. Given his patronizing attitude toward the brothers, Coffin may very well have humored them as he claimed to have humored their mother. In fact, some evidence suggests that he thought of the brothers as ignorant and primitive people whom he had conned, and that he had no intention of returning them: on his 1829 journey home with the twins, Coffin had described himself and Hunter as "owning" them.[28] Just how manipulative and calculating Coffin and Hunter actually were may never be known. However, the contract dispute clearly illustrates how the capitalist legal code had come to matter more than a person's good word.

As truly self-determining individuals, Chang and Eng declared themselves independent, but they did not get away without a symbolic thrashing from their captain. Coffin sent a fantastic version of their final meeting to James Hale, a version of events in which he reasserted his mastery over two simple-minded and childlike possessions, banishing all doubts about his authority. Hale in turn relayed the story to the twins. The letter reveals a great deal about Victorian male culture. Upon catching up with the Bunkers in Bath, New York, Captain Coffin claimed to have told them

> that it was no use to undertake to show any airs, he was their master and would exercise his authority . . . [that] he found Chang Eng indulging in all sorts of dissipation, whoring, gaming and drinking [and] that he urged the impropriety of their having connexion with women, and that Chang Eng said they had as good right to a woman as he had upon which Coffin gave Chang Eng "the damndest thrashing they ever had in their lives" and that before he left them, they acknowledged he "was perfectly right in beating them, as it was for their own good"!!

Hale refused to accept any part of this story; Coffin, he said, "is as great a liar as his wife." Aware of the twins' physical strength, he knew that Coffin could not have beaten them into submission. In a fight, Coffin would have been overwhelmed if not killed, but he was "*yet alive.*"[29]

No longer subject to a contract and Coffin's directives, the twins now set about preparing to strike out on their own and make their own choices. Engravings of the brothers made during this period of self-management project an image dramatically different from their earlier packaging. In an illustration from their 1836 brochure they are drawn as handsome men with what appear to be Western haircuts and stylish tuxedos. They look directly at the viewer, confidently poised to meet all visitors. While earlier illustrations depicted them surrounded by toys, Eng now holds a book, signifying their literacy and education. They also had Charles Harris, their trusted publicist and friend, rewrite their souvenir brochure. Retitled *A Few Particulars Concerning Chang-Eng, the United Siamese Brothers*, the 1836 pamphlet emphasized that it was "Published under Their Own Direction."

This "Account of the Siamese Twin Brothers," while essentially the same in length as the 1831 brochure, was substantially different in narrative structure and content. The twins' physical uniqueness was deemphasized. Instead, the text now detailed the everyday life of Siam, described the privileged role of Chinese merchants, discussed how "duck's eggs are a very merchantable commodity," and presented a travelogue of the twins' tours in the United States and Europe.

Most significantly, the new brochure made a special effort to refute prior statements and prejudices. Two examples provide a strong indication of the brothers' effort to counter the paternalistic narrative that had been essentially Coffin's version of their story. First, they emphatically stated that they had never intended to leave their mother and homeland permanently; "they thought it unlikely that they would be absent longer than 18 or 20 months." Indeed, although they had adopted "the American style of dress in everything [else]," they continued for many years to wear their hair long and braided in the Qing Dynasty fashion—an indication that they were keeping their option to return home open. Second, Chang and Eng now insisted on a cultural-relativist perspective. Whereas the earlier brochure had depicted Siamese society as barbaric and brutal, the new one spoke in a language comparable to that of modern-day cultural anthropologists. After describing some rituals practiced by Asian mariners, the brochure emphatically stated, "This superstitious adherence to particular days and hours appears very absurd in the detail, and many would be inclined to cry out what superstition!!! what folly!!! And yet it is no worse than the twins themselves have met with in this country." The text then proceeded to offer several examples of comparable American backwardness.[30]

As soon as they could, Chang and Eng retired from daily performances. They bought a farm in the foothills of North Carolina and married two sisters, Sallie and Adelaide Yates. If New York remained their link to civilization, prestige, and money, Mount Airy became their haven from incessant touring. In a sense they were what sociologist Paul C. P. Siu has described as "sojourners" who necessarily went on the road to support their beloved families back home. They operated in two simultaneous worlds: as pre-time-clock and pre-legalistic plantation patriarchs who were judged by their word and their mastery of the rhythms of the seasons, and as New York–centered celebrities for whom time and contracts were the ultimate determinant of success—or failure. They alternated between an urban-based commercial culture, which most prized chains of commodity transactions, and their rural homes, in which chains of affective relations between family and friends could be established beyond the glare of the commercial media.

By 1852, just after the time of Barnum's Chinese Museum, the two Bunker families had grown to such a point that it was no longer easy for everyone to live under the same roof. Eng and Sallie had six children and Chang and Adelaide now had five. Zacharias Haynes, Chang's son-in-law, later explained that

> the families lived together ten years after they were married, and of course the children could not at all times agree, and this was and would be the constant source of trouble, so long as the families remained together. . . . In truth, instances of two large families being brought up in the same house in perfect love, peace and harmony are very rare, and this is the sure cause of the families being separated.[31]

Various trial separations occurred, until in 1857 they decided to build a second house and divide their common property. Eng retained the original house, and a house for Chang's family was built a mile away. This arrangement seems to have been agreed upon for primarily practical reasons. It is unclear how much Chang and Eng desired the splitting of their households, and how much it was what the families wanted. In any case, the brothers decided to alternate between the two houses every three days, and they held to this rule rigidly until the day they died, seventeen years later. Notions of conjoined "we-ness" became separated declarations of "I."[32]

A "Self-Made Priest"

Barnum's latitude to remake himself was fundamentally different from the twins'. Not only did Barnum bring back from Europe an interest in the Orient and a renewed confidence in moneymaking, he also seems to have developed a desire to upgrade his moral reputation. In 1848 he stopped drinking and joined the activist Christian temperance movement. In June 17, 1850, Barnum decreed "NO BAR OR INTOXICATING DRINKS allowed upon the premises" of his renovated lecture hall. Instead, he served lots of ice water. Indeed, his opening and subsequently long-running melodrama *The Drunkard* punctuated his newfound abstinence from liquor. At the same time, Barnum went to great effort to secure the "Swedish Nightingale," Jenny Lind, for an unprecedented 150-concert tour. Lind, who actually was, as advertised, a celebrated singer from Sweden, impressed audiences around the country with her beautiful voice.[33] Barnum had successfully repackaged himself by sponsoring performers who would augment his status within the genteel culture.

Friends of Barnum commented that he was a "self-made priest" who often took to sermonizing and was frequently asked to speak before Universalist groups. At an 1874 banquet honoring Barnum, a Reverend Dr. Hopper remarked, "What a spiritual showman he would have made; how he would have exhibited the menagerie of the heart, in which ferocious beasts, in the forms of fiery passions, prey upon the soul." However, Barnum rejected the Puritan strictures against entertainers and entertainment that prohibited performances in several New England states, including Connecticut, well into the nineteenth century. Instead, he professed a "cheerful Christianity" in which enjoyment could be gained from "innocent amusements & recreation." His Iranistan coat of arms carried the motto "Love God and Be Merry." The lecture rooms in his various museums were designed to transform nineteenth-century theater, besmirched with bawdiness, curse words, and active audience participation, into a respectable way for middle-class families to view "moral discourses." In defending his museum against a critic, he avowed, "No vulgar word or gesture, and not a profane expression, was ever allowed on my stage! Even in Shakespeare's plays, I unflinchingly and invariably cut out vulgarity and profanity."[34] While certainly a devout Christian, Barnum rejected an ascetic and rigid Puritanism and favored a more secular, individualistic Yankee spirituality, which he viewed as universally relevant and progressive for all peoples.

It was within this spiritual worldview that Barnum judged himself and others. Barnum measured his cultural identity by the juxtaposition of the Western self against the non-Western other. From his correspondence and occasional public remarks it is possible to tease out some of his personal beliefs in this regard, beliefs that measure a hierarchy of peoples against the Protestant Yankee ideal. "It is fortunate," Barnum assured his daughter, that "*any* system of religion can be brought to enlist seriously the minds of the 'lower class, including Indians.'" Catholics were technically not idolatrous because they believed in "God and a Saviour," but they were of a "lower class" and therefore easily mollified by any type of spirituality. Indians were "lazy devils" and "a shiftless set of brutes" who were difficult to control. Jews were a "miserable" lot of "moneyless . . . brokers" who could not be trusted in real-estate transactions. Gypsies were "dirty, lazy, and *lousy*." And despite Barnum's Universalist faith, he had purchased a "nigger" on one of his early

Southern tours to serve as his valet, whom he later sold after accusing him of theft and giving him fifty lashes.[35]

Intelligence, class status, a certain willingness to do hard work, trustworthiness, and cleanliness underlined who Barnum thought he was and who he thought these others were not. His attitudes were not atypical of his background; they were part and parcel of a Yankee culture that automatically viewed the world in terms of dichotomies: heaven/hell, good/bad, civilized/uncivilized. This fixed ethnocentric cultural view shaped much of Barnum's representation of non-Western peoples.

Barnum's racial views were complicated by a Universalist and missionary faith in the individual's relationship to a Christian God. Any man could better himself materially and spiritually. For example, in writing to Moses Kimball about his act of Gypsies, Barnum stated his determination, despite a professed ambivalence, to convert them into "hard-working" entertainers who would want to perform. "I expect they are too d——d low for me to do anything with them. However, I must try, for if I don't do better than at present, I am sure to bust."[36] Although he couldn't totally control his performers in real life, at least his tightly produced performances presented successful and happy fictions that he and the public could be enticed to believe: Charles Stratton became General Tom Thumb; Che Mah, a Chinese dwarf, became a deity of "rare intellectual powers"; Chang Yu-Shing, "the Chinese Giant," became a "perfect gentleman," thoroughly "polished, refined and moral"; and a very tall African American might be promoted from a Zulu warrior in one show to a Western uniformed military figure the next.[37]

In these moral dramas, even the darkest and most uncivilized of people could, "Lord willing," be redeemed and acculturated in a proper, elite, Protestant manner. Barnum's freaks were forever being transformed into seemly Anglo-American Victorians. This repackaging of his performers from savages into princes should be understood not only as a means for Barnum to extract more money from a gullible public but, more important, as a symbolic expression of his belief that "heathens" could appear to be converted to an enlightened Christian way of life. This moral showmanship was his gift. Phineas T. Barnum turned himself into a Yankee patriarch, presiding over a world of savage, exotic creatures. Under his expert paternal guidance, his audience journeyed into and out of exhibits that helped bolster their sense of superiority and security. The journey, no matter how sensationalized, was ultimately a safe and conservative one. Western cultural norms may have been continuously challenged by the freakish "otherness" of the performers, but the core culture's rightful dominance was never questioned.

As the occidental master par excellence, Barnum wanted absolute control over all his performers. In the Bunker twins, however, he had met his match. It appears that Barnum deliberately exaggerated his association with them. He retained their image on his letterhead stationery well after their European tour with him. Publicly he made much of his association with Chang and Eng, but privately he thought them too independent, and he sensed their dislike for him. One of Eng's sons later confirmed the brothers' coolness toward Barnum. They found him "too much of a Yankee, and [he] wanted too much for his share of the money." Eng's son added, "My father and uncle were close figurers themselves."[38]

Barnum's pride in his own independence and his dislike for Chang and Eng's independence represented something deeply significant about his way of looking at personal friendships. Barnum and the Reverend Chapin felt so close a friendship for each other that they jokingly referred to themselves as "Chang and Eng." Chapin inscribed copies of books he sent Barnum, "From Eng to his friend Chang."[39] Their Chang-and-Eng pretense had a humorous dimension, but it was a private joke with a serious point. Barnum and Chapin used the Bunkers as alter egos. Like white Americans putting on blackface in minstrel shows or like participants in the secret rituals of fraternal organizations like the Masons, Barnum and Chapin may have used these exotic pseudo-identities as a means of expressing their deepest feelings of friendship for one another without threatening their very proper identities as manly individualists.[40] This private joke can also be understood as emblematic of where the boundaries of Barnum's self-image were drawn with regard to racial "others." Even as one of the culture's foremost manipulators, Barnum's personal definition of self resonated to what the twins represented. He was both constituted by this culture and one of its major shapers.

The twins remade themselves by demonstrating that they were not monsters—a terribly limiting performance venue, which drove them to early retirement—but self-possessed individuals. Barnum, however, had far more latitude. Rather than debunking stereotypes, as the twins felt compelled to do, Barnum could revel in the popular racializations of the era. Catering to self-congratulatory prejudices ultimately proved more marketable.

THE HUGE CELESTIAL, LINGUIST, SCHOLAR, GENTLEMAN. 3

THE UNQUESTIONED GOLIAH OF THE CENTURY.

CHANG, "THE CHINESE GIANT"

Undoubtedly the tallest, largest, and finest proportioned Giant the Age has produced.

STANDING NEARLY 9 FEET HIGH IN HIS STOCKING FEET.

And a full head and shoulders taller than the biggest man in the World.

HE IS NOT ONLY A MODERN TITAN

BUT COMBINES THE

STRENGTH OF HERCULES

AND THE

BEAUTY OF AN APOLLO

Chang, is an educated and cultivated gentleman, speaks seven langauges gracefully and fluently, and has exhibited in almost every portion of the civilized Globe. His parents are large Tea dealers in Pekin, China, and like their illustrious son, in affluent circumstances. They are of the ordinary size of their race,—an unusually small people.

CHANG DID NOT COMMENCE TO

GROW MUCH TILL 6 YEARS OLD

And then developed so rapidly, that at 12 he was larger than any man in his neighborhood. He manifested peculiar aptness at learning, and soon became a GREAT

Scholar and Profound Thinker

He takes delight in exhibiting his gigantic stature, and smiles with pride as he passes his arm level over the heads of the tallest visitors. His height has never been accurately ascertained, as the Celestial Race have a superstition, that so soon as one of them is measured he will die, but he is

Nearly 9 Feet High

AND HIS OUTSTRETCHED

ARMS MEASURE 8 FEET

He can lift 500 pound with ease. He is now 34 years old, and is not the

OGRE OF NURSERY TALES

But the soul of geniality, affability and kindness. He is good natured and gentle even to tenderness, and temperate in all things. He plays at Chess, Draughts and other Chinese games, and is never so happy as when doing some noble act of goodness.

POLISHED, REFINED AND MORAL

And of Colossal stature and prodigious strength, in this uncommon wonder are manifest

Every Attribute of a Perfect Gentleman

Chang, will positively appear at each exhibition, THREE TIMES DAILY, costumed in the picturesque drapery of his native land, or in the gorgeous and expensive

APPAREL OF A FRENCH CENTURION

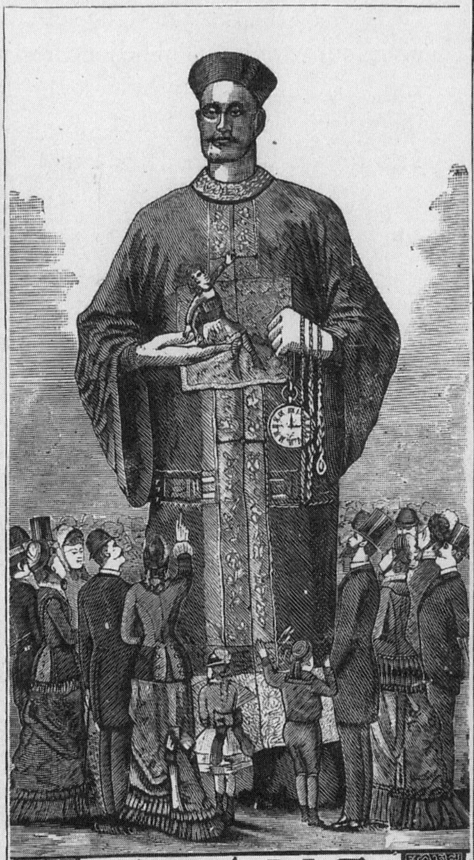

CHANG

THE CHINESE GIANT

TALLEST MAN IN THE WORLD.

He is exclusively engaged to this combination, at a

SALARY OF SIX HUNDRED DOLLARS WEEKLY

AND WILL REMAIN IN THIS COUNTRY ONLY ONE YEAR.

APPEARS AT EVERY PERFORMANCE, 10.30 A. M. and 2 and 7.30 P. M. WITHOUT EXTRA CHARGE.

Figure 19. "Chang, 'the Chinese Giant,'" advertisement, 1881. (Syracuse University, Ronald G. Becker Collection)

Figure 20. "Che Mah, the only Chinese dwarf," souvenir daguerreotype, ca. 1880s. (Wong Ching Foo Collection)

Are White People Superior?

Just how important racial typology was in Victorian science can be demonstrated by examining the public fascination with phrenology. In addition to differences in pigmentation, other physical features were thought to be fundamental indicators of racial-biological differences. Orson Squire Fowler and Lorenzo Niles Fowler pioneered the field of "applied phrenology," opening an office at 135 Nassau Street in 1835. They "read" heads, published books and the influential *American Phrenological Journal*, arranged lecture tours, assembled a "Phrenological Cabinet," or museum, and trained a growing cadre of practicing phrenologists.[41] One of their books, *Phrenology: A Practical Guide to Your Head*, amply illustrates the ways in which this science both manifested and helped to form the identity of the white middle class. How could one better judge others and understand oneself?

Phrenology was premised on the assumption that skulls divergent from the shape of certain northern and western European types were automatically of a lower order. The nose, for example, was thought to indicate the character of a person. "Flat noses," a trait commonly used in describing Asian peoples, "indicate flatness of mind and character, by indicating a poor, low organic structure." "Sharp noses," on the other hand, "indicate a quick, clear, penetrating, searching, knowing, sagacious mind."[42]

The phrenological racial hierarchy was essentially Linnaean categories made accessible and popular. In the section of the Fowlers' book on "Veneration" (defined as "devotion—respect"), the skull of a European American woman, Diana Waters, was illustrated as possessing a "large" degree of veneration. As proof of the accuracy of this science, she was said to have spent much of her life going around Philadelphia "praying and exhorting all she met to repent and pray to God." In contrast, "a Negro" whose skull was produced to show a "small" organ of veneration was described as having "ignored all religion." In this science the forehead was said to correspond to the "reflective" qualities of a person and the back of the skull to the "perceptive" qualities. "Africans," the Fowlers rationalized, "generally have full perceptives, and large Tune and Language, but retiring Causality ('Applying cause to effect'), and accordingly are deficient in reasoning capacity, yet have excellent memories and lingual and musical powers." Elsewhere, a rather grotesque drawing of the warrior-chief Blackhawk was shown to possess a "large" organ of "destructiveness" ("executiveness—force"), while the president of the First Peace Conference possessed a "small" organ. Using this

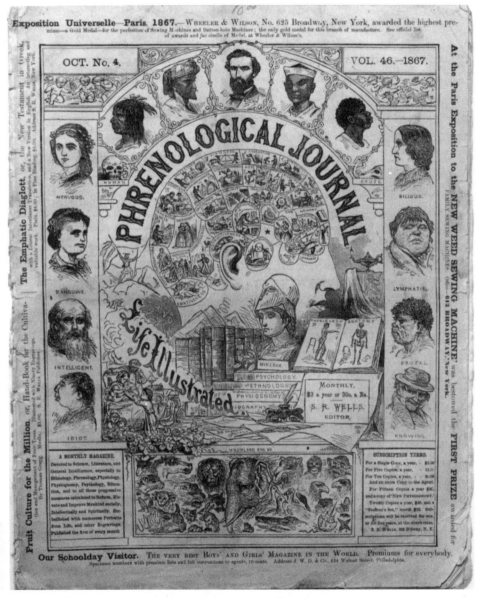

Figure 21. The "five races of mankind," represented on the cover of the *Journal of Phrenology,* published by S. R. Wells at 389 Broadway, New York, 1867. (Wong Ching Foo Collection)

drawing, the Fowlers asserted that "Indians possess extraordinary strength of the propensities and perceptives, yet have no great moral or inventive power; and, hence, have very wide, round, conical, and rather low heads, but are large over the eyes." As final proof of phrenology as "A Universal Fact," readers were asked to compare the "massive foreheads of all giant-minded men—Bacon, Franklin, Milton, etc." with the "low, retiring foreheads of idiots."[43]

Idiots, Africans, and Indians, then, were all classified as developed in terms of the baser, animal aspects of human existence, whereas Europeans and European Americans were physically constituted for the highest degree of civilization. In the process of becoming cultivated, the superior race had repressed the lower urges within and disciplined its nervous ambivalence by demoting others to savages and monsters. Such a focus on appearance as an indicator of capacity and character either reflected the assumptions of a culture or nourished such approaches to cultural definitions—or both.

Although "Mongols" were not mentioned in the Fowlers' manual, Orson Fowler did examine Chang and Eng at least twice, once in 1836 and again in 1853. Perhaps not surprisingly, he claimed to have deduced from a reading of their heads characteristics that were commonly ascribed to the "Mongol" race in the society at large. He made at least three types of observations.

First, Fowler said, the twins "furnish a striking example of the truth of phrenological science" because "they were found to be most wonderfully and strikingly *alike,* not only in size and general outline, but even in the minute development of nearly *all the phrenological organs."* This fact, he thought, explained why so many people mistakenly believed the twins to be of "one mind."[44]

Second, the twins' "general form or cast of head differs *in toto* from any Caucassion head the Editor has ever seen." The characteristics Fowler ascribed to their "nationality" or race were high "benevolence," small "destructiveness," high "veneration," little "hope," and only moderate amounts of "mirth" and "ideality." Hence, this reading explained why they were "so very tender of the lives of animals; to kill which, they consider a heinous sin" (the fact that they had been brought up as Buddhists seems never to have been factored in). It also explained why they were extremely devoted to "their religion," and why they were such "affectionate and domestic people." In contrast to Africans and Indians, and more like Caucasians, they had "large reflectives" and "deficient perceptives."[45]

Finally, Fowler reported that the twins displayed "large" organ development in terms of "ambition," "self-esteem," "imitation," and "adhesiveness." They displayed "low" development in "individuality," "dignity," and "conscientiousness" (defined as "justice, equity"). Their baser animal organs were "only moderate," their "social [organs] large," their "temperaments . . . rather coarse," and their "mental and physical movements rather slow."[46]

The twins, in sum, were said to embody the "national," or racial, characteristics of a benevolent, family-oriented, harmless people who venerated religion, were imitative, and did not have much hope for the future. Not only were Chang and Eng physically connected, but their phrenological organs indicated minimal qualities of individualism. The prevailing faith in the superiority of northern and western peoples divided the world along north-south and east-west axes. Wrapped in scientistic jargon, the occidental self was measured and judged superior to primitive and semicivilized others.

Here we see a shift in cross-cultural representations as well as a clue to the immediate popular appeal of Chang and Eng and basis of Barnum's long-term success. The Enlightenment association of the Chinese with the height of refinement and civilization was now increasingly being displaced by the conviction that they were lesser than European peoples. The new commercial regime burlesqued the older patrician verities. Within this shifting context Chang and Eng and Barnum's other acts—the Chinese giant, the Chinese dwarf—proved to be the ideal "human monsters" to be exhibited. The combination of being both racially and physically "strange" pushed the boundaries of what European Americans were used to seeing, yet at the same time it was not so transgressive of cultural norms that people were afraid. It conferred superior moral and intellectual authority upon the physical and cultural qualities of Victorian America.

By projecting tabooed, expurgated qualities onto racial others, a highly segmented hierarchy was constructed, with European Americans safely reserving their place at the top.[47] The seemingly oxymoronic view of Chinese performers as both genteel and monstrous was most troubling and ambiguous to the emerging political culture. Asians were especially difficult to pigeonhole. The eighteenth-century romantic fascination with the "Orient" had represented those vaguely defined regions of the "Indies" as an ancient domestic culture. During the antebellum period the beginnings of "modern" physical anthropology, archaeology, and biological science constructed race as an increasingly hierarchical apologia for European empire building. The older image of a cultivated and gentle people was shifting to something decidedly less flattering and more ambivalent.

Caught among these shifting paradigms of race and orientalism, John H. Van Evrie, a New York physician, erased all distinctions between Europeans and European Americans for the sake of utterly condemning blacks. In the 1850s he wrote of Caucasians, "The flowing beard, projecting forehead, oval features, erect posture and lordly presence, stamp him the master man wherever found." Evrie believed that there was inherent inequality between the races, but he was not quite sure about the Chinese. He suggested that Confucius—a stellar figure in eighteenth-century Enlightenment chinoiserie—and other ancient Chinese may actually have been Caucasian.[48] In contrast to the days of the *Empress,* when the occidental world invested the Orient with brilliant romantic notions, China was still to be admired, though not quite trusted as before. Chinese and other "Orientals" were increasingly viewed liminally in a culture of polar dualities—somewhere between civilization and savagery.

Barnum's "sights" elaborated a series of associations that reinforced what everyone presumed to know about the Chinese. The public paid twenty-five cents to see a carefully constructed performance that made their "knowledge" about China all the more tangible and real. As a commercial entrepreneur, Barnum did not so much play the role of gatekeeper of public opinion as help refine what the public felt it already knew about China. Growing up with the New England romance of the China trade, Barnum's career bridged the disastrous Opium Wars and the passage of the yellow-perilist Chinese Exclusion Act.

The Bunkers' biological and racial differences, their performances of strength and dexterity, their observation by and interaction with their audiences—all were contained within the safe and respectable boundaries of a parlor setting. As genteel monstrosities, they became a provocative and useful foil for exploring deeply troubling concerns. Once audiences had accepted that the twins were authentic and not a hoax, their display gave the public a chance to gaze at these racially and bodily different humans and sort out their own opinions.

This public's discovery of and obsessive fascination with monsters and the exotic ultimately served to reinforce the process by which boundaries delineating proper and improper Victorian identities were established. Commercialized spaces were zones in which human identity could be explored and exploited. Here the settled European American dyadic categories of male/female, human/inhuman, normal/abnormal were all up for question in life performances on the urban streetscape. Past explanations were losing power and new truths yet to be established. Within this marketplace of representations, Barnum's and the twins' identities as self-made, and ultimately lonely, men were formulated.

Chinese individuals who sought to become a part of the commercial culture clearly had to commodify themselves to cater to the orientalist marketplace. The cultural authenticity of the Tong Hook Tong Dramatic Company was not salable in this milieu, whereas the fabricated acts of Barnum were. This popular market-driven form of orientalism not only affected performers and attendees, it also became a pervasive source of popular knowledge that informed everyday life. Chinese and other Asians living in New York could strive to become self-made individuals, like George Washington and Barnum, but entrenched racial stereotyping limited the realizable options. In this sense, the twins' physical abnormality heightened perceptions of their racial differences, and the racially charged commercial marketplace impacted all who sought to enter it.

CHAPTER 7

Stereotypes
and Realities

IN 1854 BARNUM dedicated his autobiography to "the universal Yankee nation, of which I am proud to be one." Two decades later, while paying tribute to the print culture of the nineteenth century, Barnum remarked at a banquet in his honor, "Yes, without printer's ink I should have been no bigger than Tom Thumb."[1] After a lifetime of self-promotion and gaining the cooperation of journalists, Barnum was keenly aware of how he had become successful. "I am indebted to the press of the United States," he wrote to his circus partner James A. Bailey a few days before his death in 1891, "for almost every dollar which I possess and for every success as an amusement manager which I have ever achieved." Dubbing himself the "Prince of Humbugs," he defined his talents as "putting on glittering appearances . . . by which to suddenly arrest public attention and attract the public eye and ear."[2] Indeed, Barnum promoted himself as the embodiment of the mythic market-made individual: possessing no more than his own wit, he recreated himself as a wealthy, happy Christian.

Barnum was clearly aware of the conditions of his success. Print capitalism was the foundation of New York's commercial culture. Not only did it provide a means for him to publicize his various performances but, more fundamentally, vernacular print media created an urban public increasingly aware of itself as citizens of an "imagined" New York.[3] This popular print culture seeped into all aspects of everyday life in New York and came to define public knowledge. The more individuals read, the more they became part of the public culture. Public schooling, as we shall discover, not only promoted literacy but also embodied a certain view of the world that helped to secure a sense of who European Americans were and what their civilizing mission in the world was. This system of believing also became a basis of action impacting on the everyday denizens of the Fourth and Sixth Wards of lower Manhattan.

What Do You Know about China?

The revolution in print capitalism promoted popular literacy. Increasingly vernacular English replaced the Latin-based curricula of European-oriented patrician culture. The New York public school system, founded in 1842, began teaching students the rudimentary knowledge and skills necessary to make sense of the disorienting metropolis brokering goods, ideas, and people from all the world.[4] Textbooks and the popular culture came to be a primary means by which the ideology of "a universal Yankee nation" was taught.

In December 1850, Public Schools 8 and 17 tested sixty-two upper-grade students on their knowledge of geography. The young males were asked, "What do you know about silks and laces and from what country are they brought?" The young females were asked, "What do you know about teas and coffees?" All were queried, "What do you know about China?"[5] The students' answers show what they were taught and what they derived from the popular culture of the city—revealing an orientalism overlaid by both a patrician culture of distinction and a commercial culture premised on seeing for oneself.

Irene Ayers answered, "China is in the eastern part of Asia and it is noted for its Teas and Coffee[,] it is noted also for its porcelain ware and also for its Crape Shawls." To her otherwise neutral account she went on to add judgments about the people: "The Chinese are a very timid race of people and very industrious[,] their dress is very odd." For Edward Nyers, China was "an uncivilized country, in the east of Asia. It is famous for its Porcelain. Chinese are principaly Idolators. It is Famous for Tea." Another young woman confidently stated what she knew: "China is noted for tea and also for the peculiar caracter of its inhabitants, they are pagans and belong to the Worship of Fo, the Anglicized version of the Chinese term for Buddha."

Edwin Cole described the Chinese as a "peculiar" people, noting, "They are of a dark color, but not so black as the negroes." He added, "They are extremely fond of smoking the juice of the poppy called Opium and they also chew it." Twelve-year-old William H. Jackson was more moralistic in tone: "They are indolent and lazy, and are of the Mongolian race." He articulated a perspective many Westerners held on the China trade: "They are very jealous of Europeans, and there is but one port that Europeans are allowed to trade." James Ferguson was not as hostile in his reference to trade policy: "A remarkable fact connected with the Chinese is that they will not let foreigners or foreign vessels stop at their ports but one which I think is Canton, and on that account little is known about them."

Maurice Hansen gave a mixed statement accommodating a range of views bearing the mark of the striving patrician worldview. He wrote, "China is . . . thickly populated by an enterprising, active people, they call all the other nations barbarians, and although they have no commerce whatever with civilised nations yet they have acquire a pretty high degree of civilization." Thirteen-year-old Ezra Beach seemed to be the only person in the group who had actually viewed a Chinese person: "The chines are a harmless set of people, and ware their hair so long sometime as to touch the ground and some of them have very little fet. I went to the Chinees museum i had never [before seen] a chinees and i thought them quite a sight."

In contrast to the lack of geographical understanding that prevailed on the eve of the *Empress*'s departure, these schoolchildren had been required to memorize a map of the world. They not only had a simple binary sense that China was "underneath their feet" on the opposite side of the Earth but were also expected to know the names of the oceans bordering its land as well. The China trade had clearly structured much of what the students were taught and much of what they believed they knew about the nation. Forty-nine responses mentioned tea cultivation, thirteen wrote of porcelain, seven of silks, seven of shawls, and four of trade restrictions. The things desired, consumed, and needed by the United States signified the whole of Chinese culture and civilization.

The descriptions of the physical appearance of the Chinese and their "character" constitute the most interesting body of comments, lending insight into the mix of impressions these young people held at midcentury. Five noted that Chinese had long hair. Four noted that women had little feet, and six thought that both men and women had this peculiarity. Five students thought that Chinese were "odd" in one way or another. Four believed that they were uncivilized. Three noted that they were idolatrous pagans. Four boys noted the Chinese restrictions on trade. Two students noted the purported Chinese fondness for smoking and/or chewing opium, and two commented on the Chinese taste for puppy dogs, cats, rats, or other vermin. In contrast to Jackson, who characterized Chinese people as indolent or lazy, three said that they were industrious. Two students noted skin color. And despite the awareness of coveted items from China, only one person credited the Chinese with excellence in the arts, and only one said that they were civilized.

The range of comments doesn't appear to have any clear-cut correlation except one: that of gender. The male students voiced much stronger opinions about the Chinese, most of which were negative. Of the twenty-eight young women, only seven expressed a cultural opinion, five of which were negative. Of the thirty-four young men, twenty-four made judgmental statements, eighteen of which were negative. While no consensus emerged, boys had stronger opinions about Chinese appearance and character, and most of these statements were negative. Clearly, perceptions of the Chinese were a function of patrician orientalism—perceptions segregated by the gendered spheres of business and politics for men and home and sociability for women. The public schools had trained them well for the culture they would inherit.

Sometimes the students appear to have been regurgitating what they had learned in schoolbooks such as Samuel G. Goodrich's series of geography texts, beginning with *A System of Universal Geography* (1833), which conveyed both descriptive "facts" about China along with harsh judgments about the nation and its people.[6] Traces of late-eighteenth-century debates about luxuries and degeneration were also evident. Many of the students used and/or mimicked patrician adjectives, in such phrases as "splendid" shawls or "famous" teas and porcelains. Protestant-work-ethic words such as *enterprising* and *industrious* and the statement that the Chinese had acquired "a pretty high degree of civilization" all stemmed from the more positive European Enlightenment ideas of the previous century. Edwin Cole's comments on their being "peculiar," having a darker skin color, and being fond of opium, along with William Jackson's comments about their being "lazy" and "indolent," anticipated the predominant way Chinese would be described in decades to come. In this regard, Edward Nyers and Maurice Hansen were probably more representative of the 1850s than the other students in this group. They combined both negatives and positives: Chinese were "enterprising" and at the same time "odd."

In a modest way these responses embody something of the spirit of the Jacksonian era. As part of what was called a "revolution in choices," or the market revolution, public schooling greatly increased the literacy of youth throughout the United States. The information learned from reading became a way of augmenting personal power in the marketplace society. The culture encouraged young boys to cultivate independent skills of judgment. With the passage of universal white male suffrage in 1827, they would gain the responsibilities of a democratic citizenry who would be capable of voting for the interests of the propertied polity. The proliferation of popular speech and the expectation that young men would necessarily become involved in political culture certainly encouraged the feeling that their thoughts as individuals mattered and should be expressed.[7] In this sense, Ezra Beach was the prototype of the times. He went to Barnum's Chinese Museum to see Chinese for himself, forming his own independent judgment that these Chinese were "harmless" and "quite a sight."

The possibility and the act of seeing for oneself became a far more exciting and viable means of learning. Or, in the words of Louisa May Alcott's young female character in *Eight Cousins,* who had just boarded a docked clipper ship to visit with a Chinese merchant and his son, "It is a very pleasant way, and I really think I have learned more about China to-day than in all the lessons I had at school, though I used to rattle off the answers as fast as I could go. No one explained any thing to us, so all I remember is that tea and silk come from there, and the women have little bits of feet." Catherine Elizabeth Havens wrote in her diary what she had learned: "Sometimes on Saturday afternoons we go down to . . . see the pictures, and now there is a Chinese Museum down on Broadway, and wax figures of Chinese people, and it shows how prisoners are punished. Some have a board around their necks and other[s] around their feet."[8] To the degree that they experienced this commercial culture for themselves, individuals felt empowered to test and experience "reality" firsthand. This democratic leveling, however, was severely limited in its ability to comprehend cultural differences.

As the reach of American trade extended to more corners of the world, the "sights" recounted by travelers in written narratives, such as John Ledyard's account of his travels with Cook or Herman Melville's maritime novels, could be reassembled and represented in various forms as profitable, market-driven exhibitions. Individual prejudices, vested interests, and dominant identities established the basis for the commercial exploitation of difference. Those individuals and groups who did not fit the dominant Anglo-Saxon elite norm, whether by virtue of race, class, region of origin, gender, or other markers, became marketable as exotic "sights."

Direct experience in its manifold forms, offered by the commodification of goods and exhibitions, enabled Ezra Beach, Catherine Elizabeth Havens, and Louisa May Alcott's young readers to vicariously experience China and Chinese in ways far more vivid than what was written in school textbooks. Such was the appeal of the commercial culture.

Increasingly, knowledge was premised upon what people experienced directly and in common—what they saw for themselves and could communicate about with each other. And what they saw for themselves, whether on the stage or in the streets, became real, factual. In this regard, visuality became a master sense for bourgeois sensibilities; visual perception became the primary means of knowing and controlling the urban world.[9] Nevertheless, with all the faith in rational empirical observation, what and how one saw was still very much mediated by internalized structures of knowledge and power.

The print capitalism of the penny press produced textbooks, exhibit guidebooks, and newspapers that cultivated a feeling of shared experience and understanding in the chaotic metropolis. Paradoxically, this feeling of being a free occidental individual self, produced in dialogue with real and imagined oriental others, was generated by the proliferation of mechanical print mass reproduction.[10] The sensibility of individual opinion and voice being the basis for a popular culture was made possible by the formation of an urban audience of consumers. Such mass-formulated individual opinions henceforth came to have overwhelming power over the lives of Chinese New Yorkers. In contrast to the Bunkers' unique circumstances, the plight of Quimbo Appo illustrates how this print media culture impacted on a more everyday life.

Who Was the Real Quimbo Appo?

The questions of monstrosities and racial superiority helped to formulate the commercial culture of the era, echoing through the canyons of metropolitan anxiety, to newspapers, to exhibitions, to public schools, and back to public spectacles. Real Chinese and yellowface Chinese were indistinguishable in this landscape of representations playing off self and otherness. Herein the fate of that "exemplary Chinaman" Quimbo Appo would become entrapped.

Apparently all was not marital bliss between Quimbo Appo and Catherine Fitzpatrick. One of their domestic quarrels erupted in violence and made front-page headlines in the New York papers. With subsequent cycles of fights and imprisonment, violence became a way of life for Appo. Over the course of the next two decades the upstanding merchant citizen fell from grace. Yet the details of what went wrong remain vague.

One day in 1859 Quimbo Appo had returned home to his apartment below Chatham Square at 47 Oliver Street in the Fourth Ward. It seems that there was a fight between him and his wife, and their landlady, Mrs. Mary F. Fletcher, went to quiet them down. A scuffle broke out, and Fletcher was stabbed and stumbled down the tenement stairs. Neighbors gathered and, finding Fletcher dead, called for revenge. Appo was arrested, but emotions continued to run high the week after the arrest; a lynching party attempted to kidnap him. He was convicted by the jury of murder, but they "unanimously recommend[ed] him to mercy." The judge, however, for reasons not stated, sentenced him to be hanged. The governor of New York State stayed his execution and ordered a retrial.[11]

In the retrial, the reasons for Appo's temporary reprieve became obvious. Despite being fairly fluent in English, highly esteemed in the Chinese and larger communities, and a man of some means, he had not had adequate counsel. Appo had retained as his attorney an ex-judge who failed him miserably, showing up for the trial a half-hour late and being unprepared to make an opening statement. Unfamiliar with the laws of the state and the "niceties of the English language," Appo was not able to evaluate the magnitude of these and other problems of his defense.[12]

Appo took the stand, for the first time, during the retrial. He stated that he had come home to find his wife drunk after celebrating Mrs. Fletcher's birthday. Angered, he began to beat his wife; Mrs. Fletcher, and then other women in the building, came to her rescue. They hit him with their fists, one calling him a "China nigger." Another hit him with a flatiron. He admitted to having stabbed his landlady, but only in self-defense "while endeavoring to escape from her and other women." Other witnesses testifying in his behalf said that he was a man of good "peaceable" character; they confirmed that Fletcher was still alive after being stabbed, and that all the women "had been drinking intoxicating liquors to great excess." Testimony appealing to stereotypes of Irish intemperance and misogyny were used to cast Appo as a victim and the Irishwomen as his victimizers. A sympathetic reporter described Catherine Fitzpatrick as a "low Irishwoman habitually drunk who would not cook his meals and neglected him in every particular" and charged that she had just been convicted of larceny and was in jail herself. It was decided that Appo should not be hanged but should be given a prison sentence of ten years for the reduced charge of manslaughter.[13]

The testimony given in *The People of New York v. Quimbo Appo* suggests tensions over stereotypes of race, to be certain, but also over gender and class. Appo's view of what happened differed significantly from the case of the *People*. In addition, the witnesses called to testify for and against Appo represented opposing perspectives on Irish and Chinese relations, highly mediated by newspapers and the popular culture.

In the first trial the prosecution constructed a case in which a violent, irrational, and misogynist Quimbo Appo struck out at his wife. The Irishwomen in the building came to Catherine Fitzpatrick's defense, the defenseless landlady was stabbed by the crazed Appo, and Appo then escaped like a fugitive. Eight women testified in the *People's* case: two of the dead landlady's daughters, her sister who also lived in the building, the sister's friend, and four neighbors.[14]

At the retrial Appo was able to present his side of the story. In sharp contrast to the Irish female friends and relatives of Mary Fletcher, fifteen white male witnesses, all in positions of authority, testified in his behalf. A Doctor Elwood Irish testified that Appo was "an active and enterprising person—sober and honest, and sociable, quiet, and peaceable in his intercourse with his fellows and neighbors." Six local men with names like Burnham, Whyte, Neubauer, and Briggs signed a sworn affidavit supporting Irish's statement. Then six police officers, three of them sergeants, proceeded to testify that Mrs. Fletcher and the other women who had testified were known to be drunks. C. F. Williams, for example, stated that Appo had expressed "great anxiety and affection" for his wife and often complained of her "constant and excessive use of intoxicating liquors." Not only were these women represented as being habitually drunk, but they were also portrayed as unreasonably clannish to the point of not caring about justice. When the officer asked the women about what had happened, they refused to help him, stating that "they were of the same country as the deceased, and believed that it would disgrace them if they were to assist in preserving the life of a Chinese, or even to testify in his behalf."[15]

Although there were only two sides to the legal proceedings, three viewpoints were articulated. The prosecution represented the views of some neighborhood Irishwomen who sought to protect Appo's wife. The defense represented not only Quimbo Appo's views as a respected member of the Chinese community but also the class, gender, and ethnic perspective of Protestant male authority. The police who testified, after all, were the designated guardians of law and order in this Victorian city. Even though individual police officers may have been Irish, they were in this instance deracinated protectors of the dominant moral order. At this moment in time the alignment of such authority figures with Appo made all the difference in the trial's outcome. Without such support during the original trial, he had been unable to plead his position. And with such support during the retrial, the women's case was easily supplanted.

A clear hierarchy can be teased out from these legal proceedings. In 1859, Irishwomen had more authority than a lone Chinese man; however, they still had less authority than a Chinese man supported by the white male powers that be. Indeed, from a sheer class-mobility perspective, it was better for someone like Catherine Fitzpatrick to marry a Chinese merchant than to stay a single woman. As long as Victorian society still valued the imagined proto-Protestant Chinaman, she stood to gain social standing from the marriage. In this particular case, to be a working-class Irishwoman was to occupy one of the lowest positions that existed. To be a male evincing "respectable" values was to be far more powerful and important. For Appo, and probably other Chinese men, Irishwomen offered the chance of having a family away from their homeland, yet they remained terribly vulnerable. They had to behave in certain ways, ways that the real and symbolic authorities understood and found acceptable, or they could easily be victimized and marginalized. Appo's regular contacts with the police, his English-language ability, and his respectable tea-merchant status enabled him to be included within a Protestant pluralist moral economy. Yet even so, he could not stand alone, confident of his rights in the eyes of New York law. With an incompetent protector, the tardy and ill-prepared former judge, he could not even defend himself against "low-class" neighborhood Irishwomen. Clearly, both Chinese men and Irishwomen were caught in precarious positions of social status and rights. But what about the dominant culture?

At first it would appear that male Victorian authority was in firm control. Yet why the need to mobilize so many white men in Appo's behalf? Shouldn't a few have been more than enough? And why so much journalistic attention to his trial? If elite authority were so clear cut, why wasn't the adjudication of the case more straightforward?

This particular set of historical interactions was not unique. During the antebellum and Civil War period, power relations with regard to categories of race, ethnicity, gender, class, and being American were highly unstable. We need only refer to Barnum's various packagings of different cultural others, such as the Wild Men of Borneo, the Feejee Mermaid, and other abnormative performers, to appreciate the way in which these identity issues were played out in the commercialized public culture.

Which Appo was the real Appo? Like Barnum's packaging and repackaging of acts, the highly competitive newsprint media of the time played the trials both ways. At one point they were sympathetic to the white woman murdered by the violent Chinese heathen; at another point they were sympathetic to the Protestant-like Chinaman beset by lowly Irishwomen. Yet the staged and simulated stereotypes of Irishwomen, Chinese men, and Irishwomen fighting with Chinese men were always lurking in press representations and, likely as well, in the minds of the jurors, judges, and even Appo and Fitzpatrick themselves. The commercializing culture blurred the real and the stereotype to the extent that they could not be easily disentangled. Judgment and fairness were necessarily compromised by deeply embedded collective associations and memories. Was such a trial part of how stereotypes became generated? Or did stereotypes influence the verdicts? No doubt both processes were at work.

Chinese-speaking, -thinking, and -acting individuals had no long-term home in the marketplace as either citizens, consumers, or producers. They could be marketed and could market themselves within the confines of how the populace of European American consumers imagined these cultural others. Chang and Eng Bunker managed to find tremendous opportunities within commercial orientalism as long as they were willing to display their racialized "monstrous" bodies, and Quimbo Appo, for a time, managed to live the life of an "exemplary Chinaman" within the parameters of patrician orientalism. However, neither the elite culture of distinction nor the market culture of commercial stereotypes allowed enough breathing room for real, cross-cultural Chinese individuals to thrive. For the patrician and commercial cultures, easy and discrete categories of knowing avoided the layered, intercultural complexity of the creolizing port culture of lower Manhattan. Commercial orientalism profited from urban dwellers' increasingly finding their voice as a public in a chorus of mass-mediated opinions. These racially inflected opinions, as we shall see in part 3 of this book, became part and parcel of political debates formulating policy and laws.

The "Chinese Question"

By their performance ye
shall know them.

—Victor Turner

CHAPTER 8

"The Alarm"

O N JUNE 30, 1870, the gifted pro-labor editorialist John Swinton brought the "Chinese Question" to New York:

> Suddenly—by a lightning flash, as it were—the Chinese question has become the living question of the hour.
>
> It is a question not only for discussion and decision, but for action.
>
> It is a practical question in regard to industry and capital, as well as in regard to civilization, liberty, and morality.
>
> It is a question not only for to-day, but one which, if wrongly settled at this time, will be a disturbing question for ages.

At a major rally in lower Manhattan's Tompkins Square Park, laborers from the foremost trades in New York City gathered to protest the recruitment of Chinese workers to displace Irish workers in Massachusetts and New Jersey. With the flourish of rhetoric embracing white workingmen, Swinton targeted the Chinese as a national threat. "Mongolian blood is a depraved and debased blood," he declaimed.[1] Chinese New Yorkers were becoming caught up in a debate between labor and capital—about whether Chinese workers constituted "free" or "slave" labor.

Eighteen hundred seventy marked the moment at which struggles between capital and labor interpenetrated commercial culture, producing a common visual and written language in which Chinese labor would be represented in national political debates. Railways and telegraph lines now linked the regions of the continent, creating a vast market. Commercial culture helped to shape this marketplace, yet the market was not everything. As New Yorkers used the urban print and commercial culture to gain a sense of themselves as an audience with public opinions, working-class politics came to be played out in this newly constituted public arena. Print capitalism would play a major role in nationalizing the Chinese Question. Various locally produced representations of Chinese in the print media would be received and reinterpreted by this newly empowered republic of readers and voters. This new forum for political discourse constituted the third, and most powerful, form of orientalism examined in this study.[2]

After the Civil War the United States was in the midst of major social transformation. Once a peripheral colony of the British Empire, the United States had become a robust nation boasting a bourgeois industrial elite that ranked among the wealthiest in the world.[3] The end of slavery, the innovations of technology, the victory of the Northern manufacturing system, and the construction of the transcontinental railroad created the conditions for a centripetal, integrating national economy and political culture. New York was to become the economic and cultural capital of this consolidated nation. The older merchant and commercial elite, largely based in port cities and defined by their role in the exchange of goods and as cultural producers, were now joined by railroad moguls and industrialists; together they shaped the domestic and foreign policies of the United States.

The aggressive expansionist William H. Seward, Lincoln's and Johnson's secretary of state, annexed Alaska in 1867 and negotiated the Burlingame Treaty in 1868. Led by Prince Kung, China appointed New Englander Anson Burlingame as one of three ministers to represent China to the United States and Europe. Having been forced into opening its markets with the treaties negotiated after the Opium Wars, China sought to gain reciprocal rights for the Chinese in the United States. The so-called Burlingame mission was heralded by the national press with continuous and nearly unanimous acclaim. In particular, the trade interests based in the port of New York welcomed this event as signaling the dawn of new and broader trade relations between the two nations. Secretary Seward drew up the treaty while they were visiting Washington, D.C., and it was signed by both parties.[4]

As the trade-driven economy of the young republic transformed into an industrial dynamo, the uses of Chinese things, people, and ideas changed. Just as the desire for luxuries had structured the way in which the Chinese were perceived during the eighteenth century, now the desire to exploit the natural resources of the land and to industrialize the nation undergirded a new orientalist discourse. One result of the Civil War and the completion of the transcontinental rail link was to reserve Western lands for "free labor" and European American settlement. In 1871 Congress abrogated the treaty system that held Indians to be independent nations, and their vast territories were opened to railroads, homesteading, entrepreneurs, and European American immigrants. More and more Americans found themselves wage workers, even though the old Jeffersonian dream of owning one's own farm persisted.[5] At the same time, "cheap"—and seemingly limitless—Chinese labor became a highly desirable commodity for postslavery capitalists; Chinese laborers could be used to mine and cultivate the land, to develop the industrial infrastructure, and to blunt increasingly militant trade-union organizing among European American workers.

From the outset the penny press widely reported the uses and abuses of Chinese and South Asian indentured "coolie" labor—using such practices as moral lessons for the United States. *Hunt's Merchant Magazine,* for example, reported in 1856, "This traffic in Coolies is as cruel and inhuman as the African slave-trade was," and added an abolitionist moral exhortation: "Most of the ships engaged in this trade are from the ports of New York and Boston." Pro-slavery ideologues also expressed their concerns. A writer for an 1859 issue of *De Bow's Review* criticized this use of "free coolie labor" in order to defend Southern slavery. To supply "civilization" with "a little sugar and coffee," the author proclaimed (echoing Benjamin Franklin), "Christendom" exacts "a pound of flesh": "The civilized and powerful races of the earth have discovered that the degraded, barbarous, and weak races, may be induced voluntarily to reduce themselves to a slavery more cruel than any that has yet disgraced the earth, and that humanity may compound with its conscience, by pleading that the act is one of *free will.*"[6]

In contrast, Reverend William Ashmore, missionary to the Chinese, took a far more calculated approach, one that Adam Smith would have approved of:

> The Coolie trade, it will be seen, is speculation in human labor. In other words, it is reducing human labor to the list of marketable commodities—making it an object of purchase and sale, and holding it, subject to the various vicissitudes which attend stocks, provisions, dry goods and other articles of commerce. . . . Under such circumstances, a trade which should be carried on, for the purposes of furnishing, at the same time, a destitute region with labor, and a needy population with employment, would be wise and beneficent.

Ashmore had only one qualification to his proposition: "In order to be either wise or beneficent, it must be regulated on principles of justice to the parties concerned."[7] Issues of "free" versus "slave" labor, fair versus unfair contracts, and essential questions of humanity inflected the discourse. Who would be able to set the terms of wages and the composition of the work-force?

Labor versus Capital's Coolies

After the 1848 discovery of gold at Sutter's Mill in the Mexican territory of Californios, individuals from all over the world, including China, sought to strike it rich and return to their homes with greater economic security. By the late 1850s, surface deposits had already been mined clean. While few European Americans were willing to work in early industrial operations, Chinese who had been evicted and excluded from primary deposits by local law and violence were an available labor pool. They could be readily hired and managed in groups by Chinese labor contractors.

The great majority of Chinese arriving in the United States were not contract laborers. Arriving Chinese often paid for their voyage to California on what historian Him Mark Lai has called the "credit-ticket" system and worked off their debt with wages paid to them for manual labor. While abuses certainly abounded, their work arrangements were essentially those of wage laborers hired in work teams, making them among California's first industrial workers.[8]

Nonetheless, from the vantage point of the majority of independent mechanics and entrepreneurs, Chinese labor was de facto identified as "cheap labor," under the absolute control of regional railroad interests and industrialists. Denis Kearney's Workingmen's Party deemed the Chinese and the industrialists who hired them to be the enemy of the white workingman and his family. "The Chinese Must Go!" was the cry heard most often, second only to "Down with the monopolists."[9]

What became an explicitly anti-Chinese movement began as an issue of contract labor. National organized labor, as Andrew Gyory has pointed out, focused on the broader issue of eliminating the contract labor law passed in 1864.[10] These organizers had no particular interest in attacking other nationalities or racially defined groups. In late September 1868, delegates of the National Labor Union gathered in New York City to attack "private corporations" and "chartered companies" that "bring the cheap labor of Europe" over to work for them. Focused on immigrants from Europe, the congress's deliberations emphasized the unity of workers, not their nationality. The delegates opposed not immigrants but rather immigrant companies that took advantage of would-be workers' ignorance. This effort to combat contract foreign labor would define the national labor movement for years to come.

In an era in which wage work was supplanting autonomous craft production, labor saw the Civil War as a victory for some hard-fought but essential rights. Fewer individuals controlled their own means of production; as a consequence, free labor came to mean the right to sell one's own muscle and brains for fair wages under fair contracts. Such labor was threatened by other varieties. Clearly, slave labor and indentured labor were unfree and might undermine white labor's efforts to gain security and power. But what of foreign contract labor? "Cheap" labor obtained in impoverished foreign lands could be brought in by unscrupulous entrepreneurs who refused to pay American workers a decent wage.[11]

To rid the Pacific coast of Chinese workers, misrepresented as Spanish- and British-style contract "coolie" labor, was to allow resident (and white) workers a chance to fight capital on fairer terms. Politicians, labor leaders, and much grassroots support advocated ridding the region of Chinese. They focused their attention on evicting them industry by industry, town by town, with the ultimate goal of sending them all back to China. Chinese should simply not be allowed to enter or live in the United States. A revision of the United States–China treaty and immigration laws soon became organized labor's focal strategy.[12]

Workers outside the West Coast, including those in New York and other East Coast cities, were not threatened by the small pockets of Chinese living in eastern port cities. Irish and, later, other immigrants from southern and eastern Europe represented the emerging racial problems in these rising industrial cities. Yet while the Chinese Question began primarily as a West Coast labor problem, it would soon be picked up in the political debates of New York City.[13]

Andrew C. Cameron, the editor of the *Workingman's Advocate*, was one of the few labor activists outside California to perceive an impending Chinese labor "peril" once the transcontinental railroad was complete. Four months before the golden spike was driven into the soil of Promontory Point, Utah, linking west to east in 1869, Cameron wrote:

> We warn workingmen that a new and dangerous foe looms up in the far west. Already our brothers of the Pacific have to meet it, and just as soon as the Pacific railroad is completed, and trade and travel begins to flow from the east across our continent, these Chinamen will begin to swarm through the rocky mountains, like devouring locusts and spread out over the country

this side. . . . In the name of the workingmen of our common country, we demand that our government . . . forbid another Chinaman to set foot upon our shores.[14]

Even though he could not see beyond his own racial perspective, Cameron saw a sea change in the making. The railroad greatly enhanced the ability of businessmen to recruit labor from different regions and countries. Just as European immigrants and native-born Americans were beginning to flood the western regions of the country to displace Chinese labor, Chinese wage laborers could be recruited eastward from San Francisco and China to fulfill the labor needs of the rest of the nation.

Cameron's fears appeared to be realized in the Reconstruction South. Owners suddenly had to deal with a freed, wage- and land-demanding African American workforce. The editor of *St. Mary's Planter's Banner* laid out one strategy for recovery: "Small farms and white labor or large farms and coolie labor may save the land." Chinese, perceived to be docile and willing beasts of burden, could be used to punish blacks who wanted more than work for low wages on the same plantations from which they had supposedly been liberated. One planter's wife boasted, "Give us five million of Chinese laborers in the valley of the Mississippi and we can furnish the world with cotton and teach the negro his proper place." The newly assertive African Americans would then, it was supposed, change their "tune" from "forty acres and a mule" to "work nigger or starve."[15]

On July 13, 1869, two hundred delegates from Tennessee, Mississippi, Louisiana, Alabama, Georgia, South Carolina, Kentucky, Missouri, and California and representatives of the Pacific Rail Company gathered for two days at the Greenlaw Opera House to devise the "best and cheapest means of procuring Chinese laborers." The Transportation Committee stressed that orders for five hundred Chinese could be filled at fifty gold dollars per person. A Chinese Christian missionary and labor contractor, Tye Kim Orr, then assured the delegates that "agriculturists can easily be procured through proper agents. They are easily managed, being patient, industrious, docile, tractable, and obedient." The convention ended with the formation of the Mississippi Valley Immigration Labor Company, a joint stock company selling $100 shares. The delegates sought to raise $1 million and resolved to send Tye and a Louisiana businessman directly to China to begin the recruitment process. Agencies would be set up in New York City and San Francisco to make all the arrangements possible.[16]

Upon learning of these intentions, Secretary of the Treasury George S.

Boutwell sent a letter to Colonel James F. Casey, the New Orleans collector of customs. Boutwell's note warned that there was an 1862 law prohibiting American citizens from engaging in the "coolie trade." Such persons risked seizure of their vessels and/or a fine of up to $2,000 and imprisonment of up to one year. In addition, Boutwell alerted the collector that according to an 1867 circular from the Department of State, all U.S. ministers and consuls were to undertake a "full examination" of each individual laborer to certify that he was leaving voluntarily and to devote "all vigilance in the suppression of this new modification of the slave trade."[17]

A debate on the definition of *coolie* ensued. The State Department developed an official interpretation:

[The term *coolie's*] general signification was understood to be a laborer at servile work but the term has received a particular application to the class who have for many years been the subjects of the commerce known as Coolie Trade which was denounced by the unanimous resolution of both houses of Congress of January 16, 1867, as a mode of enslaving men differing from the African Slave Trade in little else than the substitution of fraud for force in obtaining its victims.

In addition, the fact of a contract between a laborer and an employer in China was perfectly acceptable as long as "the contract is not vitiated by force or fraud," and that judgment was best determined by "the local knowledge and experience of each consul." In other words, as long as overt fraud was not used in luring laborers to the United States, other means of persuasion were perfectly acceptable. Clearly favorable to the interests of capital, this policy sought only to trim the excesses of the "coolie trade" but not to change the actual practice of contract labor. As far as the U.S. government was concerned, recruiters were cleared to actively recruit Chinese laborers.[18]

In the mind of this capitalist, and no doubt others, the terms *coolie* and *Chinese labor* were interchangeable. Factory owners in St. Louis and Ohio placed orders for workers, and a Chicago businessman invited two San Francisco Chinese merchants to discuss possible commercial ventures. A General Hiram Walbridge was convinced that he would profit from the wave of the "coming man" and began planning a brand-new fleet of steamships to transport laborers from China via the almost completed Suez Canal. Cornelius Koopsmanschap sought to parlay his prior success in recruiting Chinese railroad workers into a national business. He placed the following ad in the *St. Louis Republican:*

CHINESE LABORERS—Parties wishing to employ large or small numbers of CHINESE LABORERS, may make the necessary arrangements for procuring gangs of the size required, delivered in any part of the country, by application to

KOOPMANSHCAAP [*sic*] & Co.

San Francisco, California[19]

Capital's highly publicized campaign greatly added to organized labor's anxiety about foreign competition. American workers were deluged by newspaper reports of Chinese being recruited to break strikes, to replace Irishmen, Irishwomen, African Americans—anyone their bosses had deemed uncontrollable. In New York the labor activist, lawyer, and former abolitionist Robert W. Hume of Astoria echoed the warnings of *Workingman's Advocate* editor Cameron and the California anti-Chinese movement of Denis Kearney. In August 1869 he wrote "John Chinaman":

> You sturdy tillers of the soil,
>   Prepare to leave full soon;
> For when John Chinaman come in
>   You'll find there is not room.
> Like an Egyptian locust plague,
>   Or like an eastern blight,
> He'll swarm you out of all your fields,
>   And seize them as his right.
> Let the mechanics pack his traps,
>   And ready make to flit;
> He cannot live on rats and mice,
>   And so he needs must quit.
>
> At the full cost of blood war,
>   We've garnered in a race;
> One set of serfs of late we've freed,
>   Another takes its place.
> Come friends, we'll have to leave this land
>   To nobles and to slaves;
> For, if John Chinaman come in,
>   For us—there's only graves.[20]

Despite legal rulings that distinguished "coolies" from voluntary emigrants, Hume tried to rally workers to take their stand against another race of serfs. For the moment, however, Hume's alarm did not find much resonance. Fears of the impending peril would not stir organized labor in the Northeast and Midwest till later.

Still, organized labor was concerned about the precise nature of this Chinese labor. Contract labor was a violation of the principle of free immigration. What remained ambiguous was the position of the National Labor Congress on the Chinese. Were all Chinese considered de facto coolie labor? Were they automatically understood to be a "servile race," or could they also be thought of as individuals with free will who could make their own rational, independent decisions to immigrate to the United States? Within the year the imprecision of the National Labor Congress's position would be tested.

In the first months of 1870 the Chinese Question exploded onto the national scene. In June 1870 a Colonel Calvin Sampson recruited seventy-five Chinese via the transcontinental railroad to his North Adams, Massachusetts, shoe and boot factory to break a strike of the militant shoemakers' union, the Knights of St. Crispin. Chinese laborers had been brought into the core region of the nationalizing political economy, the industrial heartland of the Northeast. How would New York City respond to the Chinese Question? The city that had witnessed the regular breaking of contracts with Chinese performers, from the Tong Hook Tong Dramatic Company to the crew of the *Keying* to Chang and Eng Bunker, would now be a primary site of debate on the fairness of contracts to procure Chinese labor.

"The Alarm"

The arrival of seventy-five Chinese Californians to North Adams, Massachusetts, in 1870 and the importation of sixty-eight Chinese Californians to South Belleville, New Jersey, after that sparked a chain reaction. Protest rallies, newspaper editorials, and political debates reverberated across sectional bounds, ultimately concluding with the passage of the 1882 Chinese Exclusion Act. Caught between labor and capital, these recruits became entangled in issues much larger than they could have imagined. Basic shifts in people's racial identities were in the making.

The events of North Adams and South Belleville, located at opposite ends of the Hudson Valley, illustrated what this age actually meant for New Yorkers. Calvin T. Sampson owned the Model Shoe Factory of North Adams. Situated in the rolling mountains of the Hoosic range in the Berkshires, North Adams was an industrialized New England mill town with thirty-eight fac-

Figure 22. "What Shall We Do with John Chinaman?" *Frank Leslie's Illustrated,*
Sept. 25, 1869. (Courtesy of Bonner Collection)

tories manufacturing a wide range of consumer goods and industrial equipment. Sampson's male and female employees were largely a mixture of native-born Americans, Irish, and French Canadians who belonged to the Knights of St. Crispin. The Crispins were a shoemaker's union, one of the largest trade unions in the country, claiming some forty thousand members in Massachusetts alone. The *Springfield Republican,* a newspaper hostile to organized labor, called them the "most domineering of trade-unions."[21]

The Crispins had been going on strike at Sampson's factory regularly since 1868. Sampson, in turn, had been sending supervisors as far afield as Canada and Maine to recruit nonunion workers. But his efforts accomplished little. Once brought to North Adams, these workers would join the Crispins and press for the rehiring of strikers. Claiming lower sales, Sampson reduced wages by 10 percent in January 1870 and denied access to the company's accounting books. The Crispins struck for no wage reduction and demanded an eight-hour working day. "I shall," Sampson swore to the Crispins, " . . . enter a wedge that will destroy your order in five years." Sampson then instructed his superintendent, George Chase, to travel to San Francisco, a trip made possible by the recent completion of the transcontinental railroad, and bring back seventy-five Chinese workers to break the stronghold the Crispins had on his factory. Chase arrived in San Francisco in mid-May. Eventually he persuaded Kwong, Chong, Wing, and Company to contract seventy-two laborers, two cooks, and one foreman, who doubled as the translator known as "Charlie" Sing.[22]

Angry Crispins, anticipating their arrival, had been waiting at the railroad station for several days. They were joined by "many peaceable townspeople, drawn out by curiosity only." When the train finally arrived and the Chinese got off, the crowd saw their "blue shirts, long cues, and queer faces," and "the air was filled with hoots and all kinds of taunting shouts." "Though the wildest threats of vengeance were shouted no general attack was made." The extra police presence, no doubt, helped maintain some order. After some rocks were thrown and two "leading offenders" were arrested, "an exciting scene of threatened riot, lasting nearly half an hour," ended with the Chinese safely ensconced in Sampson's factory. He had refitted one floor of his three-story factory as a dormitory for his new employees.[23]

One hundred miles down the Hudson Valley from Calvin Sampson's factory was the Passaic Steam Laundry factory, owned by a Captain James Hervey. Hervey had been in the laundry business for some twenty-five years and had moved to South Belleville, located in the industrializing valley along the Passaic River in northern New Jersey, in 1857. His mechanized laundry specialized in washing and ironing new shirts manufactured in the garment factories of New York City. Each week some six thousand shirts were put into his wooden cylinders to be washed and then ironed by hand. He employed about one hundred women, mainly Irish, who lived in a dormitory on the premises that was reportedly outfitted with a Roman Catholic chapel and maid service.

Hervey found it difficult to recruit workers. To reporters he explained that he made regular trips to Castle Garden looking for female German and Irish immigrants desperate for work. But once they were faced with the exhausting task of hand-ironing so many shirts at such a frantic pace for so many hours, he had trouble keeping them. Upon hearing of the North Adams "Chinese experiment," he wrote to Sampson for advice. He too then sent his foreman to employ San Francisco's Kwong, Chong, Wing, and Company in hiring laborers. They were to work for three years and be paid $30 in gold pieces per month. Two cooks accompanied them, and "Charley" Ming was their interpreter and foreman. He was paid $60 a month. Learning from the hos-

Figure 23. "The Chinese in New England—The Work-Shop," *Harper's Weekly*, July 23, 1878. Chinese men were recruited in 1870 to work at Colonel Calvin Sampson's North Adams shoe factory. (Wong Ching Foo Collection)

tile reception that had greeted the Chinese of North Adams, Hervey had his sixty-eight Chinese Californian workers travel by horse-drawn carriages in the shadow of night through the sleeping town, taken past his newly built private fence and oak gate, and secreted into his factory compound. A converted storeroom became their new home.[24]

Major daily newspaper coverage and organized protests by unions and politicians in New York City followed both arrivals. On June 30 the rally Swinton and others had organized was held in Tompkins Square Park. Sponsors built three speaker's platforms in the Lower East Side gathering place— one for German speakers and two for English-language protesters. Local unions chipped in to pay for the wood and the decorations: American flags and dozens of Chinese lanterns painted red, white, and blue. As evening approached, a crowd began to assemble. The *Tribune* reported, "From all sides of the square they came faster and faster, until, as the hour approached, the noise of their voices became like the rushing of mighty waters." Other newspaper reports indicated the participation of virtually all of the city's trades—from shoemakers to cigar makers, from bakers to bricklayers, from iron molders to painters, and "a large number of sympathetic women."[25]

After rounds of fireworks, Nelson W. Young, the president of the Workingmen's Union, addressed the crowd: "The introduction of Coolie labor is nothing but a speculation to make the rich man richer and the poor man poorer." Hall probably spoke for many in the crowd when he stated flatly that this Chinese Question was "the most important issue" facing the integrity of the workingman "in a long time." He then introduced New York City mayor A. Oakely Hall. Hall opposed the "importation of tawny slaves" by the "wicked combination of capitalists" and "man-stealers." While defending the right of Chinese to immigrate voluntarily to the United States, Hall nonetheless called them "debased in race, irreligious, and in many respects incapable of free reason." Speakers from the Tailor's Union, the Bricklayer's Union, the German-language journal *Arbeiter Union,* and others also railed, in a similar fashion. John Ennis of the Plasterer's Union, for example, spoke in Protestant terms: "At one end of Wall Street stands a magnificent temple erected for the worship of the Christian's God, and at the other end, if the Chinese obtain a foothold here, will in ten years be erected a Pagan Temple for the worship of Budhee and Confucius." At the same time, Ennis said he did not object to Chinese coming as willing émigrés, which was the basic "free-labor" position of the Republican Party. Similar rallies were held in Brooklyn, Rochester, Troy, and other locales throughout the region.[26] While speakers distinguished voluntary from forced labor and rhetorically supported the right of Chinese workers to enter freely and compete in the United States, they also conflated racial arguments with labor- and class-related arguments. Many of these same speakers made remarks that undermined their own supposedly favorable position with regard to voluntary foreign labor. The Chinese were de facto adjudged to be a backward people not really capable of becoming free, rational, and Christian laborers.

In contrast to the attempted distinctions made at the Tompkins Square rally, an "indignation meeting" held three months later to protest Captain Hervey's importation of Chinese had a decidedly bleaker and more explicitly racist tone. Held in North Arlington across the river from Hervey's residence on the evening of September 28, some nine hundred people listened to wholly anti-Chinese arguments. No distinctions were made between free and coolie labor; all Chinese were to be banned. A Dr. M. H. C. Vail of Newark moved from the question of contract to race: "Now comes this Asiatic Race to take the place of those who had come here before. We have had no trouble with the people of Europe. They come here, and mingle with us. . . . They helped to increase the wealth and prosperity of this country. They are of the same race with us." But, in contrast "these Chinese—can they ever mingle with this people? (Voices—'No, no, never!') Can they go out and in with us? ('No, no!') You answer well. . . . They are too far removed from us in every character—in everything that make up man." Referring to middle-class households who hired the Chinese as servants and cooks, Vale identi-fied Republican abolitionists as the culprits: "The people who hire this help are the ones who were the loudest mouthed against African slavery, but they hire these idolatrous slaves." But even those naive members of the white race would be sorry, for "Captain Hervey may see the time when rats are in bed with him, and a Chinese holding a mouse over his head [to force him to eat]." The good doctor closed by making a pitch for political activism. Refer-ring to local elections, he told the crowd, "You must make a gigantic effort to prevent the introduction of these heathen people; vote for no man who favors it; have nothing to do with any man who favors it." Following Vail was Michael R. Kinney, counsel of the Board of Alderman of Newark, who advocated the passage of resolutions to stop the introduction of Chinese labor. According to the *New York Star* reporter, Kinney stated, "'The only remedy for that evil is to vote the Democratic ticket.' He continued in this train, and the other speakers of the evening were few and of the same opin-ion as those who had preceded them."[27]

New Yorkers first learned of the Chinese Californians' arrival through the penny press, which increasingly played a role in the formulation of pub-lic policy. Their reactions, also recorded in the press, served as a bellwether of the changing political culture of New York City.[28] The *New York Herald* had the largest circulation of any newspaper in the nation, and its reportage provides an interesting case study of how North Adams was represented in one mass-circulation paper. The *Herald*'s first article on June 16 was a reprint of a *Boston Advertiser* feature from two days before. It was a mod-est-sized story on page 8 with the headline "The Coolies in Massachusetts, Oriental Laborers on the Soil of Massachusetts." Each succeeding day the headlines grew larger, the articles ran longer, and they were moved up nearer to the front of the paper. Clearly, James Gordon Bennett thought the issue was becoming more newsworthy as popular protests unfolded. By June 27 the headline on page 3 read:

The New Labor Movement, The Oriental Shoemakers in Massachusetts. Indignation of the Crispins Movement Towards Co-operative Manufactories and Its Probable Failure—A Secret Combination Against It by the Manufacturers, Jobbers and Leather Dealers—The Crispins in Council—A Manufacturer Addresses Them on Christianity, Morality and Co-operation—Redress to Come from Christianity and Religion, and North Through Political Action.

The article was given one and a half columns, identifying it as being, from the editor's point of view, a very important domestic issue.[29]

Bennett had established the *Herald* as the largest-circulation paper in the nation by catering primarily to the huge potential New York–area readership of European Americans, American-born and immigrant. One staffer explained that Bennett's position on issues varied with public opinion and political winds, that he went with "the party [he] believes to be the strongest." Possibly reflecting the yet-to-be-defined positions of Republicans and Democrats, Bennett waffled on the Chinese laborers' arrival in North Adams. He first expressed his continued distaste for abolitionists and how they might cause another civil war over the "pig-tailed coolie." Then he mused that cheaper shoes might be for the greater good, and he pointed out that the United States had survived the "depraved, slothful and brutal African in its midst; the "Anglo-Saxon race" could exploit the "Asiatic" or "heathen race" to its own advantage.[30]

In the past Bennett had supported the economic argument that Chinese labor was good for the country. In the 1850s and the 1860s the *New-York Times*, Horace Greeley's *Tribune*, and Edwin Lawrence Godkin's *Nation*, among other major East Coast journalist voices, spoke firmly about the economic value of Chinese and other immigrants. With labor shortages, labor could demand higher wages, thus hampering economic development. The Chinese, in this view, were to the West what the Negro was to the South and the Celt to the East. Among their chief virtues, according to Godkin's Social Darwinist thinking, was that these "barbarians" had a predisposed "fitness for servile duties and [a] want of social ambition." As "birds of passage," once Christianized, the Chinese could promote the good word in China as well as spread their taste for American goods. In 1852 Bennett maintained that anyone who questioned this wisdom must be a "free soiler, abolitionist, or worse." Bennett met a Chinese man on Vesey Street, downtown New York, and his imagination was excited by what the United States could do with this "cheap labor." "The unsurpassed value of Chinese servants promises to relieve housekeepers in our Atlantic States from the annoyances to which they are now tyrannically subjected by independent Bridget in the North and by emancipated Dinah in the South."[31] As an extension of the trade in Chinese things, Chinese people were coming to be considered in commodified terms. Their transactable utility, and not their human rights, was primary in these public-policy debates. In this sense historian Michael O'Malley's argument that race and money, "specie and species," were interrelated questions in the dominant discourse about African American freedom also helps to elucidate the debate around the Chinese Question.[32]

Bennett's views during these pro-Chinese labor years were in line with the majority of postbellum eastern editors. Buoyed by Republican free-labor ideology and the reciprocal trade and labor agreements of the 1869 Burlingame Treaty, Chinese were viewed as immigrants, albeit of an inferior pagan race, who should be allowed to compete and assimilate into the American experiment. Contrary to the trade unionists, who made a clear distinction between importation and immigration, elite gatekeepers of public opinion favored labor competition. The New-York Times argued for the importance of unfettered trade in a capitalist-driven economy. Citing Adam Smith (and reiterating the stereotype of Chinese as childlike), the Times editorialized that plentiful, cheap labor developed the higher branches of industry and elevated skilled labor: "Slavery no doubt demoralized whites as well as blacks; but the mere juxtaposition of the inferior Negro, or of the Indian never lowered the white, nor will that of the industrious child of the Central Flowery Land." Most editors agreed with Horace Greeley of the Tribune, the foremost Republican journal in the nation: "So far the benefits [of Chinese immigration] have decidedly overbalanced the evils."[33]

Eighteen seventy was, however, a moment of confusion in which older notions of free labor and free immigration coincided and conflicted with growing fears of displacement, social chaos, and unfair competition. The postbellum Northern Republican consensus was increasingly fragmented, while Democratic power in urban immigrant communities strengthened. These fundamental labor questions were also aggravated by reports filtering back from missionaries in China.

Antiforeign rebellions sparked by the Opium Wars in China further polarized American public opinion. The 1870 Tianxin murders of French missionaries drew headlines across the country. The Herald gave the incidents a distinct racial tilt that played on already established notions of despotism. For example, "Mongolian Intolerance" headed one of Bennett's editorials, a point resonant enough with those attending the North Arlington indignation meeting for Dr. Vail to claim that "the Chinese race are the only people who lift the dagger to plunge it into the Christian missionaries."[34]

As public opinion shifted, Bennett's opinions did as well. In June 1869 he printed a long letter to the editor from a man "ten years a resident of California, Oregon, Washington Territory, Vancouver Island and British Columbia [who] knows whereof he speaks"; this man wrote of the irredeemable idolatry of the Chinese, their "personal and moral habits . . . beneath [those of] any other race," and "their fondness for pork [which] may account in part for the leprosy . . . prevalent in China." Bennett finally settled on a resolutely anti-Chinese position: "Their pagan savageness appears to be impregnable to the mild influences of Christian civilization." When the facts did not coincide with his view, Bennett made them fit. In 1871 the Reverend Russell Conwell wrote a relatively mild book called *Why and How: Why the Chinese Emigrate, and the Means They Adopt for the Purpose of Reaching America.* While Conwell recounted various superstitions, customs, stories, and motivations for emigration, his tract was hardly xenophobic. However, Bennett used the release of the book as an occasion to promote his own increasingly hostile perspective. He claimed that the book proved that the Chinese Question was no longer a matter of "labor versus capital" but rather one of racial warfare. If the Chinese first displaced the Negro and then the Irish, what would happen next? "We may soon see them building our ships and houses, digging our canals, driving our city railroad cars. . . . It will thus be seen that the Chinese question interests all classes of the community . . . because there is absolutely no limit to the supply of oriental laborers, except the capacity of ships and railroads to transport them."[35]

Other editors, such as Charles Dana, the former utopian socialist, now editor of the *New York Sun,* also shifted positions in 1870. In response to the Memphis Convention of the prior year, Dana was one of the few Northern editors to take more than a businesslike position on the recruitment of Chinese labor. In the pages of the *Sun* he first waxed on about the Chinese, as "children of one common Father," being entitled to share in "His Bounty." After North Adams Dana renounced such a position as "sentimentalist." Having brought "the whole world here to share in the advantages of our superior civilization," he claimed, "Americans starve and die" through the "excess of their benevolence." Placing limits on Chinese immigration was only "simple justice" for honest workingmen. The battle lines had been clearly drawn. Dana stated that those who did not agree were "neither good Americans, good economists, good philanthropists, nor sensible men." He now believed that the position of the radical Republicans was overzealous. Contradicting his own stance of the 1860s, he rejected the notion of equal rights: "To them . . . one man is as good as another and birth, education, morality, and intellectual power count for nothing at all."[36] The fulcrum of good common sense was shifting. Race was becoming more and more an important issue.

Reconstructionists Reconsidering

The old radical Republican coalition of abolitionists, Free-Soilers, suffragettes, and freedmen were not united on what position they should take with the Chinese. The editorial board of the *National Standard* was split on this issue. Wendell Phillips took the prevailing free-labor, trade-union stance, supporting unlimited Chinese immigration while criticizing contract labor. Nominated by the National Labor Union to become governor of Massachusetts, he reiterated the traditional distinction between voluntary and nonvoluntary labor:

> The Chinese . . . will be a welcome and valuable addition to the mosaic of our Nationality. . . . But such immigration to be safe and helpful must be spontaneous. It must be the result of individual will obeying the laws of industry and the tendencies of the age. IMMIGRATION OF LABOR IS AN UNMIXED GOOD. IMPORTATION OF HUMAN FREIGHT IS AN UNMITIGATED EVIL.

But even this most ardent of crusaders for equal rights lapsed into protoracist attitudes. Phillips referred to all Chinese as "barbarous, "machinelike," and of "alien-blood," capable of "dragging down the American home to the level of the homeless street beggars of China."[37] (The description "machine-like" evoked an identification of Chinese laborers with new industrial machinery displacing skilled crafts, and for New Yorkers the reference to the homeless street beggars of China would have resonated with the memory of the Tong Hook Tong opera troupe beggars.)

Other influential reformers took different sides on the Chinese Question, depending on their attitudes toward labor and capital. Frederick Douglass agreed with Phillips's pro-immigration and anti-importation position, as did Lydia Maria Child. She qualified her stance, however, stating in a letter to the *National Standard,* "I dislike all monopolies; and a monopoly of labor seems to me as wrong, in spirit and principle, as a monopoly of grain or fruit." William Lloyd Garrison had little sympathy for workers. "Mr. Sampson," Garrison maintained, "simply asserted his unquestionable right as an employer, as against a brow-beating and exacting combination." More typical, however, among the postwar radical Republicans was William Cullen Bryant's attitude. In private correspondence he discreetly expressed his antipathy to Chinese people: "We shall be obliged to have closer relations with our pig-tailed brethren . . . ere long, but I do not contemplate it with any pleasure; I prefer the Caucasian race. The Negroes among us are a source of trouble, and there is [no] knowing what might yet happen as a consequence of the mutual jealousy of races."[38]

With the arrival of Chinese workers in the New York area, the New York–based religious organizations immediately saw them as their link to accelerating conversions in China—paving the way for Christian civilization and commerce. The Reverend and Mrs. Stephen L. Baldwin, who worked among the Chinese in Fuzhou, China, and in Hervey's plant, embodied this dual strategy.

In October and November 1870 the Halsey Street Methodist Episcopal Church of Newark paid for a sequence of one-line ads in the Newark Daily Advertiser: "HEATHEN CHINESE, / HALSEY ST. M. E. CHURCH. / REV. STEPHEN L. BALDWIN. / LECTURE ON HABITS AND CUSTOMS." Baldwin had recently returned from the M.E. Mission in Fuzhou and was on a speaking circuit in the New York metropolitan area raising funds for their salaries and continued work. The event featured a Mr. Ling Cha Cha, a "native Chinaman" Baldwin had converted. In his various lectures Baldwin spoke of the individuals and people he had touched. Arguing for the importance of prolonged work, he pointed out that he had not made a single conversion during his first ten years in China; but now there were over eight hundred full members and as many probationers. One conversion of a "native" led to many others. Baldwin spoke of a "most efficient preacher" who had been "an opium smoker and opium seller, a sorcerer and many other things that are evil." After enduring great opposition, stoning, and imprisonment, this brave individual "has been an instrument" in the converting of three to four hundred "other souls." Another success story concerned an older illiterate man of fifty-six who, upon being given a translated version of the Gospel of Matthew, learned to read this book in Chinese in seven months. Another old man, who had smoked opium for forty years, upon his conversion immediately abandoned the practice, saying, "It is all wrong, I am a servant of Jesus, I am not going to touch it again."[39]

No doubt Baldwin sincerely believed in his work and the power of moral uplift. However, by emphasizing the horrors of Chinese depravity and the power of Christianity to civilize these ignorant heathen, missionaries such as Baldwin were able to raise funds to continue their work. Emphasizing the "evil" and pagan qualities of Chinese culture and people made the conversions all the more miraculous and important.

While Stephen Baldwin worked on the foreign front, his wife, Esther E. Baldwin, was a staunch advocate for Chinese immigration. In her regularly reprinted pamphlet, *Must the Chinese Go? An Examination of the Chinese Question*, and other articles she passionately refuted exclusionist contentions. In line with Henry Ward Beecher's position of saving, not damning, the Chinese, Mrs. Baldwin argued that "far from being the worst people of the world, they are far in advance of almost every heathen nation, and set us an example of industry and justice it would do well for us to copy." Ever mindful of the importance of U.S. trade, she saw them as linked concerns: "Not only is that great empire the grandest and most promising market for our products and manufacturers, but for Christian work and civilization." In this expression of the basic faith of manifest destiny, commerce and Protestant missionary work were seen as interdependent with the "opening" of China as a free market for Western goods and Christian civilization.[40]

While radical Republicans and missionaries debated how to understand the Chinese and China, organized labor continued to be torn by countervailing currents of economic developments. Labor was at a crossroads. Both workers and manufacturers were feeling ever more uncertain about how a new equilibrium between the dignity of labor and the responsibilities of capital might be achieved. From 1870 onward Chinese laborers employed in California factories were nationally competitive in two trades: the boot- and shoemaking industry and the cigar-making industry. The Knights of St. Crispin of San Francisco made their Massachusetts brethren very much aware of Chinese-born competition. Workers responded to the nationalization of capitalist interests with national unions. The largely immigrant Cigar Makers' International Union (CMIU), based in New York, was especially keen on challenging the strong Chinese presence in San Francisco and New York. Nonunion-Chinese-made cigars threatened to undercut the price of white- and union-made cigars. In this context Calvin Sampson's and Captain Hervey's recruitment of the Chinese can best be understood as having had nationally dire implications for labor.[41]

The Language of Racial Threat

The rhetoric of this worker's movement was quite telling. Anti-Chinese placards in San Francisco construed the Chinese as enemies of progress. Mixing themes of free labor, women's rights, and antigentry sensibilities, they read, "American Trade Needs no Coolie Labor," "No Servile Labor shall Pollute our Land," "Women's Rights and no more Chinese Chambermaids," "Our Women are degraded by Coolie Labor," "We want no Slaves or Aristocrats," and "The Coolie Labor System leaves us no Alternative—Starvation or Disgrace."[42]

The agitation in California laid the groundwork for the anti-Chinese protests in North Adams and North Arlington. The Chinese labor issue provided trade unions and the Democratic Party with one more means of fragmenting the Republican consensus. A June 1870 "Letter from a North Adams Shoemaker," signed "Christopher Crispin" and printed in Bennett's *Herald*, exemplifies the cross-regional nature of the issue. Speaking in modest yet national terms, the letter began, "Being a workingman I enter my humble protest against the introduction of this system of semi-slavery into this or any other State of the Union." Referring to the Civil War, the writer continued, "We have here initiated among us a twin brother of the old iniquity which cost the country so much blood and treasure to obliterate. . . . As the old system of servile labor was the cause of desolating the fair fields and stately mansions of the South, this system may be the cause of demolishing many palatial residences and costly workshops at the East."

The presence of Democratic Party candidates at the North Arlington indignation meeting undoubtedly pointed to the urban-based party's efforts to build on anti-Chinese sentiments. Indeed, none other than the New York senator and Democratic Party boss William Marcy Tweed presented the state legislature with New York's version of anticoolie legislation. In a meeting of the Working Men's League on Third Avenue and Twelfth Street, Manhattan, resolutions were adopted for the eight-hour-day work law and the prohibition of hiring "Chinese or so-called coolie laborers in . . . this State," under penalty of a six- to twelve-month prison term or a fine of $5,000.[43]

Although a coherent anti-Chinese and counter-Republican ideology emerged in the waning days of 1870, the Republican-dominated New York state legislature had a different agenda, an amalgam of liberal free-trade and antiunion positions. *Harper's Weekly,* the respectable New York–based national newspaper whose biting cartoons by Thomas Nast eventually brought down Democratic Party "Boss" Tweed, applauded the defeat of the anti-Chinese bill. "The Chinese invasion, of which he seems so much afraid," the *Harper's* editors wrote of Tweed, "is altogether mythical. . . . Mr. Tweed presumes too much of the ignorance or the prejudices of the workingmen if he expects to delude them with such a flimsy cheat. . . . A majority of this country still adheres to the old Revolutionary doctrine that all men are free and equal before the law, and possess certain inalienable rights which even Mr. Tweed is bound to respect." The same issue featured a biting cartoon by Nast on the Chinese Question.[44]

Another voice, however, better forecast the anti-Chinese developments of the coming decade. The morning before the rally at Tompkins Square Park, there appeared on page 1 of the nation's preeminent Republican newspaper, the *New York Tribune,* a lengthy article by John Swinton entitled "The New Issue: The Chinese-American Question." In this article Swinton, an editor of the *New-York Times* and a future labor organizer, formulated what was possibly the most cogent anti-Chinese argument on the basis of race east of the Rockies to date. Writing in the tradition of an educated Victorian generalist speculating on a wide range of subject matter, Swinton articulated a pan-European American nationalism that foreshadowed what would be the dominant American racial ideology for the years to come.[45]

In contrast to the distinction New York mayor Hall and others made between coolies and free immigration, Swinton emphasized unresolvable racial differences as the primary grounds for anti-Chinese protest. In an authoritative and persuasive manner he maintained, "The deepest dividing line between men is that of *race.* Deeper than politics or religion—deeper than the contemporary differences of laws or manners, are the depths and differences of *race.*" Hence, differences between nativist and immigrant Catholics, between English-speaking and non-English-speaking European-born Americans, Republicans and Democrats, workingmen and manufacturers, did not matter nearly as much as the racial divide. "The people of the United States are of the white European race, the Japhetic stock, from which have sprung the Germanic, Celtic, and Latin varieties—all immediately related to each other by historical terms—all growing side by side for thousands of years, and all developing a progressive civilization through the changes of time." Swinton was in effect drawing upon dubious racial gene-alogies to construct a new white nationalist identity. "The life, genius and power of the American Republic is with the European race," he wrote. "All that here exists is owning to this white race, and is the work of this race, which is the best-based and best-built, the strongest and soundest, the dom-inant and predominant, the most aggressive and progressive race in the world."[46]

In Swinton's formulation, progress and civilization were equated with the destiny of the white race. Yet this bright future was threatened. Labor must unite with capital to fight the impending scourge. "The Alarm" must be sounded against the threat of "the infusion and transfusion of the Chi-nese, Mongolian or Yellow race with the White American race," for "all anthropologists and ethnologists are agreed" that the "Mongolian blood is a depraved and debased blood. The Mongolian type of humanity is an infe-rior type,—inferior in organic structure, in vital force or physical energy, and in the constitutional conditions of development." Drawing from mod-ern medicine and science a metaphor for the national body politic, Swinton asked, "Can we afford to permit the transfusion into the national veins of a blood more debased than any we have known? Can we afford to offer the opportunity for this sort of mongrelism? If there be any truth whatever in Darwin's scientific theory of Natural Selection, it must be admitted that a nation like ours would run a fearful risk from the degradation of its race—existence." Chinese immigration, of any kind—free or contract—in Swin-ton's mind meant the downfall of all that was dynamic and progressive in the United States. "In the Spanish colonies on this continent," Swinton proffered proof positive, "the European (Latin) race mingled with the Indian and the African; and we need nothing more than the direful and dismal his-tory of Mexico and Central America as commentary on the fact."[47] Swinton posed race as the primary divide in American politics and urged all whites of whatever class to follow his xenophobic banner.

Swinton's analysis of the Chinese Question dissolved the old ambivalence toward Chinese and presaged a new national consensus based on white Euro-pean American nationalism. Racial assumptions about immutable Chinese characteristics were at the foundation of this developing political culture. The fulcrum point for freedom and civil rights shifted toward segregation, emphasizing race and difference; a new common sense informed more and more New Yorkers' thinking that an anti-Chinese immigration position was perfectly reasonable, sensible, and necessary. Indeed, reasoning people like John Swinton argued, the very dignity of labor, and of capital, was dependent upon it.[48]

Swinton had considerable power as a speaker and writer, and it is instructive to examine his rhetoric in light of what anthropologist Benedict Anderson has said about the role of language in creating nationalistic "imagined communities." Swinton's language was one of scientistic racism toward Chinese and "Orientals," and in fact this language was sustained by the culture of New York City. The constellation of meanings associated with key words commonly used in the press and in everyday speech—*coolie labor, Orientals, swarthy, Johnny Coolie, pigtails, John Chinaman, imitative,* or *magical*—designated Chinese people as irreconcilably different. The term *coolie labor,* for example, which immediately raised associations with miserably exploited Peruvian and Caribbean indentured labor, was often used as a general-purpose term to denote the totality of Chinese workers, eliding significant differences of contracts among them. In this way all Chinese labor in the United States became equated with "coolieism," which was, as Bennett wrote, "but another name for African slave labor." It was a terminological sleight of hand that would soon prove fatal to any hopes for Chinese American equal rights.[49]

The terms of the prior forms of orientalism, both the patrician and the commercial, infused this political culture with a sense of vast difference. *Oriental* used in combination with *pigtail* and *swarthy* reminded readers of the racial representation of Chinese and their culture as being opposite and irreconcilable to the white Occident. The Orient in the commercial culture was associated with magic, mysticism, and conjuring abilities beyond Western comprehension. As has already been recounted, Chinese performers populated the Broadway stage. Significantly, stage stereotypes were extended beyond the proscenium arch to apply to the Chinese in North Adams. In a revealing anti-Crispin editorial statement, "Strikes and the Asiatic Element," Bennett wrote:

> The cordwainers in Massachusetts have put their foot in it. They have struck for higher wages; and what is the result? The shoe manufacturers telegraph to China or San Francisco for workmen, and presto! as if by magic, up pops a gang of Oriental pigtails, cocked and primed, and, with their unrivaled imitative powers, within forty-eight hours they commence making shoes as handily as the most expert waxend in the Commonwealth.

Presented as magical figures that might have been taken from a scene of the *Arabian Nights,* the competing Chinese laborers become emblematic of the disconcertingly instant speed of modern communication and transportation.[50] In this association, racial scapegoating serves to reduce the anxiety provoked by the "magic" of progress.

At the root of these public debates lay the question of how to categorize Chinese laborers within the naturalized hierarchy of U.S. society. New York intellectuals played a significant role in this process of categorization. Dr. John William Draper provides an excellent case study. A professor of chemistry and physiology at the University of the City of New York (later renamed New York University), Draper was himself both a product and a prime advocate of New York's developing civic culture.[51] Draper was, along with Samuel F. B. Morse, one of the most famous of New York University's faculty. He established the university's medical school, was one of the first people to take a photograph of the human face, founded the American Chemical Society, and wrote the first American intellectual history of European thought. He was a public intellectual par excellence, situated within the cultural institutions that profoundly shaped nineteenth-century New York's elite public culture.[52]

Based on a series of four lectures given at the New-York Historical Society, Draper's *Thoughts on the Future of Civil Policy of America* (1865) articulated a vision of a priesthood of expert opinion informing American domestic and foreign policies. "The aim of all science is prevision," he prefaced his book, "the foretelling of the future." With a modernist faith in the universal truthfulness of science, he used metaphysical language to communicate the predictive goals of his study: "To appreciate the working of some of those natural laws in the case of America, to divine the future tendencies of the Republic, to extract from the observations we make rules for national conduct—these are the objects to which the following pages are devoted." For example, in contrast to Europe's many different state governments and rival aristocracies, Asian "homogeneousness" supposedly fostered political despotism and individual dissipation; this homogeneity made China "conservative, and secure[d] its internal stability by producing a common direction of thought."[53] "National types" of superior, middling, and inferior "social grades" were deemed critical variables in determining the rise and fall of nations.

Combining theories of climate, racial biology, and phrenology, Draper hypothesized:

If the life of a man could be prolonged through many centuries, and he were to occupy it in making a journey over the earth from the Arctic to the Antarctic Circle, though he might have been perfectly white at first, his complexion would in succession pass through every degree of darkness, and by the time he had reached the equator toward the middle of his life, he could be perfectly black. . . . [Even] his skull would vary, and with it his intellectual powers. His forehead, reclining at the outset, would undergo rectification as he slowly advanced to more genial climes; the facial angle enlarging and reaching a maximum at the time of his residence in the temperate zone, but diminishing again, and his countenance becoming baser, as he approached the equator.[54]

Yet despite his racialist stance, Draper was no simple xenophobe. His position was that admixtures of blood could be either good or bad, depending on whether the civilization was rising or falling. In an argument that foreshadowed what crusading moralists would later say of the international port settlement of lower Manhattan, Draper contended that, for a strong and virtuous civilization, the historical consequence of such intermingling was "dissipation"—a "sapped society." Roman virtue, for example, was diluted by the various "foreign blood" lines, which happily "dissolved and [were] lost in the conterminous [sic] races." The Romans' "political forms vanished—their religious forms, their paganism, disappeared." As "the thoughts of the conquered people vanquished the thoughts of the Romans," Roman society experienced a rapid disintegration into evil. "The thing went on from bad to worse, until slave concubinage was almost universal. The accumulation of power and wealth gave rise to a universal depravity." With the creation of this "mongrel race," "ideas and dogmas, that would not have been tolerated for an instant in the pure old homogeneous Roman race, found acceptance in this adulterated, this festering mass."[55]

"With Eastern blood will necessarily come Eastern thoughts, and the attempt at Eastern social habits," Draper warned. "Social habits," of course, include sexual habits. Issues of sexuality and gender undergird Draper's theory of interracial pollution. In contrast to the European man, who virtuously makes woman "his companion," the "Asiatic makes her his toy," essentially a "slave of the man." While "the treasures of the [Asian] are placed in a harem, those of the [European] are invested in the public funds." In Draper's formulation, "Eastern" sexual habits are not only an index of depravity but also a means of cultural conquest: polygamy can foster for one man some two hundred children, "all glorying in their descent from their conquering father and speaking his tongue."[56]

Draper's natural laws thus codified popular prejudices and perceptions both about Chinese laborers and about the exotic-erotic allure of Asian women, and incorporated them into a larger theory of the social-policy implications of cross-cultural interaction. For Draper, Western civilization could hasten the climatic-racial-biological transformations of migrating Chinese with education. Fearing the social consequences of an intermingling of Pacific immigrants of the "lower social grades" with the "native American population," he advocated an all-out Americanization program for Chinese migrating into California. Public instruction was the solution to the disruption posed by migrating peoples from the lower ranks of any given society. The responsibilities of proper acculturation rested with the pulpit, the press, and, especially, the public schools. Draper exhorted "the Pacific States . . . to look to their public schools, laying broad and munificent foundations for their educational system, giving no encouragement to the use of any foreign tongue, and fusing into their mass, as thoroughly and rapidly as may be, their inevitable hybrid population."[57]

John Swinton, still writing editorials for the *New-York Times*, fervently disagreed with this Republican stance. Claiming that Draper advocated the "extensive emigration of Chinamen or other Asiatics" to the United States, Swinton maintained that "the free institutions and Christian virtues of America have a sufficiency of adverse elements to contend with already." Diversity was already causing great ills: "We have masses of vice and ignorance in all our great cities. We have four millions of degraded negroes in the South. We have political passion and religious prejudice everywhere. The strain upon the constitution is about as great as it can bear." Swinton speculated that if "there were to be a flood-tide of Chinese population . . . we should be prepared to bid farewell to republicanism and democracy." Generalizing about all Chinese, not simply the "lower social orders" that concerned Draper, Swinton claimed that they were a people "befouled with all the social vices" and having "no knowledge or appreciation of free institutions or constitutional liberty." They had "heathenish souls and heathenish propensitities." Their character, habits, and "modes of thought" were "firmly fixed by the consolidating influence of ages and ages."[58]

The alarm sounded in New York, the nation's center of commercial culture, had national impact. In New York's print media, regional commercial and political issues were weighed against national ones. Orientalist language from the West Coast was borrowed and then reinterpreted in the light of northeastern concerns. In turn, the debates and interpretations framed in the media hub of New York were critical in formulating a national political culture.

Were Chinese assimilable or not? How deeply embedded, how fixed, were their social characteristics? How much time would it take for schooling and climate to have a civilizing and physiognomic impact? The immigration-policy debates in New York at the end of the Civil War were not distinct from the far better known anti-Chinese debates in California.[59] The debates stemmed not from real numbers of real Chinese in New York or California but from the deep-seated anxieties of contending groups seeking to define American national identity. In this topsy-turvy era, what social values, what social categories could be relied on? What were the eternal, essential truths? Or were all the supposed verities merely conventional, merely expressions of the social and political structures of the culture in which they arose?[60]

Swinton's white populist racialization of Chinese (and "Asiatics") as "cheap labor" directly challenged the neatness of Draper's more European notion of a tripartite class-caste hierarchy. But for both Swinton and Draper, as for other participants in these debates, the social-policy question was never absolute—all or nothing—but one of tipping points. Writing his major policy statement in favor of American protectionism in 1869, Horace Greeley clearly articulated this nuanced argument: "As yet, our Mongolian visitors are substantially free to labor as they will and for whom they will, so long as they render due obedience to our laws. As yet, I judge that the benefits resulting from their immigration have decidedly overbalanced the evils." Yet with the imagined threat of one-third of the people on the globe wanting to fill the "empty" spaces of the Americas that were, by divine right, the "manifest destiny" of Anglo-Saxon Protestants, Greeley sounded his tipping point:

> But what has hitherto been a rivulet may at an early day become a Niagara, hurling millions instead of thousands upon us from the vast overcrowded hives of China and India, to cover not only our Pacific slope but the Great Basin, and pour in torrents through the gorges of the Rocky Mountains into the vast, inviting Valley of the Mississippi. . . . The stream of Mongol immigration may vastly enlarge itself, yet remain beneficent and fertilizing; but not if it is to work (as many apprehend) a retrograde change in our indus-

trial organization, and result in the establishment of a novel and specious Serfdom but little removed in essence from old-fashioned Slavery.[61]

For "pro"-Chinese and "anti"-Chinese advocates alike, the numbers of Chinese allowed to enter the United States could overwhelm even the most effective public schools. For such powerful New York civic figures as John William Draper and Horace Greeley, the question was not one of the indiscriminate glossing of all Chinese as "heathen," but a more finely calibrated position that differentiated Chinese in classed and sexualized terms. In effect, the two earlier traditions of American orientalism, one grounded in the patrician culture of distinction and the other tied to the popular commercial marketplace, where the masses voted with their pocketbooks, were juxtaposed in a third emergent form. What social policies, domestic and foreign, could be established for the new national moral and political economy that would enable worthy, striving individuals to achieve distinction and "happiness" while at the same time keeping the "lower social orders," with their democratic powers, from causing anarchy?[62] This third form of orientalism used the state to intervene in the shape of social policies to balance the interests of "the few" and "the many." At this time, these policy debates were yet to be fully played out. It was within the context of this redefinition of American identity and political culture that racially coded visual representations in the commercial culture both embodied the public common sense and predisposed that common sense to support domestic and foreign policies that would contain and exclude Chinese and other "Orientals."

CHAPTER 9

Visualizing
"Ah Sin"

Bret Harte's poem "Plain Language from Truthful James" (1870) tells the story of Bill Nye, a cardsharper, playing poker with Ah Sin, who feigns ignorance of the game. "I wish to remark," says Truthful James,

> And my language is plain—
> That for ways that are dark
> And for tricks that are vain
> The heathen Chinee is peculiar.

Though Harte did not intend it, "Truthful James" has most often been read as a humorous anti-Chinese poem. In the words of one nineteenth-century critic, it reveals "the low cunning which is generally found to underlie the affected simplicity of John Chinaman."[1]

Harte's use of phrases such as "ways that are dark" sets the stage for the trickery just behind the "pensive and child-like" smile of Ah Sin—"And I shall not deny," muses Truthful James, "what that name might imply." In the poem, the tables are turned on Western cleverness. Thinking he can make some quick money by gambling with an unknowing Chinese mark, Nye is the one who ends up being taken. The fact that he even cheated in the game is of little consequence to the story. Rather, Ah Sin's ability to beat Nye at Nye's own game goes to show that "we are ruined by Chinese cheap labor." Most readers interpreted this poem as a metaphor for the dangers of Chinese immigration into the United States. It was a warning to good Americans who might have been in favor of unfettered entry: Innocents beware! Or, as one biographer, put it "'Chinese cheap labor' had begun to be a war-cry; and Bret Harte had hit upon an illustration of the problem at once astonishingly simple and astonishingly strong."[2] The playful fascination with human differences transacted in the commercial culture increasingly became a weapon in the battles between capital versus labor, whiteness versus racial others, and pure versus mixed.

In this age in which "the sway of the new" flourished, not all that the eye could perceive could be counted on as reliable.[3] "The hand is quicker than the eye" captured but one aspect of the visual trickery that fascinated nineteenth-century men, women, and children. The rube eye needed to be educated about what was beneath surface appearance. As art historian Barbara Maria Stafford has demonstrated, one of the great challenges of Enlightenment intellectuals was to make the unseen visible by way of optical demonstrations. Appearances were deceptive.[4]

Bolstered by faith in their ability to pictorialize and survey all of nature and humankind, writers, artists, and inventors illustrated, photographed, and fabricated representations of the "real" for fun, education, profit, and political suasion. Those engaged in battling out the Chinese Question, pro, con, and in the middle, exploited the newly developed lithographic medium of the press to visualize their point of view. Yet the ever expanding republic of middle-class consumers purchased some images and plays while rejecting others. In the commercial culture they lionized those artists and writers whose representations more closely resonated with their prejudices; when such representations strayed from the mainstream of common perceptions, they ceased to be popular.

Visual form and content now affected public opinion, and both visuals and public opinion affected political policy. The work of three notable New York cultural figures of the post–Civil War era, Thomas Nast, Johannes Keppler, and Edward Harrigan, exemplify the changing dynamics of the power that cultural representations had over the fate of Chinese in the United States. The process of visualizing and making the imaginary "heathen Chinee" real in the commercial culture helped to pave the way for their criminalization and exclusion. As we shall see, these cultural representations would have a profound and long-lasting impact on the lives of Chinese New Yorkers and the early formation of Chinatown.

Thomas Nast and His "John Confucius"

Thomas Nast, the prolific political satirist best known for his drawings in *Harper's Weekly*, exemplifies a very different aspect of how representations

Figure 24. Ah Sin beats Bill Nye at cards, "The Heathen Chinee," 1871. Although Bret Harte had created Ah Sin to poke fun at anti-Chinese prejudice, he authorized such racial caricatures as this drawing by Sol Eytinge Jr. to accompany his poem. (Wong Ching Foo Collection)

of Chinese changed. In contrast to Harte's rather hapless artistic effort, Nast was in control of his art, political beliefs, and antipathies. Although he is remembered today for his caricatures of the Tammany tiger ousting Boss Tweed, his invention of the Democratic Party donkey and the Republican elephant, and his rosy-cheeked, rotund, and bearded Germanic Santa Claus,

Figure 25. Ca. 1870s. The stereotype of Ah Sin the trickster became pervasive in commercial popular culture. This novelty card is but one example of how Harte's character became a common reference to any Chinese man. (Wong Ching Foo Collection)

Nast was also engaged in arguing for Chinese equal rights, drawing over thirty cartoons on the subject from 1868 to 1886.

Thomas Nast was born in military barracks near Alsace in 1840. His father was a trombone player in a Bavarian regimental band who subscribed to the republican ideals bubbling up in the growing revolutionary movement. Like many "forty-eighters," the elder Nast saw the United States as the beacon of secular, liberal, Protestant, and romantic nationalist values. He sent his family to New York City in 1846 and soon joined them on Greenwich Street. As a skilled musician and German émigré, Nast's father became a member of the Philharmonic Society and played in the house band of Burton's Theater on Chambers Street. Through his father's world Nast was exposed to the constellation of cultural performances in the city. He saw Barnum's Jenny Lind at Castle Garden, sat with his father in the orchestra pit watching the latest plays, and sketched his favorite scenes. Evident in his political drawings is a strong sense of the proscenium framing his subjects. Indeed, his placement of people, their costuming, the sets, and their melodramatic poses seem to come directly out of a theatrical staging tradition.[5]

In stark contrast to what was possible for Chinese immigrants, Germans were able to begin taking part immediately in the cultural, economic, and political life of the city. Nast, for example, was first trained in drawing by the German-trained Theodore Kaufmann, a historical painter. At Kaufmann's 442 Broadway studio Nast was befriended by Alfred Fredericks, a well-known painter of the time. With Fredericks's guidance the talented Nast entered the Academy of Design on Thirteenth Street just east of Broadway. By the age of fifteen Nast felt enough confidence in his work to approach Frank Leslie, who that same year had founded the illustrated national news weekly bearing his name. Leslie was just introducing the wood-block engraving printing process in the United States. Illustrations soon enabled *Leslie's* and *Harper's Weekly* to dominate the burgeoning national market. By 1860 *Leslie's* boasted a circulation of over 160,000, with *Harper's* at 100,000. At *Leslie's* Nast could learn from a master of the process, Sol Eytinge Jr. Nast joined Eytinge, the future illustrator for Bret Harte's famous poem, and young Winslow Homer at *Harper's Weekly* in 1862. It was for his work at *Harper's* that Nast would become best known. The Civil War fostered the first generation of truly outstanding political artists, and Nast was foremost among them. The popularity and influence of his work rose with the victory of the North and fell with the failure of Reconstruction.[6] It is within this context that we can begin to approach Nast's drawings regarding the Chinese Question. Nast's radical Republican politics made him a staunch advocate of equal rights and universal suffrage, regardless of race or national origin. Yet the terms of his liberalism came with severe limits.

With his unambiguously noble "John Confucius" character, Nast consistently argued for equal rights for Chinese Americans. In his 1869 drawing "The Youngest Introducing the Oldest," Columbia plays the role of a good hostess and presents a dignified and princely robed Chinese, surrounded by Chinese crates, to European heads of state. Anson Burlingame, having completed his travail as the negotiator of the treaty bearing his name, is sitting behind the mustached Chinese ambassador. A caricature of the pope is aghast at the sight and fearfully peeks at the "heathen" from behind a pillar. "Brothers and sisters," says America, "I am happy to present to you the oldest member of the family, who deserves our better acquaintance." Alas, Nast wanted to believe that, with the great leadership of Anson Burlingame, China would become an equal among European nations—a member of the club.[7]

"Uncle Sam's Thanksgiving Dinner," drawn in 1868, further demonstrated Nast's evolving democratic iconoclasm. At a huge family table with a centerpiece celebrating "Self Government" and "Universal Suffrage," Uncle Sam is carving a turkey in front of a welcoming painting of Castle Garden, which had become New York's immigration depot. Columbia is flanked by an African American and his family and a Chinese man with his son and Japanese-garbed wife. All the nations and races of the world are represented at the table, with portraits of presidents George Washington, Abraham Lincoln, and Ulysses S. Grant looking on. "Come One Come All" and "Free and Equal," written on the bottom corners, further underscore Nast's proto-pluralist vision.[8]

Radical Republicans after the Civil War fought for equal access to secularized, but nevertheless Protestant-dominated, public institutions and insisted on the separation of church and state. In addition, reform issues such as temperance and ridding cities of corrupt (usually Democratic Party) politicians filled out their agenda. Nast's "Our Common Schools as They Are and as They May Be" sought to prevent public funds from being channeled into Catholic schools. In his top frame are the children of the world with hands joined, dancing in a joyful circle. An awkwardly drawn Chinese boy with pigtail flying is among them. In contrast, the bottom frame of "as They May Be," labeled "Sectarian Bitterness," includes racial caricatures of an Irish boy

Figure 26. Thomas Nast, *Harper's Weekly,* Nov. 20, 1869.
(Wong Ching Foo Collection)

clubbing a Jew and a black boy pulling the hair of a Chinese. In Nast's view this Old World sectarianism could be avoided if religion and government were kept separate.[9]

In contrast to the pluralism expressed by his male children, Nast's male adults have particularistic agendas. In "Church and State—No Union upon Any Terms" (1871) Nast shows Columbia at the grand building of the state rejecting the men of the world who are pulling their particular religions behind them. They are prohibited from entering the building by two soldiers holding bayoneted rifles. John Confucius, pulling a lotus-positioned "Heathen Chinee" deity, is prominently drawn among the rejected suitors. Upon the passage of the Chinese Exclusion Act by Congress in 1882, Nast drew the United States as "The Temple of Liberty" with a drawbridge. The soldiers guarding the entrance, dressed in European military outfits, are rejecting the passport of a Chinese man. The drawing is captioned "E Pluribus Unum (Except the Chinese)." In a similar vein, the 1870 drawing "Throwing Down the Ladder by Which They Rose" shows European Americans, having climbed a ladder into the United States, pushing the ladder away to prevent the Chinese just below from joining them.[10]

The most important Chinese Question drawings came in a series of seven full-page cartoons produced between 1871 and 1880, in the years leading up to exclusion when anti-Chinese feelings in California were beginning to spill over onto the national scene. These drawings clearly articulated Nast's

Figure 27. Thomas Nast, "E Pluribus Unum (Except the Chinese)," *Harper's Weekly,* Apr. 1, 1882. (Wong Ching Foo Collection)

Figure 28. Thomas Nast, "The Chinese Question," *Harper's Weekly*, Feb. 18, 1871.
(Wong Ching Foo Collection)

radical Republican and reform sensibilities: Irish and other immigrant rabble unfairly scapegoating racial groups, politicians corrupted by catering to the popular vote, and anti-Chinese agitation jeopardizing important diplomatic and trade relations with China.

February 1871 saw the publication of one of Thomas Nast's most powerful "pro-Chinese" drawings, a direct and angry response to the Chinese labor protests at Tompkins Square and North Arlington. Titled "The Chinese Question," the drawing depicts Columbia standing at center stage defending a huddled, overwhelmed Chinese American man.[11] She looks fiercely at a crowd of armed male rioters, shouting, "Hands off, gentlemen! America means fair play for all men." The rioters' faces are portrayed as threatening and animal-like, with deep-set beady eyes and menacing scowls. The leader is typical of Nast's anti-Irish caricatures; he holds a rock in one hand and a raised billy club in the other. The crowd has just burned down a "colored" orphan asylum during the New York City Draft Riots and are now ready to go after "John Chinaman." The wall of posters behind Columbia reproduces specific statements made about the Chinese; John Swinton's four objections to Chinese immigration are quoted verbatim, as is a racist statement by Wendell Phillips ("The Chinaman works cheap because he is a barbarian and seeks gratification of only the lowest, the most inevitable wants"). Democratic newspapers and trade unions are clearly represented as having stirred up hatred toward the poor "Chinaman," while a presumably Republican newspaper headlined "Crimes and Drunkeness [*sic*] / Riots by 'Pure White' Strikers / Europeans Are the Bulk of Our 'American' Pauperism" has been trampled on the ground. The same unruly mob reappears in three of the six other full-page drawings to represent the crowds supporting Senator James Blaine, the Sand Lots of San Francisco (the site of protests), and the Solid South.[12]

Racial groups were portrayed in Nast's drawings as caught between the purity and ideals of Columbia's America and the America of the unruly Democratic Party, marked by prejudice and mob violence. Nast consistently tried to draw parallels between the Chinese Question and the injustice visited upon African Americans, American Indians, and European immigrants. One February 1879 cover drawing encapsulated Nast's stand. John Confucius is looking upon a Kearney slogan, "The Chinese Must Go," while a pipe-and-rifle-toting "Red Gentleman" says, "Pale face 'fraid you crowd him out, as he did me." In the background a rather stereotyped lounging black man reclines on a bale of cotton with graffiti scrawled next to him, "My Day Is Coming." The genteel *Harper's* reader is reminded of the hypocrisy of ignorant Irish and German immigrants by a billboard covered with flyers saying, "Foreigners Not Wanted (His X Mark) Pat. Irish Esq." Lest good Americans forget, Nast has the lowest poster read "Knownothingism of the Past / 'Down with the Irish. Down with the Dutch.'" Here the exposure of hypocrisy and the appeal to a rationalistic morality were Nast's primary weapons. In a blunt and bold manner Nast attempted to pull together into an anti-anti-Chinese movement those who had fought slavery and regretted anti-Indian policies in the past or had themselves been victims of nativist prejudice.[13]

Denis Kearney, the leader of the Sand Lot protesters against the Chinese, and Senator Blaine, the ambitious anti-Chinese Republican from Maine, each appeared in four of the drawings.[14] Commenting on the demagoguery of Kearney's Workingmen's Party agitation, Nast featured Kearney front stage and center in a March 1880 cover drawing titled "The Ides of March. Don't—Put Him out of His Misery." The Irish leader is acting out a scene from Shakespeare's *Julius Caesar*, wearing a sandwich board that proclaims, "Brutus wanted! Kill me! I am prepared to die! And not only would the streets of San Francisco run in blood, but also New York, Boston, Chicago, and other eastern cities." Behind him stands a chorus of laughing caricatured Chinese; in depicting them, in carnivalesque fashion, as laughing, Nast reverses the melodramatic convention of using Chinese caricatures strictly for comic relief. Elsewhere Kearney appears as the unseen spirit urging crowds on toward violence.[15]

Nast's sharpest barbs were reserved for Senator Blaine, who is portrayed as a traitor to the grand cause. A front-page *Harper's Weekly* drawing from 1879 shows Blaine rejecting the teas, silks, porcelain, and carvings offered by John Confucius, thus trampling on the Burlingame Treaty, while catering to the ballot of a gross caricature of a black man who, though physically full-grown, is depicted in a childlike posture. Essentially Nast was saying that treaties, trade, and superior Chinese culture were not important to Blaine as long as he could gain the vote of an imbecilic, uncultivated former slave. The drawing was satirically captioned "The Civilization of Blaine," with John Confucius asking, "Am I not a man and a brother?"—the English abolitionists' slogan.[16]

In another drawing, featuring Blaine and others eating at "Kearney's Senatorial Restaurant," John Confucius is foregrounded clutching his stomach as he watches the politicians eating a "Mess of (Sand-Lot) Pottage." Confucius wonders, "How can Christians stomach such dirt?" In contrast to the mass of animal-faced workers, a neatly dressed, dignified-looking "Intelligent Workman" is shown lecturing an indignant Blaine, who is ripping a paper labeled "Chinese Cheap Labor." The poised hero/skilled craftsman is saying, "You need not plead my cause and my children's. I am able, and always have been, to take care of myself and mine; and no large military force is necessary to keep the peace, for real working-men are not rioters, strikers, and blowers."[17] The individualism of the "I am able... to take care of myself" was Nast's antidote to racism. Drawing on patrician forms of orientalist representation, he portrayed these refined Chinese as more than capable of rational self-determination in liberal capitalist society.

Historian Morton Keller was undoubtedly correct in emphasizing Nast's progressive stand on the rights of Chinese Americans and other racial minorities.[18] But it is possible to overstate this point, especially if we fail to consider the full range of Nast's drawings on the Chinese Question. He was a contradictory thinker and artist, not a simple champion of racial underdogs. Two early Nast drawings from 1870 indicate a more ambivalent stance. "The Martyrdom of St. Crispin," drawn in mid-July just weeks after the arrival of the Chinese workers in North Adams, shows a single European American shoemaker peacefully making boots. He has a halo over his head. Behind him stand two Chinese men with elongated heads holding swords labeled "Chop Sticks" and "Cheap Labor"—one of which is poised to cut the shoemaker's head off. On the background wall is written the title of John Swinton's anti-Chinese article, "The New Issue: The Chinese-American Question." In contrast to Nast's other "pro"-Chinese drawings, this statement is presented with no irony or satire. It is clearly an anti-Chinese "cheap labor" position.[19]

The issue of Chinese "cheap labor" is again stated in Nast's powerful full-page drawing of August 6 entitled "The New Comet—A Phenomenon Now Visible in All Parts of the United States." A comet in the shape of the pig-tailed head of a Chinese man is seen streaking across the nighttime sky. Bordered by an urban area with a factory "Closed by the Trade's Union Rules," a capital dome, a billboard saying "The Chinese Labor Question/The European Know Nothings Will Meet To Night," and a booth selling "Cheap Shoes," a huge crowd is out to view the phenomenon. Many hold placards, but they are of differing stances: "Down with Capital" and "The Chinese Must Be Wiped Out" are juxtaposed with "We Want Servants, Cooks, Nurses" and "This Country Is Large Enough for All." Caricatures of Irish-women and their children are in the foreground, while a "Capitalist," the "Press," "Politicians," and "Workingmen"—all of them male—are looking through giant telescopes. Unlike all Nast's other cartoons, this one does not

Figure 29. Thomas Nast, "The New Comet," *Harper's Weekly,* Aug. 6, 1870.
(Wong Ching Foo Collection)

appear to be taking a stand. Nast seems mainly to be noting the sudden appearance—and, presumably, disappearance—of the issue in national discourse. The crowd is not menacing or violent; it mainly appears to be engaged in spectatorship and debate.[20]

It can plausibly be argued that these 1870 cartoons represent the preliminary confrontation between the North Adams "cheap labor" question and Nast's equal-rights convictions, a confrontation that, once considered, was quickly resolved in favor of the Chinese. But even if this explanation is accurate, it does not explain a similar tension in his drawings of American Indians and African Americans, whom he represented sometimes as being fully dignified and suffering injustice and sometimes as undeserving of equal rights. Nast represented Indians and blacks as victims of prejudice in "'Every Dog' (No Distinction of Color) 'Has His Day' " and "'The Nigger Must Go' and 'The Chinese Must Go,'" yet he also showed them as savage, lazy, or childlike in "The New Alliance," "Patience until the Indian Is Civilized—So to Speak," "The Civilization of Blaine," and "Hard to Please the 'White

Trash.'"[21] Instead of understanding Nast's cartoons as consistently pro-underdog, we would do well to recognize his dualistic iconographic language.

Chinese laborers, in contrast to the aristocratic John Confucius, usually appear in Nast's drawings with highly exaggerated elongated heads. "Pacific Chivalry," for example, shows a fierce-looking California man with a raised tomahawk holding the pigtail of an escaping Chinese.[22] This drawing can be too easily misinterpreted as evidence of Nast's support for Chinese immigration. Yet the highly misshapen head—even giving Nast artistic credit for using the shape to emphasize the violent action—leaves the reader with a sense of Chinese as highly distorted creatures. The four Chinese men standing behind a finely drawn likeness of Denis Kearney in "The Ides of March" are also gross caricatures. Their heads and faces are quite grotesque, with huge smiles and slanted eyes and eyebrows. It could be argued that Nast was not a great figurative artist and simply did not know how to draw Chinese. If this is true, then why was John Confucius drawn in a more sympathetic manner? And what explains the consistently fine hand Nast used to draw political figures, such as Blaine, and symbolic figures, such as Columbia? These Chinamen were clearly crudely iconographic bit players drawn quickly as typically staged yellowface types.

Nast's drawings "A Paradox" and "Blaine Language" give some idea as to why these Chinese were drawn the way they were. "A Paradox" shows what would happen if the Chinese became citizens and began voting. It depicts two European American men, representing the Democratic and Republican parties, tugging at the Chinese man in the middle. The Chinese caricature in the middle, knock-kneed, with slanted eyes and open mouth, is responding limply, like a stuffed doll. His expression is everything: he is walleyed, and his queue is standing straight up in fright. The scene could easily have been copied from a comedy routine on the Bowery or Broadway stage, where Chinese cooks, laundrymen, and servants were portrayed in a burlesque manner.[23]

"Blaine Language" features the same Chinese caricature with slanted eyes and open mouth. This time he is identified as none other than "Ah Sin." At the table are Senator Blaine, cast in the role of "Truthful James," and a thuggish Irish caricature playing "Tramp Nye." In a direct quotation from Bret Harte's poem, "Truthful" Blaine is shown kicking the "Heathen Chinee" off stage.[24] While Nast probably styled his John Confucius caricature after the ambassadors of the Burlingame mission as photographed by Matthew Brady, his Chinese-worker caricature comes straight from the New York stage and Bret Harte. Instead of understanding Nast as consistently defending the Chinese against American hypocrisy and intolerance, then, it would be more accurate to understand him as also subject to the conventional racial attitudes of his day. With hindsight, it can be said that his political message communicated one thing, but his drawings revealed other attitudes as well.

Following Sir John Tenniel and John Leech of *Punch* (the premiere British humor journal established in 1841) as well as French and German practitioners, Nast adopted certain rules on how to draw people. In an Anglo-American culture preoccupied with classification, faces, head shapes, and bodies were all viewed as telling the truth about a person or group of people. The science of physiognomy was carefully studied by art students in both Britain and the United States. The various shapes of noses, eyes, jaws, and foreheads were drawn and compared with all the detailed care of a Linnaean taxonomist. Anglo-American caricatures exemplified the Victorian distinction made between the character of a person and the type. The visual artist, writer, and the physiognomist used the term *type* in essentially the same way.

In the United States, Nast carried on with the traditional Anglo-American caricature of the degraded low-class Irish, but he was faced with the additional challenge of representing other racial groups living in the United States. In genteel English society, class was primary and race secondary; racial others were part of the empire, though not living within the heart of the British Isles. The United States had a very different configuration. With a legacy of being first a colonial outpost and then a developing country, of privatizing the land of the continent's native peoples and then bringing in racial others to labor, the United States was far more racially diverse. Hence, race partially displaced class in the American hierarchy of peoples. Nast's Protestant-bound radical republicanism essentially transplanted the visual language of Anglo-American antipathy for the Irish and then folded in Indians, Chinese, and blacks. The Irish and other immigrants were depicted as violent mobs who wanted absolute power. Racial minorities were caught in their greedy designs. Nast's ideas of equal rights and universal suffrage communicated one set of ideas while at the same time his drawings, which uncritically followed the Anglo-American tradition of racial types, communicated a different set of messages.

It is in this larger context that Nast's use of Bret Harte deserves comment. In 1879 Nast evoked Bret Harte's poem "Truthful James" in two consecutive weeks. Why he was so suddenly inspired to refer to Harte's work is unclear. It is possible that one of the revivals of Harte's play *Ah Sin*, written with Samuel Clemens, was then making the circuit in New York, or, just as likely, that Nast rediscovered the poem, the 1874 "The Heathen Chinee Musical Album" by Tucker, or a playbill in his study.[25] Whatever the case may be, he was evoking the memory of a poem and a play that were read ambiguously. In "Blaine Language" Nast juxtaposed Blaine and the Irish thug against Joaquin Miller's quotations about ill and unjust treatment received by the Chinese in California. The message was clear and straightforward: Ah Sin was unfairly treated. But the week before, Nast had used Ah Sin in an opposite manner. While still excoriating Irish intolerance, represented by "Kearney's Equal Rights," a grinning Chinese mandarin or merchant is delighted by the news that Uncle Sam has come up with an anti-Chinese bill. Signs reading "No Foreign Devils Wanted" and "American Produce Market Closed" indicate Chinese prejudice against the West. The limits on the rights of Chinese in the United States become a welcome pretext for closing down the rights of American traders in China. Titled "Ah Sin Was His Name," the drawing depicts the "Heathen Chinee" as saying, "That is just what I have been longing for." Here Ah Sin is the wily victor, quite happy to keep Chinese trade away from the United States.[26] Thomas Nast understood Chinese as both victims and as racial stereotypes. Just as abolitionists were not necessarily antiracist and were sometimes even Negrophobic, Nast's stand on formal equal rights did not mean that he thought Chinese were his racial equals.

Nast's exposure to living and breathing Chinese and other racial groups was probably quite limited. His drawings indicate familiarity with the representational conventions of Chinese in literature and on stage, but not much other knowledge. His representations were limited to and typical of the mainstream political culture. Indeed, analyzing the melodramas and the pictorial arts of Nast's era helps explain both the possibilities and the limits of his radicalism. Nast's stark and powerful delineations of good and bad were commensurate with the melodramas popular on the New York stage.[27] His stock lead characters were supported by minor characters who simply provided a foil for a display of virtue or villainy. For example, noble John Confucius was depicted standing front and center, with those around him— Senator Blaine and the caricatured childlike black man—serving only to embody various types of folly. When, on the other hand, Denis Kearney was cast as a mock–Julius Caesar, the misshapen Chinese Ah Sins in the background were but the Greek chorus and were not drawn with any sympathy.

At one moment the black man or "Yellow Gentleman" would be acting the lead and would be drawn in a dignified, if victimized, manner; at another moment, one or the other would be the foil for the new lead.

Thomas Nast was the preeminent pioneer of American political drawing, in part because his talent could be developed and disseminated via the mass circulation of *Harper's Weekly*. But more important, he synthesized European political satire with the particularities of the American social experience—and in so doing created a uniquely American political art. It is worth analyzing Nast's iconography so as to understand the borrowed visual language upon which he elaborated.

For example, Nast's use of classical architectural elements, columns, and doorway finials in drawings such as "Church and State—No Union upon Any Terms" could be understood as simply reflecting the neoclassicism of the actual public buildings and monuments of New York, Washington, D.C., and other American cities. Yet his repeated placement of Columbia in these scenes, a symbolic white-robed figure with flowing hair, protecting the building of state, indicates that he was using these classical icons of republican ideology specifically to represent the highest ideals of American political culture. He was reiterating the nationalist contention that civilization had reached a zenith in American democracy, in a direct lineage from Greco-Roman culture.

More important, in sharp contrast to his racial groups, Nast's Columbia exemplifies prevailing Anglo-American ideals of beauty and strength of character. Whereas Columbia's facial features embody the visual sensibilities of the upper- and middle-class Anglo-Saxon Protestant mainstream, Nast's Irish crowds are drawn according to the conventional British caricature of the Irish as lowly and thuggish: they are unkempt and simian, with square jaws, low foreheads, and upturned noses. Moreover, whereas Columbia is always represented in Nast's drawings as a principled individual seeking justice, the Irish are generally portrayed in a crowd, with little individuation. Columbia represents the pinnacle of racial purity and individual enlightenment, the Americanized version of the British Norman-aristocratic ideal, while the Irish are reduced to mass physiognomic social types. Columbia is the ideal, and the Irish are the opposite. Yet without the one, the other has no contrast to give it meaning; each representation is dependent on the other.

Nast may have proclaimed that all the races in the United States should be able to vote, but his drawings clearly said that "equal rights" did not mean "equal standing." Just as capitalists should have the right to use Chinese labor to sustain their positions in society, so Chinese laborers should have the right to sell their labor in the most menial jobs the country offered. As many capitalists and business-oriented radical Republicans argued, the color line could drive class relationships. The white man could be elevated by colored labor. Individual characters rose to prominence within Nast's racial types. John Confucius and Senator Blaine were caught between the battle of Columbia and the likes of Denis Kearney and corrupt Tammany Hall Democrats.

At the height of his artistic powers and political influence, Nast argued fervently and effectively for his vision of a just nation. It was to be governed by the Republican Party, which represented the forces of social justice, enlightened nationalism, liberalism, social reform, and economic development. The nation was to be a virtuous one, subscribing to essentially Protestant, middle-class values. It was to be a prosperous and self-sacrificing one, united on the grounds of national well-being. As historian Morton Keller has ably pointed out, in the course of his career Nast focused on "the secessionist, the Democrat, the Negrophobe, the drunkard, [and] the inflationist" as threats to the "Radical Nation" of his ideals. Party affiliation meant everything to Nast: "The parties . . . represented not only differing political interests, but the fundamentally opposed governmental and social ideologies of the [Civil War] itself." Nast's job at *Harper's Weekly* provided him with a ready-made audience for this vision of a just nation. It was genteel, middle-class, Protestant, Republican, and primarily Northern. Yet it should also be noted that Nast's audience continued to grow because he spoke to their sensibilities, in particular political messages and, more subtly, in terms of their worldview. When Nast took on Boss Tweed, subscriptions tripled.[28]

Nast's ability to speak to and for his audience was particularly apt with respect to the confusion of race, class, and ethnicity that prevailed in the growing urban areas. In much the same way that the trade in luxury goods had allowed an earlier generation of Americans to address issues of distinction and identity, Nast's political cartoons helped his readership articulate a sense of who they were and who they weren't. What was unresolved in Nast was probably also unresolved among his readers.

As the United States entered the grip of a prolonged industrial depression that continued from 1873 to 1878, more working men and women turned to political protest as a way of pushing for social solutions. Nast's faith in his party and the nation began to erode. His anti-Irish stance became part of a larger antilabor position. By 1882, with the impending passage of the Chinese Exclusion Act, he had become disillusioned with both parties. The drawing "(Dis-) Honors Are Easy" shows "Liberty" and "Freedom to All" being threatened by political opportunism. On the verge of falling over a cliff into the ocean, the Republican elephant is shown clinging to the Democratic Tammany tiger, which is clinging in turn to the queue of a Chinese man holding on to the uprooting tree of liberty.[29]

After Reconstruction, Nast lost his hold on the public imagination. By the 1880s, the *Harper's* audience no longer wanted to be reminded of the "bloody shirt" of the Civil War. It was an audience that Nast no longer understood. His career was emblematic of the dissolution of the radical Republican vision. Parallel changes affected the representation of China and the Chinese. Older ways of thinking were receding in the face of the new urban and industrial realities of New York and the United States. As Nast's fortunes ebbed and his drawings became drained of life and meaning, Bret Harte's fortunes rose, his Ah Sin taking on a life and meaning that Harte had never intended. And Johannes Keppler, the founder of *Puck*, was poised to assume Nast's role as the nation's most popular and powerful political cartoonist. But the nation had lost an influential cultural activist, one who, though his message was mixed, had championed the cause of equal rights for African Americans and Chinese Americans.

"The Chinese Invasion" by Keppler

Nast, having had numerous fights with the *Harper's* editor over his artistic freedom of expression, greatly envied Keppler for owning his own publication—something Nast was unable to achieve until 1893. In contrast to Nast's increasingly unfashionable radical republicanism, Keppler flaunted an independence from both parties and advocated a reform sensibility resonant with the rising liberalism of the Gilded Age. *Puck*'s fortunes grew fabulously during the 1880s. Beginning in a small storefront office at 13 North William Street in 1876, the paper moved into the monumental Puck Building uptown on Houston Street in 1886.[30] Keppler's cartoons were spirited and humorous. His color lithographs freely deployed racial caricatures while also tweaking politicians for hypocrisy.

Though Keppler was a defender of the Chinese right to immigrate to the United States, his 1880 drawing "The Chinese Invasion" illustrates the shifting representation of Chinese after Harte's 1870 "Truthful James" poem.

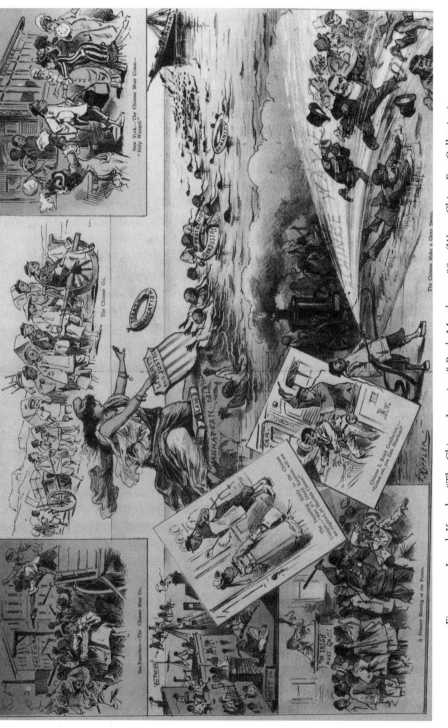

Figure 30a. Joseph Keppler, "The Chinese Invasion," *Puck*, March 12, 1880. (Wong Ching Foo Collection)

The Chinese Make a Clean Sweep.

Figure 30b. Detail of Keppler's "The Chinese Invasion."

This three-color centerfold illustration was essentially anti-Irish and nominally pro-Chinese. After being ousted by intolerant Irish and working-class mobs in San Francisco, Keppler's Chinese arrive in New York in ever greater numbers, filling Mott Street to the rooftops. This "Chinese Wave," in carnivalesque fashion, displaces the Irish—taking their jobs and beating them up. A volunteer Chinese fire company is shown washing the city clean of Mayor John Kelley, the successor to "Boss" Tweed, and the corruption of the Irish Democrats.[31]

Keppler's Chinese appear to be drawn with the same underlying physiognomic assumptions as Nast's: they have queues and oblong skulls, low foreheads and protruding jaws. However, in significant contrast to Nast's Chinese, Keppler's central image borrows on the longtime association of the Chinese with rats. As the ship of California is sinking, hordes of rats are jumping off and swimming toward Manhattan Island. Halfway there, the rats turn into Chinese men and their tails transform into queues. Keppler's Columbia, sitting on the bedrock of law, welcomes them with the shield of "Liberty and Justice" and throws out life preservers marked "Treaty Obligations," "Protection of Industry," and "Humanity."[32]

In this drawing Keppler conveys a double and countervailing message. On the one hand he is clearly standing for the rights of Chinese to be in the United States for legal, economic, and humanitarian reasons. On the other hand he fully and unquestioningly accepts the association of Chinese with rats, a subject I shall more fully explore in chapter 11. And with such an equation Keppler reinforces the notion that the Chinese are coming in hordes, quickly overpopulating the already crowded tenements of the Lower East Side. Indeed, the Chinese are represented as being so prolific that they soon take over as the Irish had done before them. Keppler satirizes the Irish while at the same time expressing some real anxiety over the new arrivals that are displacing them. The shift from Harte's Ah Sin to Keppler's rats is a telling indicator of the changing nature of the "pro-Chinese" support that culminated in the 1882 Chinese Exclusion Act. Race, physiognomy, and character were becoming so deeply intertwined in late-Victorian thought that the view of Chinese as equals or as people to be admired was becoming less and less possible in the land of "Liberty and Justice."

While it is clear that Nast's drawings represented the passing of radical republicanism and Keppler's the coming concern with urban reformism, the two artists still had a great deal in common. Both were German émigrés, and they had essentially identical underlying views of racial types. Keppler's Chinese and Irish were drawn according to the same physiognomic principles as Nast's. They caricatured crowds in essentially the same way; whether Irish or Chinese, their crowd figures were of a generic type featuring protruding, animal-like jaws. Their Chinese were drawn with high cheekbones and chimpanzee mouths, while their Irish were drawn in classic Anglo-American fashion, with square-jawed, large-nostriled, gorilla faces. In a sense Nast's and Keppler's shared physiognomic principles of drawing people far outweighed their generational and political differences.[33]

Although Keppler claimed to be in favor of Chinese immigration, his highly coded representation of the Chinese tended to turn them (like his Irish) into objects of ridicule and scorn. Keppler in a sense argued for Chinese rights through the back door. If the Irish, who were inherently so degraded a race, were to be accepted as immigrants and citizens, should not the comparably degraded race of the Chinese be granted the same status? If Nast's "The Chinese Question" was melodrama, then "The Chinese Invasion" was pure farce. Appearing on stage: Chinese men who are just as violent and narrow-minded as the Irish, Irishmen receiving their just desserts, an "ugly" Irishwoman threatening the "Haythin Chinee" in her uneducated dialect, and misguided ladies fawning over the arriving packs of rats morphing into apelike servants.[34] Keppler's audience clearly enjoyed the spectacle of these comical others burlesquing before their eyes. The self they knew was largely male, Anglo-Saxon, and genteel. They were secure and comfortable in the knowledge that they were superior to these comical figures.

Keppler's success and his genius resided in his understanding of how to appeal to this secure knowledge while making his audience laugh.

As European Americans, both Nast and Keppler enjoyed the freedom to create visual representations of racial others. Market segmentation set boundaries for both, but it did not interfere with their freedom to caricature either the Irish or the Chinese. The Irish masses were not the target audience of *Puck* (and the same was certainly true for *Harper's*); they subscribed to more sympathetic Democratic Party–oriented fare. More important than protests against Chinese exclusion, however, was the shaping of the artists' minds by the racially inscribed conventions of the time. Their arguments for tolerance operated solely within the framework of hierarchical racial science. This contradiction between explicit argument and underlying form was emblematic of the times—enlightened and modernizing, yet profoundly fixated on racial categorization as a primary means of organizing and understanding everyday life and the world.

Yet even if Nast and Keppler had seen themselves clearly enough to wish to reject these underlying physiognomic assumptions, it is unlikely that they could have maintained either their following or their freedom of expression. Even if they themselves could have transcended the racial taste of the times, it is unlikely that their constituencies could have done the same. While they professed to support Chinese immigration and equal rights, their far more powerful visual messages conveyed a message of Chinese racial inferiority. It would be only a matter of time before the rhetoric and the iconography would coincide in one united statement of Chinese unassimilability. Ironically, but understandably, this new anti-Chinese discourse would emerge from the group with which the early Chinese community intermixed both socially and culturally. The New York Irish playwright Edward Harrigan, among others, reformulated Irish-Chinese relations in a way that made the Chinese the inferior others of striving Irish Americans.

Edward Harrigan's Others

To improve their lot, aspiring Irish writers and performers took advantage of opportunities available to them in the expanding commercial culture. The publishing industry was already well established and was dominated by Protestant elites, but new and more popular forms of commercial culture were open to the Irish. As Sean Wilentz and Christine Stansell have demonstrated, the Bowery, with its accessible, popular commercial forms of entertainment, as opposed to the far more proper Broadway venues, was a dynamic commercial marketplace for mechanics, self-styled "Bowery Boys," and newly arriving immigrants. And such creative individuals as Ned Harrigan and, later, Chuck Connors, who made their careers on the Bowery stage, exemplified the way in which generations of Irish performers were able to build their success upon stereotyped representations of themselves and others in this dynamic, complex popular culture.[35]

Edward Harrigan has often been called the "American Dickens"; he and his partner Tony Hart were the "American Gilbert and Sullivan." After leaving blackface minstrelsy for variety theater in 1873, Harrigan wrote a series of plays that portrayed everyday ethnic life in the Lower East Side for the mostly male Bowery theatergoing audiences. In contrast to the gross Irish caricatures of minstrelsy, Harrigan developed Irish portraits of much greater depth and range. While he still built upon the long-established stereotypes of Hibernian laziness, brawling, and drinking, his Irish characters represented a far greater range of personalities. One of his main characters, Dan Mulligan, was a positive and realistic figure that Irish audiences could identify with. Mulligan proved so popular with audiences that Harrigan wrote and produced a series of plays that developed the protagonist into a flesh-and-blood person. As Robert Toll has pointed out, Harrigan's audiences both laughed at and laughed with his Irish. He wrote for a popular multiethnic, European American, male audience that wanted fast-paced and clear-cut contrasts. In effect, Harrigan broke through the Anglo-Protestant-dominated representational hierarchy of ethnic and racial groups by injecting a positive Irish image into the commercial theater. Via Harrigan's writing and performances, the Irish were in effect brought into the mainstream public culture.[36]

However, African Americans and Chinese were also among Harrigan's stock characters, and although his Irish representations had broken past the bounds of minstrelsy, his depictions of these other two groups had not.[37] While Denis Kearney was leading the Workingmen's Party movement against Chinese immigration on the Pacific coast, Harrigan was representing Chinese to large audiences in New York theaters. Drawing upon decades of Chinese caricatures in melodrama and minstrelsy, Harrigan regularly referred to the Chinese as part of the Lower East Side scene.

Harrigan introduced his main Chinese character in 1879, in his sketch *Mulligan Guard Chowder*.[38] "Hog-Eye," portrayed as a lustful, pidgin-English-speaking laundryman with a penchant for stealing clothing, was Harrigan's main comic antagonist to Dan Mulligan. Harrigan drew upon the well-known presence of Chinese-Irish couples and families in the Lower East Side and played out scenes pitting the oddball Chinese against dignified, if flawed, Irish heroes and heroines. In *The Mulligans' Silver Wedding*, for example, Hog-Eye is caught trying to steal Mrs. Dublin's clothes, and a comic fight ensues:

> *Mrs. Dublin:* I own that pulley line, you come over from China, you rat eater, and you put your hands on a dacent lady's property. Let go your holt of it.
>
> *Hog-Eye:* Me velly goodee man. Me likee you. Me no likee fightee.
>
> *Mrs. Dublin:* You're not half a man. Your a nagur, you eat your dinner with drum sticks. You're a monkey, you have a tail growing out of your head.
>
> *Hog-Eye:* No gettee madee. Me likee you. Makee velly goodee wifee allee same Melican ladee, Miss-ee Hog-Eye.
>
> *Mrs. Dublin:* You're a mongrel Asiatic. Would you propose the marriage lines to me. What don't ye have whiskers on your face like a man, you baboon you.
>
> *Hog-Eye:* Welly nicee ladee you. Comeetop side house somee time. Smokee pipe o mee. All-er same chinaman, all-er same, Ilish man.
>
> *Mrs. Dublin:* It's the rotten pipe you smoke. The neighbors are moving out of Mulligan Alley from the fumes of it. The likes of ye coming to a free country and walking around in petticoats and calling yourself a man, Bah, ye omadoon, ye.
>
> *Hog-Eye:* Welly good-ee pipe smok-ee, Ilish ladee smokee one pipe opium see Ilish heaven soon up quick.

After impugning Hog-Eye's manliness, or lack thereof, for not being willing to stand up to the likes of Denis Kearney, and for undermining her laundry prices, Mrs. Dublin ends the scene with a standard comic climax, a brawling "mix-up." Harrigan wrote in his stage directions, "Mrs. Dublin beats Hog-Eye, puts him in horse trough, pumps [water] on him. Policeman enters alley gate. Gets drink from back of Wee Drop Saloon passed out to him. He exits after drink laughing at fight."[39] The caricature's exaggerated appearance—with skullcap, queue, and makeup—his bumbling yet predictable attempt to lure the Irishwoman into smoking opium, his inability to compete honestly with Irish washerwomen, and his childlike demeanor typified what was presented in such entertainments to white male audiences.

There were no Chinese individuals successfully performing as minstrels or in variety shows, or writing for such venues. Small numbers, language difficulties, and societal marginalization combined to discourage such involvement in commercial theater. The Chinese had no Harrigan, Thomas Nast, or Johannes Keppler to break the bounds of the one-dimensional portrayals fostered by the commercial culture, nor was there any audience base for more realistic portrayals. Given this vacuum, Irish writers and performers like Edward Harrigan played a particularly strategic role in presuming to represent "Chinese" on the New York stage, and the representation was a decidedly racist one. How can this phenomenon of New York Irish prejudice be explained?

Given the nation's fundamental social dichotomy of white and free versus black and unfree, American social identities have been inextricably tied into a basic hierarchy of race—a hierarchy quickly complicated by other migrants and immigrants variously defined as "ethnic" or "racial" groups. Within the discourse of Irish-British relations, colonized Irish Catholics were de facto cast as an inferior race. Yet when the Irish entered the black/white discourse of the United States, they could occupy a more ambiguous position in the social hierarchy. Irish Catholics were despised by Protestant patricians yet privileged over African slaves and freed men.[40] In the face of mainstream antipathy, a positive Irish American identity was being forged within the existing (Protestant) pro-white/anti-black discourse. The classic means for Irish Catholics to defuse the longstanding Anglo-American and European-Protestant hatred toward them was to symbolically displace this valuation onto an even lower group.

It is useful to compare the hierarchies in the racial representations of Thomas Nast, Johannes Keppler, and Edward Harrigan. Nast presented the Anglo as on top, the Chinese as in the middle, and the Irish as on the bottom. Keppler had the Irish and Chinese both on the bottom fighting it out, while Harrigan had the Irish in the middle and the Chinese and African Americans below. Within this Anglo-Saxon discourse, Irish New Yorkers played a key role in fighting for the broadening of the Anglo-American identity and for the formation of a new, pan-European race of "whites." By emphasizing Irish humanness and exaggerating African and Chinese differences within the given parameters of New York commercial culture, Irish performers were able to recreate themselves in the eyes of the greater society. With large enough numbers and votes, their "otherness" could be reified in the United States into a pan-European American whiteness, precisely because of the existence of African Americans and Chinese who could be reconstituted as "others" to the Irish.

Within the arena of race, cultural representations played a decisive role in manifesting preexisting attitudes and further refining their articulation. Even when such representations were, like Bret Harte's and Thomas Nast's, not created with the explicit intention of denigrating Chinese, a naturalized hierarchy of racial relations could easily be read in them. In order to find effective and resonant means of expressing their ideas to their audiences, Harte, Nast, Keppler, and Harrigan created caricatures whose effect on American culture and identity has been long-lasting. Harte's sly, childlike Ah Sin as the Heathen Chinee, Nast's courtly John Confucius and his victimized and deformed lower-class brethren, Keppler's rat-men, and Harrigan's comical and lusty Hog-Eye have all became standard stereotypes of Chinese men. Disseminated from New York City, capital of the nation's commercial culture, these representations reached people in all parts of the United States.[41]

The caricatures created by these artists were quickly assimilated into general public and political discourse about the Chinese in America. For example, a few months after the Chinese laundry workers' arrival in South Belleville, New York City newspaper coverage began incorporating elements of Bret Harte's poem. Directly borrowing Harte's tongue-in-cheek phrase, the New York World's headlines unambiguously proclaimed the arrival of "The Heathen Chinee," and the Newark Daily Advertiser wrote of "The Heathen Chinese in Our Midst." Harte's Ah Sin was regularly invoked when referring to Captain Hervey's laundry workers. Indeed, one article spoke of their "stereotyped smile and the unmitigated chignon, which we are beginning to associate with the 'Heathen Chinee.' These men, like the Chinese depicted in illustrations of Harte's poem, did not seem very "manly." Their loose-fitting dress, shaven foreheads, and long braided hair confused reporters who were attempting to describe them for their readers. A reporter for the World, for example, wrote that he wanted to "look hard at them" so that he could "tell about their faces," which, from the ethnological point of view of the time, should reveal something about their race. "Well, they are not an uncomely race," wrote the reporter. "Some look stupid, some much like our Indians; but many have a delicate, even girlish appearance." Another reporter described them as "the dainty-fingered Chinese"; yet another stated that their celebration of the Chinese New Year evoked the image of "a room full of insane women."[42]

Reporters also focused on the pidgin English of Captain Hervey's workers. The *World* journalist reported his conversation with a "Charlie Ming" and a "Charlie Sing" as if it were verbatim. The interview begins with Hervey giving Ming permission to speak openly with the reporter, encouraging him as a father might encourage a shy child:

Mr. Harvey [*sic*]—It's all right, Charlie. Tell him all. It is to put in the newspapers, to tell the people here who you are, and tell them in California that you came safe.

Ming—He want me name? Me name Charlie.

Reporter—What is your Chinese name?

M.—Challie.

R.—No, no. What is your real China name?

M.—China name is Ming.

The other "Charlie," Ah Sing, is described in a most revealing manner: "He speaks broken English readily; but being a fast talker of swift ideas it is impossible, for your correspondent at least, to understand him when he undertakes a long explanation, though his short answers are plain enough. He reads print pretty well, dodging the hard words as a child would do." The Chinese workers' laborious and broken speech, their apparent innocence, and their childlike manner all fit the caricature that was Ah Sin.[43]

In the New York City of 1870, satirical fiction about the Chinese became indistinguishable from what now had become documented "news." Indeed, even in the halls of Congress, Ohio Representative William Mungen rose before the House and used lines from the Harte poem to denounce the presence of Chinese in the United States.[44] Popular culture had become deeply inscribed in the racial politics of the nation, thereby affecting real, living Chinese New Yorkers. From 1870 onward, China and the Chinese would be presented in an increasingly negative, even virulent fashion that culminated in a series of landmark exclusionary laws.

To treat all the work of Harte, Nast, Keppler, and Harrigan simply as inaccurate stereotypes misses a very important political shift in the actual representations. Although Keppler and Harrigan could not have disagreed more on their representations of the Irish, they reached a consensus on the Chinese. Despite their very different constituencies, both artists visualized their Chinamen as "rats." In other words, both Keppler and Harrigan show that cultural differences were coming to be understood biologically—materially and politically benefiting the formation of "white" identities over the "inferior" races of humankind. In effect, the identity of the occidental citizen was formulated in the process of European immigrants perpetuating and refining definitions of racial otherness. The power to form public opinion soon became the power to form national immigration policy. Real, living Chinese people became the casualties.

CHAPTER 10

Building
Community

In 1873 Mr. Wo Kee moved his general-goods store from Oliver near Cherry Street to above Chatham Square at 34 Mott Street. His store has generally been credited as the beginning of New York's Chinatown. The store's relocation was typical of the broad movement of the settlement's population away from the docks of the Fourth Ward up into the Sixth Ward. We now know that this store's move did not inaugurate the formation of a new community, but it did correspond with a major demographic change. The growing anti-Chinese debates in the nation had a significant impact on the nature of this settlement.

The census of 1880 reported 748 Chinese living in Manhattan, with another 143 living in Brooklyn and Newark. While still far smaller than the twenty-one thousand or more living in San Francisco, the New York City Chinese quarter was the largest east of the Sierra Nevadas. With the completion of the transcontinental rail link and the increase of anti-Chinese violence in the West, Chinese migrated east, increasing the ranks of those already there. The new arrivals added to the complexity of an already creolized, multicultural, multilayered community characteristic of the port of New York.[1]

A Continuing Settlement

From the 1850s to 1870 the uniquely mixed New York community of merchant mariners, cigar makers, Chino-Latinos, and Chinese-Irish families persisted, while witnessing internal changes. Examining the profiles for both the Fourth and Sixth Wards in 1865 shows that among the Chinese residents there were twenty-eight cigar makers, twenty-three sailors, five retailers, three stewards, two candy makers, one peddler, one cook, and one boarding-house keeper. Despite the occasional exhibition of Chinese women by Barnum and others, no Chinese woman seems to have actually settled in New York by this date, although two to three Chinese women were reported by 1870. Of these sixty-four men, eighteen (almost one-third), were married to European American women, with twenty-one children among them.[2] All the women's occupations were listed as "keeping house."[3]

The Fourth Ward still had its section of sailors, now accumulating some stability and modest wealth. Most served as cooks, stewards, and table waiters earning $20, $30, and sometimes as much as $40 per month in addition to board. Despite the *Times*'s assertion that Chinese were living "in the worst hovels," one sector of the community was doing fairly well. Thirty-five-year-old seaman William Assing, for example, lived at 66 Cherry Street with his Irish wife, Bridget Assing, age thirty-three, and their four boys: John, age fourteen, William, age six, James, age three, and George, two months. William Senior disclosed to the census taker that he had accumulated a personal wealth of $700, the equivalent of twenty-three months' pay for a sailor. Of the other six households (making up thirty-two people) in the tenement, two more were Chinese. John and Mary Ahoa had twelve-year-old Francis and three-year-old Mary. They had saved $300. John and Caroline Arwo, with their two children Orville and John, had saved $400. These sailors had clearly done well and were living among fairly comfortable Prussians, English, and Irish. One Prussian neighbor, a grocer, had saved $1,000. Nearby, James Ewing, a forty-eight-year-old Chinese ship steward, stated his personal wealth to be $800. Bridget Ewing, a thirty-eight-year-old Irishwoman, no doubt added to these savings by putting up boarders in their apartment—a West Indian sailor, an Indian cook, and two Chinese ship's stewards. Their savings were substantial for Chinese New Yorkers and others living in the crowded and modest buildings of the Fourth Ward, yet a far cry from the wealth of John Bernard, the local non-Chinese tea dealer from England, who at age forty-five had amassed $3,000.[4]

It seems plausible that these more established sailors and stewards were among the Chinese mariners who were employed on the coastal shipping routes, cited by an 1873 *New-York Times* article. Ships on these routes were generally away for shorter periods of time and were regularly scheduled. It is possible that these routes became preferred among family-oriented mariners who wanted more predictable return dates.[5] These merchant mariners were among the earliest Chinese to enter service-sector work, predating the lower-paid landlocked domestic workers in New York.

Whereas some Chinese sailors, in what can now count as a twenty-year-old Chinese settlement, seem to have done well, a dramatic shift was evident in another corner of the Fourth Ward. In what was probably the Franklin Square area, where sailors John Canaugh, John Asam, and Singmer Dosia once lived, there resided a cluster of nineteen Chinese cigar makers in three dwellings. Among them, seventeen gave John as their first name, with only one adopting a totally Anglo name (John Williams), and five married to Anglo or Irishwomen. None listed personal wealth; one couple had a sixteen-year-old apprentice Irish sailmaker as a boarder, and the lone peddler in the area was the elderly John Auchung, who boarded in Ann Murphy's apartment. At fifty-four, Auchung was the oldest Chinese New Yorker listed in the census.

In contrast to the impoverished cigar peddlers of 1855, the strong presence of cigar makers indicates that some Chinese men had managed to enter a trade with decent pay. Paid as piecework and requiring not inconsiderable skill to do well, cigar making offered more opportunity for higher earnings. By the 1870s the annual wages for male cigar makers in the Fourth Ward ranged from $350 to as much as $1,000, making the pay at least as good as that of sailors.[6] The trade had the added advantage of being locally based, requiring relatively little capital to open one's own shop. Cigar making was a skill in high demand throughout U.S. urban areas.[7]

During this time the cigar-making trade was highly fraternal, organized with ethnically protective apprenticeship customs. The first Chinese to enter the trade arrived by way of their contract labor in Cuba. Of the four grades of cigars, clear Havanas made in Cuba with island-grown leaves and wrappers gained a reputation as the best that could be bought anywhere. As the worldwide demand grew, Cuban cigar makers suffered shortages of skilled wrappers. In the 1860s they actively recruited Chinese laborers off the torturous sugar plantations into their workshops, situated in six port cities. By way of Cuban–New York trade routes, some came to New York and were hired "immediately" by early entrepreneurial Cuban New Yorkers. Indeed, such a phenomenon led one 1870 *New York Daily Tribune* article to claim that all two hundred of the Chinese in New York were from Havana.[8]

Other Chinese may have gained access to the trade because cigar making was just in the process of becoming "bastardized." In the 1870s this once "noble" male enclave of artisanal pride and independence was being rationalized and mechanized. For the crudely made stogies and the "dirty, deadend" aspects of stemming and stripping, women were increasingly hired at low wages. New York City manufacturers were among the first to deskill the trade and make it more of a segmented, assembly-line process. Other Chinese in New York may very well have entered factories such as these, thereby joining the handful of African American workers hired in the industry down south and Chinese cigar makers in San Francisco.[9]

It seems likely that at least two levels of skill, and income, operated within the community of New York's Chinese cigar makers. The first level, making top dollar, were the Cuban Chinese making "clear Havanas" and "seed and Havanas." Other less-skilled Chinese probably made stogies and five-cent cigars, or they possibly did the low-end work in factory operations. James Baptiste, the Chinese Portuguese man who in 1869 worked as a house servant, told a New-York Times reporter that skilled Chinese wrappers demanded and received $15 to $16 per thousand, whereas Germans were paid $8 to $9. The most skillful could earn $20 to $25 per week. The Chinese, it was said, were especially good at cigar making because of "their natural quickness and deftness of finger."[10]

Comparing the 1870 census data with the figures from 1855 reveals suggestive patterns. Besides the rise of cigar makers and retailers, we find about the same percentage of Chinese men marrying Irish or "English" women, indicating some ongoing desire to put down roots in New York and have families.[11] Common was the example of Charles Samuels and his "auburn-haired Hibernian wife," or that of John and Susan Acco who ran a boardinghouse; he was Chinese, she British, and their two-year-old daughter had been born in "Buenos Ayre." Typical of a time in which racial categories were in constant flux, the census takers did not categorize these Anglo- or Irish-Chinese children in a consistent way. "Mulatto," a term most often applied to West Indian interracial marriages, was sometimes used. Other times these people were considered "white" or "Chinese." This Chinese-Irish pattern continued through the balance of the nineteenth century in sufficient numbers for Harper's Weekly in 1890 to prominently feature one such union in a double centerfold spread. A reporter for the Tribune remarked, "It is very curious to hear the little half-breed children running about the rooms and alternately talking Irish to their mothers and Chinese to their fathers."[12]

Contrary to the alarms sounded by policy analysts about the dangers of polygamous, tyrannical patriarchs spawning two hundred obedient children, census records and anecdotal information suggest that couples had only a few children. Indeed, it was frequently stated in newspaper articles citing Irish spouses (Quimbo Appo notwithstanding) that the Chinese were "good to their wives" in comparison with some Irishmen.[13] In these articles, reporters clearly demonstrated their racial thinking. During a Chinese New Year's celebration an inquiring *New York Sun* reporter visited a clubhouse at 34 Mott Street: "A young and pretty Irish girl, scarcely over eighteen, opened the door. She was neatly attired, bright colored shawl over [one] shoulder," with a Chinese husband at her side. "What-ee want?" the husband asked. Unable to make him understand, the reporter turned to the girl, who explained:

"Today we had a nice dinner, chickens and such things, and the men and their wives are now smoking and drinking sour wine. The wives are all Irish girls. I'm married." "What, married to a Chinaman?" "Certainly," she answered proudly, "married two weeks today." Then laughing outright she went on to say that the Chinamen were all good "fellows," that they work hard, go to night school, and are devoted to their wives.[14]

These women, speaking an English more comprehensible to newspaper reporters, often served as the cross-cultural translators and interpreters to mainstream society. A male *New York World* reporter conceded, "It must be confessed that [John Chinaman's] taste is good. The object of his choice is seldom devoid of personal attractions, and when John keeps house with her the house is well and neatly kept." Visiting an apartment at 39 Baxter, the reporter met the unnamed Irish wives of Ah Muk and Ching Si, who invited him in to see one of their abodes, which he described in some surprise as "scrupulously clean and handsomely furnished." When asked, "How did you come to marry Chinamen?" Mrs. Ah Muk laughed, but Mrs. Ching Si was indignant: "Because we like 'em, of course, why shouldn't we?" When the reporter suggested that they should be, "in accordance with the nature of things," married to white men, Mrs. Ching Si said that their husbands were as white as anybody and a good deal whiter than many of their neighbors. Mrs. Ah Muk then displayed her sleeping child, adding, "Joe is his name. . . . He don't look like a Chinaboy, does he, when he's asleep? His eyes show it, though, when he's awake."[15] The reporter clearly found these port intermixtures suspect. His language hints at the ways in which whiteness, interethnic children, and normality were contested in everyday conversation and in the print media.

While the rate of Chinese-Irish marriage was constant, a subtle but telling shift can be teased out of the census data. In 1855, of the eleven Chinese who simply transliterated their Chinese name, such as An Son, Zi Ting, or An Too, none was said to be married. Of the thirteen with Chinese last names and European American first names, such as John A. Ching or John Asam, six were married. And of the thirteen with Western first and last names, five were married. By 1870 the balance of names shifted dramatically. Only five men (none of whom was married) had Chinese first and last names, and only six men had Western first and last names. Fifty-four had adopted Western first names with some version of their Chinese last name. Of that total, sixteen were married (to Irishwomen). If these small numbers can tell us anything, they suggest a coalescing consensus on how to negotiate a cross-cultural world. After three decades of experimentation, bicultural names seem to have become the most comfortable accommodation to the culture of New York.

It is difficult to know how much these cross-cultural marriages and Christian naming strategies represented an intention to stay. Given traditional patriarchal practices of polygamy, most common among gentry and well-to-do merchants, these men could very possibly have had a wife and children in China or elsewhere in the diaspora. Having children with their Irish wives did not necessarily indicate a commitment to settling permanently in the United States, but it did represent a deepening of roots in New York that began to rival ties to and memories of their home villages in China. Their marriages, children, and names indicated complex adaptive bicultural experiences.

One enigmatic, but no doubt significant, pattern was the frequent adoption of the name John. In the 1855 census over half of the Chinese listed were named John, and in the 1870 census over two-thirds were so named. No doubt part of this phenomenon is that John was a very popular Anglo-American name. In 1857 on the ship *W. V. Moses* of Bath, for example, as many as one-quarter of the all-European crew were named John. This does not, however, account for the greater-than-average popularity of the name among Chinese.[16] It is unclear whether this name was given by missionaries, ship captains, or other parties, or whether it was a Christian name of choice among the Chinese themselves. Among the Chinese men who married and fathered children, many apparently felt that this was a good name to give their sons; over half were listed as such. Furthermore, "Old John" was the nickname given an otherwise unnamed seventy-four-year-old Chinese man who stated that he had been in the United States since 1828.[17]

The interesting twist to this John phenomenon was the contemporaneous use of the name John Chinaman. Probably coined as an equivalent to Jack Tar and John Bull, it was in use as early as 1845 and by 1869 was flourishing in the New York press, with titles in *Times* and *Herald* editorials like "John Chinaman—What Shall We Do with Him?" and "Sambo versus John Chinaman—The California Republican." An 1871 song entitled "John Chinaman, Esquire," was published and distributed nationally.[18] A stereotypic term like *celestial* and the earlier *mandarins, John* was used both in ordinary references to any Chinese man and in patronizing or humorous contexts. It was generally not used in an overtly hostile fashion like *chink* or *heathen Chinee.*

One clear indicator of whether Chinese New Yorkers were thinking of staying or returning to China was the degree to which they endured the involved process of becoming U.S. citizens. In one section of the Sixth Ward three Chinese men living in the same building listed themselves in the 1870 census as American citizens of some means. Charles Ahchung and John Miller were both married, both seamen, and both had savings of $500. In contrast, John Ahtong was a "Segar" maker and, at age forty-five, was one of the older members of the community. Being the only Chinese in the quarter to have claimed citizenship, these men may have been friends who encouraged one another to naturalize, or they may have moved into the same building, recognizing in one another some personal similarities of wealth and citizenship. It may be impossible to ascertain what their motives for living together were; nevertheless, they were among a small but significant group of Chinese New Yorkers who decided to become U.S. citizens.

Artist S. G. McCutcheon, while illustrating local coverage for the November 1880 presidential race between Garfield and Arthur, sketched a Chinese man waiting with an Irishman and an African American man to cast their votes. Titled "The First Chinese Vote," the illustration offers clear evidence that before the 1882 Chinese Exclusion Act there was at least one politically engaged Chinese New Yorker among a population that has been characterized by historian Gunther Barth as never intending to stay in the United States. According to an 1881 *New York Herald* article, James Baptiste was the first Chinese naturalized in New York State. However, other newspaper accounts hold that distinction as more likely to belong to "Old John," who "was the first of his race to become naturalized."[19] The earliest naturalization records do not bear the names of either of these men, but they do include the names of other Chinese.

In 1860 John Charley, living on the barque *Virginia* docked at Pier 39 at West and Christopher Streets, accompanied by James Keefe of Brooklyn, came before the New York Court of Common Pleas and renounced his allegiance to the "Emperor of China" with an X. In 1866 sailor George Abut signed his X, with Wood Sampson looking on as witness. A year later John A. Wing, accompanied by his already naturalized brother, James E. Wing, became a citizen. Both lived at 65 Cherry Street, both identified themselves as mariners, and both signed their names in fluent English script. In 1868 John Afoo and Luke R. Yee, both of 1 Baxter Street, put their X's on Afoo's court papers. Four years later Chino-Latino cigar maker Bernard Leipong of 100 Mott Street, accompanied by Eloy Molina, became a citizen. None of these men was listed in the 1870 census records, which indicates either a high level of transience or a high level of census-taking inaccuracy (or both). William Assing, the sailor living with his family at 66 Cherry Street cited in the 1870 census, however, became a citizen in 1873. Apparently he had invested some of his savings and had become a "hotelkeeper." In all, at least ten Chinese were U.S. citizens by 1868, somewhere between one of six or one of fifteen naturalized, depending on the number of Chinese who actually lived in the area. Among lower Manhattan immigrant contemporaries, this was not an insignificant rate. Few of their many thousands of Irish neighbors, for example, were listed in either 1855 or 1870 as having becoming naturalized.[20]

As indicated by marriages, families, name changes, and naturalization, a significant number of the early Chinese New Yorkers intended to settle in their adopted home. These early Chinese New Yorkers were, to varying degrees, settlers and sojourners, actively keeping in touch with their home villages in China *and* building new lives in the city. However, with the increased migration of the Chinese eastward from 1870 on, distinctive new developments began to emerge.

New Diversity, New Patterns

From the 1850s to the 1870s a striking move inland progressed into the area above Chatham Square that was soon to become known as the "Chinese quarter." The movement up into the Sixth Ward, bound by Chatham Street, the Bowery, Walker, and Broadway, echoed the occupational and household patterns of the Fourth Ward but also marked a greater complexity of community organization: service-sector work dramatically increased, and a number of small businesses created the beginnings of a core commercial district.

This ward went from having no Chinese in 1850 to listing thirty-eight adult residents in 1870 and well over a hundred in 1880. In 1870, twenty were sailors, nine were cigar makers, one was a ship's cook, two were confectioners, and five were retailers. In 1880 the Sixth Ward boasted an increase in numbers and in the diversity of occupations. There were now twenty-nine cigar makers, indicating a dramatic increase in Chinese involvement in that industry. While the number of stewards (one) and sailors (two) remained small, eleven cooks appeared. They probably worked in clubhouses and community-oriented restaurants. While no laundries were recorded in 1870, ten laundry operators and workers were recorded in 1880. In addition, there were three boardinghouse operators listed in 1880. Besides these service-sector jobs, an entire small-business network emerged. There were six storekeepers and six grocers, several clerks and bookkeepers, two tea merchants, one doctor, one barber, one cigar dealer, one interpreter, and one opium dealer. This concentration of stores gave visibility to the settlement to outside observers.

This census profile is compatible with a *New-York Times* reporter's description. In 1873 the reporter estimated that some five hundred Chinese lived in New York City, making a living by "serving in hotels, club-houses, and on steam-boats as cooks and stewards, by the manufacture of cigars and the sale of that peculiar preparation known as Chinese candy." Sailors and laundry workers, for some reason, were omitted from this listing of occupations, suggesting that the actual numbers of Chinese New Yorkers may have been greater than the reporter estimated, and probably fluctuated with incoming and outgoing mariners. Immediately evident to the roving *Times* reporter were two "clubs," one "joss" house or shrine, three to four boardinghouses, a Chinese doctor from New Orleans at 66 Cherry Street, and one opium "saloon" on Donovan's Lane.[21]

The candy makers John Auong and Doon Shing were likely to have made the "Chinese candy" referred to by the *Times* reporter as "that peculiar concoction." Chinese American lecturer and journalist Wong Ching Foo has cited Chinese candy makers operating as early as 1864. An 1868 *Harper's Weekly* drawing shows a ragged Chinese peddler selling something labeled

CHINESE CANDY MAN.

Figure 31. A Chinese candy seller, *Harper's Weekly,* Sept. 19, 1868. Making and selling Chinese-style candies became one way to earn a living in New York City. (Courtesy of Bonner Collection) "rock candy," perhaps a local version of the brown-sugar treat often made in southern China, where sugar cane was grown in great quantities. Rock candy was not uncommon in British culture, however. So if whatever was being peddled needed a sign to identify it, it must have been something less familiar. Homemade peanut candy, with sesame seeds and brown sugar, and *gaigengtong*, or "chicken neck candy," were popular street-stand items for tourists in the 1900s. At least one vendor sold "pineapple candy" for a penny a piece or five cents per bag. It was made from water and white or brown sugar, boiled, stirred, seasoned with "pineapple water from a doctor's store," cooled, and coated with melted sugar.[22] Given that the making of brown-sugar rock candy or other candies required very little start-up capital, it would have been a plausible niche for some enterprising Chinese to create.

The early appearance of confectionery manufactures represented New York Chinese creatively exploring new ways of making a living in relation to non-Chinese customers. A *Scribner's Monthly* writer commented, "We taste and find the flavor very pleasant, which seems to be the opinion of others, for the purchasers are many." The reporter especially noted this "brown faced Asiatic" peddler's fluency in English, his "Christianly short" haircut, and his shrewd eagerness to please: "The smiling vender keeps his stand scrupulously clean with a wet cloth, which he politely offers to us to wipe our sticky fingers on, and we come away with an improved opinion of John Chinaman's courtesy and neatness."[23] Cleanliness, conversion, courteousness, and the speaking of English were all positively associated in this one account. These peddlers had begun to understand that they shared something with their neighbors—here a taste for sweets—and that this, along with various other communicative survival skills, could be transculturated into a means to a living.

The emergence of retailers, as a step beyond street peddling, is perhaps the most significant occupational development indicated by the 1870 census. Three of the Chinese New Yorkers listed in 1870 sold cigars, one candy, and one fruit. We do not know how small or large their operations were. All we can truly tell from the census is that some distinction was made between peddlers and retailers. It would seem fair to guess that those who had established a regular stand or store were considered to be in the latter category. The presence of retailers like Ah Sue, who operated his tobacco and candy store from 1847 until his death in 1864, suggests that Chinese who owned and operated small businesses were serving non-Chinese as much as, if not more than, the local Chinese community. These may very well have been neighborhood-type stores that responded to a range of tastes, with no one ethnic clientele (although they must have carried some Chinese goods for the local settlement). In the best of Lower East Side traditions, the mixing of immigrants automatically brought about a mixing of cultural goods as well.[24]

Wo Kee, who moved his store to 34 Mott Street in 1873, was described as an "enterprising Hong Kong merchant" who was born in 1846. Mr. Kee had started with an investment of $40. At first the business was said to be bad, but it began to pick up. With partners, he soon bought the entire 8 Mott Street building, to which he moved. A *New York Sun* reporter's description of the emporium offers a sense of the role the store played in the life of the community: "Somewhere near a million different things" were crammed into the front parlor and back room of a former residential building. Amid the Chinese medicines, foodstuffs, teas ("some of them exquisite and much more expensive than any American stores sell"), silks, jade bracelets, incense, and Chinese clothing, Wo Kee presided over a space that would accommodate only a few customers at a time. He was described as a courteous, round-faced man with a mustache who invited visitors to partake of a pot of tea.[25] This general store provided a range of provisions that any laundry worker or house servant who did not live in the core area might need between visits. And, at Chatham Square—a transportation hub—this lower Mott Street location was relatively convenient.

The store's relocation was typical of the general movement of the population center away from the docks of the Fourth Ward to the Sixth Ward above Chatham Square. Chinese were already living on Baxter Street as early as 1868. Boardinghouses, mutual aid associations, a shrine, and now stores seem to have moved up into or first established themselves in this area. One can only speculate as to why this geographical shift began to happen. The pioneer generation of sailors, cooks, stewards, peddlers, and cigar workers seems to have done modestly well in making a living, marrying, having children, and saving some money. Small retail operations became possible. As the formation of organizations and stores required larger investments, locations farther away from the transience and poverty of the docks became more desirable. As noted earlier, the classic New York housing settlement pattern was for better-established people to live inland and move farther uptown, enticed by developers, leaving downtown and dock-area buildings unimproved for the poorest and most recent immigrants and workers.[26] The move to the Sixth Ward may have been a part of this general pattern.

Mr. Wo Kee played a critical multipurpose role for the metropolitan area's increasing number of scattered Chinese. Merchants and their stores were the hub of community activity. In addition to selling necessities, store owners put up those who needed lodging, lent money, served as druggists, and performed various other support functions. They were often literate in both Chinese and English and handled the critical functions of letter writing for business matters and personal correspondence. Such stores would also receive and send mail. The rapid increase of hand laundries in Manhattan made such stores indispensable lifelines to friends, family, and community. Indeed, with the absence of traditional Chinese civil-service appointees, merchants such as Wo Kee played a key social and leadership role. He was a founding trustee of the mutual aid association Poonlon Kun Cee. He also represented the community to reporters and often greeted Chinese newcomers.[27]

The Wo Kee store may also have come to represent the beginning of Chinatown because it stood in the midst of a population explosion. The estimated stable core of 150 who lived in the Chinese settlement for some fifteen years had more than tripled by 1873. Five hundred Chinese were said to live in New York at the time of the opening of Wo Kee's store.[28] Three developments most likely accounted for this rapid increase: the 1869 completion of the transcontinental railroad, the increased anti-Chinese violence on the West Coast, and the recruitment of Chinese laborers to the East Coast. As the railroads were completed, up to twenty thousand Chinese found themselves out of work. Few could afford the tickets for the railroad they were instrumental in building. Some actually walked eastward from Promontory Point. Occasionally rate wars between the Central Pacific Railroad and the Pacific Mail Steamship Company would bring about spurts of Chinese arrivals.[29] They settled in urban areas large and small throughout the Midwest and eventually the East Coast. Twenty-four-year-old Chu Fung Wing was among those who made an eastward migration to New York in 1869. He was later to be recognized as a pioneer community builder and leader of Chinatown. Referring to the mounting anti-Chinese hostilities along the Pacific coast, James Baptiste told a reporter that "as long as the Kearney agitation continued," Chinese would be coming to New York.[30]

In 1870 the medical doctor June Ling Wau set up a practice at 40 East Fourteenth Street with an interpreter, two druggists, and a personal servant. As was typical, Dr. June came from a family of doctors. He had practiced for some thirty years. He brought "several thousand pounds" of some three hundred medicines from China via San Francisco, where he had previously practiced. Described by a *New York Standard* reporter as small, wearing white linen trousers and a loose black silk jacket without sleeves, he set up regular hours from 9 A.M. to noon, 2 P.M. to 5 P.M., and 7 P.M. to 9 P.M., charging $3 for a single consultation and $10 for repeated visits over a week, plus the cost of the drugs used. He was credited with having cured partial paralysis, diseased livers and kidneys, listlessness, general debility, and inflammation of the lungs. Apparently he built up a substantial clientele among "many of the richest ladies of the City" but had to close down his business in 1873 because the Customs House refused to admit what they deemed the "poisonous drugs and revolting salves" he used. A *New-York Times* reporter was highly skeptical of the efficacy of Dr. June's non-Western techniques. He described the good doctor as "professing to cure all manner of diseases" and managing to attract "credulous patients."[31] Like the experience of the Tong Hook Tong opera troupe, the practices of authentic Chinese culture were highly vulnerable in New York City. Candy and cigar entrepreneurs could survive by adapting to local tastes, but a doctor who actually helped even elite New Yorkers get better could not survive. Dr. June's customs experience foreshadowed government policies to come.

Despite the large numbers of residents still living below Chatham Square, the social center of the community seems to have formed above it, along Mott and Baxter Streets, including several pioneering organizations that made up the foundation of the contemporary Chinese community. According to a *New-York Times* reporter, 13 Mott Street had a large basement boardinghouse furnished by the proprietor "in a manner which is no doubt agreeable to his peculiar customers, but which to an American mind certainly conveys no idea of comfort." Board partitions divided the space into six separate areas. The rear had a cooking and eating space with "a long wooden table, greasy, and covered with innumerable dishes." The front had "a general reception room" with "dilapidated sofa," broken-down cane-bottom chairs, and "strangely colored and printed paper peculiar to the Chinese." The remaining four rooms were filled with ten wooden bedsteads "over which a few coarse bed-clothes were thrown." Although these quarters were quite typical of poor, new-immigrant living conditions in lower Manhattan, these reporters tended to equate them specifically with the Chinese.[32] Like the racial analysis correlating climate to pigmentation, living environments were believed to embody the essence of different peoples as well.

Perhaps most significant was the founding of two clubs that had been organized "to aid members in distress, and to extend a helping hand to young Chinese who might come as strangers to the City." The recently formed Poonlon Kun Cee was located at what had formerly been Wo Kee's 34 Mott Street building. The layout was similar to the boardinghouses of 1855 except that it had more space. The basement entrance opened onto two rooms, one for gaming and one for lounging and eating. However, instead of the boardinghouse-apartment arrangement, with fixed-berth dormitories located within this same social space, in this building the sleeping quarters were moved onto floors above. Typical of the buildings and the male immigrant use of the area, there were "three dark and badly-ventilated" rooms with eleven beds for twenty-two people. On the second floor were four small rooms occupied by several youth busily engaged in making cigars. Fifty members were said to pay dues to this association.[33]

The other unnamed club at 12 Baxter Street was described as having a smaller membership and less commodious sleeping quarters in the basement. On the street level, however, was established the first community shrine. On the ground floor, entering directly from the street, "a badly-lighted, musty room, some 20 feet long by 12 wide," was observed by the *Times* reporter. Facing the windows against the opposite wall was a high altar flanked by a pair of large lanterns suspended from the ceiling. Brass censers burning incense, a pair of stuffed birds, and a kerosene lamp were observed on the altar table in front of a portrait described as "Buddha, his song, and the evil one." The six long wooden benches between the window and altar could accommodate up to thirty people. This club and "joss house" was also visited and portrayed by the *Harper's* artist Winslow Homer.[34]

The two clubs were pretty much the same. The spaces may have appeared cramped and fetid to genteel journalists, but they served as home to many Chinese. They attracted transient waiters and stewards of coastwise steamships. When in port they could stop by to socialize or pay an optional fee for room and board. Local residents paid twenty-five to fifty cents a week to gain membership privileges. They could come to eat, gamble, socialize, hear news from abroad, and feel at home. Fees and dues were collected by a regularly elected finance committee that determined aid for members in distress and newcomers.

The mutual aid association not only welcomed strangers to town but also provided deceased members with proper burials. Having bought a plot of land at Green-Wood Cemetery, the parklike Victorian cemetery in Brooklyn, indigent members would be buried at the society's expense. Whenever

Figure 32. Winslow Homer, "The Chinese in New York—Scene in a Baxter Street Club-House," *Harper's Weekly*, Mar. 7, 1874. This was Homer's representation of one of the founding community organizations of early Chinese in the Sixth Ward. (Wong Ching Foo Collection)

possible, dead bodies were sent back to home villages for burial. In the corner of the Baxter Street association a candle dimly lit a picture of a young Chinese boy draped in red satin paper and Chinese characters. When the *Times* reporter asked an elderly man about the shrine, he replied, "Ah! Chinee no great monument in marble. That good boy he die! Chinese friends in big, strange land, for three months burn candle; make him a little memory here."[35]

These early mutual aid societies were remarkable, multipurpose spaces. Though similar to boardinghouses, they represented a collective level of organization rather than that of an individual entrepreneur. Brought together by some shared background or interest, investments and memberships would pay for the rent of the space. Within, a complex of overlapping activities took place, ranging from festivities to burial, temporary lodging to gaming, self-government to social welfare, smoking and eating to producing consumer goods. The two organizations encapsulated the work, sleep, play, and spiritual needs of Chinese New Yorkers in a communal setting run not by one person but by an elected and rotating committee. Such spaces fostered friendships, celebrated group memories, and nurtured the future survival of the community.

Two additional operations were established at this early date, poles apart yet both egregiously misunderstood in the decades to come. The Chinese Freemasons organization, or the Sam Hop Hui *(Sanhohui)*, was located at the foot of Mott Street. Its articles of incorporation in New York State named its purpose as being to promote "mutual friendship, brotherly love and servitude to the supreme being by mutual succor in distress and aid in sickness, poverty, adversity and affliction." Or, as Quong Lee, a clerk at Wo Kee's store, explained, it was comparable to a Masonic order: "Both blood brotherhood, both secular, both mechanic, not real mechanic but ideal mechanic."[36]

Commonly assumed in the United States to be a criminal organization, the Sam Hop Hui was an underground oppositional society reputedly founded by Buddhist monks in the early seventeenth century, during the early years of the Manchu (Qing) Dynasty, to work toward returning China to Chinese (Han) rule. Because many overseas southern Chinese who were members of the organization had had experiences with European colonialism in Southeast Asia and the Americas, the organization forged a strong antiforeign, nationalist worldview. The Sam Hop Hui, referred to by the press as the "Order and Brotherhood of Masons," would be regularly involved in various nationalist and revolutionary movements in China, including the 1911 republican revolution. In order to adapt to American society, members of the brotherhood borrowed the name and some of the language of the Masons. They were sworn to secrecy. For the New York press, this secrecy was both fascinating and frustrating. For the emerging Chinese community, however, it was one of the few resources available to protect members from social injustice. Yet in a situation in which they had limited power to influence mainstream politics or racist assaults, the Sam Hop Hui mainly dealt with internal community matters. Wang A. Ling (a.k.a. Leeng), who later changed his name to Tom Lee, James Baptiste, Domingo DeLuce, Wang Gee, and Tom Yee were listed as the founding trustees of the New York chapter, Lee later emerging as a powerful figure in New York's Chinatown.[37]

Opium smoking also attracted immense attention. The press often focused on a small opium room operated on Baxter Street by the man whom non-Chinese called "Old John." On Donovan's Lane, "a miserable little alley opening from Baxter Street," a small twelve- by six-foot opium "saloon" operated. A slanting board shelf attached lengthwise to one of the walls accommodated up to four smokers. An older man and a youth were found smoking by a reporter. The young man had just finished serving as an officer's steward on the steamer *Juniata*. In 1874, while on assignment for *Harper's Weekly,* artist Winslow Homer picked this modest space for one of his illustrations representing "The Chinese in New York," the first article and illustration the newsweekly did on this community.[38]

While few Chinese were addicted to the drug, opium smoking was, as we shall see, often cited as proof of the depravity of all Chinese, later justifying their exclusion. It is worth noting here the irony that it was the Chinese who came to be identified with opium when it was the British and the Americans who trafficked in it. Reporters never linked the city's opium trade merchants, who flooded China with the drug and helped to precipitate the Opium Wars, with their coverage of these Chinese smokers.

Missionary Chinese

Besides the survival education learned on the streets of the international district, aspiring Chinese relied on Christian programs to improve themselves. Missionaries based in the Fourth Ward, Sixth Ward, and elsewhere became a primary means for learning about and accessing Western culture. English-language courses were the biggest lure used to attract Chinese into the mission. At least as early as 1869, Mr. and Mrs. Railback, heading up the Five

Points House of Industry, enrolled four men and one woman in an evening English class. In a letter to the editorial section of the *New York Tribune* the Railbacks testified to their intelligence and eagerness to learn English. "In a single evening," the letter asserted, "most of them become quite familiar with the alphabet, and in another evening learn to spell short words. Their aptness in learning I think very remarkable." In their view these Chinese represented model proto-Protestants and warranted Christian charity: "They are docile, industrious and frugal; are eminently polite, kindly and generous." Hence, it became the Railbacks' policy to help accommodate them to New York: "Since they are in all human probability, to become a very large element in our population, on the completion of the railroads to the Pacific, it seemed to me well to consider at once how to meet them, and what to do for them, that they may be made a desirable acquisition."[39] The choice of the decidedly nonreligious term *acquisition* is telling; it suggests purchasable conveniences, reminiscent of patricians' luxury goods (or, as we shall soon discover, the perceived role of Chinese as natural-born house servants).

The Five Points Mission was built in 1853 by the Fourth Avenue Presbyterian Church on the site of the infamous Old Brewery at 155 Worth, which sensationalist crusader George Foster described as a dangerous residence of several hundred Irish and African New Yorkers intermingling in sin. This Protestant mission represented an outpost dedicated to the moral cleansing of the polyglot port-culture district. Moral redeemability became a key argument "favoring" Chinese. Railback was reputedly "one of the most faithful and successful chaplains of colored regiments" during the Civil War, and the Chinese were believed to be eminently ripe for Protestant conversion.[40] The mission's annual Chinese New Year's party became a widely covered media event and was used by the Railbacks and subsequent missionaries to demonstrate the virtues and acculturability of the Chinese in New York. Chinese dishes were described, Chinese music performed, speeches in both Chinese and English made. In 1870 the mission sponsored a "Christmas Reunion" of its Chinese students. Fifty came to "represent the better class" of the Railbacks' students. "At 7 o'clock in the evening they assembled in one of the large parlors of the institution which has been tastily decorated for the occasion with a select company of the invited guests." Chinese foods and Christmas tree decorations commingled, including a "huge Santa Claus" who "walked into the room and relieving the tree of its dainties, proceeded to distribute them to the students amid great hilarity."[41] The Chinese New Year was now supplemented by the celebration of a Christian holiday.

Conversion stories became an ongoing feature of the Five Points Mission. By 1875 a Reverend Folsom, formerly a missionary in China, headed the operation. The missionaries hired a suite of rooms at 525 Pearl Street, near Centre, to hold English classes and open a reading room featuring Chinese- and English-language Bibles, newspapers, and books. Here, it was proclaimed, the Chinese "can enjoy more freedom and comfort than in their homes, surrounded as they are by many baneful influences." Citing the fallacious yet prevalent notion that these Chinese were "isolated," the missionaries "hoped these rooms may become a kind of exchange where they may hear of chances of employment and gain other useful information." Testifying to the value of this work, the mission's organizers claimed, "In a few months their natural perseverance and anxiety to learn enable them to read and speak English fluently; and [there is] proof that religious teaching not lost for several had professed Christian faith."[42]

Articles like this one consistently praised these Chinese "scholars" for their intelligence and their quickness to learn Western culture. Drawing upon prevailing notions of phrenology, the Railbacks described a Choy Awah, who waited on the captain of a ship, as having "one of the most intelligent faces of any we have seen among the natives of the Celestial Empire. He has a clear, bright eye, and his features are more regular than most of the Chinamen we usually see." He was represented as eagerly explaining how camphor sap was harvested from trees, what cinnamon was, and how tea leaves were cured. Having established his affability and usefulness, the Railbacks then allowed him to voice his, and their, indignation at overt anti-Chinese prejudice. Declaring, "Me stay in New York," he explained why he no longer wore Chinese clothing in public: "Me no like to; small men on street they throw stones; they humbug me; they put dirt on my face; me wear 'Merican clothes." If this account of what Choy said and how he said it is accurate, the phrasing is telling of his cultural mixing. "Small men" may mean boys, but I believe it more likely to be Choy's translation of the Confucian term for petty, immoral, uneducated persons. What with his use of the term *humbug* and his adaptive clothing strategy, this description clearly reveals some of the decidedly nonisolated learning that was going on.[43]

In July 1870 a Chinese magician performed for a mix of Chinese Five Points students and invited guests. In the chapel filled with "saffron-skinned, long haired wanderers from the antipodes," a Mr. Kan Chuk (alternatively reported as "Hang Chow") performed as "Dr. Ah Foon," the "renowned Chinese prophet of Toulum [California]." He began with some Christian hymns,

Figure 33. "The Chinese School in Mott Street," New York, *Harper's Weekly,* July 19, 1879. Learning English at Protestant missions became one means for Chinese to find jobs as house servants in patrician homes. (Wong Ching Foo Collection)

juggled, and caused a teacup to float in midair, a doll to get up and walk, snakes and pigeons to come out of impossible places, and lemonade to flow from empty cups. Joking about how "Merica man laugh at China man because he eat rat," he made a rat out of a handkerchief. Born in 1850, Kan Chuk had worked as a carpenter and cabinetmaker in Hong Kong, went to Cuba in 1867, shipped as a cook to Rio, and somehow ended up coming to New York "to see his brother."[44] In contrast to the Bowery commercial venues with their stereotypic representations of Chinese, Kan Chuk was one of the first performers to appear before an audience of Chinese New Yorkers, performing in a largely Chinese manner and explicitly mocking attitudes of the dominant society. A Chinese-community audience was emerging where it had not quite yet existed for the ill-fated Tong Hook Tong performers.

In 1878 Moy Jin Kee was celebrated as a "well educated" and "intelligent Chinaman" working for H. C. Parkes, a Chinese- and Japanese-goods dealer on Front Street. Moy was a member of the Methodist Episcopal Church, other members of which had "formed a plan" to send him to the Drew Theological Seminary to make him a missionary. When asked if there was hope for Christianizing the Chinese, Moy answered affirmatively: "Yes, great hope. Seventeen thousand were baptized in the Methodist Church in Canton within three months. If the Chinese in this country were not forced to go back to China they would be more willing to embrace Christianity. . . . My brother is a Baptist and I have three friends in the city who are Congregationalists."[45]

The missions, with all their self-righteous moralism, provided one of the few acceptable mainstream public spaces within the international port district that was not tainted with explicitly anti-Chinese judgments. Indeed, these Victorian Protestants created a Chinese community divide. These Christianized—or, more accurately, missionary-associated—Chinese, represented as intelligent, articulate, moral, and good, came to distinguish themselves from their unacculturated brethren. Or, as the Railbacks claimed, "Our Chinese do not use opium, and look down with a kind of scorn upon those who do, saying 'They are no good Chinamen.'"[46] Whether this purported scorn was hurtful or not, it gave some Chinese tremendous access to the dominant Protestant culture, access they otherwise would not have had. Interestingly, Moy Jin Kee offered a sort of Sinicized mirror of John William Draper's analysis of the three ranks of men in society: "There are three classes in China, all of whom have different ancestors. They are the Chinese, the Tartars [referring to the Manchu invaders] and the Coolies. . . . Out of the 1,800 Chinamen in this city not more than 20 are Chinamen, properly called. The better class do not come here because they do not get . . . 'kind treatment.'" The "coolies" were described as "half breeds arising from intermarriage" who "come as hired laborers not as persons intending to gain citizenship." Speaking from the point of view of a diasporic merchant, Moy said, "I would like to cut off my cue, bring my wife here, now living in Canton, if I could acquire property and be protected in its use and transmit it to my family."[47] In declaring his readiness to be a self-possessed individual of property, Moy also betrayed his own class-bound attitudes, privileging his own position to the detriment of other Chinese.

Chinese who learned Western ways—those who came to be called John, who learned English, became Christians, and wore Western clothing—understood these efforts as demonstrations of their willingness to accommodate themselves to Anglo-American life. Christian European Americans would then perceive these Chinese as more civilized and less threateningly different. This adaptive pattern, however, would soon be unsettled by the Chinese Question. In July 1878, Charles Miller, a forty-year-old Chinese man married to an Irishwoman who had been a resident of New York for twenty-eight years, applied to a Judge Choate for naturalization. His application was denied on the grounds of a California ruling stating that Chinese were not white and therefore were not eligible for citizenship. The editors of the *Herald* concurred: "The law is wise. Charles Miller may be an excellent man, but it is not well that citizenship should be offered to all the races of the world." The matter was not closed, however. Later that year Judge Larremore ruled that a Wong Ah Yee, a cigar maker on Baxter Street and a six-year resident of New York who had two years earlier married an Irishwoman at Transfiguration Church, was qualified to become a citizen. He was described by the *New York Sun* reporter as being "of unusual intelligence" and as wearing "American costume." The judge's clerk explained the ruling: "If negroes are admitted, and all other foreigners, I don't know upon what ground we could put a refusal to Chinamen. The constitution provides for no other classes of color than white or black and I hold that Chinamen must come within one or the other." The *New York Herald* reported that Wong celebrated his victory by inviting his fellow naturalized citizens to a Thanksgiving dinner at Thomas Ah Yee's restaurant at 20 Mott Street. John Ah Woh, naturalized since 1863, William Assing, and Tom Lee all showed up, eating sliced turkey with chopsticks. Ah Woh, a "tobacco folder" at 6 Baxter Street, had voted in every election since his naturalization.[48]

A few months later Larremore granted Charles Wing the rights of citizenship, with Wong Lee serving as the witness. Wing was typical of the Chinese who first settled in New York. He was a cigar maker who lived in a rear tenement at 49 Bayard Street. He left China when he was sixteen, lived in Havana for a year, and then came to New York. He studied English at night and attended the Seaman's Church on Madison Street, but he complained that business was bad and spoke of moving to Key West, Florida, to run a grocery store with a friend. Apparently Wong Ah Yee's highly publicized naturalization case, and the loud rumblings of Chinese exclusion, had sparked a trend. Fourteen Chinese New Yorkers became citizens by March 1880, and some two hundred filed their intention of becoming citizens. Tellingly, all fourteen granted citizenship were "converts to Christianity."[49]

Service Workers

New York's genteel middle class constantly complained about "the servant problem." Irish female house servants were said to be "unreliable" and "too demanding." Chinese manservants were explored as one possible solution.[50] Indeed, the Five Points missionaries made it a point to have the *Evening Post* reporter help promote their efforts to place Chinese men as house servants: "It is hoped these rooms may become a kind of exchange where they may hear of chances of employment and gain other useful information." A journalist confirmed, "The capability and fidelity [of Chinese] in housework and outdoor labor have been well tested in California and elsewhere and will no doubt be appreciated here," concluding, "Offerings of employment should go to Miss Goodrich, 140 W. 15th St." In an 1880 *New-York Times* article James Baptiste was quoted as stating that Chinese house servants worked for between $18 and $30 a month, rates 25–30 percent higher than the wages paid to "Irish or German girls." Nonetheless, upon hearing of an employment service that could help locate Chinese workers, "several ladies from Madison Avenue and other fashionable uptown quarters" visited Mott Street to look for the agency. That day they were to leave disappointed, but Chinese men continued to be offered as a convenient solution to this household dilemma.[51] In effect, the Five Points Mission's religious and language training prepared Chinese men to deal with the cross-cultural demands of serving middle-class European Americans.

Chinese servants working outside the Fourth and Sixth Wards appear to account for a demographic shift that can be detected in the census records. In 1870 approximately half of the Chinese lived in the Fourth and Sixth Wards' core area. However, by 1880 less than one-fifth lived in the Chinese core, and four-fifths lived throughout the city.[52] While the statistical demographic work remains to be done, it appears that the great majority of these non-core-area Chinese worked as house servants and laundry workers. This rise of service work signaled important shifts in the New York community's development. While earlier service work—as cooks or stewards, for example—was performed on ships that landed in New York, this new pattern of service work was landlocked and resulted in a necessarily decentralized settlement pattern. As such, the shift represented two terribly important changes in the work options of Chinese New Yorkers. First, migrating Chinese men brought transplanted California occupational innovations to New

Figure 34. Chinese English-language students serving the meal at a Five Points Mission holiday party, 1870. (Wong Ching Foo Collection)

York soil. Second, Chinese hand laundries would become the foundation of the New York Chinese community to come.

What was it like to be a Chinese servant in New York during the nineteenth century? The surviving documents from an 1869 New York State Supreme Court case provide some hints about one person's experience. One John Amoy petitioned the court for a habeas corpus hearing of a countryman. Employed as a house servant at 26 Twenty-third Street, a nineteen-year-old Fou Afung was "imprisoned and detained of his liberty" by his boss, Migel Adamas. Afung was apparently not permitted to leave the house or to "hold any communications with his friends."[53] Just who was Adamas? Could he have been a Cuban who brought Amoy to New York as an indentured servant? I have yet to find the documents that would reveal how the case was resolved; it is clear, however, that of those living outside the core area, some were occupied as house servants and were cut off from the core settlement. In the face of these difficult odds, at least John Amoy was sufficiently aware of the law and willing to use the U.S. courts to protect Afung's personal rights. Yet despite these valiant efforts at asserting their claims as Americans with guaranteed individual rights, the larger cultural associations of Chinese servitude with families of wealth and the very category of being a "servant" were soon to prove an overwhelming obstacle.

Little is known about Chinese house servants in New York, but more is known about the development of Chinese-operated hand laundries. The ten "laundrymen" who show up in the 1880 census represented the means by which Chinese would survive racism in the coming decades. They were the future of the community. Wong Ching Foo, the fully bilingual journalist who wrote about and defended Chinese in New York, estimated that by 1888 there were over two thousand laundries in New York City, some eight hundred to nine hundred in Brooklyn, and some one hundred in Jersey City. In 1898 journalist Louis Beck estimated that there were some eight thousand Chinese laundry operators and workers in the greater metropolitan region, comprising fully half of the Chinese New York population.[54] What were the origins of laundries in New York, and why hand laundries?

Hand laundries emerged in the 1870s. Between 1870 and 1872, some three hundred Chinese laborers were recruited from California to work in Captain James B. Hervey's Passaic Steam Laundry in South Belleville, New Jersey. They were brought in because, in Hervey's view, the young Irishwomen in his employ were prone to striking and would "get $20 or $30 in their pockets" and then be "above their work and clear out." The Chinese substitutes proved to be just as militant and independent. Many left the operation after their contracts expired and opened laundries in the Newark–New York region.[55] The same year the Chinese arrived in the Passaic Valley, Ong Yung, reportedly the brother of a South Belleville laundry worker, opened what one journalist referred to as the first Chinese "washee washee" in Manhattan, located off Chatham Square on Catherine and East Broadway. Said to be ambitious, he began a series of hand laundries in Manhattan and became quite wealthy, returning to China three times that decade. According to Wong Ching Foo, "their cousins and other relatives came so rapidly that in a few years nearly every street and avenue in New York became filled with Chinese laundries, and the flaming red signs of Wah Sing, One Lung, and Goon Hi Fay Toy dangled floriously in great numbers."[56] Thus was inaugurated a major industry in New York. By 1876 two hand laundries were listed in a business directory, Lee Hung at 83 Canal Street and Lee Sing at 99 Canal Street. The next year thirty laundries paid to be listed. And in 1879 one *New York Sun* reporter claimed that there were at least two hundred hand laundries in Manhattan. Until the repeal of exclusionary laws and the advent of home washers and dryers in the 1960s, Chinese hand laundries were to constitute the major occupation of Chinese in New York.

The shift from Chinese working in areas related to the maritime trades to laundry work in New York reveals a great deal about the changing structure of attitudes toward Chinese. Images of the China trade and the association of Chinese with valued luxuries were being displaced by an opposite association. Chinese were becoming synonymous with the laundry trade and the washing of soiled clothing. "The question has frequently been asked by Americans," journalist Wong Ching Foo noted, "'Do these Chinamen wash clothes in China? How is it that nearly all who come here enter the laundry business? Do they love it?'" He responded with a keen insight into why Chinese took on this occupation:

> No, they do not love it any more than any other kind of labor. . . . Laundry work in China is invariably done by women, and when a man steps into a woman's occupation he loses his social standing. They become laundrymen here simply because there is no other occupation by which they can make money as surely and quickly. The prejudice against the race has much to do with it. . . . Here in New York as yet there is no other alternative. Many an able-minded man as well as skillful mechanic who came to America to better his condition may be found wielding polishing-irons in a New York Chinese laundry.[57]

The first Chinese hand laundries in the United States appeared in California in the 1850s. The "prejudice against the race" pushed many Pacific coast Chinese from a variety of occupations into this relatively noncompetitive, low-status occupation. It was both a creative and a limiting response to systematic occupational evictions, and it became the prototype work of Chinese moving east. Middle-class Americans always seemed to need laundries, and genteel Victorians tended to look most favorably upon the Chinese for this work. From the point of view of the Chinese entrepreneur, the start-up cost was fairly low, and contact with non-Chinese could be kept to a minimum. The main expenditures were a stove, tubs for washing, a drying line, a sign, and a sleeping area. One hundred dollars was all that was needed to set oneself up in this small business. In addition, the occupation was flexible and therefore suitable to people moving from city to city looking for better situations. A washhouse could easily be established and then sold to another Chinese.

The prevalence of the occupation in New York suggests that many of the migrants from the Pacific coast took up this vocation and that other job opportunities were severely limited. As sociologist Paul Chang Pang Siu has pointed out, the niche was not without its social complexities. While providing many Chinese Americans with a means of subsistence, it also isolated Chinese from the mainstream of American society, helping to foster a "sojourner" mentality. Laundries depended on middle-class communities outside the Chinese settlement to survive. While spreading out into such neighborhoods throughout the metropolis, racialized ignorance and violence effectively ghettoized these Chinese. Most lived in the back of the shop. Even when they made enough money to rent a separate apartment, prejudice was such that they could rarely find a place to rent.[58]

In sharp contrast to the earlier pattern of Chinese-Irish couples and families who were settling in New York City, the Chinese hand-laundry business became both a means of protecting Chinese from the prejudice of the larger society and a constrictive space that kept Chinese disconnected from the world around them. "Under the [restrictive] race and ethnic situation," Siu posits, "the Chinese immigrants were driven to make a choice, and they founded the laundry as a form of accommodation to the situation. But, since its establishment [in the 1850s] the laundry has served to isolate the laundryman and, therefore, has created a type of personality which is directly contrary to the expectation of assimilation."[59] Although the occupation was formed from the crucible of anti-Chinese racism and the need to eke out a livelihood, Chinese who took on this occupation easily created a cultural nationalist personality that resisted adoption of the American way of life. As embodied in the story of Ong Yung, Chinese laundry operators and workers largely worked to save money to send back to their families and then retired to their home villages.[60]

However, there were notable exceptions in New York. As a spillover of port-culture intermarriages, one laundryman, Ah Lin Wang, and his Irish wife had a baby, and the press publicized their differences on what to name the child. She supposedly wanted to call the boy Dennis, but they settled on Andrew Jackson. This "human interest" squib appeared just at the time anti-Chinese leader Denis Kearney was in the news for being arrested once again.[61]

Anti-Chinese violence further reinforced this pronounced defensive pattern of occupational isolation. In 1879, for example, Wah Sing and Lee Ing were walking near their laundry on 114 Third Avenue when one of them had his wallet picked by a woman who came up from behind them. They chased her and retrieved the wallet. She screamed, whereupon a crowd gathered and began to beat the innocent victims. Wah Sing was drawing a knife to protect himself when someone from the crowd shot him, lodging a bullet in his cheek. Lee Ing was wrongfully arrested but later released. Commenting on this incident, Jim Lee, a laundry owner at 3 Houston Street, voiced what must have been the common frustration of all Chinese in New York. "It's a miserable outrage," he told a *New York World* reporter. "People treat us as if we were savages. . . . They tried to bring a woman they regarded as a criminal to a station house and turn her over to the police. An ignorant mob interfered with them and rescued the woman and came near killing Wah Sing, who is one of the most peaceable men living." Just a week later another incident was reported in which Ah Long and Ah Lee, who operated a laundry on Third Avenue between Eighty-fourth and Eighty-fifth Streets, ran out to catch boys who had been throwing bricks at their shop. The father of one of the boys then knocked Ah Long down with a blow to the head, and Ah Lee emerged from the laundry with a revolver. No arrests were made.[62] The nature of laundry work was lonely enough, but with the added pressure of random street violence against their persons and stores, many Chinese took further refuge within the sojourner mentality.

Isolated and longing for company, Chinese laundry operators and workers provided the economic basis for the development of a commercial core area in the Sixth Ward. Business from those living in the immediate neighborhood would not have been enough to support the stores and groceries on lower Mott Street. Laundry operators and workers would go to Mott Street every Sunday to purchase what they needed for the week ahead. This would also be a time to socialize, to escape into gambling or opium smoking, or to catch up on news from home villages. The commercial and political cultures of the city kept Chinese New Yorkers segregated from the mainstream life of the city as perpetual others.

"A Heathen Missionary"

On May 7, 1877, a young Chinese man publicized as a Buddhist missionary lectured at Steinway Hall on the "Damnation of the Heathen." The *New-York Times* had stated the week before that this man, Wong Ching Foo (Huang Qingfu), was a "native missionary" who was "on the errand of converting the 40,000,000 Christians of this country to Buddhism." Fully bilingual, Wong spoke "in a clear, loud voice, and with a faultless accent, although his sentences were at times stilted or inverted." This was one of some eighty lectures scheduled on the tour arranged for Wong Ching Foo by Madame Helena Blavatsky, the doyenne of Americans probing Asian spiritualisms.[63] During an era in which lectures became a popular forum for middle-class public discourse, Wong's Steinway Hall appearance was the first time a Chinese perspective on the differences between China and the United States was articulated on a New York City stage. Wong Ching Foo was the closest thing the Chinese community had to someone who could speak in their behalf in the English language. The reportedly "low" audience turnout at Steinway Hall of two hundred people, however, indicated that the public was not especially interested in the thoughts of a real Chinese individual—no matter how articulate—if they competed against far more powerful caricatures flourishing in the commercial culture.[64]

This lecture tour constituted Wong Ching Foo's second visit to the United States and marked the beginning of his career as an activist and a gadfly. By his own account, Wong was the son of a fairly successful officer in the Chinese army. He had been educated in a private school in Shanghai and was in the United States for a year in 1869. Upon his return to China he served as an English-language interpreter for the imperial court. He formed an anti-opium society that was suppressed by the Chinese government. He then escaped to a British missionary post in Hong Kong. Upon learning his identity, the missionaries locked him up and called the police. Wong managed to escape once more, this time via a vessel to San Francisco that was carrying two hundred Chinese women in steerage to serve as prostitutes in the largely male Chinese community. Troubled by the plight of these women, he organized to rectify the situation. With the aid of the Reverend Otis Gibson, Wong said he helped the women in steerage gain freedom and raised money to send them back.[65]

Although he came from a very different class and regional background from his overseas compatriots, Wong detested the Westerners' sense of superiority over China and came to champion Chinese in the Americas. In 1874 he expressed strong nationalist sentiments in a letter to the *New-York Times* noting the plight of a Chinese man who had escaped from a Cuban sugar cane plantation: "The continual instances brought under my notice of the helpless condition of my own countrymen in foreign lands fill my heart with grief." Writing as a man of strong patriotic feelings, he linked the situation of overseas Chinese to that of a weak Manchu-ruled government:

Figure 35. Wong Ching Foo, *Harper's Weekly*, Mar. 26, 1877. Wong was an outspoken critic of stereotypes Americans held of China and Chinese Americans. (Wong Ching Foo Collection)

Heretofore I have refrained from speaking of the wrongs committed upon the Chinese, which are passed unnoticed by the present ruling power in China, because I disliked to lower my country in the estimation of other nations. But the manner in which my fellow citizens are everywhere neglected compels me to speak out the truth regarding our present Tartar rulers. I do so in order that I may justify the revolutionists, who are now persecuted in every part of China and at the same time enlist sympathy for my countrymen who have been inveigled from their homes. In no period of the history of the Chinese Empire has she suffered so much from political corruption as during the present time. . . . Within the past twenty-five years at least 100,000 Chinese have been kidnapped in the treaty ports of China, and not infrequently these crimes are perpetrated in the very face of the authorities, and yet no effort is made by the Government to help its suffering thousands who are to-day in slavery.

A corrupt regime of "Tartar rulers," in Wong's estimation, was directly responsible for the enslavement of so many Chinese in the coolie trade. (This was an analysis that many Chinese American activists would echo over the coming decades.) Wong's call for the support of "revolutionists" to rid the nation of foreign despotism was resonant with the political objectives of various secret societies such as the Sam Hop Hui, which his friend Tom Lee founded in 1880 and to which he himself may very well have belonged. "May we hope that the time will soon come when China shall be governed by its own loyal citizens and justice given to its people," Wong wrote. It was a position consistent with the Sam Hop Hui slogan, "Oppose the Qing, Restore the Ming."[66]

At Steinway Hall, Wong flatly stated that missionaries were misinforming the American public about China so as to "obtain contributions" for the Foreign Board of Missions. He said that he was not a Buddhist missionary, as was widely publicized, but that it was his desire to "simply explain the doctrines of his faith." He quipped, "I never knew that rats and puppies were good to eat until I was told by American people."[67] His lecture, as reported by a journalist, confronted the stereotypes and discrimination imposed upon Chinese in the United States:

If mistakes were entertained here about such simple matters as the diet of the Chinese, he argued, then much greater errors of belief would prevail in respect to their religion and other abstruse matters. Intelligent men, he said, must necessarily believe in a God, and as proof that there were intelligent men in China he reminded his audience that 450 million people lived under a good government and committed fewer crimes than one-tenth the number living under the American flag. God, he claimed, had given to every race of men a system of revelation according to their peculiar wants and their peculiar nature, and the practice of sending out missionaries to other nations only tended to confound matters in religion.[68]

Attempting to counter the representation of Chinese as idol worshipers and therefore pagan, Wong explained, with the insight of a cultural anthropologist, that Chinese "knelt before images as symbols of their religion, as the Catholics knelt to the cross, and in the same spirit." He then commented on the "opposite" natures of China and the United States to apparently good humorous effect on the audience. In the words of the *New York Tribune* reporter:

> In America a gentleman removed his hat in society; the man who did that in China would be counted a barbarian. Here we shook our friends by the hand and made them suffer for making our acquaintance; in China a man clasped his own hands and tortured himself for his friend. "Which is the more civilized way?" asked the speaker, and the audience laughed. At meals in America soup was eaten first, in China it was the last dish to be partaken of. Here wine was drunk cold; there it was made steaming hot. Here when a man called upon a friend he immediately inquired after the health of his wife; there a wife is considered too insignificant a creature to mention. Here men marry recklessly; there they had to be careful because they could not get divorces so easily.

National differences were laid out and then relativized in a manner quite contrary to the simplistic Victorian polarities of absolute good and bad. Wong insisted on the need to respect and understand the cultural and historical peculiarities of each society. In response to Christian missionary charges of heathenish pagan worship, Wong countered that the "Chinese worshipped but one true God—the Supreme and All-powerful Ruler of the universe," and that they had "inherited from Confucius and their other sages as pure and noble a system of morals as that contained in the New Testament." The "idols" that missionaries railed against with "a dozen or more eyes and arms, and similar accompaniments" were not literal representations. Instead they symbolized the "all-seeing and all-powerful attributes of the deity which were common to all nations which believed in one God." Confucius, Wong pointed out, lived some 550 years before Christ. Therefore "the plagiarism, if any, must be ascribed to the latter."[69]

Those who attended the lecture seem to have been quite sympathetic to Wong's point of view. Many were probably friends and colleagues of Madame Blavatsky. However, as a *Tribune* reporter commented, "The audience appeared like a handful of people in the large hall." The small turnout, a Colonel Olcott observed, indicated that New Yorkers "didn't care whether the heathens were damned or not." It is more likely, however, judging from the editorial response of *Harper's Weekly*, that Olcott's perception of apathy should be understood as a general desire not to dignify Wong's arguments. *Harper's* editors were quite offended by his point of view. "If Mr. Wong Ching Foo had taken the pains to inquire a little into the real condition of American ideas respecting China and the Chinese," they stated, "he would have discovered that he has no occasion to be quite so smart and flippant in his criticisms."[70] While Wong's articulate and impassioned lectures add an important element to our understanding of Chinese Americans, he was not terribly effective. Wong's counterrepresentational efforts had a very limited impact. His arguments did not fall easily into the existing discourse on China, the Chinese, or racial hierarchy. Wong's insistence on the relativism of cultural and historical differences fell on deaf ears in New York City's increasingly tense and bounded commercial marketplace, at the moment when the city and the nation were abandoning the radical Republican dream of racial equality in the postwar South. In New York's commercial culture, Wong Ching Foo had little power supporting his perceptions and knowledge.

As might be imagined, bicultural tensions were not necessarily easy to negotiate. Census data, crew lists, naturalization records, and non-Chinese media representations do not readily allow us to penetrate the silences of these Chinese Americans, to hear their point of view expressed in their own words and life stories. We do not yet understand how difficult and/or rewarding their negotiations between Chinese and American, between Guangdongese and New York cultures, may have been. We do know, however, despite the promise of earlier cross-cultural experiences embodied by Chinese-Irish families settling as port-culture New Yorkers, that another set of social relations came to predominate.

The servant Fou Afung's detainment by his boss was but one of many instances already recounted: the regular breaching of legal contracts with Chinese performers, the plight of the impoverished actor-peddlers, and the displaying of Miss Pwan Ye Koo all indicate bitter experiences that we may never be able to fully tell. The rise of the institution of laundry work in the

1870s, above and beyond all other occupations in New York City, gives clear indication of an increasingly hostile racial climate that prefigured the emergence of a protective and ghettoized Chinese enclave. Chinese New Yorkers were increasingly treated as an undesirable and unassimilable race of people. Chinese efforts at mixing into the multinational culture of lower Manhattan's port culture were to be deeply discouraged.

The flourishing exchange cultures of the China trade and chinoiserie outlined in part 1 of this book and the production and reproduction of a variety of commercialized images and identities explored in part 2 were now combined into a powerful culture of otherness that precluded any effective self-representation of a Chinese American sensibility. Chinese New Yorkers were simply marginalized and had limited voice in the mainstream work and political culture of the city. Their efforts to engage in a two-way conversation were limited by the nature of the hierarchy of New York civic culture, combined with a stereotypic commercial culture driven by consumer demands and racial biases. Increasingly, Chinese New Yorkers were limited in their choices. When properly Christianized, they gained jobs as house servants. If they remained sojourners in their ghettoized living places and work, they might have a chance of making a living. Even for the biculturally literate and highly communicative Wong Ching Foo, horizons were severely limited. The earlier culture—the era of the merchant Chong collecting errant debts, the era of the Bunker twins' being so unusual that they could gain some control over their destiny, the era of a mixed culture of Chinese and Irish and others—was now increasingly eclipsed by the use of the Chinese in political debates about labor, class, race, and what it meant to be American.

CHAPTER 11

Descent
to Darkness

A S THE CHINESE COMMUNITY GREW and be-
gan to create its own businesses and organizations, the many New York daily
newspapers regularly reported on this small but curious settlement. Newspaper coverage constituted what was probably the single most influential
body of written and visual material representing Chinese and the Chinese
quarter to the New York public. From the late-1860s on through the 1880s,
paralleling the early development of Chinatown, newspaper features increasingly emphasized the association of Chinese with filth and the practices of
opium smoking, gambling, and racial intermingling—increasingly taking on
a moralistic tone, showing readers the inside of a criminal and dangerous
culture. Between the decade before and the decade after the arrival of Chinese
workers in North Adams and South Belleville, the character of newspaper
representations of the Chinese quarter changed, the tone of easy-going tolerance giving way to one of trepidation and fear. These currents had deep
resonance in the political culture of New York City, a resonance that would
ultimately give impetus to the middle-class support of national anti-Chinese legislation.

Dangerous Dens

At midcentury the newspaper coverage of Chinese New Yorker life was often
anecdotal and humorous. A *Frank Leslie's* article written in 1858 by "Doe-
sticks," for example, referred to opium and domino playing in a lighthearted
manner. Having "secured the friendly services of an intelligent officer of the
police to pilot us on our uncertain way," the reporter, a friend, and an illustrator made their way to Cherry and James Streets to find a "nest of cocoa-

nut heads." After climbing "a flight of narrow, dirty stairs, into the upper story of one of the filthiest tenement houses of the vicinity," they found lots of tobacco and opium smoke, peculiar sleeping habits, people socializing and working, and very crowded conditions. Having taken some puffs on the pipe, the journalist's friend announced that "he was Swang-Pang-Jang, the father of the Sun and Moon, and own cousin to the Milky Way; and he called for dinner and mentioned tom-cat fricassee as a dish to be provided, with bull-pup potpie to follow, and also declared his intention of throwing Old Spectacle out of the window if all wasn't ready in two minutes." The tone of the article was more burlesque than judgmental, but this was soon to change.[1]

In a December 1869 issue of the *New York Tribune*, editor Horace Greeley featured an article entitled "Our Pagan Population. The Chinese Considered without Reference to 'Caste.' Among the Dens of Baxter Street—A Celestial Habitation. Opium Smoking—It Produces Consumption. The Chinese Club Room—A 'Pigtail' Interviewed. A Row—Schools—'Anoder Brudder.'" Greeley's intrepid reporter went to the police station for a police escort. They then descended from "Captain Jourdan's precinct station house down that most filthy and iniquitous of all thoroughfares in the metropolis—Baxter Street." After passing "rickety dens in which human beings breed and die," amid "wretched women, in tattered garments, shivering with cold, innoculated with rum and speckled with chronic sores of debauchery and vice," and "frightful yells and . . . blasphemous oaths—flying through the air as thick as hail," the reporter arrived at 14 Baxter Street. "In such a quarter as this, where everything is of the lowest and most vulgar description, the Chinese live." One of the "inmates" answered their knock:

> Amid the fumes of opium, the foul smells of deoxogenized air, and the thick vapory clouds of an apartment that had little acquaintance with the external atmosphere, the first impression was one of extreme novelty. . . . It is sometimes within man's fortitude to behold degradation and misery; but when foul smells are added, when his ear is filled with jargon, his taste attacked by a revolting nausea, and his feelings triumphed over by a chill of loathing, the conquest of his physical powers is complete.

The article proceeds to describe the face of a Chinese man in proto–Fu Manchuesque terms:

> Look at his face! His complexion was a dusky brown, his features cast in the ugliest mould possible, turning out a model which had for its chief characteristic an excrescence [of] a nose; two small mountains, known as cheek-

Figure 36. "A Growing Metropolitan Evil," *Frank Leslie's Illustrated,* May 12, 1883.
The representation of innocent white women victimized by nonwhite men has been
a persistent means by which groups have been demonized and scapegoated.
(Wong Ching Foo Collection)

bones; two deep valleys, in physiognomy styled dimples; two caverns from which gleamed the dying pupils of eyes suffering the eclipse of a long continued habit of opium smoking; a frightful crater whence now and then shot out a tongue emitting eruptions of spittle; a broad expanse of brow that may have typified the Black Sea; a slight promontory for a chin; a couple of peninsular shaped ears; all combining with an expression that pictured a vexation of the body, a convulsion of nature.[2]

Within this world the Chinese and their habitat embodied filth, disease, sexual mixing, and all that was repulsive to the Victorian middle-class sensibility.

Even the most pro-Chinese of newspapers, the *New-York Times,* became increasingly fixated on the Chinese quarter as primarily a site of opium smoking, gambling, violence, and little else; the ever temperate patrician-oriented *Times* began featuring opium smoking and "pagan worship" in its subtitles. One 1878 article was entitled "Pining for Their Poison. Two Chinese Prisoners Yearning for Opium. How a Times Reporter Got Some for Them at Ah Que's Bazaar in Baxter Street—The Merchant, His Home, His Wife, and His Pipe." The article recounted the arrest of "four wretched and dirty Chinamen" who were put behind bars for selling cigars on which no revenue tax had been paid. Out of pity, the reporter procured opium for them to smoke in prison from "a lean, lank, saturnine fellow, with a yellow, jaundiced-looking eye and a skin like parchment."[3]

In 1879 the *Daily Graphic* had fully criminalized the representation of Chinese and the Chinese quarter. In recounting the raid of a "Chinese gambling den," the *Graphic* headlined, "The Moon-Eyed Gamblers. The Raid by the Police on a Chinese Establishment. Thirty-one Prisoners Arraigned before a Police Justice and Discharged." In what appears to be one of the first raids on gambling in Chinatown, Captain Brogan explained that the police "might as well make an example of the heathen as of the Christian law breaker." Though there was no formal complaint, the police decided to "raid the place on their own information." Some forty-seven police officers surrounded the Chinese grocery at 18 Mott Street, which had a gambling and opium-smoking room in the rear. "It is one of the places which are popularly supposed to abound in pickled rat, edible dog and savory candles, but whose main source of income is really derived from the lucrative but forbidden opium traffic." A grand total of $3 in American money and "nearly twice as much in Chinese" was seized along with "un-understandable gambling implements, by means of which it would greatly puzzle the average

Caucasian to either win or lose his money, unless he were exposed to Ah Sin's vain tricks." The next day, all thirty-one prisoners were released by the judge for "an absence of proof" that they had been engaged in anything but "some private amusement such as is not uncommon in the best clubs and in private houses."[4]

These journalistic descriptions were often accompanied by visual representations of opium dens. In an October 1881 issue of *Harper's Weekly*, J. W. Alexander etched a powerful full-page drawing of "American Opium-Smokers—Interior of a New York Opium Den." While the good middle-class business-oriented readers of *Harper's* had been exposed to the connection between Chinese and opium dens, they had not seen such dramatic evidence of the corruption of otherwise well-dressed European Americans "hitting the pipe." A rather ghastly-looking Chinese man is entering a darkened, smoke-filled room with a tray of the poison. The room frames six men, one woman, and one skull-like face caught in various stages of intoxication; all are white. The same basic theme was reiterated eighteen months later in a more refined and powerful way by *Frank Leslie's Illustrated*. The front page of a May 1883 issue depicted another smoky, darkened room with a Chinese man bringing in a tray with opium. But instead of so many white men, we see only the faces of three white women, one holding a pipe and nodding out. The caption read, "A Growing Metropolitan Evil—Scene in an Opium Den, in Pell Street, Frequented by Working-Girls."[5] Chinese men not only harmed their own women with barbaric practices such as foot-binding, they were out to corrupt American women as well.

"Do Chinese Eat Rats?"

> Chinkie, Chinkie, Chinaman,
> Sitting on the fence;
> Trying to make a dollar
> Out of fifteen cents
> Chink, Chink, Chinaman
> Eats dead rats;
> Eats them up
> Like gingersnaps.[6]

The association of Chinese and rats was not an invention of Joseph Keppler or Edward Harrigan. The identification had its American origins in children's textbooks decades earlier, and by the 1870s and 1880s it had become a dominant popular image in San Francisco, New York, and the rest of the nation. When public issues such as the Chinese Question were played out in the commercial realm, individuals expressed their political positions not only through the electoral process but also through the selection of cultural representations. The "revolution of choices" of the nineteenth century also included the choice to consume and identify with a set of politicized racial attitudes.[7] The print culture created a means by which readers could engage in contemplating an image of the acceptable citizen.

The association of Chinese with rats and other animals had long been featured in American popular culture. The image can be traced in the public domain to as early as the 1840s. Samuel Griswold Goodrich's *The Child's Second Book of History* (1840) included a picture that would remain etched in the memories of generations of American schoolchildren. The image was captioned "Chinese selling rats." The text read:

> Many parts of China is so thickly settled, that nothing which will support life is thrown away. Puppies, rats and mice are constantly hawked about the streets for sale. A favorite dish with the great is made of birds' nests of a particular kind, composed of glutinous substances. The common articles of food are rice, vegetables, fish, poultry and pork. Among the Tartars, horse flesh is a favorite food. Tea is an universal beverage.[8]

The chatty history lessons of Goodrich's popular *Peter Parley's Universal History* text reiterated these claims from 1853 to 1886. Generations of American youth were deeply influenced by such associations. As we saw in chapter 7, New York City schoolchildren of 1850 already knew what to think about China and the Chinese. Two children noted that the Chinese "eat mice and pupies" or "live on dogs, rats, cats and other vermin for want of anything else."[9] From here it was only a small (but significant) leap of imagination to the claim that rats, "like gingersnaps," were everyday preferred fare.

Such images were certainly not limited to child-oriented materials. They circulated throughout the commercial culture—in newspapers, trade cards, labels, songs, and on stage. In 1853 the New York publication *Yankee Notions* lightheartedly featured a rotund Chinese caricature named "Chi-chin-choo" who relished rat soup, roast pup, and the "Landlady's favorite Tabby." Another drawing, "Uncle Sam's Chrystal Palace Restaurat!!" showed a choking John Chinaman with Uncle Sam speculating, "I suppose that pup he's jest eat has got to fighting with that cat he had for breakfast, or is huntin them rats I made him a present of yesterday."[10]

The linkage of the Chinese with rats—specifically, with eating rats—was an undeniably powerful image in the Victorian imagination.[11] The proliferation of the image in the popular culture should be understood not only as a manifestation of public opinion but also as having the power to forge a coherent working-class and middle-class consensus about Chinese exclusion and containment.

An 1883 *New-York Times* article provides a rare insight into how the association of Chinese and rats was played out in Victorian discourse. The piece was headlined "Mott Street Chinamen Angry / They Deny That They Eat Rats—Chung Kee Threatens a Slander Suit." The fact that the *Times* was one of the few papers that still held pro-Chinese editorial policies makes the implications of the text all the more complex.[12]

The article begins with the question "Do the Chinese eat rats?" The unnamed reporter acknowledges the standard contention of geography texts and the "old wood-cut of a Chinaman peddling rodents, strung by the tails to a rack." Although "the Chinese have always indignantly denied the charge," the reporter confirms that "a large portion of the community believe implicitly that Chinamen love rats as Western people love poultry." The article responds to the charge of Dr. Charles Kaemmerer, of 20 East Thirteenth Street, that the "Chinamen" living at 5 Mott Street, in the words of the reporter, "killed and cooked rats and cats in the yard, and . . . disposed of the offal by throwing it into the yard of No. 199 Worth street." Five Mott Street happened to be occupied by a Mr. Wong, who ran the Chung Kee grocery store and lived above the store. Wong had apparently lived in New York for several years and was "quite wealthy." He was the head of the Wong Family Association, and his store was their headquarters.

Kaemmerer, a former sanitary inspector for the city and conspicuously identified as "a short, stout, excitable Frenchman upwards of 50 years of age and a resident of this City for a quarter of a century," was visiting his friend Cepirlo, and for some reason he converted this visit into a sanitary inspection. Kaemmerer apparently noticed, in the words of the reporter, a "very peculiar odor" coming from the courtyard and saw "some Chinamen standing there handling some things that looked like very small cats or very large rats." But the "stench" was so terrible that Kaemmerer demurred from further examination. This was the basis of his complaint. Upon further inquiry,

Figure 37. "Uncle Sam's Chrystal Palace Restaurat!!" *Yankee Notions,* June 1853.
The early representations of the stereotype of Chinese eating rats were
relatively playful. (Courtesy of Bonner Collection)

the reporter found that Cepirlo gave a different version of the story. According to Cepirlo, the doctor did not actually see the cats, but Cepirlo's son saw two dead cats outside the kitchen window, which were later removed by a Chinese man. The son claimed to have seen a Chinese cook "skin the animals, cut off their heads, chop their bodies into small pieces, and put them into a pot." He did not see any of the meat eaten but did claim to have seen the meat picked from the bones after boiling.

Kaemmerer's complaint led to a sanitary inspection by a Dr. Vermtiye, who found no odor from the kitchen, "no offal in the yard, no cat or rat skins, and no stench." Looking into the open window of the kitchen next door, he determined that the Chinese chef was making "a stew of salted Chinese turnips, soft-shelled crabs, and pigs ears." In the reporter's words, "The cook was as deft as a hotel *chef,* and did his work with much care and cleanliness. He shelled fresh peas, sliced a wholesome-looking cabbage head, and peeled fresh potatoes whose skins were almost white. There was nothing suggestive of rats or cats about the place and the doctor said that he should report that there was no cause for complaint."

Under closer scrutiny, the reporter's story doesn't quite hold up. It is difficult to sort out what was really said to the reporter and what he claimed the protagonists told him. It seems unlikely that the inspector compared the cook with a hotel chef or used such words as *wholesome*. These rather didactic elaborations seem more likely to have originated in the reporter's skeptical attitude toward the complainants and his interrelated preference for extolling the virtues and innocence of the Chinese. Kaemmerer's version of the story was that he was offended by the "peculiar odor" and overpowering "stench" of the backyard, indicating that the meat was rotting in the August heat. Yet Kaemmerer insisted on telling the reporter that the French were not bothered by the notion of Chinese eating cats or rats. Indeed, the French inspector stated, "In Paris the Frenchmen ate rats during the siege. We eat dogs and horses, and cats are served for rabbits in almost every restaurant in Paris. I once ate part of a cat in this City [New York], and I liked it. I thought it was a French hare until several days afterward. The meat was sweet and it tasted very good." What makes this disclaimer by Kaemmerer interesting is that he was pointedly stating that he was not making a cultural judgment about the Chinese eating such things. The reporter, on the other hand, was not impressed by these eating habits, which he may have thought were indicative of the peculiar excesses of French culinary indulgence.

Given these statements, it seems unlikely that Kaemmerer or anyone else actually saw cats or rats being butchered. There was plenty of testimony to give lie to this claim. The reporter was skeptical, the city inspector found no evidence, and Mr. Wong angrily denied the charge. Indeed, in true American fashion, he threatened to sue Dr. Kaemmerer for slander. The reporter asked several Chinese if "cat meat was ever used for food or in the preparation of Chinese medicines." Several answered that "cats and rats were never eaten but that a nostrum was made of cat's meat." They emphasized, however, that "it was not made in America but was imported from China."

Wong Ching Foo, now the editor of the bilingual (and short-lived) New York–based *Chinese American* newspaper, boldly countered these accusations with a reward of $500 to anyone who could prove that Chinese ate rats or cats. Wong said that he had traveled all over China and had never heard of a native eating a rat or a cat. While acknowledging that Chinese ate dog meat, he stated that the only circumstance in which he could imagine Chinese eating rats and cats would be in a time of famine, when "they ate anything to keep from starving." Furthermore, he maintained, there was no necessity for the Chinese to eat such foods in the United States. Citing the adequate salaries of laundry workers, he contended that "they can all afford to buy the best that the market affords."[13]

Despite the skeptical manner in which these complaints were reported and the dubious truthfulness of the specific complaints, two elements of this story underscore the mainstream American sense that Chinese people were capable of such strangeness: first, the mainstream culture saw exoticism, and second, the unaccustomed odors associated with Chinese and the Chinese quarter also signaled incomprehensible repulsion. The boy's claims to have seen cats being chopped up was consonant with mainstream American perceptions of odd Chinese food habits. Given the pervasiveness of caricatured representations of Chinese eating rats and puppies, it may not have been such a leap of imagination for the son to have truly thought he saw a cat being chopped up, especially having seen two dead cats laid out the day before. It seems likely the boy simply did not know what the Chinese cook was cutting up, and he therefore assumed it to be a flesh that he believed, via the popular culture of the time, Chinese diners relished.

What did even the most open-minded of Americans know about the foods Wong Ching Foo described as being displayed in New York's Chinese stores? Such foods—dried ducks' feet stuffed with chicken liver wrapped with prepared entrails, oysters dried hard as stone, shad in oil, pork in sugar, old eggs of duck, dried cabbage, salted turnips, and "hundreds of other things which are unheard of by the enterprising American gastronomer"—must have looked quite "peculiar."[14] Americans of this era were at once fascinated and intimidated by the complexity and variety of Chinese foodways. Louis Beck, in his 1898 book *New York's Chinatown*—the first attempt at an in-depth examination of New York's Chinese—responded to this ambiguous anxiety by devoting many pages to Chinese foodways, Mott Street restaurants, and recipes for these strange dishes, including a section titled "How to Cook Rice."[15] Cepirlo's son may very well have thought he was telling the truth and simply did not understand what he was seeing. What became a citywide issue of rats and inferior races may have originated in the anxiety of a simple inability to recognize a different culture's food.

By the 1880s, the representations associating Chinese with rats that were already in common circulation were starting to become far more negative.

A generic trade card of 1881, brightly printed in three colors (black, red, and blue), shows a salacious, bony-headed Chinese caricature and a ferocious-looking guard dog, both eyeing a cage containing two huge white rats. In this image—captioned "Two minds with but a single thought / Two hearts that beat as one"—the association of Chinese with rats had taken a decided turn for the worse. Indeed, Chinese were now shown competing with "lower"-order, nonhuman animals.[16] The sense that Chinese would eat rats "for want of anything else" had given way to the belief that these heathen actually relished rodents and ate them by choice. This leap of imagination was made by stage performers and writers as well as visual artists. The shift can be seen in the contrast between Septimus Winner's song "The Coolie Chinee," written and performed in 1871, and Frank Dumont's "The Chinee Laundry Man," written in 1880 and performed from that year on.

Winner, an accomplished songwriter, musician, and performer, wrote "The Coolie Chinee" as a "humorous song" that emphasized the fanciful, storybook nature of his subject. The song describes the peculiar customs of a Chinese servant and the predictable disasters that follow his hiring. "He would never sit like the rest of us did, But down on the floor squat[t]ed he." The servant cheats at cards as Ah Sin had done, and he uses a silk hat for a "basket to market." And, of course, naively assuming that his own "Chinese" ways are the ways of the world, "for dinner he gave us our little pet cat" and "supper he made from a cussed old rat." The song emphasizes the servant's childlike naiveté and lack of sophistication. While explicitly anticoolie, it is at the same time playful.[17]

In contrast, New York novelist and playwright Frank Dumont's popular song "The Chinee Laundry Man," written some nine years later, has a more cutting edge. This piece was performed "with wonderful success" by Charles Backus. Different versions of the song have different lyrical variations, but one version heavily emphasizes rats:

> Me comee from Hong Kong, Chinee,
> To workee for de Mellican man,
> Me no can talkee much English,
> Me speakee you de best I can.
> Me workee all day in laundry,
> For ching chong dats his name,
> Me catchee all de rats in de market,
> Makee potpie alle same. . . .

> Me soon gettee money velly plenty,
> And wantee gettee nice littee wifee . . .
> Me feedee her on rice and opium,
> Me buyee nice littee house—
> For dinee me fixee de rat-trap,
> To catchee nice littee mouse,
> Mousee, good mousee, alle same, nice mousee
> Littee mousee, big rat, so big.

One can imagine how Backus must have toyed with his audience while singing these last few lines. Unlike Winner, who referred to his Chinese character in the third person, Backus actually took on the persona (and no doubt the odd costuming) of a Chinese. His use of pidgin dialect was typical of a trend in New York stage representations of Chinese characters. By turning himself into a three-dimensional caricature, Backus could further tease and disgust his audience, trying out various versions of the song to gauge which specific lyrics had the greatest effect. Clearly, in this version of the lyrics he overemphasized the association of Chinese with rats in order to elicit a response from the audience.

While Winner's lyrics focused on the strange customs of the Chinese, Dumont's song seems to emphasize a willful choice and imposition of Chinese ways onto American life: even while living in the land of plentiful red meats, Chinese immigrants still actively prefer the rat and the mouse. Besides being a source of humor, this association signaled to the audience the undesirability of these "peculiar" and backward people. One version of another verse reiterates Joseph Keppler's carnivalesque image of Chinese feeling so comfortable in the United States that they begin taking over:

> Me no go backee to China,
> Me doee welly well out here;
> Me cheatee de melican gamblee,
> Me drinkee sourkroutee and beer
> Me soon become a cit'zen,
> And votee just likee me please,
> By'm by me gette a good jobbee
> To workee on de policc! (gong)
> Police! (gong) Much clubee! (gong.)[18]

Like Bret Harte's "Truthful James" poem and Johannes Keppler's "pro"-Chinese pieces, both of these songs use humor to emphasize the strangeness

Figure 38. "Rough on Rats," poison label, ca. 1870s–80s. Stereotypes could easily be commercialized to sell products. (Warshaw Collection of Business Americana, Archives Center, NMAH, Smithsonian Institution)

of the Chinese. But the tone of Dumont's lyrics indicates a shift toward a decidedly more negative, even hostile, portrayal. The innocent Chinese who squats on the floor while eating or mistakes a silk hat for a grocery basket has given way to a threatening Chinese who takes over by the rat, the vote, and the policeman's club.

In 1898 a Protestant missionary, E. R. Donehoo, recalled in the *Charities Review* one of his most striking childhood memories of the Chinese. The memory involved an event that occurred in Sunday school during a lecture on the importance of foreign missions, when an image projected by a lantern slide appeared of "a Chinaman reposing on a couch." Donehoo recalled, "Suddenly there emerged from the gloom a monster rat, whereupon the Chinaman opened his capacious jaws, and the rat aforesaid made a wild plunge down his throat. Soon another rat appeared and disappeared in like manner, and another, and still another." At once horrified and entertained, "we youngsters screamed with delight and kept encoring the performance, so that the 'professor' was obliged to curtail the Biblical features of the program in order that we might feast our eyes on the rat-eating Chinaman." This recollection presumably had some motivating role in the good minister's subsequent decision to enter missionary work, but most significant for the discussion at hand is the shift from the notion of Chinese eating rats for survival to the representation in later decades of a Chinaman gorging himself on live rats in a feeding frenzy.[19]

This imagery was pervasive enough for an enterprising Jersey City exterminator to promote his "Rough on Rats" products with an anti-Chinese message. To demonstrate the effectiveness of his rat poison, he illustrated his product with an oddly dressed, clubfooted Chinese caricature holding up a huge rat poised headfirst for ingestion, fur and all. The line "They Must Go!" was a tongue-in-cheek double entendre, an appropriation of the Pacific coast anti-Chinese slogan "The Chinese Must Go." A Kansas manufacturer, the Good Luck Liniment Company, actually named its poison the "Chinese Rat Destroyer" and used a similar visual logo. That company's slogan read, "The greatest known destroyer of rats, mice, and all vermin. They devour it eagerly and once eaten death is certain." Ads like these cleverly argued for ridding the nation of the rat-loving Chinese.[20]

If it was believed that Chinese relished eating rats, it was not difficult to imagine them capable of consuming anything and everything. For anti-Chinese agitators, this representation of the Chinese as indiscriminate and ravenous eaters was easily translated into a symbolic devouring of the

Figure 39. "The Problem Solved," poster, White and Bauer, San Francisco, ca. 1870s. A Chinese grotesque is here depicted as the ravenous consumer of everything in sight. This highly charged political cartoon appealed to a variety of mainstream cultural anxieties. (Wong Ching Foo Collection)

United States. A copyrighted drawing published by two San Francisco "News Agents" illustrates the national danger—the "Great Fear of the Period." In contrast to Nast's anti-Irish sentiments and Kearney's anti-Chinese actions, this drawing expresses a blanket anti-foreignism; it is both anti-Irish and anti-Chinese. Entitled "The Problem Solved," the three-part drawing first shows Uncle Sam being swallowed from both ends—from the head by a prognathous Irish caricature on the Atlantic coast and from the feet by an equally prognathous Chinese caricature on the Pacific coast. Uncle Sam having been finished off, the ultimate winner of the contest proves to be the Chinese eater, who is now shown consuming the Irishman, and wearing his hat as well. In a bit of mock–Social Darwinism, it is not "survival of the fittest" but survival of the most ravenous.[21]

The alluring middle-class association of Chinese labor with saving white labor from drudgery also carried over the threshold of the Victorian household—as did the anxieties associated with the dangers of these Chinese male bodies. While still displaying Chinese porcelains and luxuries in the parlor, Victorians were ever more anxious about hiring Chinese servants and cooks. After all, who knew what they might introduce into the intimate backstage areas of the household? Thus, from the 1870s to the end of the century, the Chinese Servant Question became an issue hotly debated among Victorian families vexed by the problem of finding tractable household labor.

M. T. Caldor's 1873 play *Curiosity* offers an example of how this anxiety was played out on the commercial stage. The play features "Ah Sin" as the mischievous and totally untrustworthy Chinese house servant. When "Mrs. Woebegone" complains, "You know I haven't got but this one pair of hands for all the work in this house," "Mrs. Sprightly" replies, "Why, my dear creature, there's no need of your being so cast down. Haven't you heard the good news that rejoices the hearts of all the housekeepers in the land? No more ruling of helpless mistresses by lady Bridgets or saucy Dinahs. Is it possible you haven't read in the newspapers about the great revolution that is to take place? About the coming man who is to relieve all our perplexities?" Enter Ah Sin, who, betraying the playwright's ignorance, salutes them with a "salam." Ah Sin proceeds to wreak havoc in the household, serving a visiting grand duke vinegar as if it were wine and then tying Mrs. Woebegone to a chair with apron strings and making "grotesque gestures" at her.[22]

The Shadow Metropolis

Perceptions about the place of Chinese in American society were shaped in part by the Victorian notion of the hierarchy of the body as mirrored in the spaces of both the household and the city. At the top of the bodily hierarchy were the intellect and the spirit, which corresponded to the parlor, the library, and the music room—the most important rooms of the household. The genitals, anus, and their associated functions represented the lower bodily stratum; in the household they were to be concealed from any gaze or other sensory exposure, and the tasks associated with them—cleaning, washing, stooping, and the like—were to be performed by those deemed suited for lowly work. These bodily and household hierarchies were in turn mapped outward onto the streetscape along a lateral uptown/downtown axis: on the one hand, the civic centers, courts, churches, public libraries, and clubs frequented by properly acculturated middle-class and elite Anglo-European New Yorkers; on the other hand, the slums—filthy dens of iniquity and vice, infested with disease and vermin and occupied by racial others.

Just as references to the lower body and the releasing of bodily noises were repressed and "forgotten" by the new bourgeoisie, the city's "low" became what Stallybrass and White have termed "a site of obsessive preoccupation." Projecting away from the idealized purity of their own bodies, Victorians focused on eliminating urban "filth"—the slum, the ragpicker, the prostitute, the sewer, the rat, and the racial other. The explosion of nineteenth-century books about the "lights" and "shadows" of New York City, among other Anglo-American cities, is quite telling in this regard. Borrowing conventions and titles from a tradition traceable back to sixteenth-century Great Britain, books such as George G. Foster's *New York by Gas-Light, with Here and There a Streak of Sunshine* (1850), Matthew Hale Smith's *Sunshine and Shadow in New York* (1868), James Dabney McCabe's two books *Lights and Shadows of New York Life* (1872) and *New York by Sunlight and Gaslight* (1882), and Helen Campbell's *Darkness and Daylight, or Lights and Shadows of New York Life* (1892) correlated the Victorian sensibility with a hierarchy of spatial relations in the streetscape.[23]

These books tried to make sense of the new city and its peoples. Historian John Kasson has pointed out that the rise of the nineteenth-century city, with all the pressures of migration, urbanization, and immigration, created enormous anxiety for the dominant classes. Traditional customs and meanings associated with proper relations between social groups were being challenged by the sheer numbers of people populating Manhattan Island. From 1860 to 1890, New York City—still before the annexation of Brooklyn and the other boroughs—tripled in size from some 813,000 to 2.5 million, of which the great majority were living in poverty. Foster's 1850 book illustrates the obsessive fascination such writers brought to their observation of the urban poor. His investigation sought to "penetrate beneath the thick veil of night and lay bare the fearful mysteries of darkness in the metropolis—the festivities of prostitution, the orgies of pauperism, the haunts of theft and murder, the scenes of drunkenness and beastly debauch and all the sad realities that go to make up the lower stratum—the underground story—of life in New York!" Similarly, minister Peter Stryker's "gaslight" tours of the Lower East Side (1866) emphasized the racial and sexual intermixing of the city's poor. Visiting tenements with officers of the law, he found moral degeneracy flourishing everywhere he looked—"people of both sexes and every shade of color herding together, exhibiting less taste and refinement than the brute creation."[24]

Foster's and Stryker's vicarious and puritanical semiotics—connecting poverty and darkness, sexuality and pauperism, degeneracy and racial inter-mingling—exemplifies the Victorian association of the lower body and sex-uality with the lower orders of the city. This association was established well before a noticeable Chinese community had taken root in the city. In fact, Chinese at midcentury were still associated with high refinement and the cultivation of what was good and enlightened about New York City. Weren't the Chinese luxuries that the wealthy and prominent collected and displayed proof positive of their good taste and refinement? By the 1880s, however, Chinatown was beginning to be identified as one of the shadowy parts of the city. James McCabe described Chinatown in 1882 in a chapter entitled "Life under the Shadow." McCabe first takes the reader to "Ragpickers Row" on Mulberry just off Bayard, "the most wretched haunt occupied by human beings in the New World," where "the exterior of the building is wretched enough; the interior is equally so." He then moves on to Baxter Street, "an-other scene of misery, and, alas, of crime," which is also "the centre of the Italian and Chinese colonies." McCabe reports that "it is a terrible neigh-borhood, and at night even the police venture into it with caution." This area is the "headquarters of the Mongolians" with their "gaming houses and opium dens." The Chinese, he says, "are inveterate gamblers, and one of their chief dissipations consists in stupefying themselves by smoking opium."[25]

The sunlight-and-shadow genre sought to redefine the cultural geogra-phy of the entire city—ranking the streetscape and its citizens from a par-ticular moral vantage point. In such writings, Chinese New Yorkers, their living spaces, and the Chinese quarter were consistently described as the opposite of the ideal Victorian individual, Victorian household, and Victorian city. This spatial remapping of New York City was not simply geographical in the narrowest sense of the term but essentially cultural and socioeco-nomic.[26] The reformation of the senses of the urban elite necessitated new thresholds of tolerance and intolerance. What would disgust, shame, embar-rass and what would please, comfort, and flatter became reformulated. As urban problems worsened, the Chinese quarter of New York increasingly became the embodiment of all that was deviant and contrary to the dominant cultural idea. The evil Chinese man flourished, like the rat, in all that was opposed to and subversive of Western civilization.

Exclusion

On April 29 and 30, 1882, New York City newspapers reported on the U.S. Senate's passage of the Chinese Exclusion Act, which prohibited any Chinese "laborers" from immigrating into the United States for ten years. The editorial response of the steadfastly Republican and "pro"-Chinese *New-York Times* was remarkably mild. The editors' commentary on what they referred to as the "New Chinese Bill" simply offered details about the version of the bill passed, some of the debate, the vote, and the president's impending decision. The other Republican paper, the *New York Tribune*, devoted only eight lines to the story, simply noting, in matter-of-fact language, the fact of the bill's passage. These two pro-Chinese papers, which for a decade had played such an active role in the debates on the Chinese Question, expressed no moral outrage about or political disagreement with what had happened in the nation's capital.[27]

Only the *New York Evening Post*, the smallest of the three elite Republican dailies, expressed any remorse or concern. "It is melancholy to relate that the Republicans get no political capital out of it," the paper reported; while the Democratic senators voted overwhelmingly for the bill, the Republicans were split in their opposition. Laying the blame for the anti-Chinese sentiment upon irrational Pacific coast politicians, the long editorial stated, "Everything about this Chinese agitation is characterized by the most delightful absurdity." The editors ended by attempting to remind Republicans of their once radical heritage: "We trust in dealing with all these [anti-Chinese] movements, Republicans will remember their old faith in the power of the United States Government to protect every human being living under its flag in the enjoyment of life, liberty, and the pursuit of happiness."[28]

The anti-Chinese bill clearly represented a defeat for what the Republican Party had fought for since the Civil War. What explains the odd complacency of the *Times* and the *Tribune*? Let us consider the bill in more detail. Congressional representatives from New York City and Brooklyn voted eight to one in favor of exclusion, in contrast to the rest of the state, which voted eight to six in favor. In other words, despite the small numbers of Chinese in the city, the city's politicians responded as if there were an immediate threat.[29] New York senators Lapham of Canandaigua and Miller of Herkimer represented traditional Republican interests. Over the series of votes that first passed a twenty-year ban (vetoed by President Arthur) and then the revised ten-year legislation, the two senators voted to modify the language of the Chinese Exclusion Act to accommodate trade interests and the entry of skilled laborers, augmenting the position of capital in its battles against organized labor.[30]

The battle lines were clearly drawn. The first bill posed continued trade with China and the immigration of skilled labor against Chinese exclusion. Those arguing for exclusion supported a boycott of all Chinese labor in a fashion reminiscent of the tea boycott. The Burlingame Treaty, and subsequent versions of it, became the center of controversy. As Senator Bayard from Delaware explained matters, the treaty had been the work of merchant interests who "saw but one thing—a profitable commerce, and they rushed with haste into a treaty that considered Americans and Chinamen as if they were all of the same race, habits, and characteristics—all equally and alike entitled and fitted to become citizens of the Republic of the United States." Drawing upon the language of the commercial marketplace, the senator declared the Burlingame Treaty "a humbug." Americans had been taken in: "I can recall the procession of the embassy as it swept like a grand circus over the United States, and know what it meant and know what it did, and now you see its fruits."[31]

However, in the course of the congressional debates, trade and exclusion would both be justified. As passed by the Senate and later signed by the president, the language and specifics of the Chinese Exclusion Act were the product of a three-way negotiation process involving the bill's congressional advocates, President Arthur, who wanted to protect prior treaty agreements so as not to jeopardize trade, and various currents of public sentiment. "In the opinion of the government of the United States," the bill opened, "the coming of the Chinese laborers to this country endangers the good order of certain localities within the territory thereof." The phrase "good order" will be discussed below, but the key phrase in this sentence is "Chinese laborers," which was defined in a special way. Contrary to popular usage of the time, wherein *laborer* denoted manual or unskilled labor, section 15 of the bill defined the phrase "Chinese laborers" to mean "both skilled and unskilled laborers and Chinese employed in mining." The earlier national debates distinguishing voluntary and involuntary foreign labor had become divorced from the Chinese Question; all Chinese laborers were now defined as incapable of rationally and freely deciding their own fates. President Arthur had vetoed a previous version of the act because of its potential violation of prior treaty agreements that were vital to U.S. trade interests in China. "Pro"-Chinese concerns centered around protecting the immigration rights of elite Chinese, or those who were merchants, diplomats, scholars, students, teachers, and travelers. The rights of genteel and upstanding Chinese—Chinese of the sort whom patricians had long romanticized and whom Thomas Nast had depicted as "John Confucius"—were supposedly protected in this bill. This constituted a Republican victory of sorts. Americans who were "pro"-Chinese were able to insist on class being the ultimate arbiter of an otherwise racial piece of legislation. Although these exempted individuals were technically free to immigrate, the bill stipulated in section 14 that "no State court of the United States shall admit Chinese to citizenship, and all laws in conflict with this act are hereby repealed."[32]

While at first glance this withdrawal of naturalization rights from all Chinese, including the elite, appears to contradict the more open-minded, pro-Chinese position, the legislation was in fact compatible with the consensus of the Gilded Age political culture of New York City and the nation. Amid the rapid and profound social transformations of the Age of Capital, the Chinese Question came to symbolize the general problem of social instability. The question's resolution, therefore, would restore "good order" in behalf of the greatest good for the general public, irrespective of human-rights issues. The dominant Victorian cultural associations of the Chinese with rats, opium, and everything antithetical to Anglo-Dutch-German Protestant (and now Irish Catholic) American civilization were expressed in the provisions of the Chinese Exclusion Act and related laws of the time. Not only were all Chinese made legally ineligible to become a part of the American body politic, they were classified with other categories that genteel Victorians now found disgusting and abnormal; this included opium addicts, polygamists (Mormons), convicts, "idiots," and "paupers." In the minds of elected officials, the Chinese bill was grouped with the "Polygamy bill" and the passage of immigration laws limiting the rights of those classified as convicts, "idiots," or paupers to enter the United States.[33]

Ironically, on the very day on which the Chinese bill was passed in the Senate, a commercial treaty with China was signed prohibiting the exporting of opium to the United States. Just as Victorian New Yorkers expelled all that had become vile to them into the shadows of the downtown streetscape, populist politicians now legally expelled all that they believed threatened American core values. Within this broad moralistic discourse, the pro-Chinese were just as ready to scapegoat cultural "others" as were the anti-Chinese. Americans had arrived at a new consensus: Chinese were by definition alien, foreign to the United States of America.

The struggles of journalist, lecturer, and activist Wong Ching Foo in New York were indicative of the limits faced even by an educated and rather Westernized "John Confucius."[34] In 1883, after an eighty-lecture tour across the United States, Wong decided to settle in New York City and begin a weekly newspaper called the *Chinese American*. "Our aim," Wong wrote, "is to make this paper supply the long felt want of our countrymen, of whom not one in a thousand can read a word of English. . . . We shall find room for the wants of our readers, in their dealings with Americans or with each other."[35] Note for a moment the significant timing of this event. Just one year after the passage of the Chinese Exclusion Act, we have for the first time in recorded history the use of the term *Chinese American* by an activist expatriate intellectual who sought to use his language and cross-cultural skills to publish a newspaper that spoke to the needs of ordinary Chinese workers and merchants.

Wong repeatedly sparred, in print and in person, with that infamous Irish-immigrant anti-Chinese agitator Denis Kearney. In the summer of 1883, upon the announcement of Kearney's speaking engagement at Cooper Union's Great Hall, Wong announced that he challenged Kearney to a duel to the death: "I give him his choice of chop-sticks, Irish potatoes or Krupp guns." Kearney retorted in the press, "I'm not to be deterred from this work by the low blackguard vaporings of Chin Foo, Ah Coon, Kee Yah, Hung Fat, Fi Fong or any other representative of Asia's almond-eyed lepers." In 1887 Kearney once again spoke at the Great Hall for two hours to an audience of several hundred men and four women—all supporters, except for the five Chinese New Yorkers who sat in the front row, Wong among them. During Kearney's tirade about China as a nation of liars and lepers, Wong repeatedly stood up and confronted him from the audience. He was drowned out by the howls and hoots of the crowd. Kearney victoriously proclaimed, "No Chinese shall speak in the same house with me!"[36]

Though silenced in such public spaces, Wong still found a voice in the liberal Republican press. He wrote two important articles in 1888, "The Chinese in the United States" for the *Chautauquan* and "The Chinese in New York" for *Cosmopolitan*. Yet by the century's end he had still not succeeded

Figure 40. "No more Chinese cheap labor, Celluloid Cuffs, Collars & Bosoms,"
trade card advertisement for Fashion Parlor at 14th Street and Broadway,
New York, ca. 1880s. (Wong Ching Foo Collection)

in creating a specifically Chinese American civil-rights movement, and he returned to China to join the revolutionary movement there.[37]

Chinese New Yorkers, who began their settlement in the city amid many possibilities for creating a creolized downtown culture, were now legally forced to remain perpetual foreigners. Chinese women were effectively denied entry under the rules of the new bill, thereby greatly limiting the future possibility of Chinese American families.[38] Furthermore, only the children of a Chinese person born in the United States could become citizens. In essence, Chinese were excluded from the social, cultural, economic, and political life of the city and the nation. In New York the exclusion law also meant that Chinese would remain marginalized in the commercial culture of the city. Wong Ching Foo would never get sufficient readers to create an alternative Chinese-oriented newspaper. Nor would cultural performers such as the Tong Hook Tong Dramatic Company ever have a real chance to make the kind of transition that Edward Harrigan made when he bridged the Irish American audience with the pan-Christian, pan–European American Bowery audiences of the 1880s. What prevailed was the freedom of the dominant culture to represent Chinese and other Asians in yellow-face. The practice of non-Chinese representing Chinese in American commercial and political venues was already firmly rooted in New York City's community culture. But the passage of the Chinese Exclusion Act further fueled and consolidated this tradition.

Racism, exclusion, and segregation in the United States nurtured bitterness in the hearts of Chinese Americans. The only viable option for energetic and concerned Chinese New Yorkers, whether they liked it or not, was to look to their homeland for sources of political strength. Overseas Chinese, including many New Yorkers, were to play important roles in supporting the revolutionary nationalist movements to come.

Between the Revolutionary War and the Gilded Age, New York City had become the most powerful metropolis of the nation. Its population, its concentration of individual and corporate wealth, and its political power made it the dynamo that drove the nation's progress. Its ever rebuilding spatial environment, constantly making itself anew, and its central role in communications and cultural production largely defined American modernity. In contrast, Guangzhou, the once fabled destination of the *Empress of China*, was now but a treaty port controlled by Western and Japanese world powers. Chinatown, the shadow community of the great metropolis, came to represent all that was low and vile in Victorian genteel urban culture.[39]

CHAPTER 12

Appo's Demise

A YEAR AFTER THE PASSAGE of the Chinese Exclusion Act, Quimbo Appo was screaming that he was being harassed by the "Fenian Party" and that, for political reasons, the Democrats had conspired with the governor to delay his release from the Matteawan State Hospital for the Criminally Insane.

A doctor's typed notes documented the regularly drugged patient's statements over the years:

Mar. 30, 1885. Has delusion that he has been, and is now, suffering for the cause of Ireland and that he must suffer until she is free.

Feb. 26, 1890. Is at times irritable and always preserves a sense of his own importance. . . . He believes that he has grand hotels, palaces, servants and horses outside of the asylum; says he is King of the World and has power over the sun, the wind, and over day and night, and that he is omnipotent. Often he is very happy in his delusions and says he is a Second God.

Nov. 7, 1893. Claims to have power of taking away votes.

Sept. 9, 1895. Imagines that he owns ten hotels and all the laundries in the country.

Jan. 4, 1899. Imagines that he owns Madison Square Garden. . . . Says he was the first Chinaman that ever came to America and while in China he ran the largest tea trade of any man in that country.

Jan. 2, 1907. He says that he is the World Law and has immense sums of money, has a number of hotels in New York City where his National Palace is located. Says that he has many gun boats on the Hudson River and that soon 400,000 boxers are coming to this institution, [who will] raze it to the ground and release him.[1]

What had happened to this man? Represented as "exemplary" in the 1850s, he had become known as the "Chinese devil man" by the time of his death in 1912.[2] Why?

Quimbo Appo's fall from grace embodied the profound shift in the attitude of New Yorkers toward the Chinese and the imagined "Indies." Appo's life spanned three distinctive, overlapping phases of New York's history: from one rooted in the China trade and the passion for Chinese luxury goods and chinoiserie, to a market-mediated antebellum period of relatively open, complex, and countervailing representations, to a post-Reconstruction period of criminalization, ghettoization, and political exclusion.

Charged with the killing of his landlady in 1859 and convicted of manslaughter, Appo was pardoned in 1863. He was released from prison and moved back to lower Manhattan. His wife, Catherine Fitzpatrick, had left New York after the trial, taking their daughter with her to California, where her brother lived, but their ship was wrecked off the Pacific coast; all were killed. Their son, George Washington Appo, had been left behind to be raised on Donovan's Lane.[3]

If Appo wasn't a man accustomed to using physical force before he went to prison, he appears to have become prone to fights after his release. He was accused and convicted of "justifiable homicide" in the killing of a Lizzie Williams, for which he served one year. Now identified by newspapers as the "notorious Chinese ruffian," he was later found guilty of assault in a fight and sentenced to five years in prison. He was pardoned in 1875, then convicted again for brutally kicking a German woman. Six months later he set up a cigar stand but was arrested for not bearing the required tax stamp license.[4]

In 1876 Appo committed another homicide, in an incident that typified all his acts of violence and was perversely reminiscent of Bret Harte's Ah Sin. While lodged at a boardinghouse on Chatham Street, he played checkers with a man named Kelly. Appo was proud of his skill at checkers, and he beat the man several times, winning small wagers with each game. Eventually Appo went to bed, while the much larger Kelly went off angrily and had a few drinks. Later Kelly returned to the lodging house, dragged Appo out of bed, blackened his eye, and kicked him down the stairs. Appo drew his penknife and stabbed the approaching Kelly three times. Kelly died, and Appo was once again convicted of manslaughter, this time receiving a seven-year sentence. He was sent to Auburn State Prison but during his sentence was transferred to the Matteawan facility for the criminally insane.[5]

Real-life events following fiction was not just coincidental; experience as lived was undoubtedly influenced by developing stereotypes, popular representations in the commercial culture, and the dominant political culture of the city. The sympathy for Appo expressed earlier by reporters had now turned into hatred. Partly, no doubt, this shift reflects Appo's later pattern of involvement with violence, but it was also indicative of a larger change in the representation of Chinese between the 1850s and 1880s. The *New-York Times* called Appo "one of the most desperate criminals in the city." The *New York Herald* described him as "a fiend in human shape." And the *New York Tribune* wrote about him in specifically racial terms. Appo's actions, according to Horace Greeley, were "an instance of the uncurbed barbarian temper of the East brought into collision with the colder habits of our Saxon civilization." Appo's criminality was used not only as an argument for more stringent laws to keep recidivist criminals in jail, but also as evidence that all Chinese immigration should be curbed.[6]

It is clear that Quimbo Appo had become a violent man. But what precipitated this behavior? Was he insane? And if so, what made him insane? No definitive answer can be found, but it is obvious that the crossing of uncharted cultural boundaries was a key factor in Appo's descent. Even for a leader of the early Chinese settlement who spoke eloquently to newspaper reporters, being different was fraught with unforeseen dangers.[7]

Quimbo Appo's patient records, logged over his twenty-four years of incarceration in the Matteawan prison hospital, provide invaluable insights into Appo's life experience, with telling hints about the nature of his attributed "mania with delusions." The prison notes describing Appo's behavior indicate that he was easily agitated and probably became delusional during his confinement at the Auburn State Prison, the year prior to his transfer to Matteawan. At the age of fifty-five Appo was described as being five feet three inches tall, 140 pounds, copper-colored, and a Roman Catholic; he was "well built and has evidently been possessed of great bodily vigor and muscular strength." He had an enlarged prostate that apparently caused "frequent and difficult" bowel movements at night. He slept and ate irregularly. He was quite lucid "on some subjects." The entry concerning "Previous habits of life, Temperate or Intemperate?" indicated that he was a "Moderate Drinker." To the question "Is the patient addicted to self abuse [masturbation]?" the doctor gave the less than exact answer "Probably." (In Victorian science masturbation was commonly thought to be a cause of insanity, especially among women.) And in response to "Does the Patient use Tobacco or Opium in any form?" the answer "Chews tobacco" was entered. Having little hair and no teeth, Appo regularly demanded that "the State ought to allow him" a new hairpiece and false teeth, but to no avail.[8]

Despite the representation of Appo by the media as an irredeemably violent criminal, he had not been subjected to mechanical restraint or treated with drugs at Auburn. During his twenty-four years at Matteawan he did express anger on numerous occasions, the fact being duly noted in his records. For example, when no false teeth were given to him, he asked guards to tell the state comptroller that if there were any further refusals Appo would "fix him." The records indicate that when he felt slighted or provoked he would respond by becoming irritable, swearing, or threatening violence, whereupon he would be injected with a sedative. Under sedation he would have hallucinations, such as of "quantities of tobacco upon the floor and in his pockets."[9]

As to how Appo explained his own violent behavior, the doctor gave this account:

> Patient says that ever since the close of the late Civil War he has received revelation from the spirits and "ciples" (disciples) and that he has had assurances from these sources that whatever he should consider it right to do would be considered a good act by God Almighty, no matter what it might be in the light of the human law. He further says that he has been the special subject of the "temptations" by evil spirits for many years and that these "tengatations," as he calls them, have been the source of all his crimes. He says that whenever one of these temptation has been about to beset him, he has been forewarned by spirits and assured that he would come out all "light" (right) in the end, no matter what he did; and, on studying the homicides he has committed, it will be found that in nearly all, some aggravating act of the victim led to the commission of the crime and to a mitigation of the punishment. From his frequent escapes from capital punishment, patient has acquired the delusions that no one can kill him or seriously injure him; and from his many years' imprisonment (18) he regards himself as a protegee of the State. . . . Patient is a devout Roman Catholic; expresses himself as ready to die at any time and says he is "going to Heaven, sure."[10]

While it would be easy to diagnose Appo in contemporary terms as having delusions of grandeur and a persecution complex, such an analysis would tend to underestimate the powerful social influences of his time. Appo's patient records are full of late-nineteenth-century scientific language premised on racially charged notions of biological determinism. In striking contrast to the judgment of the *New-York Times* reporter who characterized Appo as a shrewd and most intelligent businessman, this examining doctor authoritatively stated that Appo "has many of the characteristics of the Mongolian type," and that "he is possessed of little or no education and is of an inferior order of intelligent development, resembling in many respects a child." Like Harte's Ah Sin and all the pidgin-English-speaking and child-like "Chinamen" of popular culture, Appo was described within a scientifically "proven" racial hierarchy. As evidenced by their once great culture, Chinese were clearly superior to lowly Africans, who were thought to be suspended in the "foetal" stage of human development, but far inferior to European-originated whites who were considered full adults. As if to prove these qualitative racial determinations, the doctor described Appo as having a "small and well shaped" head. He also attached a full page of twenty-four "cephalometrical" measurements of Appo's head, including circumference, volume, "great transverse diameter," facial angle, and "angle of prognathism," all expressed in centimeters.[11]

As further evidence of Appo's irrational nature, the doctor recorded examples of his delusions. The loss of a game of checkers was said to be due to the machinations of a political or professional party of one type or another—"Abe Lincoln's Party," the "Doctor's Party," the "Superintendent's Party," or the "Fenian's Party." The doctor also reported that fellow inmates purposely teased Appo because they enjoyed "listening to his 'pidgin' English."[12] His irritability made it easy for others to provoke him into putting on what could be described as a mock-yellowface show, replete with the comic and childish expressions of an Ah Sin.

Contrary to the medical representation of him as somehow being imprisoned by his biological racialness, however, Appo clearly exemplified strong intercultural influences. The doctor's notations indicate that Appo had Western tattoos on both arms, probably a practice of sailors who had visited international port cities. According to one prison admission record, the left forearm featured "the Goddess of Liberty & the Crucifixion" and the right forearm displayed a "Spanish dancing Girl & Girl with a flag & emblem skull & cross bones."[13] Appo did not shave his head, nor did he wear a queue such as all Chinese men, even those overseas, were subject to wear. Indeed, he had adopted the distinctly European and American custom of wearing a wig. He had become so imbued with Roman Catholicism that even his delusional fantasies were punctuated with Catholic imagery; he reported having a vision of the Virgin Mary. In this regard Appo's experience was remarkably similar to that of John Hu, the Jesuit convert committed to an asylum in France in 1723. Both of these Chinese Christians experienced their faith too vividly and too excessively to seem "normal." At other times Appo's delusions centered on European and American politics. He became preoccupied with the Irish, by turns fearing and identifying with them. In 1885 he so identified with the Irish that he believed he was "suffering for the cause of Ireland and that he must suffer until she is free."[14]

Even Appo's mounting delusions of grandeur were a mix of Chinese and American fantasies. He at once told all who would listen that he and his son owned countless New York hotels, including a "National Palace," and that he also owned "all the laundries in the country." While claiming to be the "real Emperor of China" with over "four hundred of the prettiest wives that China ever produced," he also insisted that his son was the president of the United States and was worth "billions of dollars." He believed that he was both a despotic emperor who held all others as his slaves and a wealthy capitalist who owned vast properties.[15]

Appo's responses were clearly extreme, yet the social pressures he felt were quite real. Many political parties, "Fenians," and professional authorities were indeed hostile to Chinese. When Appo lashed out in this climate of mounting racial hostility and rebelled against those who he thought did him an injustice, he was declared first a criminal and then insane. If Appo was not insane when he entered Matteawan, he surely was by the time of his death.

In 1882, the year in which the Chinese Exclusion Act was passed by the United States Congress, Appo complained to prison officials that he should have been released but that "the Democratic party" was in conspiracy against him and had prevailed upon the governor to withhold his commutation of sentence for political reasons.[16] In a sense, Appo was quite correct. His seven-year term had indeed been completed by that date, and although he did not realize it, he would never be released. In an oddly insightful way, Appo had diagnosed the source of his woes. Shifting political winds had indeed conspired against him, though of course not in the personal way of his paranoid imaginings.

What was the danger that Quimbo Appo had come to represent to society? Appo, like the Irishwomen who had relations with nonwhite men, had transgressed the reformulating racial boundaries of lower Manhattan. If Appo had committed his crimes of passion and violence within the confines of the Chinese settlement, it is doubtful that they would have received any public notice. Appo's crimes, however, were directed at the non-Chinese with whom he lived and came into contact. A free-spirited and intelligent individual acting in his own behalf, he was viewed as a danger that had to be controlled. And, as a cultural symbol of racial impurity, a "miscegenator," he had to be made marginal and criminalized.[17] In this sense, Appo's fears about Fenians, Democrats, and politicians trying to get him were not entirely delusional. These fears were grounded in actual power dynamics occurring in lower Manhattan. His fall from grace, his degradation from respected merchant and spokesman to loathsome "Chinese devil man," was not entirely of his own doing.

Over the years, from the New York tea shop to prison, Appo's hybrid, multifaceted life became increasingly limited. Both scientific and popular yellowface stereotypes were used to measure his normality. In effect, his efforts to cross cultural borders became a source of amusement and terrible fascination that ultimately had to be punished. The signals to the Chinese community were clear: within Anglo-American orientalism, Chinese would forever be viewed as foreigners. Settling and intermingling was discouraged.

Quimbo Appo and, by extension, other Chinese New Yorkers came to be represented as either Dr. Jekylls or Mr. Hydes. Yet it was in the historical terrain *between* such Victorian polarities as light and shadow, good and evil, that the true experience of Chinese in New York was actually lived. Quimbo Appo began his life in New York as a respected tea merchant who demonstrated shrewd business skills and spoke to the press on behalf of the needy in the small Chinese settlement. His actions were sufficiently admired by reporters to be described as "exemplary"—praised because he was thought to embody the Protestant, mercantile values of striving so prized by the patrician culture of distinction. Later, Appo's life on trial exemplified the crosscurrents of the popular commercial culture. Whatever he did or did not do to his landlady was represented by the penny press to the fascinated public eager to see—or read—for themselves. Ultimately the spectacle of Appo as the "Chinese devil man" was fed to the sensation-seeking urban republic of consumers. Appo was permanently imprisoned at the same time the Chinese Question was being contested in the political culture of New York.

At stake was the issue of how domestic and international policies, such as definitions of "free labor," immigration laws, and missionary strategies, were to be fashioned. After Reconstruction the "heathen Chinee" were cast out from the body politic, along with African Americans (who were nevertheless entitled to vote), indigenous Indians, and others. In the demise and marginalization of these groups, a white Americanism was born, inaugurating the "American Century." These distinctly New York—and later national—cultures of distinction, of seeing for oneself, and of white nationalism formulated the basis for various orientalist exchanges transacted through New York. The China trade, the commercial stage and media culture, and the mediation of competing political interests into public policies framed the experiences of real Chinese entering, settling, and passing through the port of New York.

Common sense in this democratic public culture was never a simple consensual process. Knowledge about nature and humankind that represented itself as "scientific" intermingled with popular notions, creating "self-evident" truths. Those who had property and wealth, those who voted, those who counted as paying consumers, and those who organized to wield political clout articulated their perspectives on Chinese and China in relation to their own identities. By 1882 three coexisting yet distinct forms of orientalism had resulted, each of which would play a role in shaping the passage and enactment of the Chinese exclusion law. For better and for worse, Quimbo Appo lived through, but did not survive, all three forms of orientalism.

The "American Century"

F ROM THE TIME OF THIS NATION'S FIGHT against
British colonialism until the passage of the Chinese Exclusion Act, the perception and representation of China and the Chinese were part of how
New Yorkers—and, indeed, Americans generally—defined who they were
and were not. Over these hundred years the specific nature of this orientalism changed according to the changing needs of the nationalist self. George
Washington, Phineas T. Barnum, and John Swinton were all self-made individuals who used Chinese things, ideas, and people to suit their own agendas. Merchant Chong, the Bunker twins, and Wong Ching Foo were not any
less their own men, yet each was subject to the claustrophobic ways in which
they were perceived and treated. The American imitation and emulation of
Chinese luxuries decade by decade was complicated by a powerful commercial culture that represented otherness as a commodity to be purchased by
the buying public. With the rise of a destined sense of American civilization,
the Chinese were cast as the embodiment of slavish imitators—the opposite
of free and happy Americans.

American Protestants preaching salvation, individualism, and progress
not only proselytized the Chinese of midcentury New York—among other
"heathen" settlements in the Americas—but in the decades to come also
became prominent in the U.S. involvement in China.[1] The dawn of what
media mogul Henry Luce, himself the son of missionaries in China, termed
the "American Century" prompted an even more covetous and judgmental
gaze at the "oldest" civilization.[2] This would be the era in which American
values and goods heralded freedom and progress around the world, but especially in Asia. For better and for worse, new transcultural contact zones in

coastal cities under American influence developed variations on New York's port life.

The possibilities of communicating across cultures would continue to be highly skewed. Perceptions of the Orient would be plagued by severe ethnocentric and racist judgments. Indeed, the Western practice of mimicking, ventriloquizing, and copying Chinese things, people, and ideas at the beginning of the new nation was displaced by mounting charges that the Chinese were simply copying and pirating American creative and material properties. A fierce, possession-driven individualism, which continues to this day, would be the standard against which the Chinese and Chinese government were measured.[3]

The 1911 revolution in China overthrowing the Manchus and dynastic rule ended the practice of the *ketou*—the traditional act of deference that has come into English as *kowtow*. And recurrent cultural and political movements since that time, including the 1949 communist revolution, have demonstrated the ongoing refusal of various individuals and groups of Chinese to blindly respect authoritarian rule. Yet the association of Chinese people with slavishness and Chinese political authority with despotism continues to blind Americans to the nuances of different political cultural traditions. In American culture the word *kowtow* has been used as a synonym for complete obedience. New Yorker and attorney for the GTE Corporation William T. Barr, for example, clearly expressed his resistance to government by invoking this word. In an interview given to the *New York Times*, he stated, "I'm not a bomb thrower by any means, but my basic philosophy is that you don't get anywhere by kowtowing to regulators."[4] Barr's deployment of this orientalist term, so rich with negative associations of un-American foreignness, helped to gloss over fundamental questions about GTE's enormous wealth and power. *Ketou*, unmoored from its original and specific Chinese usage, has become a free-floating association signifying any constraint to an American's pursuit of life, liberty, and happiness. Now even the American government could be tainted with this orientalist brush.

Indeed, we are living in another era in which consuming desires, globalizing trade, and notions of despotism are once again being played out. The nation's early debates about virtue and corruption, consumption and restraint, propriety and impropriety, normality and deviance, when viewed in these cross-cultural terms, can become an uncanny, revealing resource to help us rethink the present.

It must be stated that the times have changed. We have a growing, albeit still small, population of Asian Americans. New York City has still not elected a person of Asian descent to the city council, nor have most mainstream cultural organizations brought on an Asian as a trustee. But New York now features many Chinese and Asian American professors, fashion designers, students, architects, playwrights, doctors, journalists, developers, philanthropists, and aspiring strivers. Wong Ching Foo would now have a newspaper-buying public, the Bunker twins would have been separated at birth, Pwan Ye Koo, with speech lessons, could be anchoring the evening television news, and Quimbo Appo would have received marriage counseling. In this sense, the world of the nineteenth century has passed.

At the same time, the deeper cultural-political patterns I have written about in this book remain largely intact. Too independent Asian "dragons," small, medium, and large, loom in American nightmares. The elimination of racially based immigration quotas has renewed fears of alien hordes overwhelming the nation. And instances of anti–Asian American violence are on the rise. American conglomerates continue to seek entry into the fabled China market and decry "inscrutable" business practices, while ethnocentric moralizers continue to attempt to reshape Chinese political culture from afar. Indeed, scholar-policymaker Samuel P. Huntington's influential book proposing an impending "clash of civilizations" returns us to terminology and ideas typical of the nineteenth century.[5]

If we look more closely at the coverage of New York and the nation's Chinese community, even deeper patterns remain the same. Recent immigration preference categories favor professionals and increasingly discourage the entry of skilled and unskilled blue-collar workers. The media feature successful and wealthy Chinese and other Asians in a model-minority manner that recalls Thomas Nast's John Confucius, whereas many of the working poor continue to be cast as subservient, unsophisticated, and living in constant fear of criminal gangs and severe community leaders. At the same time, as long as the cultural structures of racial "otherness" continue to flourish, a model citizen can easily be degraded and represented as a corrupting, foreign influence.[6]

In the shadows of Victorian New York the foundations of the Chinese community that would be known as Chinatown were being defined. But contrary to the mainstream impression that this enclave existed solely because of some in-group clannishness, blithely isolated from the rest of the city, the community's very existence was established in the crucible of racism and the failed possibilities of cross-cultural understanding. The history of Chinatown and how it emerged and developed, therefore, was shaped not so much by the actual presence of Chinese in the metropolis as by their systemic erasure and omnipresent "otherness" in New York before Chinatown.

NOTES

Preface

1. For Benjamin's idea of a "philosophical history," see Walter Benjamin, "Theses on the Philosophy of History," in *Illuminations: Walter Benjamin, Essays and Reflections*, ed. Hannah Arendt, trans. Harry Zorn (New York: Schocken, 1969), 253–64; Susan Buck-Morss, *The Dialectics of Seeing* (Cambridge: MIT Press, 1989), 55, 217–21; and Michael W. Jennings, *Dialectical Images: Walter Benjamin's Theory of Literary Criticism* (Ithaca: Cornell Univ. Press, 1987), 52.

2. David Arkush and Leo O. Lee, *Land without Ghosts: Chinese Impressions of America from the Mid-Nineteenth Century to the Present* (Berkeley: Univ. of California Press, 1989).

Introduction

1. Alexander Saxton, *The Indispensable Enemy: Labor and the Anti-Chinese Movement in California* (Berkeley: Univ. of California Press, 1971).

2. Henry R. Luce, "The American Century," *Life*, Feb. 17, 1941, 61–65. For a discussion contextualizing the phrase and the *Life* magazine essay, see W. A. Swanberg, *Luce and His Empire* (New York: Charles Scribner's Sons, 1972), 180–83.

3. Western stereotypes about China and Chinese people have been a major area of study. Unfortunately, few of these discussions are historically grounded. For a sampling, see William W. Appleton, *A Cycle of Cathay: The Chinese Vogue in England during the Seventeenth and Eighteenth Centuries* (New York: Columbia Univ. Press, 1951); William P. Fenn, *Ah Sin and His Brethren in American Literature* (Peiping: College of Chinese Studies, with California College in China, 1933); John Burt Foster, "China and the Chinese in American Literature, 1850–1950" (Ph.D. diss., Univ. of Illinois, Urbana, 1952); Harold R. Isaacs, *Scratches on Our Minds: American Images of China and India* (New York: John Day, 1958); Raymond Dawson, *The Chinese Chameleon: An Analysis of European Conceptions of Chinese Civilization* (London: Oxford Univ. Press, 1967); William F. Wu, *The Yellow Peril: Chinese Americans in American Fiction, 1850–1940* (Hamden, Conn.: Archon Books, 1982); Philip P. Choy, Lorraine Dong, and Marlon K. Hom, *The Coming Man: Nineteenth Century American Perceptions of the Chinese* (Seattle: Univ. of Washington Press, 1994); Arthur Bonner, *Alas! What Brought Thee Hither? The Chinese in New York, 1800–1950* (Madison, N.J.: Farleigh Dickinson Univ. Press, 1997); and James S. Moy, *Marginal Sights: Staging the Chinese in America* (Iowa City: Univ. of Iowa Press, 1993).

4. Said's definition of orientalism serves as an adaptable starting point for coming

to understand the relationship between the rising self-made man and the Western uses of Chinese things, people, and ideas. Edward W. Said, *Orientalism* (New York: Pantheon, 1978), 2–3. In addition to Said's formulation of the Occident, see James G. Carrier, ed., *Occidentalism: Images of the West* (Oxford: Oxford Univ. Press, 1995), and especially Couze Venn, *Occidentalism and Its Discontents* (London: New Ethnicities Unit, Univ. of East London, 1993). I seek to situate the phenomenon of orientalism in time and place. Said's theory is vulnerable to criticisms of ahistoricity—a charge made especially by historical materialists. For more on the elaboration and critique of Said's concept, see Lisa Lowe, *Critical Terrains: French and British Orientalisms* (Ithaca: Cornell Univ. Press, 1991); John M. MacKenzie, *Orientalism: History, Theory, and the Arts* (Manchester: Manchester Univ. Press, 1995); Aijaz Ahmad, "Orientalism and After," in *Colonial Discourse and Post-colonial Theory,* ed. Patrick Williams and Laura Chrisman (New York: Columbia Univ. Press, 1994), 163; and Aijaz Ahmad, *In Theory: Classes, Nations, Literatures* (London: Verso, 1992). See also Said's response to critics and subsequent elaboration: Edward W. Said, *Culture and Imperialism* (New York: Vintage Books, 1994), xxiv–xxv.

One of my frustrations in this study is not having the chance also to examine the dynamics of gender and sexuality with relation to orientalism, racism, and class. However, a number of important recent studies should be read to complicate this study further: Avtar Brah, *Cartographies of Diaspora: Contesting Identities* (London: Routledge, 1996); Reina Lewis, *Gendering Orientalism: Race, Femininity, and Representation* (London: Routledge, 1996); Mrinalini Sinha, *Colonial Masculinity: The "Manly Englishman" and the "Effeminate Bengali" in the Late Nineteenth Century* (Manchester: Manchester Univ. Press, 1995); and Meyda Yegenoglu, *Colonial Fantasies: Towards a Feminist Reading of Orientalism* (Cambridge: Cambridge Univ. Press, 1998).

Perhaps too obvious a point, but one that should nevertheless be made explicit, Said's work and this study are also influenced by the epistemological questions explored by the work of Michel Foucault.

5. For an example of the theory of the westward advance of civilization, see E. L. Magoon, *Westward Empire, or the Great Drama of Human Progress* (New York, 1856), 414.

6. French sociologist Emile Durkheim argued that "society builds a framework of knowledge only at its inception." Emile Durkheim and Marcel Mauss, *Primitive Classification* (Chicago: Univ. of Chicago Press, 1963). For a provocative study on how this insight has been applied to the founding of U.S. race and ethnic relations, see Richard Williams, *Hierarchical Structures and Social Value: The Creation of Black and Irish Identities in the United States* (Cambridge: Cambridge Univ. Press, 1990), 5–6.

7. Eric J. Hobsbawm, *The Age of Revolution, 1789–1848* (New York: Vintage Books, 1992). I use the term *Western modernity* to specify what Marshall Berman has defined as "a mode of vital experience—experience of space and time, of the self and others, of life's possibilities and perils—that is shared by men and women all over the world today"; it is a kind of experience in which, quoting Karl Marx, "all that is solid melts into air." Marshall Berman, *All That Is Solid Melts into Air: The Experience of Modernity* (New York: Simon and Schuster, 1982), 15–36. For more on the definition of "expe-

rience," see Miriam Hansen, Foreword, in *Public Sphere and Experience* by Oscar Negt and Alexander Kluge, trans. Peter Labanyi, Jamie Owen Daniel, and Assenka Oksiloff (Minneapolis: Univ. of Minnesota Press, 1993), xv–xx.

8. Hobsbawm, *Revolution*, 28.

9. Ibid., 53–76; Joyce Appleby, *Capitalism and a New Social Order: The Republican Vision of the 1790s* (New York: New York Univ. Press, 1984), 22.

10. Gordon S. Wood, *The Radicalism of the American Revolution* (New York: Knopf, 1992), 350; Appleby, *Capitalism,* 15–20, 95–97. It is well worth examining Schama's critique of the theories that treat all emergent middle classes as "bourgeois" (in the traditions of Marx and Weber) and his discussion of how the term does not quite represent the Dutch middle class during the height of Dutch international empire building. Simon Schama, *The Embarrassment of Riches: An Interpretation of Dutch Culture in the Golden Age* (New York: Vintage Books, 1987), 6–9, 297, 391, 489. Sociologist Colin Campbell's brilliant extrapolation and challenge to Weber's 1904–5 classic *The Protestant Ethic and the Spirit of Capitalism* is the theoretical frame that best suits the historical evidence I have gathered herein in regard to the use of Chinese things, people, and ideas within the racialized class dynamics of New York City. Campbell examines the historical trajectory of the twin Protestant ethics of pietism as it developed into romanticism and bohemianism in the "modern" era, thus laying the basis for contemporary capitalist consumerism. This study can be understood as an examination of how those twin ethics played out in the port of New York among the patricians, the commercial middle class, and the white ethnic working class. Colin Campbell, *The Romantic Ethic and the Spirit of Modern Consumerism* (Oxford: Blackwell Publishers, 1987). For a political-science perspective, see Barry Alan Shain, *The Myth of American Individualism: The Protestant Origins of American Political Thought* (Princeton: Princeton Univ. Press, 1994).

The discussion of the "dual revolutions" and the concept of individual freedom borrows heavily from Appleby's framing of liberty in the historiographic debates about the persistence of republicanism and the rise of liberal capitalism, as well as Thomas Holt's examination of this question with regard to Jamaican slavery, emancipation, and national independence. This study builds on their characterization of the bourgeois liberal individual in relation to problems of racialized otherness. Thomas C. Holt, *The Problem of Freedom: Race, Labor, and Politics in Jamaica and Britain, 1832–1938* (Baltimore: Johns Hopkins Univ. Press, 1984), 3–9.

11. Hobsbawm, *Revolution*, 189, 20–22. See also Robert Nisbet, *History of the Idea of Progress* (New Brunswick, N.J.: Transaction Publishers, 1994).

12. Appleby, *Capitalism,* 79–105. According to Appleby, Thomas Jefferson's defeat of the Federalists "endowed American capitalism with the moral force of [the people's] vision of a social order of free and independent men," the "people" being defined as "ordinary men, political parvenus, outsiders, interlopers, mere voters without office" (104). Appleby defines this early form of capitalism as "a particular system for producing and distributing the material goods that sustain and embellish life" that relied "upon individual initiative and the absence of authoritarian direction" (22). "Money becomes capital through the changed intentions of those with the money, that is with

the decision to invest rather than spend or hoard wealth" (23). See also Joyce Appleby, *Liberalism and Republicanism in the Historical Imagination* (Cambridge: Harvard Univ. Press, 1992), 1–33, 160–87.

13. Holt, *Problem*, 4; Appleby, *Capitalism*, 15–20.

14. Appleby, *Capitalism*, 19–22, 34–37; James Tully, *A Discourse on Property: John Locke and His Adversaries* (Cambridge: Cambridge Univ. Press, 1980); Herman Lebovics, "The Uses of America in Locke's *Second Treatise of Government*," *Journal of the History of Ideas* 47 (Oct.–Dec. 1986): 567–81. I thank Herman Lebovics for his helpful comments on the debates interpreting Locke.

15. The findings of this study have led me not only to an understanding of the property-bound nature of early U.S. society but also to a perspective that critiques the gender- and race-boundedness of the European liberal social contract. For two recent studies focused on the historical and epistemological particularities of this social contract, see Carole Pateman, *The Sexual Contract* (Stanford: Stanford Univ. Press, 1988), and Charles W. Mills, *The Racial Contract* (Ithaca: Cornell Univ. Press, 1997).

16. Holt, *Problem*, 5.

17. Benjamin B. Ringer, *"We the People" and Others: Duality and America's Treatment of Its Racial Minorities* (New York: Tavistock Publications, 1983); Holt, *Problem*, 5. On the history of Western individualism, see Steven Lukes, *Individualism* (London: Basil Blackwell, 1973). The classic study on Protestantism and capitalism is, of course, Max Weber's *The Protestant Ethic and the Spirit of Capitalism*, trans. Talcott Parsons (New York: Charles Scribner's Sons, 1958). For studies on alienation and the rise of capitalism, see István Mészáros, *Marx's Theory of Alienation* (London: Merlin Press, 1970), and Bertell Ollman, *Alienation: Marx's Conception of Man in Capitalist Society* (Cambridge: Cambridge Univ. Press, 1971).

18. Albert O. Hirschman, *The Passions and the Interests: Political Arguments for Capitalism before Its Triumph* (Princeton: Princeton Univ. Press, 1977).

19. C. B. MacPherson, *The Political Theory of Possessive Individualism: Hobbes to Locke* (Oxford: Clarendon Press, 1962), 60. John Dunn, among others, has challenged MacPherson's analysis of the *Two Treatises of Government*. My concern is not so much to offer one interpretation of Locke over another, but to understand how Locke's ideas were used to justify the powerful rising claims of individualism and property rights as they related to the formation of American identity in juxtaposition to how China was perceived. John Locke was not simply a theoretician; he was an investor in the slave trade, and he was also involved in investments in the East India Company. See John Dunn, *The Political Thought of John Locke* (Cambridge: Cambridge Univ. Press, 1969); Neal Wood, *The Politics of Locke's Philosophy* (Berkeley: Univ. of California Press, 1983), 115 n. 91; Wayne Glausser, "Three Approaches to Locke and the Slave Trade," *Journal of the History of Ideas* 51 (Apr.–June 1990): 199–216; Barbara Arneil, *John Locke and America: The Defense of English Colonialism* (Oxford: Clarendon Press, 1996); and James Tully, "Rediscovering America: The *Two Treatises* and Aboriginal Rights," in *Locke's Philosophy: Content and Context*, ed. G. A. J. Rogers (Oxford: Clarendon Press, 1994), 165–96.

20. Reginald Horsman, *Race and Manifest Destiny: The Origins of American*

Racial Anglo-Saxonism (Cambridge: Harvard Univ. Press, 1981). For a discussion of the inner tensions of what has been called "republican virtue," see J. G. A. Pocock, *The Machiavellian Moment: Florentine Political Thought and the Atlantic Republican Tradition* (Princeton: Princeton Univ. Press, 1975), 506–26. For a discussion of the relationship between a waning republicanism and waxing liberalism, see Appleby, *Liberalism*, 17–23, 320–39.

21. The classic study that frames the nineteenth century is Eric J. Hobsbawm's trilogy. In addition to *The Age of Revolution*, see *The Age of Capital, 1848–1875* (New York: Vintage Books, 1996), and *The Age of Empire, 1875–1914* (New York: Vintage Books, 1989).

22. Many studies discuss the impact of European and European American judgments on a particular racialized group. For example, Winthrop Jordan's class study *White over Black: American Attitudes towards the Negro, 1550–1812* (New York: Penguin, 1968) discusses this unilateral phenomenon in relation to Africans and African Americans. For a study centered more on the formation of occidentalist anthropology and how such a theory and practice thereby represented and acted upon cultural others, see George W. Stocking Jr., *Victorian Anthropology* (New York: Free Press, 1987). Sinha's case study on the colonial dynamics of the "manly Englishman" and the "effeminate Bengali" babu clearly illustrates how these power relations were gendered and sexualized. (*Babu* is traditionally a term of respect like *Master* or *Mr.* used to address certain persons of distinction.) Sinha, *Colonial Masculinity*, 15–22.

23. This formulation of "zones" derives from the work of cultural geographers. See Edward J. Soja, *The Postmodern Geographies* (New York: Verso, 1989), and the various studies of Yi Fu Tuan. A port-culture zone is comparable to the frontier zones delineated by John Mack Faragher, *Daniel Boone: The Life and Legend of an American Pioneer* (New York: Holt, 1992), and Richard White, *The Middle Ground: Indians, Empires, and Republics in the Great Lakes Region, 1650–1815* (Cambridge: Cambridge Univ. Press, 1991); and to the Mexican-U.S. border zones explored by Guillermo Gomez-Peña, *The New World Border: Prophecies, Poems, and Loqueras for the End of the Century* (San Francisco: City Lights, 1996), and Carlos Velez-Ibenez, *Border Visions: Mexican Cultures of the Southwestern United States* (Tucson: Univ. of Arizona Press, 1996). The concept of cross-cultural contact, translation, and communication are related to the ideas of Dean MacCannell, *The Tourist: A New Theory of the Leisure Class* (New York: Schocken, 1976); Mary Louise Pratt, *Imperial Eyes: Travel Writing and Transculturation* (London: Routledge, 1992); Linda Young, *Crosstalk and Culture in Sino-American Communications* (Cambridge: Cambridge Univ. Press, 1994); Tejaswini Niranjana, *Siting Translation: History, Post-structuralism, and the Colonial Context* (Berkeley: Univ. of California Press, 1992); and Vincente L. Rafael, *Contracting Colonialism: Translation and Christian Conversion in Tagalog Society under Early Spanish Rule* (Durham, N.C.: Duke Univ. Press, 1992). For a study that begins to explore the historical role of port cultures and mariners in the African diaspora, see Paul Gilroy, *The Black Atlantic: Modernity and Double Consciousness* (Cambridge: Harvard Univ. Press, 1993).

24. For interpretations tied to the expansion of bourgeois individualism and its

encounter with African Americans and Native Americans, see Arneil, *John Locke;* Glausser, "Three Approaches"; and Tully, "Rediscovering America," 165–96.

25. I use the term *contact zone* in a sense that is more general than Mary Louise Pratt's definition. See Pratt, *Imperial Eyes,* 6.

26. Here I have adapted Michael Omi and Howard Winant's concept of "racial formations" to describe variant cultural formulations of orientalism. The term *formation* is used to indicate a dynamic social historical process in which meanings and categories are politically generated and transmuted. Michael Omi and Howard Winant, *Racial Formation in the United States from the 1960s to the 1980s* (New York: Routledge and Kegan Paul, 1986), 4–5.

27. On the Western phenomenon of mimesis, see Gunter Gebauer and Christoph Wulf, *Mimesis: Culture, Art, Society,* trans. Don Reneau (Berkeley: Univ. of California Press, 1992).

28. Alain Grosrichard, *The Sultan's Court: European Fantasies of the East,* trans. Liz Heron (London: Verso, 1998).

Chapter 1: Porcelain, Tea, and Revolution

1. *Pennsylvania Evening Post,* July 13, 1776; *New York Herald,* July 10, Aug. 28, 1876; I. N. P. Stokes, *The Iconography of Manhattan Island, 1498–1909* (New York: Dodd, 1915–28), 2:992. The statue was unveiled on August 16, 1770. Thomas Jefferson Wertenbaker, *Father Knickerbocker Rebels: New York City during the Revolution* (New York: Charles Scribner's Sons, 1969).

2. Wertenbaker, *Knickerbocker,* 76–87; Stokes, *Iconography,* 2:991–99, 1001; William H. W. Sabine, ed. *Historical Memoirs from 16 March 1763 to 25 July 1778 of William Smith* (New York: New York Times and Arno Press, 1969). "Hardship, exposure" from *Kemble's Journal,* quoted in Stokes, *Iconography,* 2:999.

3. Franklin Knight, *Monuments of Washington's Patriotism Containing a Fac Simile of His Public Accounts Kept during the Revolutionary War, June 1775–June 1783* (Washington D.C., 1844), 4:471; Douglas Southall Freeman, *George Washington: A Biography* (New York: Charles Scribner's Sons, 1948), 1:52. *Damask* was commonly used to refer to a richly patterned fabric that originally derived from Damascus markets defined as part of "the Orient." Josiah Wedgwood, the British porcelain maker, described "burnt china" as a ceramic with gold burned into it. Eliza Meteyard, *The Life of Josiah Wedgwood* (London, 1865), 1:372.

4. Susan Gray Detweiler, *George Washington's Chinaware* (New York: Harry N. Abrams, 1982), 65.

5. Stokes, *Iconography,* 2:1002; Wertenbaker, *Knickerbocker,* 91–97.

6. George Washington, *The Writings of George Washington from the Original Manuscript Sources, 1745–1799,* ed. John C. Fitzpatrick (Washington, D.C.: United States Government Printing Office, 1931–44), 8:194, 16:321.

7. By 1763, British entrepreneur Josiah Wedgwood had pioneered a lead-glazed faux porcelain earthenware of a cream color. The style became increasingly popular among the British aristocracy and was inexpensive enough to be affordable to the mid-

dle classes. Indeed, at the height of the Revolutionary War, Washington constantly sought out "queensware"—the distinctive ivory-colored ceramics that Wedgwood named after Queen Charlotte, wife of George III. Detweiler, *Chinaware*, 53–54, 57, 62. For insights on Washington's aspirations to be a gentleman, see Paul K. Longmore, *The Invention of George Washington* (Berkeley: Univ. of California Press, 1988), 6–7, 9, 14–15.

8. For the divides of wealth in Virginia, see Freeman, *George Washington*, 1:40–52, 73–189. For personal revelations gained with surveying, see George Washington, *Diaries of George Washington*, ed. John C. Fitzpatrick (Boston: Houghton Mifflin, 1925), 1:8.

9. [Dr.] Alexander Hamilton, *Gentleman's Progress: Itinerarium of Dr. Alexander Hamilton*, ed. Carl Bridenbaugh (Chapel Hill: Univ. of North Carolina Press, 1948), 8. For an excellent synthetic study on the meaning of early American material culture, see Richard L. Bushman, *The Refinement of America: Persons, Houses, Cities* (New York: Alfred A. Knopf, 1992), 76.

10. The patricians' abhorrence of rural backwardness also applied to their perceptions of craftsmen and unskilled urban labor. Samuel Johnson's *Dictionary of the English Language* defined *mechanic* as "mean, servile; of mean occupation." Alexander McDougall, a leader of the Sons of Liberty and a Scottish Presbyterian who rose from milkman and apprentice sailor to become a major general in the Continental Army, noted that he constantly had to fend off attacks on his character because of his origins. See Roger J. Champagne, *Alexander McDougall and the American Revolution in New York* (Schenectady: New York State American Revolution Bicentennial Commission in Conjunction with Union College Press, 1975), 136.

11. G. S. Wood, *Radicalism*, 27, 198.

12. For a discussion of how American culture was and became even further Anglicized, see Jack P. Greene, *Pursuits of Happiness: The Social Development of Early Modern British Colonies and the Formation of American Culture* (Chapel Hill: Univ. of North Carolina Press, 1988).

13. George Washington to Richard Washington, Dec. 6, 1755, George Washington Papers, Manuscripts Division, Library of Congress. One hundred such merchants worked in London for much of the century, their numbers peaking in the 1760s. In addition to porcelain, these merchants sold large quantities of tea, chocolate, snuff, arrack, fans, lacquered cabinets, and tea tables. In a sense these stores became the embodiment of the East Indies and Americas trade, with perceptual confusion stemming from the indiscriminate intermingling of goods sold. Aubrey J. Toppin, "The China Trade and Some London Chinamen," *English Ceramic Circles Transactions* 3 (1935): 36–37, 45. Detweiler points out that the term *china* generally referred to porcelains made in Ching-te Chen (Jingdezhen). Detweiler, *Chinaware*, 31. This confusion about Asia and the tendency to conflate different Asian peoples and cultures continues throughout European and American history to the present day. See John Kuo Wei Tchen, "Believing Is Seeing: Transforming Orientalism and the Occidental Gaze," in *Asia/America: Identities in Contemporary Art* (New York: New Press, 1994), 12–25.

14. T. H. Breen, "'Baubles of Britain': The American and Consumer Revolutions of

the Eighteenth Century," *Past and Present* 119 (May 1988): 73–104; Diane diZerega Wall, *The Archeology of Gender: Separating the Spheres in Urban America* (New York: Plenum Press, 1994), 127–50.

15. Hugh Honour, *Chinoiserie: The Vision of Cathay* (New York: Harper and Row, 1961), 5–8; Dawson, *Chinese Chameleon*, 106–31; Ellen Paul Denker, *After the Chinese Taste: China's Influence in America, 1730–1930* (Salem: Peabody Museum of Salem, 1985), 1–8.

16. Anne H. Wharton, "Washington's New York Residence in 1789," *Lippincott's Monthly Magazine*, May 1889, 741–45; Detweiler, *Chinaware*, 106.

17. Henry B. Hoffman, "President Washington's Cherry Street Residence," *New-York Historical Society Quarterly Bulletin* 23 (July 1939): 95–97.

18. Wharton, "Residence," 742, 744.

19. Washington, *Writings*, 30: 443–45; Morris (Paris) to GW, Jan. 24, 1790, George Washington Papers, Manuscripts Division, Library of Congress, vol. 22 (Commercial Letters).

20. Detweiler, *Chinaware*, 109, 120–35.

21. Pierre Bourdieu, *Distinction: A Social Critique of the Judgement of Taste* (Cambridge: Harvard Univ. Press, 1984), 1–7; see also Leora Auslander, *Taste and Power: Furnishing Modern France* (Berkeley: Univ. of California Press, 1996); La Rochefoucauld-Liancourt quoted in Bayrd Still, *Mirror for Gotham* (New York: New York Univ. Press, 1956), 67; Grant Thornburn, *Forty Years' Residence in America* (Boston, 1834), 20–21.

22. Bushman, *Refinement*, 110–22.

23. Gordon S. Wood, *The Creation of the American Republic, 1776–1787* (New York: Norton, 1969), 36; Catharine Macaulay, *An Address to the People of England, Scotland, and Ireland, on the Present Important Crisis of Affairs* (London, 1775), 9; Tobias Smollet, quoted in John Sekora, *Luxury: The Concept in Western Thought, Eden to Smollet* (Baltimore: Johns Hopkins Univ. Press, 1977), 84; *Columbia Magazine* 4 (Apr. 1790): 245–48.

24. Sekora, *Luxury*, 84; Rodris Roth, "Tea-Drinking in Eighteenth-Century America: Its Etiquette and Equipage," in *Material Life in America, 1600–1860*, ed. Robert Blair St. George (Boston: Northeastern Univ. Press, 1988), 440; William H. Ukers, *All about Tea* (New York: Tea and Coffee Trade Journal Company, 1935), 389. On feminine perceptions, see Leonard Blussé, *Strange Company: Chinese Settlers, Mestizo Women, and the Dutch in VOC Batavia* (Dordrecht, The Netherlands: Foris Publications Holland, 1986).

25. David Hume, "On Luxury," in *Political Discourses* (Edinburgh, 1752), 32–34. Emmanuel Chukwudi Eze maintains that Hume, as typical of many European intellectuals of that time, believed in white superiority and nonwhite inferiority. See Emmanuel Chukwudi Eze, ed., *Race and the Enlightenment* (Oxford: Blackwell Publishers, 1997), 5, 29–33.

26. Sekora, *Luxury*, 61. By 1725 the Society for the Reformation of Manners, focusing on southeastern England, claimed over ninety-one thousand arrests for violation of these consumption laws. However, such regulation became increasingly difficult with the domestic circulation of the spoils of British colonialism. For a useful his-

tory of sumptuary laws in Europe, see Alan Hunt, *Governance of the Consuming Passions* (New York: St. Martin's Press, 1996). See also Frances Elizabeth Baldwin, *Sumptuary Legislation and Personal Regulation in England* (Baltimore: Johns Hopkins Univ. Press, 1926), 195.

27. Breen, "Baubles," 86–87. See also Edmund S. Morgan and Helen M. Morgan, *The Stamp Act Crisis: Prologue to Revolution* (Chapel Hill: Univ. of North Carolina, 1953), and T. H. Breen, "An Empire of Goods: The Anglicization of Colonial America, 1690–1776," *Journal of British Studies* 25 (1986): 467–99.

28. Charles M. Andrews, "Boston Merchants and the Non-importation Movement," *Trans. of the Colonial Society Massachusetts* 19 (1916–17): 92; "New York Sons of Liberty Resolutions on Tea," Nov. 29, 1773, in *Documents of American History*, ed. Henry Steele Commager (Englewood Cliffs, N.J.: Prentice-Hall, 1988), 1:70.

29. *New York Journal*, Oct. 14, 1773. The pen name is possibly chosen from John Hampden (1594–1643), an English politician and leader of Parliament against Charles I. He raised troops for Parliament and was killed during the English Civil War. On McDougall, see Roger J. Champagne, *Alexander McDougall and the American Revolution in New York* (Schenectady: New York State American Revolution Bicentennial Commission in Conjunction with Union College Press, 1975).

30. *New York Journal*, Oct. 14, 1773. Here *slavery* is used not to denote the practice of slavery itself but rather in the metaphorical sense of losing control of one's "natural rights" to buy and sell. Scevola, or Scaevola, was a Greek philosopher. Classical references like this were common among the eighteenth-century British and their colonials, who were fascinated by the Greek and Roman empires.

31. Diana diZerega Wall, "At Home in New York: Changing Family Life among the Propertied in the Late Eighteenth and Early Nineteenth Centuries" (Ph.D. diss., New York Univ., 1987), 253, 255. See also Elizabeth Blackmar, *Manhattan for Rent, 1785–1850* (Ithaca: Cornell Univ. Press, 1989), 52.

32. Abbé Robin, *New Travels through North America: In a Series of Letters. . . in the Year 1781* (1783; reprint New York: New York Times, 1969), 23. For a study of British women's uses of the tea table, see Elizabeth Kowaleski-Wallace, *Consuming Subjects: Women, Shopping, and Business in the Eighteenth Century* (New York: Columbia Univ. Press, 1997), 19–72. See also Karen Halttunen, *Confidence Men and Painted Women: A Study of Middle-Class Culture in America, 1830–1870* (New Haven: Yale Univ. Press, 1982). On the intertwined relationship between gender-bounded roles in Victorian society, see Mary Poovey, *Uneven Developments: The Ideological Work of Gender in Mid-Victorian England* (Chicago: Univ. of Chicago Press, 1988). The use of Chinese things to mark distinction within such a highly gender-inflected context deserves further study.

33. Thomas Bender, *New York Intellect* (Baltimore: Johns Hopkins Univ. Press, 1987), 9–45; Bushman, *Refinement*, 84; Gertrude E. Noyes, *Bibliography of Courtesy and Conduct Books in Seventeenth Century England* (New Haven: Tuttle, Morehouse, and Taylor, 1937), 11; Antoine de Courtin, *The Rules of Civility, or Certain Ways of Deportment Observed in France amongst All Persons of Quality upon Several Occasions* (London, 1678), 69–75.

34. John Adams, *Diary and Autobiography of John Adams*, ed. L. H. Butterfield (Cambridge: Belknap Press of Harvard Univ. Press, 1961–66), 1:129, 2:113–14, 386–87.

35. Prints and Photographs Division, Library of Congress, illustrated in Roth, "Tea-Drinking," 453. Having "a dish of tea" could also be a subject of satire regarding materialistic excess. See John Smith, "A Little Teatable Chitchat, a la Mode, or an Ancient Discovery Reduced to Modern Practice" (1781) in *Dramas from the American Theatre, 1762–1909*, ed. Richard Moody (Cleveland: World Publishing, 1966), 9–10.

36. Marcel Mauss, *The Gift: The Form and Reason for Exchange in Archaic Societies*, trans. W. D. Halls (New York: W. W. Norton, 1990), 8–14; James G. Carrier, *Gifts and Commodities: Exchange and Western Capitalism since 1700* (London: Routledge, 1995), 24–38.

37. Bushman, *Refinement*, 88.

38. Wall, *At Home*, 255. For an excellent discussion of George Washington's elaborate use of porcelains in mealtime rituals, see Detweiler, *Chinaware*, 103–18.

39. Bender, *Intellect*, 40; Benjamin, "The Work of Art in the Age of Mechanical Reproduction," in *Illuminations*, 222–25; Bourdieu, *Distinction*, 1–7. For more on the European style of chinoiserie, see Dawn Jacobson, *Chinoiserie* (London: Phaidon, 1993), and Honour, *Chinoiserie*. For a discussion of American chinoiserie, see Denker, *Chinese Taste*, 1–8.

40. For a compatible analysis, see Gillian Brown, *Domestic Individualism: Imagining Self in Nineteenth-Century America* (Berkeley: Univ. of California Press, 1990), 38–60.

41. Annette B. Weiner, *Inalienable Possessions: The Paradox of Keeping-While-Giving* (Berkeley: Univ. of California Press, 1992), 6–12.

42. Jacob Ernest Cook, *Alexander Hamilton* (New York: Charles Scribner and Sons, 1982), 1–8, 18–19; Saul K. Padover, *The Mind of Alexander Hamilton* (New York: Harper and Brothers, 1958), 31.

43. Historian Nancy Cott has noted that childrearing practice shifted during this period from "physical coercion to psychological maneuvering," restraining passions by instilling individual self-control. Within this worldview, childhood education demanded the shaping of desires and training in how to manage commodities. Girls in particular were trained in the arts of conversation, discernment, and appropriating commodities into meaningful possessions. See Nancy Cott, "Notes toward an Interpretation of Antebellum Childrearing," *Psychohistory Review* 7, no. 4 (1973): 20, and Bernard Wishy, *The Child and the Republic: The Dawn of American Child Nurture* (Philadelphia: Univ. of Pennsylvania Press, 1967), 181. See also Ashis Nandy, *The Intimate Enemy: Loss and Recovery of Self under Colonialism* (Delhi: Oxford Univ. Press, 1983), 15.

44. Jill T. Matas, *Unstable Bodies: Victorian Representations of Sexuality and Maternity* (Manchester: Manchester Univ. Press, 1995).

45. William James, *The Principles of Psychology* (New York, 1890), 293.

46. Father Du Halde's four-volume study was the most influential of the few books about China circulating in the European American colonies and the United States during the eighteenth century. Jean Baptiste Du Halde, *The General History of China, Containing a Geographical, Historical, Chronological, Political, and Physical Descrip-*

tion of the Empire of China (London, 1736). On the early American interest in Confucianism, see A. Owen Aldridge, *The Dragon and the Eagle: The Presence of China in the American Enlightenment* (Detroit: Wayne State Univ. Press, 1993), 23–46. In the same volume (144–60) Aldridge has also carefully analyzed the influence of Voltaire and the physiocrats on early U.S. political intellectuals. See also Lewis A. Maverick, *China a Model for Europe* (San Antonio, Tex.: Paul Anderson, 1946).

47. Benjamin Franklin, *The Papers of Benjamin Franklin*, ed. Leonard W. Labaree (New Haven: Yale Univ. Press, 1959–78), 6:77; *Poor Richard Improved* (Philadelphia, 1765), 12:11–12, 16:200, 17:107, 18:188, 19:268, 19:317, and 19:323; American Philosophical Society, *Transactions* 3 (1793): 8–10.

48. Franklin, *Papers*, 21:173; American Philosophical Society, *Transactions* 1 (1768): xix.

49. E. Millicent Sowerby, *Catalogue of the Library of Thomas Jefferson* (Washington, D.C.: Library of Congress, 1952–59), 1:132–38; Frederick Doveton Nichols and Ralph E. Griswold, *Thomas Jefferson, Landscape Architect* (Charlottesville: University Press of Virginia, 1977); Jefferson to Mr. Joseph Milligan, Apr. 6, 1816, in *The Life and Selected Writings of Thomas Jefferson*, ed. Adrienne Koch and William Peden (New York: Random House, 1944), 663; Count Antoine Louis Claude Destutt de Tracy, *A Treatise on Political Economy*, trans. Thomas Jefferson (New York: A. M. Kelley, 1970), 35–36, 46, 71–72.

50. Alexander Hamilton, *Alexander Hamilton's Pay Book*, ed. E. P. Panagopoulos (Detroit: Wayne State Univ. Press, 1961), 4–5, 36–37, 45, 42–43.

51. George C. D. Odell, *Annals of the New York Stage* (1931; reprint New York: AMS Press, 1970), 1:135, 199, 201, 242; Fenn, *Ah Sin*, xxvi, 101; Chen Shou-yi, "The Chinese Orphan: A Yuan Play," *Tien Hsia Monthly* 3 (Sept. 1936): 114.

52. Robert M. Dell and Charles A. Huguenin, "Vermont's Royall Tyler in New York's John Street Theatre: A Theatrical Hoax Exploded," *Vermont History* 38 (spring 1970): 105.

53. William Whitehead, Esq., Poet-Laureate, Spoken by Mr. Holland, quoted in Arthur Murphy, *The Orphan of China, a Tragedy, as Performed at the Theatre-Royal, Drury-Lane* (London, 1797), xiii.

54. S. Chen, "Orphan," 89–115. The Wade-Giles transliteration of the Chinese is *Chao-shih-ku-erh*, translated as "The Little Orphan of the House of Chao."

55. Aldridge, *Dragon*, 21, 95.

56. S. Chen, "Orphan," 91–93. The play was typical of the Chinese operatic tradition. The actors introduced themselves to the audience upon first appearing on stage. Sets would have been simple, and musicians would have sat in the wings. Dialogue, spoken or sung in a highly stylized manner, would have been intermixed with a range of arm, leg, and head movements and percussive, wind, and stringed instrumental music. The play clearly emphasized the Confucian values of filial piety, loyalty to virtuous superiors, and avenging injustice.

57. For historical context, see Allardyce Nicoll, *A History of Late Eighteenth-Century Drama, 1750–1800* (Cambridge: Cambridge Univ. Press, 1927), 335.

58. Cited in S. Chen, "Orphan," 93, 96–97, 109. See also Appleton, *Cycle*, 84.

59. In 1750 Rousseau offered China as disproof of the value of learning. If learning, upon which the Chinese placed such high value, could triumph over corruption, then China should have long since become a wise, free, and all-powerful society. China has not managed to achieve this, ergo what use are literature and science? Appleton, *Cycle*, 85; S. Chen, "Orphan," 105–6.

60. S. Chen, "Orphan," 109, 111. See also Murphy, *Orphan*, 85–86.

61. S. Chen, "Orphan," 113.

62. Murphy, *Orphan*, 88–89.

63. Appleton, *Cycle*, 88–89.

64. Murphy, *Orphan*, 89.

65. Gouverneur Morris to Charles Thomson, Dec. 30, 1783, Charles Thomson Papers, Library of Congress.

66. *Compact Edition of the Oxford English Dictionary* (OED) (Oxford: Oxford Univ. Press, 1971), s.v. "exchange"; Georg Simmel, *The Philosophy of Money*, trans. Tom Bottomore, ed. David Frisby (London: Routledge, 1990), 78.

67. William M. Reddy, *Money and Liberty in Modern Europe: A Critique of Historical Understanding* (Cambridge: Cambridge Univ. Press, 1987), 64–65, 88, 199. In *Treatise*, xvi, 6, Count Destutt de Tracy defined society as "purely and solely a continual succession of exchanges. It is never anything else, in any epoch of its duration, from its commencement the most unformed, to its greatest perfection."

68. *OED*, s.v. "superfluities"; Lars Magnusson, *Mercantilism: The Shaping of an Economic Language* (London: Routledge, 1994), 6; Adam Smith, *The Wealth of Nations* (London: Penguin Books, 1970), 472.

69. Holden Furber, *Rival Empires of Trade in the Orient, 1600–1800* (Minneapolis: Univ. of Minnesota Press, 1976), 2, 7, 17, 24, 127, 330; Immanuel Wallerstein, *The Modern World System* (New York: Academic Press, 1974), 132.

Chapter 2: What Does China Want?

1. Samuel Shaw, *The Journals of Major Samuel Shaw, the First American Consul at Canton*, ed. Josiah Quincy (Boston, 1847), 100.

2. William Appleman Williams, *Empire as a Way of Life* (New York: Oxford Univ. Press, 1980), 42.

3. Sidney Pomerantz, *New York: An American City, 1783–1803* (New York: Columbia Univ. Press, 1938), 148. Clarence Ver Steeg, "Financing and Outfitting the First United States Ship to China," *Pacific Historical Review* 22 (1953): 12. For the classic account of the commercial expansion of the port of New York, see Robert Greenhalgh Albion, *The Rise of New York Port, 1815–1860* (1939; reprint Boston: Northeastern Univ. Press, 1984).

4. P. C. F. Smith, *The Empress of China* (Philadelphia: Philadelphia Maritime Museum, 1984), 15–19.

5. John Ledyard, *John Ledyard's Journal of Captain Cook's Last Voyage*, ed. James Kenneth Munford (Corvallis: Oregon State Univ., 1963), 200. For examples of recent scholarship and controversy about Cook, see Marshall D. Sahlins, *How "Natives"*

Think: About Captain Cook, for Example (Chicago: Univ. of Chicago Press, 1995), and a sharp critique by Gananath Obeyesekere, *The Apotheosis of Captain Cook: European Mythmaking in the Pacific* (Princeton: Princeton Univ. Press, 1997).

6. Ibid., xxxvii, 5. Cook's official account came out a year after Ledyard's. Virtually every crew member had kept a journal of the trip, but all such notes were confiscated by the ship's officers before landing in Macao. This effort at controlling details of the voyage was calculated to safeguard Cook's publication as the official account of the voyage. According to biographer James Kenneth Munford, Ledyard's book was also the first to be copyrighted in the United States. Ironically, Ledyard had himself plagiarized entire sections of the anonymously published log of a shipmate named Rickman.

7. P. C. F. Smith, *Empress*, 17.

8. *Pennsylvania Packet*, Sept. 9, 1783; Ver Steeg, "Financing," 4.

9. P. C. F. Smith, *Empress*, 43.

10. Thomas Elliot Norton, *The Fur Trade in Colonial New York, 1686–1776* (Madison: Univ. of Wisconsin Press, 1974), 217–20.

11. Mary Gallagher, "Charting a New Course for the China Trade: The Late Eighteenth-Century American Model" (1996), Robert Morris Papers, Queens College, City Univ. of New York, 2–4; Robert Morris, *The Papers of Robert Morris, 1781–1784,* ed. Elizabeth M. Nuxoll and Mary A. Gallagher (Pittsburgh: Univ. of Pittsburgh Press, 1996), 8:872–73 n. 5. I wish to thank Mary Gallagher and Elizabeth Nuxoll for their helpful suggestions. For an insightful study of a contemporary of Morris involved in the China trade, see Jonathan Goldstein, *Philadelphia and the China Trade, 1682–1846: Commercial, Cultural, and Attitudinal Effects* (University Park: Pennsylvania State Univ. Press, 1978). For a description of Chinese goods imported into U.S. homes, see Carl L. Crossman, *The China Trade: Export Paintings, Furniture, Silver, and Other Objects* (Princeton: Pyne Press, 1972).

12. P. C. F. Smith, *Empress*, 20–23; Gallagher, "Charting," 3–4, 5.

13. Ver Steeg, "Financing," 3–4; Gallagher, "Charting," 3–4; P. C. F. Smith, *Empress*, 20.

14. Gallagher, "Charting," 5–6; P. C. F. Smith, *Empress*, 20, 44–48. For more on Duer, see Robert F. Jones, "The Public Career of William Duer: Rebel, Federalist Politician, Entrepreneur, and Speculator, 1775–1792" (Ph.D. diss., Univ. of Notre Dame, 1967).

15. P. C. F. Smith, *Empress*, 29.

16. Morris, *Papers*, 8:873 n. 7.

17. Gallagher, "Charting," 6.

18. William Duer to John Holker, Dec. 3, 1783, cited in Morris, *Papers*, 8:870.

19. Gallagher, "Charting," 9.

20. Morris, *Papers*, 8:878 n. 50, 879 n. 54.

21. Maritime scholar P. C. F. Smith's otherwise informative work discusses ginseng in a condescending fashion. See P. C. F. Smith, *Empress*, 33. The Greenbies wrote that ginseng was "not therapeutic in any sense, but purely psychic." Sydney Greenbie and Marjorie Barstow Greenbie, *Gold of Ophir* (Clinton, Mass.: Colonial Press, 1937), 31. In an era in which Western medicine still used leeches in bloodletting, such attitudes

were clearly ethnocentric. On the historical uses of ginseng, see E. N. Anderson, *The Food of China* (New Haven: Yale Univ. Press, 1988), 113, 230, 235–36, and Edward H. Schafer, "T'ang," in *Food in Chinese Culture: Anthropological and Historical Perspectives*, ed. K. C. Chang (New Haven: Yale Univ. Press, 1977), 111–12.

22. P. C. F. Smith, *Empress*, 34–35. For the medicinal uses of ginseng, see James A. Duke, *Ginseng: A Concise Handbook* (Algonac, Mich.: Reference Publications, 1989).

23. Major Jelles Fonda, letter, 13 Sept. 1774, and "An Indian Book," Fonda Collection, New-York Historical Society, New York; Barent Sanders, July 24, 25, 28, Aug. 2, 4, 5, 1800, Sanders Collection, New-York Historical Society; P. C. F. Smith, *Empress*, 35–36.

24. Feb. 10, 1784, Parker Papers, Massachusetts Historical Society; P. C. F. Smith, *Empress*, 36–42, 155.

25. For comparison purposes, Ver Steeg has noted that the sales price of the second largest iron works in the United States (which included thirty thousand acres of land) in 1781 was $240,000, and the initial capitalization of the Bank of North America was $400,000. Ver Steeg, "Financing," 8–9.

26. P. C. F. Smith, *Empress*, 3–5. The weather during the winter of 1784 is also described in David M. Ludlum, *Early American Winters, 1604–1820* (Boston: American Meteorological Society, 1966), 64–66.

27. Captain John Green, "Journal of an Intended Voyage . . . ," Jan. 25, 1784, John Green Papers, Philadelphia Maritime Museum.

28. Shaw, *Journals*, 21, 58.

29. Ibid., 112.

30. P. C. F. Smith, *Empress*, 64, 191–92; Holker Papers, reels 12, 13, 16, Manuscripts Division, Library of Congress.

31. Dec. 7, 28, 1784, William Duer Papers, New-York Historical Society; P. C. F. Smith, *Empress*, 221–22, 235–49. Here the word *honour* was used in a very particular Hobbesian sense that linked being propertied to individual character. In *Leviathan* Hobbes maintained, "The manifestation of the Value we set on one another is that which is commonly called Honouring, and Dishonouring. To Value a man at a high rate, is to Honour him. . . . Nor does it alter the case of Honour, whether an action (so it be great and difficult, and consequently a signe of much power,) be just or unjust: for Honour consisteth onely in the opinion of Power." Quoted in MacPherson, *Political Theory of Possessive Individualism*, 242. As legal scholar Morton Horwitz has noted, exchange chains among merchants increasingly abstracted the tangible ownership of real material property into an exchange of promises. Morton Horwitz, *The Transformation of American Law* (Cambridge: Harvard Univ. Press, 1977), 31–62.

32. *OED*, s.v. "Indies," 1416; Raynal quoted in Donald Lach, *Asia in the Making of Europe* (Chicago: Univ. of Chicago Press, 1965), 1:4; logbook title from P. C. F. Smith, *Empress*, 8.

33. Green, "Journal," Jan. 25, 1784, entry.

34. *New York Packet*, Feb. 23, 1784; Pomerantz, *New York*, 444.

35. P. C. F. Smith, *Empress*, xiii.

36. Shaw, *Journals*, 160–67. Apparently this sense of camaraderie extended even

over the War of 1812. Silas Holbrook stated, "Notwithstanding the war between the two nations, there was no hostility betwen [*sic*] the Americans and the English in Canton." [Silas Holbrook], *Sketches by a Traveller* (Boston, 1830), 42.

37. Charges of roguery, piracy, and shrewdness all, of course, became part of cross-cultural vocabulary in this age of international trade and colonialism. However, some of these charges lived on to become entrenched stereotypes that often affected the course of events. Chinese knavery came to take on the persona of "Ah Sin" from 1870 onward. For more on this, see chapter 9.

38. Shaw, *Journals*, 183. For essays on the colonial, cross-cultural dynamics of pidgin English, see Dell Hymes, ed., *Pidginization and Creolization of Languages* (Cambridge: Cambridge Univ. Press, 1971). Sidney W. Mintz's essay therein, "The Socio-Historical Background to Pidginization and Creolization," 481–96, is particularly suggestive for comparable cross-cultural dynamics occurring in Pacific and Indian Ocean ports. For a more contemporary discussion, see L. Young, *Crosstalk*, 1–27.

39. This pattern of perception of the "good" and "bad" other is consistent with how Pacific islanders, other Asian peoples, Asian Americans, Africans and African Americans, Native Americans, indigenous peoples, and Mexican Americans have been portrayed in the colonial Western imagination. For a sampling of these studies, see Roy Harvey Pearce, *Savagism and Civilization: A Study of the Indian and the American Mind* (Berkeley: Univ. of California Press, 1988); George M. Frederickson, *The Black Image in the White Mind: The Debate on Afro-American Character and Destiny, 1817–1914* (New York: Harper and Row, 1971); and Bernard Smith, *European Vision and the South Pacific* (New Haven: Yale Univ. Press, 1975).

40. Freeman Hunt, *Worth and Wealth: A Collection of Maxims, Morals, and Miscellanies for Merchants and Men of Business* (New York, 1856), 82, 110. On Chinese merchants' perennial indebtedness, see Kuo-Tung Anthony Ch'en, *The Chinese Insolvency of the Chinese Hong Merchants, 1760–1843* (Taipei: Institute of Economics Academia Sinica, 1990).

41. Indeed, these Western traders came to view China in a manner paralleling Montesquieu's formulation of "oriental despotism." Despotism, he theorized in his 1746 *The Spirit of the Laws*, was determined by land and climate. Virtuous republics, like the much idealized Greece, were small urban port cultures located in a hospitable clime and responsive to popular will. Despotic empires, on the other hand, were fostered in torrid, endless land masses where authoritarian fear ruled the few and the many. The emperor owned all property and people. The people in such lands were de facto servile. Brendan O'Leary, *The Asiatic Mode of Production* (London: Basil Blackwell, 1989), 43. My own analysis freely borrows from O'Leary and Lowe yet synthesizes their important insights in a manner different from theirs. See O'Leary, *Asiatic Mode*, 60–65, and L. Lowe, *Critical Terrains*, 60–74. For a Lacanian analysis of "oriental despotism," see Grosrichard, *Sultan's Court*.

42. Erasmus Doolittle, "Recollections of China," in [Holbrook], *Sketches*, 25; Amasa Delano, *A Narrative of Voyages and Travels* (Boston, 1817), 542; Stuart Creighton Miller, *The Unwelcome Immigrant: The American Image of the Chinese, 1785–1882* (Berkeley: Univ. of California Press, 1969), 24–26. For a discussion of contemporary

versions of this same basic judgment of "despotism," see John Kuo Wei Tchen, "Pluralism and Hierarchy: 'Whiz Kids,' 'The Chinese Question,' and Relations of Power in New York City," in *Beyond Pluralism: Essays on the Definition of Groups and Group Identities in American History*, ed. Edward Landsman and Wendy Katkin (Urbana: Univ. of Illinois Press, 1998).

43. John Locke, *An Essay Concerning Human Understanding*, ed. Peter H. Nidditch (Oxford: Clarendon Press, 1975), 1:iv, 22.

44. O'Leary, *Asiatic Mode*, 43. In this context, the European and Anglo-American critique of male "oriental despotism" was part of the antipatriarchal liberal movement for what Carole Pateman has called "the fraternal social contract." Carole Pateman, *The Disorder of Women* (Stanford: Stanford Univ. Press, 1989), 33–57.

45. On this point, see Glausser, "Three Approaches," 204–15, and N. Wood, *Politics*, 117, 140, 145. See also Appleby, *Liberalism*, 9–10.

46. Unbeknownst to Robert Morris, Daniel Parker had agreed to allow Shaw and Randall the "captain's privilege" to conduct their own private trade in addition to the sponsored shipment. This was a common incentive offered to ship captains at the time. See Gallagher, "Charting," 1.

47. *New York News Dispatch*, May 10, 1785.

48. P. C. F. Smith, *Empress*, 64, 191–92.

49. After additional business dealings, Robert Morris ended up in debtor's prison and died there in 1806. Duer too ended his life in debtor's prison, in 1799. And after a lucrative career as a China trader and as the first consul to China, Shaw died at the age of thirty-nine in 1794. Ibid., 248.

Chapter 3: The Port's Rise

1. Walter Barrett [Joseph A. Scoville], *The Old Merchants of New York* (New York, 1863–66), 3:6–10, 4:8; Kenneth Wiggins Porter, *John Jacob Astor: Business Man* (Cambridge: Harvard Univ. Press, 1931), 1:144–50, 424–28; Thomas LaFargue, "Some Early Chinese Visitors to the United States," *T'ien Hsia Monthly* 11 (Oct.–Nov. 1949): 128–39; *Commercial Advertiser*, Aug. 13, 1808.

2. Jefferson to Gallatin, July 25, Aug. 15, 1808, Thomas Jefferson Papers, Manuscripts Division, Library of Congress.

3. For a sampling of how this story has been retold over time, see Michael H. Hunt, *The Making of a Special Relationship: The United States and China to 1914* (New York: Columbia Univ. Press, 1983), 13, 322 n. 14; Tyler Dennett, *Americans in Eastern Asia: A Critical Study of the Policy of the United States with Reference to China, Japan, and Korea in the Nineteenth Century* (New York: Macmillan, 1922), 77–78; Charles C. Stelle, "American Trade in Opium to China, Prior to 1820," *Pacific Historical Review* 11 (Dec. 1940): 434; Loren Fessler, *Chinese in America: Stereotyped Past, Changing Present* (New York: Vantage, 1983), 6; Mike Berger, "New York Chinatown," Chinese Chamber of Commerce of New York, Fiftieth Anniversary Issue (New York, 1957), 28; and C. Y. Chu, *Meiguo Huaqiao Gaishi* [A History of Chinese People in America] (New York: China Times, 1975), 9.

4. "Columbus" to James Madison, Aug. 11, 1808, Papers of Albert Gallatin, box 6, New-York Historical Society. A letter written to Secretary of Treasury Albert Gallatin from "Punqua Wingchong" thanking him for his permission to return to China is also included. Punqua Wingchong to Albert Gallatin, Feb. 15, 1809, Papers of Albert Gallatin, box 6.

5. K. Ch'en, *Insolvency*, 20, 322–27, 345–48. For studies on Chinese hong merchants, see Dilip Kumar Basu, "Asian Merchants and Western Trade: A Comparative Study of Calcutta and Canton, 1800–1840" (Ph.D. diss., Univ. of California, Berkeley, 1975), and Hosea Ballou Morse, *The Chronicles of the East India Company Trading to China*, 5 vols. (Cambridge: Harvard Univ. Press, 1926–29).

6. Appleby, *Liberalism*, 291–319.

7. Charles Sellars, *The Market Revolution: Jacksonian America, 1815–1846* (New York: Oxford Univ. Press, 1991), 22; Alfred F. Young, *The Democratic Republicans of New York: The Origins, 1763–1797* (Chapel Hill: Univ. of North Carolina Press, 1967), 216–17.

8. For an excellent historical overview of this time period, see Sellars, *Market*, 3–33. On the theoretical basis of Jefferson's trade policies, see Destutt de Tracy, *Treatise*.

9. Craig R. Hanyan, "China and the Erie Canal," *Business History Review* 35 (1961): 558–66.

10. Sellars, *Market*, 41–44; Albion, *New York Port*, 76–94, 95–121; Robert Ernst, *Immigrant Life in New York City, 1825–1863* (New York: Kings Crown Press, 1949), 14, 118 n. 16.

11. Ira Rosenwaike, *Population History of New York City* (Syracuse: Univ. of Syracuse, 1972), 15–19. For a major new study on the British strategy to disrupt the intra-Asian trade, which ultimately resulted in the Opium Wars, see Sucheta Mazumdar, *Sugar and Society in China: Peasants, Technology, and the World Market* (Cambridge: Harvard Univ. Press, 1998). For a fundamental retheorization of world trade systems, see John H. Wills Jr., "Maritime Asia, 1500–1800: The Interactive Emergence of European Domination," *American Historical Review* 98 (Feb. 1993): 83–105, and Andre Gunder Frank, *ReOrient: Global Economy in the Asian Age* (Berkeley: Univ. of California Press, 1998).

12. For more on Girard, see Goldstein, *Philadelphia and the China Trade*, 8–9, 12, 25, 35, 41–46, 37, 52–61, 69.

13. New York–based Amasa Delano noted in his memoirs that as many as fourteen ships were anchored at the Falkland Island Massafuero. He estimated that this single site accounted for 3.5 million sealskins sold between 1793 and 1807. Kenneth Scott Latourette, *The History of Early Relations between the United States and China, 1784–1844* (New Haven: Yale Univ. Press, 1917), 40.

14. Ibid., 42, 72–73; Porter, *Astor*, 1:292, 312, 314–16, 2:589, 595, 601. Another source claims that Astor's first trip to Canton was in 1800 and that he was the first American trader to arrive in Canton. The celebratory 1915 biography by Gebhard is not fully reliable on its historical details. Elizabeth L. Gebhard, *The Life and Ventures of the Original John Jacob Astor* (Hudson, N.Y.: Bryan Printing Company, 1915), 127–35.

15. Jacques M. Downs, "American Merchants and the China Opium Trade, 1800–1840," *Business History Review* 17 (winter 1968): 425; Porter, *Astor*, 2:600–601, 604–5, 613–16; Stelle, "Opium," 443. For details on Astor's bringing opium into New York City, see Porter, *Astor*, 2:628 n. 64.

16. Porter, *Astor*, 2:605.

17. Ibid., 613–18. For an example of the statement of American innocence and British culpability in regard to the opium trade, see David Sanctuary Howard, *New York and the China Trade* (New York: New-York Historical Society, 1984), 43. A picul was 100 cattie, or 133⅓ pounds. Turkish opium was packed in chests that contained one picul each. Stelle, "Opium," 432 n. 35.

18. Downs, "American Merchants," 418–44; Stelle, "Opium," 425; Michael Greenberg, *British Trade and the Opening of China, 1800–1842* (New York: Monthly Review Press, 1979), 50, 104, 105, 106–7.

19. Stelle, "Opium," 425; Greenberg, *British Trade*, 50, 104, 105, 106–7.

20. For the classic English-language discussion of the Opium War from the perspective of Commissioner Lin, see Arthur Waley, *The Opium War through Chinese Eyes* (Stanford: Stanford Univ. Press, 1958). See also Downs, "American Merchants," 433.

21. Yen-p'ing Hao, *The Commercial Revolution in Nineteenth-Century China* (Berkeley: Univ. of California Press, 1986), 112; Downs, "Merchants," 418, 432, 435, 440; Basil Lubbock, *The Opium Clippers* (Boston: Brown, Son, and Ferguson, 1933); Howard, *New York*, 46–48. For the amounts of opium shipped to China from 1800 to 1839, see Greenberg, *British Trade*, 221.

22. Lubbock, *Opium Clippers*, 320–21. On the relationship between the U.S. involvement in the opium trade and the coolie trade, see Robert J. Schwendinger, *Ocean of Bitter Dreams: Maritime Relations between China and the United States, 1850–1915* (Tucson, Ariz.: Westernlore Press, 1988), 7–64.

23. Howard, *New York*, 30; Downs, "Merchants," 430; Porter, *Astor*, 2:615–16; Stelle, "Opium," 436–37.

24. John R. Spears, *Captain Nathaniel Brown Palmer: An Old Time Sailor of the Sea* (Stonington, Conn.: Stonington Historical Society, 1996), 168–82.

25. The origins of the word *coolie* have not been definitively researched. It is clear that the word is related to both South Asian and Chinese words describing hired laborers. The *Oxford English Dictionary* identifies as one of the word's origins the Tamil *kuli*, referring to "hire, payment for occasional menial work." *OED*, s.v. "coolie." Whatever the word's origins, these manual laborers were pulled into an international colonial system of plantation labor recruitment.

26. Evelyn Hu-DeHart, "Chinese Coolie Labor in Cuba and Peru in the Nineteenth Century: Free Labor or Neoslavery?" paper presented at the Latin American Studies Association's Fifteenth International Congress, San Juan, Puerto Rico, Sept. 21–23, 1989; Walton Look Lai, *Indentured Labor, Caribbean Sugar: Chinese and Indian Migrants to the British West Indies, 1838–1918* (Baltimore: Johns Hopkins Univ. Press, 1993); Arnold Joseph Meagher, "The Introduction of Chinese Laborers to Latin America and the 'Coolie Trade,' 1847–1874" (Ph.D. diss., Univ. of California, Davis, 1975).

For an important study on the issue of slavery and indentureship, see Mary Turner, ed., *From Chattel Slaves to Wage Slaves: The Dynamics of Labour Bargaining in the Americas* (London: James Currey, 1995), and David Northrup, *Indentured Labor in the Age of Imperialism, 1834–1922* (Cambridge: Cambridge Univ. Press, 1995). I thank Evelyn Hu-Dehart for sharing her unpublished paper with me.

27. Basil Lubbock, *Coolie Ships and Oil Sailers* (Glasgow: Brown, Son, and Ferguson, 1955), 17, 36.

28. *Hunt's Merchant Magazine*, May 1856, 649 (includes *Journal of Commerce* reference); Daniel Henderson, *Yankee Ships in China Seas* (New York: Hastings House, 1946), 186; Robert J. Schwendinger, *International Port of Call* (Woodland Hills, Calif.: Windsor Publications, 1984), 62. For more on the smuggling of Chinese laborers in Chinese port cities, see Zhu Jieqing, *Dongnaya Huaqiao Shi* [A History of Overseas Chinese in Southeast Asia] (Beijing: Gaoden Jiaoyu Chubashe, 1990), 128–32. I thank Renqiu Yu for this reference.

29. *Harper's New Monthly Magazine* 29 (June 1861): 1–10. Schwendinger has estimated that mortality rates ranged from 11 percent to 22 percent of all "coolies" shipped. Schwendinger, *International*, 62.

30. Robert Lee Boughton Jr., "From Clipper Ship to Clipper Ship: A History of W. R. Grace and Co." (senior thesis, Princeton Univ., 1942), 9.

31. Cecilia Mendez, "Los Chinos culies en la explotacion del guano en el Peru" [The Use of Chinese Coolies in the Exploitation of Guano in Peru], *Primer Seminario sobre Poblaciones Immigrantes*, vol. 2 (Lima: Consejo Nacionale de Ciencia y Tecnologia, 1988), 91–107 (I thank Evelyn Hu-DeHart for this citation); Marquis James, *Merchant Adventurer: The Story of W. R. Grace* (Wilmington, Del.: Scholarly Resources, 1993), 28. James's study is a company-sponsored biography. See also Lawrence A. Clayton, *Grace: W. R. Grace and Co.—The Formative Years, 1850–1930* (Ottawa, Ill.: Jameson Books, 1985).

32. Henderson, *Yankee Ships*, 187.

33. D. J. Williamson to Secretary of State, Callao, Sept. 20, 1870 (no. 11), Consular Despatches, Callao 6, quoted by Watt Stewart, *Chinese Bondage in Peru: A History of the Chinese Coolie in Peru, 1849–1874* (Durham, N.C.: Duke Univ. Press, 1951), 97–98.

34. M. James, *Merchant Adventurer*, 14, 15, 18; William Kooiman, *The Grace Ships, 1869–1969* (Point Reyes, Calif.: Komar Publishing, 1990), 1–2; Boughton, "Clipper Ship," 9, 19–22.

35. Ernst, *Immigrant*, 14, 118 n.16.

36. Blackmar, *Manhattan*, 14–43; Ernst, *Immigrant*, 14, 38.

37. Blackmar, *Manhattan*, 77–84; Bushman, *Refinement*, 118–22.

38. Mantuas were loose gowns worn by European women in the seventeenth and eighteenth centuries.

39. "Of Domestic Affairs Anterior to the Revolution," *Valentine's Manual* (1858), 517–25.

40. This section is based primarily on Elizabeth Blackmar's excellent study of the development of a real estate market in New York City. Blackmar, *Manhattan*, 38–40, 50, 75–80.

41. Ibid., 79. Coffeehouses were places to conduct business, but they could not compete with hotels and taverns as a venue for formal social events. Bushman, *Refinement*, 163–64.

42. Will of John Jacob Astor, New-York Historical Society, Jan. 11, 1845.

43. William Reddy has described this nexus of money and power as creating a force field allowing "the rich to discipline the poor through their bodies and through their sense of familial or other social duty." Reddy, *Money*, 68, 199.

44. The term *moral economy* derives from E. P. Thompson and is most fully explicated in his *Customs in Common* (London: Merlin Press, 1991).

45. Bender, *Intellect*, 27–28, 34, 41.

46. Ibid., 119–20.

47. Ibid., 45–51.

48. Porter, *Astor*, 2:620.

49. Bender, *Intellect*, 49–51, 47, 74, 113–14, 119–20, 123, 134–35, 279; Albion, *New York Port*, 241, 257; Howard, *New York*, 30.

50. *Crockery and Glass Journal* 3 (May 25, 1876): 15, quoted in J. G. Stradling, "American Ceramics and the Philadelphia Centennial," *Antiques*, July 1976, 150. On the exposition, see Richard Kenin, "Introduction," in *A Facsimile of Frank Leslie's Illustrated Historical Register of the Centennial Exposition, 1876* (New York: Paddington Press, 1974), and Robert W. Rydell, *All the World's a Fair: Visions of Empire at American International Expositions, 1876–1916* (Chicago: Univ. of Chicago Press, 1984), 29–32. 51. Ralph Sessions, "The Image Business: Shop and Cigar Store Figures in America," *Folk Art Magazine*, winter 1996–97, 54–60. Shop figures were carved by the same craftsmen who carved the figureheads on ships.

52. Jenny Young, *The Ceramic Art: A Compendium of the History and Manufacture of Pottery and Porcelain* (New York, 1879), 478, 442.

Chapter 4: A Pioneer Settlement

1. *New York Herald*, July 24, 15, 1847.

2. Dan Schiller, *Objectivity and the News: The Public and the Rise of Commercial Journalism* (Philadelphia: Univ. of Pennsylvania Press, 1981), 12–75; Sellars, *Market*, 385–86.

3. On print culture, see Benedict Anderson, *Imagined Communities: Reflections on the Origins and Spread of Nationalism* (London: Verso, 1983), 15–16, 41–47.

4. *New York Herald*, July 15, 1847; Stokes, *Iconography*, 3:1804 ("usual hospitalities," "new era"); *Morning Courier and New York Enquirer*, July 12–13, 1847; "Visit to the Chinese Junk," *Chamber's Edinburgh Journal* 10 (1848): 40–41; Rodman Gilder, *The Battery* (Boston: Houghton Mifflin, 1936), 183–85. The most thorough and reliable description of the craft can be found in H. H. Brindley, "The 'Keying,'" *Mariner's Mirror*, 1922, 309–11.

5. *Morning Courier and New York Enquirer*, July 13, 1847. The "mandarin's" name was variously spelled Eesing, Hesing, and Keesing by the New York and British press. The Crystal Palace exhibition was in 1851. Apparently Captain Kellett displayed keen

entrepreneurial foresight in purchasing the Chinese vessel and touring with it so many years in advance of the exhibition.

6. *New York Enquirer*, Sept. 10, 1847; "Visit to the Chinese Junk," 40–41; Brindley, "Keying," 311; "The Chinese Junk," *Holden's Dollar Magazine*, Apr. 1848, 252.

7. Philip Hone, *The Diary of Philip Hone, 1828–1851*, ed. Allan Nevins (New York: Dodd, Mead, and Co., 1936), entry for July 29, 1847; *New York Herald*, July 21, 1847; Heiser Papers, New-York Historical Society, cited in Gilder, *Battery*, 183–85. It remains unclear if Heiser and French actually promoted the ship's display and shared in all the profits.

8. *New York Herald*, July 24, 26, Aug. 6, 9, 1847.

9. Ibid., July 28, 31, Aug. 4, 10, 12, 1847.

10. Ibid., Aug. 28, 31, 1847.

11. Ibid., July 15, 27, 1847. The phrase "astonishment proof countenances" refers to the perceived lack of facial expression.

12. *New York Herald*, Aug. 31, Sept. 4, 1847. According to the New York County Clerk's office, the Court of Special Sessions handled misdemeanors and cleared out its transcripts every twenty years.

13. Ibid., Sept. 4, 1847. There are differing accounts as to where the Chinese crew joined the ship. These testimonies speak of Canton, and another source speaks of Hong Kong. Much depends on whether we are to believe the story of Captain Kellett smuggling the ship out of Canton and picking up crew members in Hong Kong.

14. *New York Evening Express*, Sept. 6, 1847; *New York Herald*, Sept. 4, 1847. According to other sources, the crew's "mutinous" attitudes after St. Helena and contrary winds forced the captain's decision to sail for New York rather than Liverpool. A *Globe* article stated that when the ship first arrived at New York, the crew claimed that their wages had not been paid since their hiring, and that they should be sent back right away. Brindley, "Keying," 311, 313–14.

15. "Sailing of the Chinese Sailors, Belonging to the Cochin China Junk," *American Magazine*, Nov. 13, 1847, 726–27.

16. Ibid., 728.

17. *New York Herald*, Aug. 31, 1847. The *Evening Express* stated this point of view even more strongly: "Ching Ching since his arrival in Gotham knows how to smoke segars, drink soda water, carry a cane and cultivate a moustache (along with a queue), ride in the omnibuses and eject, in tolerable good English, a dozen oaths in as many minutes." *New York Evening Express*, Sept. 2, 1847.

18. Charles Husband, "Racist Humour and Racist Ideology in British Television, or I Laughed Till You Cried," in *Humour in Society: Resistance and Control*, ed. Chris Powell and George E. C. Paton (London: Macmillan Press, 1988), 155–56. See also Alan Dundes, *Cracking Jokes: Studies of Sick Humor Cycles and Stereotypes* (Berkeley: Ten Speed Press, 1987).

19. "Visit to the Chinese Junk," 40–41; Norman Brouwer, "New York's Unusual Visitor: The Junk *Keying*," *Seaport Magazine*, spring 1991, 18.

20. Brindley, "Keying," 312.

21. Blackmar, *Manhattan*, 94–100.

22. Ibid., 101.

23. Ibid., 99. For more on the Sixth Ward, see Carol Groneman Pernicone, "'The Bloody Ould Sixth': A Social Analysis of a New York City Working-Class Community in the Mid-Nineteenth Century" (Ph.D. diss., Univ. of Rochester, 1973).

24. Timothy J. Gilfoyle, *City of Eros: New York City, Prostitution, and the Commercialization of Sex, 1790–1920* (New York: W. W. Norton, 1992), 38.

25. Graham Hodges, "'Desirable Companions and Lovers': Irish and African Americans in the Sixth Ward, 1830–1870," in *The New York Irish*, ed. Ronald H. Bayor and Timothy J. Meagher (Baltimore: Johns Hopkins Univ. Press, 1996), 106–24; Shane White, *Somewhat More Independent: The End of Slavery in New York City, 1770–1810* (Athens: Univ. of Georgia Press, 1991), 84, 116, 160, 173; Gilfoyle, *City of Eros*, 41.

26. Sean Wilentz, *Chants Democratic: New York City and the Rise of the American Working Class, 1788–1850* (Oxford: Oxford Univ. Press, 1984), 256. See also Marina E. Espina, *Filipinos in Louisiana* (New Orleans: A. F. Laborde and Sons, 1988), 1.

27. Among a few of the works open to this interpretation I would include Wilentz, *Chants Democratic*; Christine Stansell, *City of Women: Sex and Class in New York, 1789–1860* (New York: Knopf, 1986); Gilfoyle, *City of Eros;* and George Chauncey, *Gay New York: Gender, Urban Culture, and the Making of the Gay Male World, 1890–1940* (New York: Basic Books, 1994).

28. Prime quoted in Ernst, *Immigrant*, 40–41. On "pidgin" dialects, see Hymes, *Pidginization*. See also Mary Neth, "Cultural Conflict and Cultural Mixing: Tap Dance and American Popular Culture," paper presented at the Organization of American Historians' Annual Meeting, 1993.

29. Letter from Rev. E. W. Syle, *Spirit of Missions*, Aug. 1854, 323–28.

30. Ibid., 324–26.

31. Rosenwaike, *Population*, 16–17; Third Ward, Fourth Ward, and Fifth Ward volumes, 1855, *New York State Census Manuscripts*, Manhattan County Clerks Office. Unfortunately the 1855 census seems to be the only surviving New York State manuscripts from the nineteenth century. The addresses of the households are not indicated, only the order in which the households were visited by the census takers. The following paragraphs, unless otherwise indicated, draw upon data from the 1855 census.

32. "Ah" is a familiar form of address used among friends and family. Many Westerners mistook this salutation as part of the person's formal name.

33. *New-York Times*, Dec. 26, 1856.

34. *Yankee Notions* 7 (Mar. 1858).

35. M. Berger, "Chinatown," 28.

36. Fessler, *Chinese*, 8, 2; Him Mark Lai, Joe Huang, and Don Wong, *The Chinese of America, 1785–1980* (San Francisco: Chinese Culture Foundation, 1980), 12; Goldstein, *Philadelphia and the China Trade*, 74–75; Crew Lists, Port of New York, 1835 and 1847, record group 35, National Archives.

37. Lai, Huang, and Wong, *Chinese*, 12; William Lytle Schurz, *The Manila Galleon* (New York: Dutton, 1939); C. R. Boxer, "Notes on Chinese Abroad in the Late Ming and Early Manchu Periods, Compiled from Contemporary European Sources (1500–

1750)," *T'ien Hsia Monthly* 9 (Aug.–Dec. 1939); H. H. Dubs and R. S. Smith, "The Chinese in Mexico City in 1635," *Far Eastern Quarterly* 1 (Aug. 1942): 387–89. For a suggestive study on gendered Chinese-Dutch-Indonesian port interactions, see Blussé, *Strange Company.* See also Espina, *Filipinos in Louisiana,* 1.

38. Albion, *New York Port,* 200; Lubbock, *Opium Clippers,* 1–29; John King Fairbanks, *Trade and Diplomacy on the China Coast: The Opening of the Treaty Ports, 1842–1854* (Cambridge: Harvard Univ. Press, 1964), 63–73; Schwendinger, *Ocean of Bitter Dreams,* 7–17.

39. *New-York Times,* Dec. 26, 1856; "The Coolie Trade," *De Bow's Review* 27 (Sept. 1859): 296–321.

40. For a sampling of coverage at this time, see "The Coolie Trade," *Hunt's Merchant Magazine,* May 1856, 649; "The Slave Trade," *Tait's Edinburgh Magazine,"* June 1857, 321–27; "Coolies—Cuba and Emancipation," *De Bow's Review,* Apr. 1857, 414–19.

41. Crew Lists, 1847.

42. *New-York Times,* Dec. 26, 1856, June 20, 1859.

43. *New York Tribune,* June 21, 1885.

44. Ibid.

45. Alvin F. Harlow, *Old Bowery Days* (New York: D. Appleton, 1931), 392. What is now called Park Row from City Hall to Chatham Square was then called Chatham Street.

46. Patricia Cooper, *Once a Cigar Maker: Men, Women, and Work Culture in American Cigar Factories, 1900–1919* (Urbana: Univ. of Illinois Press, 1987), 11.

47. *Yankee Notions* 3 (Apr. 1854), 6 (Oct. 1857); *Ballou's Pictorial,* July 18, 1857.

48. *New-York Times,* Dec. 26, 1856.

49. Ibid.

50. Ibid., Feb. 16, 1874; Chu, *Meiguo,* 50.

51. Warner M. Van Norden, *Who's Who of the Chinese in New York* (New York: Warner Van Norden, 1918), 33, 65.

52. Lois Rodecape, "Celestial Drama in the Golden Hills: The Chinese Theatre in California, 1849–1869," *California Historical Quarterly* 23 (1944): 101; Ronald Riddle, *Flying Dragons, Flowing Streams: Music in the Life of San Francisco's Chinatown* (Westport, Conn.: Greenwood Press, 1983), 18; *New York Herald,* June 29, 1853. Leong actually verified his statements to the *New York Herald* reporter with his signature.

53. Leong's statement from *New York Herald,* June 29, 1853; *Alta California,* Oct. 20, 1852; Rodecape, "Drama," 102–3.

54. Full details of the contract appear in *New York Herald,* June 29, 1853.

55. Ibid.

56. Ibid.; *New York Evening Post,* May 24, 1853.

57. *New York Herald,* May 22, 1853. For more on Garrick's plays, see Appleton, *Cycle,* 76–81.

58. *New York Evening Post,* May 24, 1853.

59. *New York Tribune Semiweekly,* May 24, 1853. It was not until the 1916 production of "The Yellow Jacket" that Chinese theatrical forms were taken on their own

terms by the New York theater, and not until Thornton Wilder's 1938 "Our Town" that such techniques were adapted and used in a nonexotic presentational format.

60. *New York Herald*, June 29, 1853.

61. Ibid.

62. Ibid.; *New York Evening Post*, July 2, 1853; *New York Herald*, July 27, 1853.

63. *New York Evening Post*, Aug. 17, Sept. 3, 1853; Syle, *Spirit of Missions*, Aug. 1854, 323–28.

64. Syle, *Spirit of Missions*, Aug. 1854, 323–28.

65. Gutzlaff had proposed that Americans emulate the Prussian practice of sending missionaries on opium-trading vessels. Speaking several dialects of Chinese with some fluency, Gutzlaff took two unauthorized trips into the Chinese countryside in 1831 and 1833. He published his diary as Charles Gutzlaff, *The Journal of Two Voyages along the Coast of China, in 1831 and 1832* (New York, 1833). He also published *Sketch of Chinese History, Ancient and Modern* (New York, 1834). For background on Gutzlaff, see Clifton Jackson Phillips, *Protestant America and the Pagan World: The First Half Century of the American Board of Commissioners for Foreign Missions, 1810–1860* (Cambridge: East Asian Research Center, Harvard Univ. Press, 1969), 178, 183–85.

66. *New York Tribune*, Oct. 23, 1876. On events involving Zhusan (Chusan) Island, see Fairbanks, *Trade and Diplomacy*, 58, 59, 81, 82, 90, 94, 121, 135n, 156, 286, 333; Syle, *Spirit of Missions*, Aug. 1854, 323–28.

67. Syle, *Spirit of Missions*, Aug. 1854, 323–28.

68. *New-York Times*, Dec. 26, 1856.

69. Ibid.; Albion, *New York Port*, 201; Latourette, *Relations*, 76–77; Syle, *Spirit of Missions*, Aug. 1854, 339–43.

70. *New-York Times*, Dec. 26, 1856.

71. *New York Tribune*, Apr. 19, 1856. Reverend Syle gathered about thirty Chinese men for Christian religious sermons at St. George's Episcopal Church on Beekman Street. Several members of the congregation, which included individuals of some wealth, vowed that "something must be done [for] these poor fellows." A committee of ten raised $2,500, which enabled twenty-two former troupe members to be sent to California and four to Guangzhou. Syle's concern, however, did not mean that he found these souls to be virtuous. "Their personal character," Syle wrote, "was so little to be relied on that to have introduced them into families as servants would have been at the risk of transplanting into our homes some of the worst vices of heathendom." Unless they converted to Christianity, they could not be trusted. Syle's charity, spurred on by pity, was bound by a limited tolerance. *Church Journal*, Aug. 24, 1854.

72. Evelyn Nakano Glenn's notion of "strategies" is useful here. Evelyn Nakano Glenn, *Issei, Nisei, War Bride: Three Generations of Japanese American Women in Domestic Service* (Philadelphia: Temple Univ. Press, 1986), xiii, 17, 141–64.

73. Christopher Hibbert, *The Dragon Wakes: China and the West, 1793–1911* (London: Longman Group, 1970), 245. Ward returned to the United States to align himself with the Southern secession at the beginning of the American Civil War.

74. Matthew Calbraith Perry, *The Japan Expedition, 1852–54*, ed. Roger Pineau (Washington, D.C.: Smithsonian Institution Press, 1968). For a general study of U.S.

empire building in the Pacific, see Arthur Power Dudden, *The American Pacific from the Old China Trade to the Present* (New York: Oxford Univ. Press, 1992).

75. Dudden, *American Pacific*, 3–21; T. Dennett, *Americans*, 343.

76. Milton Mackie, "The Chinaman, Domestic, Scholastic, Iconoclastic, and Imperial," *Putnam's Monthly* 9 (Apr. 1857): 339; *Yankee Notions* 6 (Oct. 1857).

77. The image had become so common that it threatened to symbolize all Chinese, and "respectable" Chinese felt compelled to dissociate themselves from it. Recall the 1856 petition that appeared in the *New York Tribune*, signed by thirty-seven self-appointed betters of the Chinese community who, embarrassed and angered, sought to draw a clear boundary between themselves and their fallen countrymen. Horace Greeley's accompanying editorial thanked the "Chinese gentlemen . . . as to the character of their ex-countrymen who support a paltry and disreputable existence." While acknowledging that there were "genuine objects of charity," individuals who had been "struck down by wasting sickness" or widows "paralyzed by sore bereavement," Greeley portrayed these Chinese as examples of moral depravity—people who harbored "evil appetites and ignoble desires." *New York Tribune*, Apr. 22, 1856.

78. M.F., "On a Chinaman in Broadway," *United States Democratic Review* 35 (May 1855): 411–12.

79. Mackie, "Chinaman," 337–38.

80. *New York Evening Post*, Apr. 14, 1856; *Brother Jonathan*, Apr. 26, 1856.

Chapter 5: "Edifying Curiosities"

1. Odell, *Stage* 4:584–85, 5:57, 6:275; *New York Evening Post*, Jan. 31, Feb. 7, 1853. For more on the "Feejee Mermaid" hoax, see Neil Harris, *Humbug: The Art of P. T. Barnum* (Chicago: Univ. of Chicago Press, 1973), 62–67.

2. "Wild Men of Borneo," Ronald G. Becker Collection, Special Collections, Syracuse Univ. Library. On the "Wild Men of Borneo," see Robert Bogdan, *Freak Show: Presenting Human Oddities for Amusement and Profit* (Chicago: Univ. of Chicago Press, 1988), 121–27; for more on people with microcephaly being put on display, see 111–12.

3. I am indebted to Donald Lowe's concept of "bourgeois perception" and how a sense of time and space became transformed in this new perceptual universe. See Donald Lowe, *The History of Bourgeois Perception* (Chicago: Univ. of Chicago Press, 1982), 35–85. See also Martin Meisel, *Realizations: Narrative, Pictorial, and Theatrical Arts in Nineteenth-Century England* (Princeton: Princeton Univ. Press, 1983), 17–90.

4. Jonathan Crary, *Techniques of the Observer: On Vision and Modernity in the Nineteenth Century* (Cambridge: MIT Press, 1990), 112–13; Susan R. Horton, "Were They Having Fun Yet?" in *Victorian Literature and the Victorian Visual Imagination*, ed. Carol T. Christ and John O. Jordan (Berkeley: Univ. of California Press, 1995), 5; Tchen, "Believing Is Seeing." For a brief history of "oriental conjuring," see Sidney W. Clarke, "The Annals of Conjuring," *Magic Wand*, Dec. 1928. For more examples of orientalism in the practice of Western magical performances, see William Doerflinger, ed.,

The Magic Catalogue: A Guide to the Wonderful World of Magic (New York: Dutton, 1977), plates 6, 9, 12, 13, pp. 21, 26, 28–30, 35, 191, 214, 222–24.

5. I believe that such nineteenth-century urban experiences are an extension of the eighteenth-century patrician aesthetic concept of the "sublime." For more on this, see Andrew Ashfield and Peter de Bolla, eds., *The Sublime: A Reader in British Eighteenth-Century Aesthetic Theory* (Cambridge: Cambridge Univ. Press, 1996), 1–16. For more on the phenomenon of Western travel literature, see Pratt, *Imperial Eyes.*

6. *OED*, s.v. "curiosity" and "curio."

7. Jordan, *White over Black*, 216; Arthur O. Lovejoy. *The Great Chain of Being: A Study of the History of an Idea* (Cambridge: Harvard Univ. Press, 1936).

8. Steven Jay Gould, *The Mismeasure of Man* (New York: W. W. Norton, 1981), 134–35. Queues were imposed on the Chinese as a sign of submission by invading Manchus during the Qing Dynasty. See also David Gordon White, *Myths of the Dog-Man* (Chicago: Univ. of Chicago Press, 1991), and Partha Mitter, *Much Maligned Monsters: A History of European Reactions to Indian Art* (Chicago: Univ. of Chicago Press, 1992). On Aristotle's phrase *lusus naturae* or "joke of nature," see Peter Stallybrass and Allon White, *The Politics and Poetics of Transgression* (London: Methuen, 1986), 27–43, 62–66, and Jean-Christophe Agnew, *Worlds Apart: The Market and the Theater in Anglo-American Thought, 1550–1750* (Cambridge: Cambridge Univ. Press, 1986), 46–56.

9. Andrea Stulman Dennett, *Weird and Wonderful: The Dime Museum in America* (New York: New York Univ. Press, 1997), 1–22; Henry P. Tappan, *A Step from the New World to the Old, and Back Again* (New York, 1852), 1:100, cited in Harris, *Humbug*, 33.

10. Edward K. Spann, *The New Metropolis: New York City, 1840–1857* (New York: Columbia Univ. Press, 1981), 1–22; William R. Taylor, *In Pursuit of Gotham: The Commerce and Culture of New York City* (New York: Oxford Univ. Press, 1992), 74–75, 90; Robert W. Snyder, *The Voice of the City: Vaudeville and Popular Culture in New York* (New York: Oxford Univ. Press, 1989), xiv–xvi; Bender, *Intellect*, 57.

11. Judy Yung, *Chinese Women in America: A Pictorial History* (Seattle: Univ. of Washington Press, 1986), 14.

12. Odell, *Stage*, 4:42.

13. Ibid., 43; *New-York Times*, Nov. 12, 1834.

14. Odell, *Stage*, 4:42, 43, 106, 107, 177, 186, 5:398.

15. New York had become the major headquarters for overseas missionary activity. See C. J. Phillips, *Protestant America.*

16. Denker, *Chinese Taste*, 2–8.

17. For various perspectives on the Western practice of displaying non-Western peoples and cultures in museums, see Ivan Karp and Steven D. Levine, eds., *Exhibiting Culture: The Poetics and Politics of Museum Display* (Washington, D.C.: Smithsonian Institution Press, 1991).

18. Judy Yung's research on Marie Seise, the first known Chinese woman immigrant to the United States, and on women sold by impoverished parents to overseas prostitution rings supports this claim. See Yung, *Chinese Women*, 14, 18.

19. Kay Hunter, *Duet for a Lifetime* (New York: Coward-McCann, 1964), 35. Known in the United States as Chang and Eng, they explained to James Hale that their names should be pronounced "Chun" and "In." [James Hale], *A Few Particulars Concerning Chang-Eng, the United Siamese Brothers, Published under Their Own Direction* (New York, 1836), 4.

20. The *Boston Daily Courier*, Sept. 1, 1829, announced the twins' arrival as a "Great Natural Curiosity."

21. Hale to "H[arris] & C[hang]E[ng]," Nov. 4, 1832, and Hale to "H & CE," Nov. 14, 1832, Chang and Eng Bunker Collection, North Carolina State Archives; Irving Wallace and Amy Wallace, *The Two: A Biography* (New York: Bantam, 1978). Biographical articles and books on the twins have generally been patronizing in tone. A 1933 *New Yorker* article presented them as quick-learning, simple, fun-loving, and practical. Kay Hunter's 1964 biography, *Duet for a Lifetime*, represented them in a similar "positive" light. Irving and Amy Wallace's 1978 mass-market biography, *The Two*, is by far the best-researched and most fair-minded treatment of Chang and Eng. In contrast to Hunter, the Wallaces did not hesitate to describe conflict and problems.

22. Robert Hunter is credited as the first British merchant to base his operations in Siam. His family made its money from Virginia tobacco but was forced to leave after the Revolution, returning to Glasgow. It was Hunter who "discovered" the twins and involved Coffin. Wallace and Wallace, *The Two*, 35, 48–49, 55. Bristowe claimed that four thousand people "flocked" to every performance. W. S. Bristowe, "Robert Hunter in Siam," *History Today*, Feb. 1974, 92.

23. *Boston Patriot*, Aug. 17, 1829; *Aurora and Pennsylvanian Gazette*, Oct. 24, 1829; *London News*, Nov. 22, 1829.

24. Wallace and Wallace, *The Two*, 81.

25. *New York Courier and Enquirer*, Sept. 22, 1829.

26. Harris to Davis, Mar. 2, 1832, Chang and Eng Bunker Collection, North Carolina State Archives ("rooms," "a show"); "The United Brothers, Chang-Eng," Broadside Collection, American Philosophical Society, Philadelphia.

27. *New York Evening Post*, Sept. 19, 21, 1829.

28. Wallace and Wallace, *The Two*, 57–58.

29. *New York Courier and Enquirer*, Sept. 22, 1829; James W. Hale, ed., *An Historical Account of the Siamese Twin Brothers, from Actual Observations* (New York, 1831), 3. For other examples of medical statements made public, see Dr. John C. Warren, "Siamese Youths," Broadside Collection, American Philosophical Society, Philadelphia; "Extracts from a paper read before the Royal Society, London, Apr. 1st, by G. B. Bolton, Esq.," in Hale, *Historical Account*, 13.

30. Wallace and Wallace, *The Two*, 70–72.

31. [Hale], *Few Particulars*, 12.

32. Wallace and Wallace, *The Two*, 98–99.

33. Ibid., 111–13.

34. John M. Elliot, "Eng-Chang" (New York, 1839), New-York Historical Society Collection.

35. Hale, *Historical Account*, frontispiece.

36. See the N. Whitlock illustration in K. Hunter, *Duet*, after p. 32.

37. [Hale], *Few Particulars*, 5–6, 7–8, 9.

38. Yi Fu Tuan, *Dominance and Affection: The Making of Pets* (New Haven: Yale Univ. Press, 1984), 2–15.

39. Dunn's collection opened in Philadelphia in 1837 and was moved to London in 1840. There is some confusion over Dunn's collection having been purchased by Barnum. Having conducted an item-by-item comparison, I conclude that they were not the same collection. For a discussion of one of the nation's earliest museums (Charles Wilson Peale's 1786 museum) and its role in the formation of early American nationalism among patricians, see David R. Brigham, *Public Culture in the Early Republic: Peale's Museum and Its Audience* (Washington D.C.: Smithsonian Press, 1995). For an overview of East Asian fine art collections in the United States during this early period, see Warren I. Cohen, *East Asian Art and American Culture: A Study in International Relations* (New York: Columbia Univ. Press, 1992), 1–34.

40. Latourette, *Relations*, 134, 119, 133–44; T. Dennett, *Americans*, 108–13.

41. United States Bureau of the Census, 1850 (Washington, D.C.); *Doggett's New York City Directory, 1850–1856* (New York, 1850–56); *Rode's New York City Directory, 1850–1856* (New York, 1850–56); *Trow's New York City Directory, 1850–1856* (New York, 1850–56); Blackmar, *Manhattan*, 206–7.

42. John R. Peters Jr., *Guide to, or Descriptive Catalogue of the Chinese Museum* (New York, 1849), hereafter cited as *Guide* (1849); [John R. Peters Jr.], *Barnum's Chinese Museum* (New York, 1850). See also John R. Peters Jr., *Guide to, or Descriptive Catalogue of the Chinese Museum of the Marlboro' Chapel* (Boston, 1845), hereafter cited as *Guide* (1845).

43. T. Dennett, *Americans*, 142; C. J. Phillips, *Protestant America*, 190–93, 194, 202, 276.

44. All descriptions of the exhibition are from Peters, *Guide* (1849).

45. Miller, *Unwelcome*, 8, 43–44, 49, 51–52, 53–54, 58, 112.

46. *New York Herald*, Jan. 2, 1849; J. H. Lanman, "The Chinese Museum in Boston," *Hunt's Merchant Magazine* 14 (1846): 347.

47. *New York Herald*, Jan. 17, 1849.

48. Gary Kulik, "Designing the Past: History-Museum Exhibitions from Peale to the Present," in *History Museums in the United States: A Critical Assessment*, ed. Warren Leon and Roy Rosenzweig (Urbana: Univ. of Illinois Press, 1989), 4–5.

49. This relationship to collected objects is explored by James Clifford in a different context. James Clifford, *The Predicament of Culture: Twentieth-Century Ethnography, Literature, and Art* (Cambridge: Harvard Univ. Press, 1988), 217.

50. [Peters], *Barnum's Museum*, 12, 14, 17.

51. Ibid., 16–17, 38–43, 53.

52. This phenomenon provided the undergirding for the shift of public opinion Harold Isaacs and Stuart Creighton Miller have written about. See Isaacs, *Scratches*, 71, and Miller, *Unwelcome*, 83–85.

53. Barnum has been synonymous with "humbug," entrepreneurial slickness, and the saying "There's a sucker born every minute." Arthur H. Saxon, Barnum's most

recent biographer, does not believe that this saying was Barnum's. A. H. Saxon, *P. T. Barnum: The Legend and the Man* (New York: Columbia Univ. Press, 1989), 334–37. Robert Bogdan's important book on the transformation of people with physical abnormalities into "freak shows" by dime-museum and circus showmen does discuss the issue of racism. Bogdan, *Freak Show*, 6, 28, 106, 177, 197, 278. See also Rydell, *All the World's a Fair*, and Bernth Lindfors, "Circus Africans," *Journal of American Culture* 6 (summer 1983): 9–14.

54. "Barnum's Chinese Museum" advertisement, *New York Herald*, Apr. 21, 1850. For ads on the opening of "The Great Chinese Museum," see *New York Herald*, Jan. 1, 1849, under "Amusements." For Barnum's overprinting of Peters's New York edition of the Chinese Museum catalogue, see Peters, *Guide* (1849), and [Peters], *Barnum's Museum*. See also Peters, *Guide* (1845). For the closing date of Barnum's Chinese Museum, see *New York Tribune*, July 17–Aug. 15, 1850. A *New York Sunday Mercury* article cited by Barnum stated that Barnum had "enlarged and otherwise remodelled" Peters's Chinese Museum. However, judging from the catalogue, there is no indication of any change in the collection. [Peters], *Barnum's Museum*, 206; *New York Sunday Mercury*, Apr. 21, 1850. Some time between July 23 and August 15, the Chinese Museum evidently left 539 Broadway, which was subsequently referred to as the "Chinese Assembly Rooms."

55. This quotation was listed under "Opinions of the Press" in Barnum's slightly revised imprint of Peters's catalogue. Even in the case of paid advertisements, he cited them in his catalogue as actual "opinions" of reviewers. For example, the *New York Sun*, Apr. 22, 1850, and *New York Tribune*, Apr. 22, 1850, quotations were both paid ads. [Peters], *Barnum's Museum*, 205–6. For comments on how newspaper editors "accommodated" Barnum's "puffs" and "genuine" news items, see Saxon, *Legend*, 75.

56. *New York Tribune*, Apr. 29, 1850.

57. [Peters], *Barnum's Museum*, 205–6. Like other Chinese names, Pwan Ye Koo's name was spelled differently in different newspapers.

58. Ibid., 6.

59. Ibid., 6, 205–6.

60. Ibid., 6. On the role of the translator, see P. T. Barnum to Moses Kimball, Aug. 26, 1850, Boston Athenaeum Library.

61. *New York Tribune*, Apr. 29, May 8, 1850.

62. For example, see "Ballad Soiree," *New York Tribune*, Apr. 24, 1850; "Chinese Rooms," *New York Tribune*, Aug. 15, 1850.

63. *New York Herald*, Apr. 21, 1850; *New York Tribune*, Apr. 29, May 8, 1850; *New-York Times*, June 16, 1850.

64. [Peters], *Barnum's Museum*, 205; *New York Sun*, Apr. 22, 1850; Barnum to Kimball, P. T. Barnum manuscripts, Manuscripts and Rare Books Room, New York Public Library (the letter is incorrectly annotated as having been written in 1856).

65. Barnum to Kimball, P. T. Barnum manuscripts, Manuscripts and Rare Books Room, New York Public Library; Bogdan, *Freak Show*, 94–116.

66. Phineas T. Barnum, *Selected Letters of P. T. Barnum*, ed. A. H. Saxon (New York: Columbia Univ. Press, 1983), 13.

67. Ibid., 41, 38, 39. We do not know how much he rented Peters's Chinese Museum for, nor the associated space, renovation, and maintenance costs of 539 Broadway.

68. *Blackwood's Edinburgh Magazine*, July 1852, 105. The reporter asserted that the "Ching Ching"'s were "indescribably funny" when they argued, and were of a "dirty tribe"; one was a "thief." He concluded with a rhetorical flourish: "Who will deny that it is our 'manifest destiny' to teach them how to progress?" *New York Evening Express*, Sept. 2, 1847.

69. Nicoll, *Late Eighteenth-Century Drama*, 335; Fenn, *Ah Sin*, xxvi, 101.

70. Odell, *Stage*, 4:503–4, 7:230, 9:277, 6:586. This is a particularly early reference to Chinese hand launderers. Chinese laundries did not begin to appear in New York until the 1870s. For background on Chinese laundry operators, see Paul C. P. Siu, *The Chinese Laundryman: A Study of Social Isolation*, ed. John Kuo Wei Tchen (New York: New York Univ. Press, 1987).

71. Odell, *Stage*, 5:584, 587, 6:263, 330–31.

72. Doerflinger, *Magic*, 1–18; Christ and Jordan, *Victorian Literature*, xix; Horton, "Were They Having Fun Yet?" 3.

73. *OED*, s.v. "stereotype"; Benjamin, "Age of Mechanical Reproduction," in *Illuminations*, 219. Robert Wiebe called described this Jacksonian-inflected era as one of populist "choice culture." Robert H. Wiebe, *The Opening of American Society* (New York: Alfred A. Knopf, 1984).

74. *Yankee Notions* 7 (Mar. 1858). Burlesque cross-ethnic "mix-ups" became a standard genre of early New York print media and stage. See Robert Secor, "Ethnic Humor in Early American Jest Books" in *A Mixed Race: Ethnicity in Early America*, ed. Frank Shuffelton (New York: Oxford Univ. Press, 1993), 163–93.

75. Charley White, *The Chinese Wash Man*, is cited in Odell, *Stage*, 6:586; Edward Harrigan, *The Mulligan's Silver Wedding* (1881), Edward Harrigan Papers, Manuscripts and Archives Section, New York Public Library.

76. George M. Baker, "New Brooms Sweep Clean," in *The Social Stage: Original Dramas, Comedies, Burlesques, and Entertainments for Home Recreation, Schools, and Public Exhibitions* (New York, 1870), 263.

77. John Kuo Wei Tchen, "Modernizing White Patriarchy: Re-viewing D. W. Griffith's Film *Broken Blossoms*," *Moving the Image: Asian Pacific Americans in the Media Arts*, ed. Russell Leong (Los Angeles: UCLA and Visual Communications, 1991), 133–43.

Chapter 6: Self-Possessed Men

1. Wiebe, *American Society*, 143–67. For more on American individualism, see Wai-chee Dimock, *Empire for Liberty: Melville and the Poetics of Individualism* (Princeton: Princeton Univ. Press, 1989), 3, 7; Richard O. Curry and Karl E. Valois, "The Emergence of an Individualistic Ethos in American Society," in *American Chameleon: Individualism in Trans-national Context*, ed. Richard O. Curry and Lawrence B. Goodheart (Kent, Ohio: Kent State Univ. Press, 1991), 29; Lukes, *Individualism*, 88–93.

2. The twins worked with Barnum on three occasions: a one-month stint at the

American Museum in 1860, a three-week booking eight years later at Wood's Museum and Theater, and an eight-month grand tour of Europe beginning later that year. From the outset, however, the Bunkers did not like Barnum, and Barnum did not like them. Wallace and Wallace, *The Two*, 240.

3. Harris, *Humbug*, 11, 3, 17. See also William R. Taylor, *Cavalier and Yankee: The Old South and American National Character* (Cambridge: Harvard Univ. Press, 1979).

4. Halttunen, *Confidence Men*, 28.

5. Daniel T. Rodgers, *The Work Ethic in Industrial America, 1850–1920* (Chicago: Univ. of Chicago Press, 1974), 7–15.

6. Saxon, *Legend*, 47–50; Harris, *Humbug*, 14.

7. Saxon, *Legend*, 162.

8. Richard D. Altick, *The Shows of London* (Cambridge: Harvard Univ. Press, 1978), 236; Saxon, *Legend*, 130–34.

9. Patrick Conner, *Oriental Architecture in the West* (London: Thames and Hudson, 1979), 131–53; John Nash, *Views of the Royal Pavilion* (London: Pavilion Books, 1991).

10. Saxon, *Legend*, 157. See also *New Haven Columbia Register*, Nov. 13, 1847. Saxon states that the letterhead of Iranistan was what persuaded Jenny Lind to sign with Barnum on her American tour. Saxon, *Letters*, 66.

11. Jesse Franklin Graves, "The Siamese Twins as Told by Judge Jesse Franklin Graves, 1829–1894," unpublished manuscript, North Carolina State Archives, n.d., 1, 7; Wallace and Wallace, *The Two*, 4, 11, 16–17, 25; [Hale], *Few Particulars*, 4–5.

12. Wallace and Wallace, *The Two*, 65.

13. K. Hunter, *Duet*, 21; Wallace and Wallace, *The Two*, 11; [Hale], *Few Particulars*, 2, 3, 4.

14. David K. Wyatt, *Thailand: A Short History* (New Haven: Yale Univ. Press, 1982), 2–3. See also George W. Skinner, *Chinese Society in Thailand: An Analytic History* (New York: Cornell Univ. Press, 1957). If Chang and Eng had maintained a strong Chinese identity it would be plausible, then, that their names were actually Chinese. This possibility seems to be confirmed by the recent appearance of what was purportedly their original contract with Captain Abel Coffin. Contract between Chang and Eng and Robert Hunter, Apr. 1, 1829, Bangkok [sic], Surry County Historical Society, North Carolina.

15. K. Hunter, *Duet*, 75. A variation of this apocryphal story is told in Wallace and Wallace, *The Two*, 185.

16. Declaration of Naturalization, Wilkes Co., N.C., Superior Court Minutes, Fall Term 1839, Chang and Eng Bunker Collection, North Carolina State Archives; Graves, "Twins," 11–12; Wallace and Wallace, *The Two*, 143, 185.

17. Wallace and Wallace, *The Two*, 65, 67.

18. K. Hunter, *Duet*, 53; Wallace and Wallace, *The Two*, 110.

19. Harris to Davis, York, Pa., Apr. 11, 1832, Chang and Eng Bunker Collection, North Carolina State Archives.

20. Ibid.

21. Wallace and Wallace, *The Two*, 135.

22. Harris to Davis, Buffalo, N.Y., May 29, 1832, Chang and Eng Bunker Collection, North Carolina State Archives; Wallace and Wallace, *The Two*, 136–38.

23. CE to Davis, Auburn, N.Y., July 4, 1832, Chang and Eng Bunker Collection, North Carolina State Archives; Wallace and Wallace, *The Two*, 149.

24. CE to Davis (no location cited), July 11, 1832, Chang and Eng Bunker Collection, North Carolina State Archives; Wallace and Wallace, *The Two*, 151. Emphasis in original.

25. Wallace and Wallace, *The Two*, 153.

26. Harris to Davis and CE to Davis, Rochester, N.Y., June 15, 1832, Chang and Eng Bunker Collection, North Carolina State Archives; Graves, "Twins," 10.

27. The purported original contract, which surfaced in 1977, was much less precise. It was clearly written to promote Coffin's best interests:

We the undersigned Chang & Eng agree [illegible] & engage ourselves with our own free will & consent (also that we have the free will & consent of our Parents and the King of our country) to go with Captn Abel Coffin to America and Europe and remain with him wherever he chooses until the expiration of the time agreed upon between Captn Coffin and the Gov't of our country; and that He according to promise will return us to our Parents & friends any time within five (5) years, and that Captn Coffin will allow us from His Profits ten Spanish P'Month, and pay all our expenses and nothing is to be deducted from the money allowed our mother dated in Bangkok first day of Apr. one Thousand Eight Hundred twenty nine.

Contract between Chang & Eng and Robert Hunter, Apr. 1, 1829, Bangkock [*sic*], Surry County Historical Society, North Carolina; *Winston Salem Journal*, Aug. 6, 1977.

28. K. Hunter, *Duet*, 35.

29. Wallace and Wallace, *The Two*, 154–55. It was ironic that Coffin, who so fervently advocated proper behavior and good manners, also fantasized such monstrous intolerance and insensitivity. See K. Hunter, *Duet*, 36.

30. [Hale], *Few Particulars*, 1, 3, 6, 13.

31. Wallace and Wallace, *The Two*, 245.

32. Ibid., 247, 146.

33. Harris, *Humbug*, 111–42.

34. Saxon, *Legend*, 51, 55, 158, 105–7; Saxon, *Letters*, 281, 42–44; "Mr Barnum on Museums," *Nation*, Aug. 10, 1865.

35. Saxon, *Legend*, 56, 84, 100; Saxon, *Letters*, 24.

36. Saxon, *Letters*, 15.

37. From the late-1860s onward, Barnum often retained Chang Yu-Sing, "the Chinese Giant," said to be nearly nine feet tall and weighing over four hundred pounds. In the advertisement, Barnum had the artist further exaggerate Chang's size by drawing him three times the height of the "normal" Westerners standing around him. Barnum also booked Che Mah, twenty-eight inches tall and weighing forty pounds, "the only Chinese dwarf," in the 1880s Barnum and Bailey circus tours. Like Chang, Che Mah was dressed in ornate, aristocratic Chinese garb, and he wore a queue reported to be

thirteen feet long. A color advertising poster depicted Che Mah as a Buddha-like deity before whom superstitious Chinese men bowed in obeisance. See Bogdan, *Freak Show,* 99, 113, 165; "Chang, the Chinese Giant," broadside, P. T. Barnum's Greatest Show on Earth, 1881, Ronald G. Becker Collection; "Chang-Yu-Sing, The Chinese Giant," photograph, Ronald G. Becker Collection; "Chemah, the diminutive Chinese dwarf," poster, Barnum and Bailey Circus, n.d., Barnum Collection, Bridgeport Public Library; Eisenman photographs, Ronald G. Becker Collection.

38. Letterhead stationery, P. T. Barnum to Moses Kimball, Feb. 18, 1871, Shelburne Museum, reproduced in Saxon, *Letters;* Wallace and Wallace, *The Two,* 257–58; Archie Robertson, "Chang-Eng's American Heritage," *Life,* Aug. 11, 1951, 78.

39. Saxon, *Legend,* 53.

40. Jean H. Baker, *Affairs of Party: The Political Culture of Northern Democrats in the Mid-Nineteenth Century* (Ithaca: Cornell Univ. Press, 1983), 220; Mark C. Carnes, *Secret Ritual and Manhood in Victorian America* (New Haven: Yale Univ. Press, 1989), 120–27, 156–58.

41. Horsman, *Race and Manifest Destiny,* 56–57, 120–21; Andrew E. Norman, "Introduction," in *Phrenology: A Practical Guide to Your Head,* by Orson S. Fowler and Lorenzo N. Fowler (New York: Chelsea House, 1969), vi–vii. In contrast to the fifty cents the twins charged for someone to see them, the Fowlers charged $1 for a standard chart reading and $3 for a full-scale handwritten analysis.

42. John D. Davies, *Phrenology, Fad and Science: A Nineteenth-Century American Crusade* (New Haven: Yale Univ. Press, 1955), 6–11, 38–39.

43. Fowler and Fowler, *Phrenology,* 60, 133, 99.

44. Orson Fowler, "The Phrenological Character of Chang and Eng, the Siamese Twins, with a Likeness," *American Phrenological Journal* 8 (1846): 316.

45. Wallace and Wallace, *The Two,* 231.

46. Ibid; Fowler and Fowler, *Phrenology,* 317.

47. The psychoanalytic literature on the projection of interior conflicts onto non-self others is worth noting here. Melanie Klein, for example, elaborated a Freudian theory of projection and introjection between the self and others. Melanie Klein, *Love, Guilt, and Reparation and Other Works, 1921–1945* (New York: Free Press, 1975).

48. John H. Van Evrie, *Negroes and Negro "Slavery": The First an Inferior Race, the Latter Its Normal Condition* (New York, 1861), 44, 47, 80.

Chapter 7: Stereotypes and Realities

1. Saxon, *Legend,* 8; Saxon, *Letters,* 332.

2. Saxon, *Legend,* 76, 77.

3. B. Anderson, *Imagined Communities,* 15–16, 41–47; Lucien Febvre and Henri-Jean Martin, *The Coming of the Book: The Impact of Printing, 1450–1800,* trans. David Gerard, ed. Geoffrey Nowell-Smith and David Wootton (London: Verso, 1984), 248–332. For how vernacular, elite, and middle-range oral and print literacy played out in the United States, see Kenneth Cmiel, *Democratic Eloquence: The Fight over Popular Speech in Nineteenth-Century America* (New York: William Morrow, 1990), and

Michael Schudson, *Discovering the New: A Social History of American Newspapers* (New York: Basic Books, 1978).

4. Ira Katznelson and Margaret Weir, *Schooling For All: Class, Race, and the Decline of the Democratic Ideal* (New York: Basic Books, 1985), 10, 18, 24, 178–79.

5. Beekman Papers, New-York Historical Society.

6. John A. Sahli, "An Analysis of Early American Geography Textbooks, 1784–1840" (Ph.D. diss., Univ. of Pittsburgh, 1941), 150; Miller, *Unwelcome*, 94.

7. Wiebe, *American Society*, 308–13; Edward Pessen, *Jacksonian America: Society, Personality, and Politics* (Urbana: Univ. of Illinois Press, 1969), 62; Cmiel, *Eloquence*, 14–15. For how this democratic individualism expressed itself religiously, see Nathan O. Hatch, *The Democratization of American Christianity* (New Haven: Yale Univ. Press, 1989), 13–14.

8. Louisa May Alcott, *Eight Cousins* (Cleveland: World Publishing, 1948), 74; Catherine Elizabeth Havens, *Diary of a Little Girl in Old New York* (New York: H. C. Brown, 1920), 129. Alcott (1832–88) grew up with the China trade and experienced its impact on the patrician culture.

9. D. Lowe, *Bourgeois Perception*, 17–35.

10. Benjamin, "Age of Mechanical Reproduction," in *Illuminations*.

11. Louis Joseph Beck, *New York's Chinatown: An Historical Presentation of Its People and Places* (New York, 1898), 9; Return of Quimbo Appo, New York Supreme Court, 1–19, New York County Clerk's Office; *New York Herald*, Mar. 9, 10, Apr. 11, 1859; *New York Tribune*, Mar. 9, 18, Apr. 12, 1859; *New-York Times*, Mar. 9, 10, Apr. 12, 1859.

12. Return of Quimbo Appo, 18–19.

13. Ibid., 20–35; *Brother Jonathan*, July 2, Nov. 19, 1859, Mar. 3, 1860; *National Police Gazette*, May 14, 1859; *New York Herald*, Feb. 22, 1860.

14. Return of Quimbo Appo, 1–12, 13.

15. Ibid., 20.

Chapter 8: "The Alarm"

1. John Swinton, "The New Issue: The Chinese-American Question," *New York Tribune*, June 30, 1870; John Swinton, *The New Issue: The Chinese-American Question* (New York, 1870), 3, 6. For more on Swinton, see Sender Garlin, *John Swinton, American Radical, 1829–1901* (New York: American Institute for Marxist Studies, 1976); Sender Garlin, *Three American Radicals: John Swinton, Crusading Editor, Charles P. Steinmetz, Scientist and Socialist, William Dean Howells and the Haymarket Era* (Boulder, Colo.: Westview Press, 1991); and David Quigley, "Reconstructing Democracy: Politics and Ideas in New York City, 1865–1880" (Ph.D. diss., New York Univ., 1997), 167–70, 212–15, 286–88, 320–24.

2. On the relation between the rise of print media and the rise of U.S. nationalism, see David Waldstreicher, "Rites of Rebellion, Rites of Assent: Celebrations, Print Culture, and the Origins of American Nationalism," *Journal of American History* 82 (June 1995): 37–61.

3. Hobsbawm, *Capital*, 135–54; Wallerstein, *World*, 3:3–53; Karl Polanyi, *The Great Transformation* (Boston: Beacon Press, 1944), 163–77.

4. Department of State Documents, 1863, ser. no. 1181, ser. no. 1364; 1868, ser. no. 1316, ser. no. 1445. For a sampling of the press coverage, see *Harper's Weekly*, May 30, 1868; *Nation*, Sept. 10, 1868, Oct. 14, 1869, Jan. 6, 1870; and *Alta California*, Apr. 29, 30, 1868. On Anson Burlingame, see Frederick Wells Williams, *Anson Burlingame and the First Chinese Mission to Foreign Powers* (New York: Scribner's, 1912). On William Seward, see Ernest N. Paolino, *The Foundations of the American Empire: William H. Seward and U.S. Foreign Policy* (Ithaca: Cornell Univ. Press, 1973).

5. Eric Foner, *Reconstruction: America's Unfinished Revolution, 1863–1877* (New York: Harper and Row, 1988), 463, 460–61; Wallerstein, *World*, 3:22–24.

6. *Hunt's Merchant Magazine*, May 1856; *De Bow's Review* 27 (Sept. 1859): 297, 315.

7. Rev. Wm. Ashmore, "The Chinese Coolie Trade," *Christian Review* 27 (1862).

8. On the distinctions between the contract labor and the "credit-ticket" system, see Lai, Huang, and Wong, *Chinese*, 18.

9. John Kuo Wei Tchen, *Genthe's Photographs of San Francisco's Old Chinatown, 1895–1906* (New York: Dover Publications, 1984), 6–9.

10. Andrew Gyory, "Rolling in the Dirt: The Origins of the Chinese Exclusion Act and the Politics of Racism, 1870–1882" (Ph.D. diss., Univ. of Massachusetts, Amherst, 1991), 1–105.

11. Ibid., 29–33; Eric Foner, *Free Soil, Free Labor, Free Men: The Ideology of the Republican Party before the Civil War* (New York: Oxford Univ. Press, 1970). For a discussion of the distinctions and similarities between slave labor and wage labor in the transition from slavery to free labor, see Nigel Bolland, "Proto-Proletarians? Slave Wages in the Americas," in *Chattel Slaves to Wage Slaves*, ed. Turner, 123–47.

12. Saxton, *Indispensable Enemy*, 55–60, 62–66, 68–91; Gwendolyn Mink, *Old Labor and New Immigrants in American Political Development: Union, Party, and State, 1875–1920* (Ithaca: Cornell Univ. Press, 1986), 92–97, 165–66. See also Elmer Sandemeyer, *The Anti-Chinese Movement in California* (Urbana: Univ. of Illinois Press, 1973), and Mary Roberts Coolidge, *Chinese Immigration* (New York: Henry Holt, 1909).

13. Ernst, *Immigrant Life*, 12–47; Iver Bernstein, *The New York City Draft Riots: Their Significance for American Society and Politics in the Age of the Civil War* (New York: Oxford Univ. Press, 1990), 112–13, 181; Thomas Kessner, *The Golden Door: Italian and Jewish Immigrant Mobility in New York City, 1880–1915* (New York: Oxford Univ. Press, 1977), 3–23; David Ward, *Poverty, Ethnicity, and the American City, 1840–1925: Changing Conceptions of the Slum and the Ghetto* (Cambridge: Cambridge Univ. Press, 1989), 13–44.

14. *Workingman's Advocate*, Feb. 6, 1869, 2.

15. Foner, *Reconstruction*, 419–20; Gunther Barth, *Bitter Strength: A History of the Chinese in the United States, 1850–1870* (Cambridge: Harvard Univ. Press, 1969), 188–89.

16. Barth, *Bitter Strength*, 190–91; Lucy M. Cohen, *Chinese in the Post–Civil War*

South: A People without a History (Baton Rouge: Louisiana State Univ., 1984), 65–67, 69–70, 71; *New York Tribune*, July 15, 1869. Cohen (68–70) offers the most detailed description of Tye and the Memphis Convention.

17. *New Orleans Daily Picayune*, June 27, 1869; "Coolie Trade Prohibited, Koopsmanschap Enterprise Contrary to Law," *New-York Times*, July 24, 1869; "A Chapter on the Coolie Trade," *Harper's New Monthly Magazine* 29 (June 1861): 1–10.

18. J. C. B. Davis, Assistant Secretary of State, to C. M. Goulding, Jan. 20, 1870, record group 59, Instructions to Consuls, Department of State, National Archives.

19. *New York Sun*, July 21, Aug. 16, 1869; *New York Tribune*, July 21, 29, Aug. 9, 13, 1869; *Omaha Herald*, quoted in *New York Tribune*, Aug. 14, 1869.

20. Gyory, "Rolling," 44–45.

21. *History of Berkshire County, Massachusetts* (New York, 1885), 1:536, 577; W. F. Spear, *History of North Adams, Massachusetts, 1749–1885* (North Adams, 1885), 83–85; "A Model Shoe Factory," *Adams Transcript*, Mar. 24, 1870; *Springfield Republican*, June 10, 18, 1870.

22. Gyory, "Rolling," 57–58; Frederick Rudolf, "Chinamen in Yankeedom: Antiunionism in Massachusetts in 1870," *American Historical Review* 53 (Oct. 1947): 7–9, 12–13.

23. *Berkshire County*, 1:536, 577; Rudolf, "Chinamen," 2–28; *New York Herald*, June 16, 1870.

24. *Newark Daily Advertiser*, Sept. 22, 1870; *New York World*, Sept. 22, 1870; *Frank Leslie's Illustrated*, Mar. 11, 1971. Although Hervey's factory was commonly referred to as being in South Belleville, New Jersey, it was actually located in North Arlington, New Jersey. To avoid confusion, however, I will generally use "South Belleville."

25. *New York Tribune*, July 1, 1870; *New York Sun*, July 1, 1870.

26. *New York Sun*, July 1, 1870; *New York Herald*, July 1, 1870; *New York Tribune*, July 1, 1870, *New York World*, July 1, 1870.

27. *New York World*, Sept. 29, 1870; *New York Star*, Sept. 29, 1870.

28. Miller, *Unwelcome*, 145.

29. *New York Herald*, June 16, 27, 1870.

30. Ibid., June 16, 21, 23, 27, 1870.

31. Foner, *Reconstruction*, 261, 272–73; Miller, *Unwelcome*, 168; *New-York Times*, Oct. 5, 1852; *New York Herald*, Apr. 26, 1852, Dec. 12, 1853, July 5, 15, 1868, Aug. 3, 14, 1869.

32. Michael O'Malley, "Specie and Species: Race and the Money Question in Nineteenth-Century America," *American Historical Review* 99, no. 2 (1994): 369–95. See also Nell Irwin Painter, "Thinking about the Languages of Money and Race: A Response to Michael O'Malley, 'Specie and Species'," *American Historical Review* 99, no. 2 (1994): 399.

33. *New-York Times*, Aug. 18, 1869. For similar ideological arguments expressed by West Coast entrepreneurs, see Crocker's testimony. Charles Crocker, *Report of Committees of the Senate of the United States for the Second Session of the Forty-fourth Congress, 1876–1877* (Washington, D.C., 1877), 3:666–68. See also *Albany Evening Journal*, July 21, 1869; Miller, *Unwelcome*, 172.

34. *New York World,* Sept. 29, 1870; *New York Star,* Sept. 29, 1870.

35. Russell H. Conwell, *Why and How: Why the Chinese Emigrate, and the Means They Adopt for the Purpose of Reaching America—With Sketches of Travel, Amusing Incidents, Social Customs, &c.* (Boston, 1871); Miller, *Unwelcome,* 182–83; *New York Herald,* May 12, June 11, 1869, May 12, 29, June 26, Oct. 6, 25, 1870; *New York World,* Sept. 29, 1870.

36. Candace Stone, *Dana and the Sun* (New York: Dodd, Mead, and Co., 1938), 341–42; Foner, *Reconstruction,* 225, 481.

37. Wendell Phillips, "The Chinese," *National Standard,* July 30, 1870.

38. Lydia Maria Child, letter, *National Standard,* Sept. 7, 1870; William Lloyd Garrison, "Hostility to the Chinese," *New York Independent,* Aug. 18, 1870; Bryant to Miss J. Dewey, Jan. 21, 1875, in Parke Godwin, *A Biography of William Cullen Bryant, with Extracts from His Private Correspondence* (1883; reprint New York: Russell and Russell, 1967), 2:360.

39. *Newark Daily Advertiser,* Oct. 8, 10, 21, Nov. 22, 1870. Advertisements for the talk borrowed from Bret Harte's poem "Truthful James," which is discussed in chapter 9.

40. Ibid.; Mrs. S. L. Baldwin, "The Chinese in America," *Christian Advocate* 66 (May 26, 1887): 4–5; Mrs. S. L. Baldwin, *Must the Chinese Go? An Examination of the Chinese Question* (New York, 1890); Miller, *Unwelcome,* 77; *New York Tribune,* Dec. 7, 1885; *New York Herald,* Sept. 30, 1870.

41. Mink, *Old Labor,* 77–79; Coolidge, *Chinese,* 357–77. For the most detailed study on the Chinese American occupational structure of that time period, see Ping Chiu, *Chinese Labor in California, 1850–1880* (Madison: Wisconsin State Historical Society, 1963).

42. Mink, *Old Labor,* 78–79; Sandemeyer, *Anti-Chinese,* 47–48.

43. *New York Herald,* June 24, 1870; *New-York Times,* Dec. 2, 1870. The anti-anti-Irish and anti-nonwhite stance was to become a hallmark in Democratic Party politics. See J. Baker, *Affairs of Party,* 212–58.

44. *Harper's Weekly,* Feb. 18, 1871; *New York Herald,* Feb. 3, 1871.

45. Swinton, *New Issue; New York Tribune,* June 30, Aug. 27, 1870; Marc Ross, "John Swinton, Journalist and Reformer: The Active Years, 1857–1887," Ph.D. diss, New York Univ., 1969.

46. Swinton, *New Issue,* cover, 6–8. For more on Swinton, see Norman J. Ware, *The Labor Movement in the United States, 1860–1895: A Study in Democracy* (New York: D. Appleton and Co., 1929); Gary M. Fink, ed., *Biographical Dictionary of American Labor Leaders* (Westport, Conn.: Greenwood Press, 1974), 346–47; Dumas Malone, ed., *Dictionary of American Biography* (New York: Charles Scribner's Sons, 1936), 252; and James Grant Wilson and John Fiske, eds., *Appleton's Cyclopaedia of American Biography* (New York, 1889). For a more contemporary biographical sketch of Swinton, see Garlin, *Three American Radicals.*

47. Swinton, *New Issue,* cover, 6–8.

48. Gyory, "Rolling," 75. While I appreciate Gyory's analysis of the differences between Swinton's position and much of the trade-union movement, I believe he un-

derestimates how much the labor movement soon went in the direction of Swinton's 1870 position.

49. B. Anderson, *Imagined*, 129–40; *New York Herald*, June 18, 1870.

50. *New York Herald*, June 18, 1870.

51. John William Draper, *Thoughts on the Future Civil Policy of America* (New York, 1865), 94.

52. On Draper, see Bender, *Intellect*, 106–7; on the civic-cultural aspirations and failures of the University of the City of New York (or New York University), see ibid., 90–104.

53. Draper, *Thoughts*, iv, 107.

54. Ibid., 102–6, 143–44.

55. Ibid., 108–9, 11–12.

56. Ibid., 172–73, 112–13.

57. Ibid., 273, 115–26, 145, 172.

58. Editorial, *New-York Times*, Sept. 3, 1865. See also editorials, *New-York Times*, May 17, June 7, 1868.

59. For the "California thesis" argument, see Coolidge, *Chinese*.

60. O'Malley, "Specie and Species," 377–78.

61. Horace Greeley, *Essays Designed to Elucidate the Science of Political Economy* . . . (Philadelphia, 1869), 83.

62. Lawrence W. Levine, *Highbrow Lowbrow: The Emergence of Cultural Hierarchy in America* (Cambridge: Harvard Univ. Press, 1988).

Chapter 9: Visualizing "Ah Sin"

1. Bret Harte, "Plain Language from Truthful James," *Overland Monthly* 5 (Sept. 1870): 287–88; Robert Ford, *American Humorists* (London, 1897), 85, quoted in Fenn, *Ah Sin*, xiii.

2. Henry W. Boynton, *Bret Harte* (New York: McLure, Philips, 1903), 111–14, quoted in Fenn, *Ah Sin*, xiii.

3. Peter Gay, *The Bourgeois Experience: Victoria to Freud* (New York: Oxford Univ. Press, 1984), vol. 1, *Education of the Senses*, 45–56.

4. Barbara Maria Stafford, *Body Criticism: Imaging the Unseen in Enlightenment Art and Medicine* (Cambridge: MIT Press, 1991), 2. Eric Lott addresses these complex dynamics between audience and performers, blacks and whites. Eric Lott, *Love and Theft: Blackface Minstrelsy and the American Working Class* (New York: Oxford Univ. Press, 1993).

5. Albert B. Paine, *Thomas Nast* (New York: Chelsea House, 1980), 5–15.

6. Ibid., 16–18, 21, 28–29; Morton Keller, *The Art and Politics of Thomas Nast* (New York: Oxford Univ. Press, 1968), 6–9, 11–38, 39–45. The American appetite for political art was first whetted by the patriotic enthusiasms stirred by the War of 1812. This early political art celebrated the rise of American nationalism and mused on the foibles of party politicians. The figures of Columbia, representing Protestant-inflected freedom, civilization, and enlightenment, and Uncle Sam (also known as Brother Jonathan)

first appeared at this time. The Civil War became the great thematic vehicle for the next generation of graphic artists.

7. *Harper's Weekly,* Nov. 20, 1868.

8. Ibid., July 18, 1868. The Chinese man in this drawing is essentially the same as "John Confucius," even though Nast did not use that name for the character until March 8, 1879. For example, see *Harper's Weekly,* July 18, 1868, Mar. 8, 1879. "John Confucius" was probably modeled on one of the two Chinese ambassadors, "Chih-Tajin" and "Sun-Tajin," who had come to the United States with Anson Burlingame the month before. A woodcut based on a photograph by Mathew Brady was published in June 1868. The hat with feather tassels, the moustaches, and the high cheekbones were incorporated into Nast's drawing "The Chinese Embassy," *Harper's Weekly,* June 13, 1868. For a similar image of the same grouping, see also "Chinese Embassy to Foreign Powers," a steel engraving print by Johnson, Fry, and Co. of New York City, Wong Ching Foo Collection.

9. *Harper's Weekly,* Feb. 26, 1870.

10. Ibid., Feb. 25, 1871, Apr. 1, 1882, July 23, 1870.

11. Ibid., Feb. 18, 1871.

12. Ibid., Sept. 13, Mar. 22, 1879, Jan. 31, 1880.

13. Ibid., Feb. 8, 1879.

14. For Kearney and Blaine, see ibid., Feb. 8, Mar. 8, 15, 22, Sept. 13, 1879, Jan. 21, Mar. 20, 1880.

15. Ibid., Mar. 20 1880. On the carnivalesque, see Stallybrass and White, *Transgression,* 6–20.

16. *Harper's Weekly,* Mar. 8, 1879.

17. Ibid., Mar. 15, 1879.

18. Keller, *Nast,* 217–21.

19. *Harper's Weekly,* July 16, 1870.

20. Ibid., Aug. 6, 1870.

21. Ibid., Feb. 8, Sept. 13, 1879, July 29, 1876, Dec. 28, 1878, Mar. 8, 1879, Apr. 10, 1878.

22. Ibid., Aug. 7, 1869.

23. Ibid., May 22, 1880. For more on the stage and visual-representational phenomenon of yellowface, see Tchen, "Believing Is Seeing," 15–18. On the phenomenon of impersonation, see Elaine K. Ginsberg, "The Politics of Passing," in *Passing and the Fictions of Identity,* ed. Elaine K. Ginsberg (Durham, N.C.: Duke Univ. Press, 1996), 1–18.

24. *Harper's Weekly,* Mar. 15, 1879.

25. On July 31, 1876, *Ah Sin* opened at Augustin Daly's Fifth Avenue Theater starring Charles T. Parsloe Jr., "the great impersonator of Chinese character." Foster, *Literature,* 28–29; Stuart W. Hyde, "The Chinese Stereotype in American Melodrama," *California Historical Society Quarterly* 5 (1955): 362.

26. *Harper's Weekly,* Mar. 8, 15, 1879.

27. David Grimstead, *Melodrama Unveiled: American Theater and Culture, 1800–1850* (Berkeley: Univ. of California Press, 1987).

28. Keller, *Nast*, 111, 110, 40, 243.

29. Paine, *Nast*, 217–21; *Harper's Weekly*, May 20, 1882.

30. Keller, *Nast*, 326; Paine, *Nast*, 122–23; Richard Samuel West, *Satire on Stone: The Political Cartoons of Joseph Keppler* (Urbana: Univ. of Illinois Press, 1988), 125–28.

31. Mayor Kelley appears in Keppler, "King or Clown—Which?" *Puck*, Aug. 13, 1879.

32. *Puck*, Mar. 12, 1880. The anti-Irish, anti-worker, pro–Chinese immigration stand expressed in this drawing was repeated in Keppler's "Uncle Sam's Lodging House," *Puck*, June 7, 1882, and F. Gratz's "The Anti-Chinese Wall," n.d., Wong Ching Foo Collection.

33. West, *Satire*, 5–8, 28–29, 64; Lewis Perry Curtis, *Apes and Angels: The Irishman in Victorian Caricature* (Washington, D.C.: Smithsonian Institution Press, 1971), 58–67.

34. An opponent of women's suffrage, Keppler also mocked women in this cartoon. The hopelessly naive genteel women who welcome the Chinese off the train from San Francisco are as much an object of humor as the grotesque Irishwoman, unsuitably dressed in stylish clothing, whom the Chinese cook has just displaced.

35. Wilentz, *Chants*, 257–71; Stansell, *City of Women*, 89–101. For a fuller discussion of the relations and representation of Irish and Chinese in New York, see John Kuo Wei Tchen, "Quimbo Appo's Fear of Fenians: Chinese-Irish-Anglo Relations in New York City," in *The New York Irish*, ed. Ronald H. Bayor and Timothy J. Meagher (Baltimore: Johns Hopkins Univ. Press, 1996), 125–52.

36. Robert C. Toll, *Blacking Up: The Minstrel Show in Nineteenth-Century America* (New York: Oxford Univ. Press, 1974), 177–79. For an excellent analysis of the role of blackface in American culture, see Lott, *Love and Theft*. See also Richard Moody, *Ned Harrigan: From Corlear's Hook to Herald Square* (Chicago: Nelson-Hall, 1980), 5, 170.

37. J. Baker, *Affairs of Party*, 212–60; Alexander Saxton, *The Rise and Fall of the White Republic* (New York: Verso, 1990), 165–82.

38. Edward Harrigan, *Mulligan Guard Chowder*, 1879, Edward Harrigan Papers, Manuscripts and Archives Section, New York Public Library.

39. Harrigan, *The Mulligans' Silver Wedding*, act 2, scene 7. See also Edward Harrigan, *The O'Reagans*, 1886, Edward Harrigan Papers, Manuscripts and Archives Section, New York Public Library.

40. David R. Roediger, *The Wages of Whiteness: Race and the Making of the American Working Class* (New York: Verso, 1991), 133–63; R. Williams, *Hierarchical Structures*, 131–47.

41. For more on stereotypes, see Wu, *Yellow Peril*.

42. "A 'Heathen Chinee' in Love," *Newark Daily Advertiser*, Jan. 20, 1870; "The Heathen Chinee," *New York World*, Sept. 22, 1870; "The Heathen Chinee in Our Midst," *Newark Daily Advertiser*, Sept. 22, 1870; "The Chinese Puzzle," *New York Star*, Sept. 29, 1870; "The Chinese Puzzle," *New York World*, Sept. 29, 1870; "Belleville Chinamen's New Year's," *Newark Daily Advertiser*, Feb. 17, 1871; "A Chinese Holi-

day," *Newark Daily Advertiser,* Dec. 20, 1872; "The Heathen Chinee Love Case," *Newark Daily Advertiser,* Jan. 21, 873.

43. "The Heathen Chinee," *New York World,* Sept. 22, 1870; "Orientalism in New England," *New York Herald,* June 19, 1870. "Charlie" was commonly used to refer to any Chinese laundry worker.

44. This discussion of how Ah Sin became a part of the popular political imagination is largely based on the work of William P. Fenn. Fenn, *Ah Sin,* xi–xii, 45–47. For examples of how Ah Sin is referenced, see Hon. William Mungen, speech before the House of Representatives, *Congressional Globe,* 41st Cong., 3rd sess., 1871, 43, pt. 1: 354; *New York Tribune,* Oct. 1, 1870. See also "The Heathen Chinee," sheet music, words by Bret Harte, music by Henry Tucker (New York, 1871).

Chapter 10: Building Community

1. Federal Census Manuscripts, New York County, 1880 (Washington, D.C.). According to the 1855, 1865, and 1870 Census Manuscripts, the absolute numbers of Chinese remained fairly steady. In the 1855 census, 64 Chinese were listed in New York City; in 1865, 63 were counted; in 1870, 65 were recorded. These numbers were neither large nor growing. How reliable were these counts? It seems reasonable to assume that immigrants who did not speak English might be underreported because of the simple inability of the census taker to locate and communicate with them. In addition, sailors and non-home-based working households were probably significantly underreported. New York–based sailors who lived in boardinghouses when in port were probably not reported. Moreover, hired as government functionaries with varying degrees of dedication and knowledge, the European American census takers brought their own biases to these temporary and politically connected jobs. Chinese, in brief, were probably more heavily undercounted than their European American neighbors.

2. Federal Census Manuscripts, New York County, 1870 (Washington, D.C.). Unless otherwise noted, the information in this chapter is gathered from this source.

3. "Keeping house" most likely denoted unpaid labor, which sometimes meant that the women took care of the home and family and sometimes meant that they also managed the room and food of boarders. *New York Daily Tribune,* Oct. 8, 1870.

4. Ibid.

5. *New-York Times,* Dec. 26, 1873.

6. Federal Census Manuscripts, Fourth Ward Manufacturers, New York County, 1870.

7. Cooper, *Once a Cigar Maker,* 10–40.

8. *New York Tribune,* June 21, 1885; *New York Daily Tribune,* Oct. 8, 1870. A Colorado newspaper blurb reiterated the 1870 *Tribune* article's erroneous claim: "By a careful estimate the number of Chinese in New York City is placed at only 200. The number has been diminished rather than increased since the 1st of January. Not enough have come in to offset those who have gone away. All the Chinamen come from Havana. In no instance is one known to have come from San Francisco." *Daily Central City Register* (Colorado), Oct. 20, 1870.

9. Cooper, *Once a Cigar Maker*, 15; Wilentz, *Chants*, 128; Saxton, *Indispensable Enemy*, 6.

10. *New York Herald*, Dec. 26, 1869; *New-York Times*, Mar. 6, 1880; Federal Census Manuscripts, 1880. The 1880 U.S. census indicated that cigar workers were the largest occupation in the Chinese core settlement area (30 percent). See also *New York Daily Tribune*, Oct. 8, 1870, May 8, 1877.

11. Naturalization Records, 1792–1906, New York Supreme Court, New York County Clerk's Office. Many of the women citing England as their country of origin were likely to have been Irish. U.S. naturalization policy required Irish to list England as the country of citizenship they were renouncing loyalty to. At least one unnamed Chinese woman, "very well looking for an oriental, and possessing a mass of jet-black hair at the back of her head," possibly the first to be a resident of the city, was married to a Chinese man in 1869. They ran a boardinghouse for Chinese sailors. *New York Tribune*, Jan. 4, 1869.

12. *New-York Times*, Dec. 26, 1873; *New York Tribune*, May 8, 1877; *Harper's Weekly*, Nov. 22, 1890; *New York Tribune*, Jan. 4, 1869. See the 1855 and 1865 census profiles to see the different ways in which Chinese were classified.

13. For example, see Wong Chin Foo, "The Chinese in New York," *Cosmopolitan* 5 (1888): 308. Although Wong's name was transliterated as "Chin" it should more properly have been "Ching." I thank Him Mark Lai for pointing this out to me.

14. *New York Sun*, Feb. 16, 1874.

15. *New York World*, Jan. 30, 1877.

16. 1857 and 1880 Crew Lists, Port of New York, National Archives. The name seems to have decreased in popularity by 1880. In two sample crew lists from that year, one had only eight of sixty-two named John, and the other only seven of fifty-one.

17. *New York Tribune*, Sept. 6, 1875.

18. *New-York Times*, June 29, 1869; *New York Herald*, July 24, 1869; *Girls, Don't Fool with Cupid*, Songster (New York, 1871). An American lieutenant, John B. Dale, while serving in China on the *Constitution* in 1845, sketched a scene of two men trading. He titled the drawing "John Chinaman trading with Jack Tar." See Jean Gordon Lee, *Philadelphians and the China Trade, 1784–1844* (Philadelphia: Philadelphia Museum of Art, 1984), 40.

19. S. G. McCutcheon, "Scenes and Incidents of Election Day in New York," *Harper's Weekly*, Nov. 13, 1880; Barth, *Bitter Strength*, 180; *New York Herald*, Jan. 20, 1881; *New York Tribune*, Sept. 6, 1875.

20. Naturalization Records, 1792–1906. These wards were known for housing recent immigrants. It may be that as Irish arrivals improved their lot, they moved uptown and also became citizens.

21. *New-York Times*, Dec. 26, 1873.

22. "Chinese Candy Man," *Harper's Weekly*, Sept. 19, 1868.

23. *Scribner's Monthly* 1 (Dec. 1870): 121–22.

24. *Harper's Weekly*, for example, referred to the food in a lower Manhattan "low restaurant" as being "promiscuous" in national cuisines. "Along the Docks," *Harper's Weekly*, suppl., Oct. 21, 1871. For a discussion of the immigrant Lower East Sider's pen-

chant for sugar in later decades, see Elizabeth Ewen, *Immigrant Women in the Land of Dollars: Life and Culture on the Lower East Side, 1890–1925* (New York: Monthly Review Press, 1985), 173–74.

25. Beck, *Chinatown*, 11; C. F. Wong, "New York," 311; *New York Tribune*, June 21, 1885; Federal Census Manuscripts, 1880; *New York Tribune*, June 21, 1885; *New York Sun*, Mar. 7, 1880.

26. Blackmar, *Manhattan*, 197.

27. *New-York Times*, Mar. 21, 1879; *New York Sun*, June 29, 1879.

28. *New York Tribune*, June 21, 1885.

29. Siu, *Chinese Laundryman*, 53; Leavitt Burham, "Chinese Coolies Crossing the Missouri River," *Harper's Weekly*, Jan. 22, 1870; *New-York Times*, Mar. 4, 1880.

30. Van Norden, *Who's Who of the Chinese*, 31; *New-York Times*, Mar. 6, 1880.

31. *Frank Leslie's Illustrated*, June 4, 1870; *New York Herald*, June 4, 1870; *New York Standard*, June 4, 1870; *New-York Times*, Dec. 26, 1873.

32. *New-York Times*, Dec. 26, 1873. For photographs of living conditions throughout this part of lower Manhattan, see Jacob Riis, *How the Other Half Lives* (New York: Dover Publications, 1984).

33. *New-York Times*, Dec. 26, 1873.

34. The "Chinese in New York" article accompanying the Homer drawing describes the altar paintings as depicting a "trio of Buddhist gods." The central figure, however, appears to be Guangung, the god of war and literature. *Harper's Weekly*, Mar. 7, 1874; *New-York Times*, Dec. 26, 1873.

35. According to historian Him Mark Lai, the practice of sending bones back to China began in San Francisco as early as 1857. As yet, it is unknown when this practice began in New York.

36. *New-York Times*, July 8, 1880. In this context *mechanic* was used to refer to skilled workingmen.

37. *New-York Times*, July 8, 1880; *New York Sun*, Mar. 7, 1880. On the *Sanhohui* (Sam Hop Hui), see Jean Chesneaux, *Secret Societies in China in the Nineteenth and Twentieth Centuries*, trans. Gillian Nettle (Ann Arbor: Univ. of Michigan Press, 1971), 13–35.

38. *New York World*, Feb. 28, 1880; Winslow Homer, "The Chinese in New York: Scene in a Baxter Street Club-House," *Harper's Weekly*, Mar. 7, 1874.

39. *New York Tribune*, Feb. 21, 1869.

40. Ibid., Oct. 5, 1869.

41. *Frank Leslie's Illustrated*, Jan. 22, 1870.

42. *New York Evening Post*, May 27, 1875.

43. *New York Tribune*, Feb. 21, 1869. The Confucian term for petty individuals of low morality is literally "small men," or *xiao ren*.

44. *New York World*, July 7, 1870; *New York Herald*, July 7, 1870; *New-York Times*, July 7, 1870.

45. *New York Tribune*, Feb. 27, 1879.

46. Ibid., Feb. 21, 1869.

47. Ibid., Feb. 27, 1879.

48. In 1789 the authors of the United States Constitution limited citizenship to "white" men of property and stipulated that naturalization should take a period of five years. In 1798, during a period of antiforeignism, the waiting period for naturalization was extended from five to fifteen years. Three years later Jefferson was able to reverse the ruling back to five years. From 1800 to 1830, twenty-one of twenty-seven states extended voting rights to all taxpaying white males. New York amended its constitution in 1821. The Fifteenth Amendment, ratified in 1870, stated that the vote could not be denied on the basis of race or a person's previous condition of servitude. *New York Herald,* July 11, Nov. 28, 30, 1878; *New York Sun,* Nov. 29, 1878; *New-York Times,* July 7, 1878.

49. *New York World,* Mar. 23, 1879; *New York Tribune,* Mar. 24, 1879. See also *New-York Times,* July 7, 1878; *New York World,* Mar. 5, 1880.

50. *New-York Times,* Mar. 6, 1880; Hasia Diner, *Erin's Daughters in America: Irish Immigrant Women in the Nineteenth Century* (Baltimore: Johns Hopkins Univ. Press, 1983), 80, 85–86.

51. *Evening Post,* May 17, 1875; *New-York Times,* Mar. 6, 1880. See also Harriet P. Spofford, *The Servant Girl Question,* ed. Leon Stein (Salem, N.H.: Ager, 1977). Chinese men commonly served as house servants in California.

52. For the distribution of Chinese living in New York County and around the state, see the 1855 and 1865 census profiles.

53. "In the Matter of the Petition of Fou Afung," New York Supreme Court, June 19, 1869, New York County Clerk's Office.

54. C. F. Wong, "New York," 297–98; Beck, *Chinatown,* 57–58.

55. Federal Writer's Project, "A History of Belleville," n.d., Belleville Public Library, 61–67; John Kuo Wei Tchen, "Eight Pound Livelihood: A History of Chinese Laundry Workers in the United States," exhibition, New York Chinatown History Project, 1983, Museum of Chinese in the Americas, New York.

56. *New York Tribune,* June 21, 1885; C. F. Wong, "New York," 297.

57. C. F. Wong, "New York," 298.

58. The major study on Chinese laundry operators is by the son of a laundry man. Siu, *Chinese Laundryman,* 23–43.

59. Ibid., 429.

60. For a full discussion of this social interactionalist process, see John Kuo Wei Tchen, editor's introduction to ibid., xxxii–xxxiii. It is worth noting that Chinese fishing families on the Pacific coast did not adopt a sojourning mentality. See Sandy Lydon, *Chinese Gold: The Chinese in the Monterey Bay Region* (Capitola, Calif.: Capitola Book Company, 1985), 22–23.

61. *New York Herald,* Mar. 28, 1880.

62. *New York World,* July 12, 18, 1879.

63. Sylvia Cranston, *HPB: The Extraordinary Life and Influence of Helena Blavatsky, Founder of the Modern Theosophical Movement* (New York: G. P. Putnam's Sons, 1993), 55–63, 80–101, 168–78. Madame Blavatsky's sponsorship of Wong should be understood as part of the broader fascination many notable Americans had with Buddhism and Asian religions, especially among the Transcendentalists. For example, see

Emerson's "Oversoul" and "Self Reliance," in *Ralph Waldo Emerson: Essays, Poems, Addresses,* ed. Gordon H. Haight (New York: Walter J. Black, 1941), 205–23, 119–46.

64. *New-York Times,* Apr. 30, 1877, *New York Herald,* May 8, 1877.

65. Ibid.

66. *New-York Times,* Aug. 17, 1874.

67. Ibid.

68. *Harper's Weekly,* May 26, 1877; *New York Herald,* May 8, 1877. It is interesting to note that Wong described the Chinese government as "good" even though three years earlier he had emphasized the corruption of the empire.

69. *New York Tribune,* May 8, Apr. 30, 1877.

70. *Harper's Weekly,* May 26, 1877.

Chapter 11: Descent to Darkness

1. *Frank Leslie's Illustrated,* Feb. 6, 1858.

2. *New York Tribune,* Dec. 26, 1869.

3. *New-York Times,* Dec. 26, 1856, June 20, 1859, Dec. 26, 1873, Feb. 16, 1874, Aug. 11, 1878. The coverage in the *Times* became increasingly negative.

4. *Daily Graphic,* Mar. 18, 1873, Mar. 26, 1879. See also the *Daily Graphic's* Mar. 28, 1879, follow-up feature on different Chinese gambling games.

5. *Harper's Weekly,* Oct. 8, 1881; *Frank Leslie's Illustrated,* May 12, 19, 1883. For a comparable discussion of this phenomenon in the Victorian villainization of Chinese and opium in London's Limehouse District (East End), see Virginia Berridge and Griffith Edwards, *Opium and the People: Opiate Use in Nineteenth-Century England* (New Haven: Yale Univ. Press, 1987), 195–205.

6. Bonner, *Alas,* 16.

7. Wiebe, *American Society,* 338–40.

8. Samuel Goodrich, *The Child's Second Book of History* (Boston, 1840), 166. Generations of children were taught by this book through 1886. Cultural differences were explained in terms of inferiority: "The people are not nice about what they eat. Dead puppy-dogs are publicly sold in the streets for food. Rats and mice are frequently eaten. There is a sort of bird's nest which is made into a jelly and is considered a great delicacy" (165–66). See also *New-York Times,* June 20, 1859, in which the reporter noted in subdued language the assumption that Chinese New Yorkers ate rats: "The cooking was done in an adjoining room, out of which there issued an odor of soup, whether of rats or shin-bones we could not distinguish."

9. Beekman Papers, New-York Historical Society.

10. *Yankee Notions* 2 (June and July 1853).

11. Was there an actual basis for this association? The nature of one's diet, in China as elsewhere, depended largely on one's class position and on the bounty of any given locale and season. In the 1880s China boasted a population of some 450 million people to the United States' 40 million. The Chinese had domesticated pigs and dogs for meat in the Neolithic era and were known to hunt wild animals, notably deer and rabbits. They also occasionally hunted wild dog, wild boar, wild horse, bear, badger, tiger, pan-

ther, fox, antelope, and what one historian has called the "common rat" and the "bamboo rat." Historical records indicate that Chinese aristocrats of the Tang Dynasty were known to eat specially prepared dishes of "bamboo rats" and newborn rats along with elephants, pythons, and turtles as delicacies. In A.D. 759 the price of a single rat rose to 4,000 taels cash. Given these economics of red-meat consumption, rats (among other wild animals) were primarily limited to the epicurean proclivities of the elites. The practice of eating rats was sufficiently rare that one eminent food historian of China never saw this practice in his many years of field work. See E. N. Anderson, *Food*, ix. See also *New York Tribune*, May 8, 1877; K. C. Chang, "Ancient China," and Schafer, "T'ang," both in *Food*, ed. Chang, 29, 100–102, 107–8. For a modern and rather sensationalist account of Chinese eating rats written by a Chinese American journalist, see Melinda Liu, "Pass a Snake, Hold the Rat," *Newsweek*, July 29, 1991, 35.

12. *New-York Times*, Aug. 1, 1882. All the following quotations are from this article.

13. Wong Chin Foo, "The Chinese in the United States," *Chautauquan* 9 (Nov. 1888): 216.

14. Ibid.

15. Beck, *Chinatown*, 45–57.

16. "Two minds with but a single thought / Two hearts that beat as one," 1881, Wong Ching Foo Collection.

17. Septimus Winner, "The Coolie Chinee," sheet music (Philadelphia, 1871).

18. [Frank Dumont], "The Chinee Laundry Man," sheet music (Philadelphia, 1871). There is also a tamer, more edited version by Frank Dumont, "The Chinee Laundryman," sheet music (Philadelphia, 1880), reprinted in Lester S. Levy, *Flashes of Merriment: A Century of Humorous Songs in America, 1805–1905* (Norman: Univ. of Oklahoma, 1971), 157–58.

19. E. R. Donehoo, "John Chinaman," *Charities Review* 7 (Jan. 1898): 914.

20. Hal Morgan, *Symbols of America* (New York: Viking, 1986); Jamily Alray, *"Rough on Rats": The 1887 Dream Book and Almanac—A Facsimile of the Original Edition* (New York: Random House, 1971).

21. "The Problem Solved," poster (San Francisco: White and Bauer, n.d.), facsimile in Wong Ching Foo Collection. As Andrew Gyory has properly pointed out, Chinese were associated with a range of animals. I have singled out the association with rats as the most prevalent and instrumental of the identifications. The other common stereotype related to insatiable eating was the portrayal of Chinese as grasshoppers. For more on these associations, see Gyory, "Rolling," 155–60 (grasshoppers on 156).

22. M. T. Caldor, *Curiosity*, in *English and American Drama of the Nineteenth Century*, ed. Allardyce Nicoll and George Freedley (Chester, Vt.: Readex, 1965–84). For a discussion of the hiring of Chinese men as the solution to the shortage of reliable female servants in the Northeast, see Spofford, *Servant Girl*, 165, 167–81.

23. Stallybrass and White, *Transgression*, 145; George G. Foster, *New York by Gas-Light, with Here and There a Streak of Sunshine* (New York, 1850); Matthew Hale Smith, *Sunshine and Shadow in New York* (Hartford, Conn., 1868); James Dabney McCabe, *Lights and Shadows of New York Life* (Philadelphia, 1872) and *New York by*

Sunlight and Gaslight (Philadelphia, 1882); Helen Campbell, *Darkness and Daylight, or Lights and Shadows of New York Life* (Hartford, Conn., 1892).

24. John F. Kasson, *Rudeness and Civility: Manners in Nineteenth-Century America* (New York: Hill and Wang, 1990), 78; Rosenwaike, *Population*, 63; G. G. Foster, *New York by Gas-Light*, 5; Peter Stryker, *The Lower Depths of the Great American Metropolis* (New York, 1866), 3, 4.

25. McCabe, *New York by Sunlight and Gaslight*, 584, 590.

26. For an analysis of the cultural geography of power, see Dolores Hayden, *The Power of Place* (Cambridge: MIT Press, 1995).

27. *New-York Times*, Apr. 29, 1882; *New York Tribune*, Apr. 29, 1882.

28. *New York Evening Post*, Apr. 29, 1882.

29. *Congressional Record*, 47th Cong., 1st sess., 1882, 13, pt. 3: 2973–74.

30. For their voting records, see ibid., pt. 2: 1428, 1707, 1716, 1749–51.

31. Ibid., pt. 3: 2616.

32. *New-York Times*, Apr. 29, 1882.

33. Ibid., Apr. 28, 29, 1882; Keith Melder, "Becoming American: Citizenship," in *A Nation of Nations*, ed. Peter C. Marzio (New York: Harper and Row, 1976), 300.

34. *New-York Times*, Aug. 17, 1874; *New York World*, Apr. 29, 1877.

35. *Chinese American*, Feb. 3, 1883.

36. *New York Tribune*, July 20, 23, 1883; *New-York Times*, Oct. 19, 1887; *New York Tribune*, Oct. 19, 1887.

37. Qingsong Zhang, "The Origins of the Chinese Americanization Movement: Wong Chin Foo and the Chinese Equal Rights League," in *Claiming America: Constructing Chinese American Identities during the Exclusion Era* (Philadelphia: Temple Univ. Press, 1998), 41–63.

38. For the exclusion law's impact on Chinese women, see Sucheng Chan, "The Exclusion of Chinese Women, 1870–1943," in *Entry Denied: Exclusion and the Chinese Community in America, 1882–1943*, ed. Sucheng Chan (Philadelphia: Temple Univ. Press, 1992), 94–146.

39. David C. Hammack, *Power and Society: Greater New York at the Turn of the Century* (New York: Columbia Univ. Press, 1982), 6–7.

Chapter 12: Appo's Demise

1. Appo, Quimbo, Case File 456, Certificate of Insanity, State of New York—Matteawan State Hospital Records, New York State Archives, Albany, 3, 4, 5, 6, 9 (hereafter referred to as "patient notes"). The mention of "boxers" pertains to the Boxer Rebellion in China.

2. "'Devil' Appo's Son, Thought Dead, Is Alive," *New York World*, June 24, 1912.

3. *New York Herald*, Dec. 26, 1869.

4. *New York Tribune*, Oct. 23, 1876; *New York World*, Oct. 22, 1876.

5. *New York Herald*, Oct. 22, 29, 1876; *New-York Times*, Oct. 21, 23, 25, 1876; *New York Tribune*, Oct. 21, 23, 25, 1876; *New York World*, Oct. 21, 22, 1876, June 29, 1912.

6. *New-York Times,* Oct. 21, 23, 25, 1876; *New York Herald,* Oct. 22, 1876; *New York Tribune,* Oct. 21, 23, 25, 1876; *New York World,* June 29, 1912.

7. I admire the tack of Elaine Showalter's analysis of women and madness in Victorian culture and agree with her that a serious historical study must neither romanticize madness and totally identify with the condition nor accept at face value the linking of madness and gender (or of madness and race). Elaine Showalter, *The Female Malady: Women, Madness, and English Culture, 1830–1980* (New York: Viking Penguin, 1985), 5. For background on the pre–Civil War practices of identifying and imprisoning the insane, see David J. Rothman, *The Discovery of the Asylum: Social Order and Disorder in the New Republic* (Boston: Little, Brown, and Co., 1971).

8. Appo, patient notes, "Description &c. of patient," introductory notes; Showalter, *Female Malady,* 37, 75.

9. Appo, patient notes, Oct. 4, 1878, Jan. 1, 1879.

10. Ibid., introductory notes.

11. Ibid.

12. Ibid.

13. Quimbo Appo, Sing Sing Inmate Admission Register (B0143-80), New York State Archives, 22 Dec. 1876, vol. 14, 161. I would like to thank Timothy Gilfoyle for providing me this information.

14. Appo, patient notes, Jan. 1, June 10, 1879, Feb. 26, 1880, Mar. 30, 1885; Jonathan D. Spence, *The Question of Hu* (New York: Vintage, 1989).

15. Appo, patient notes, Aug. 23, 1893, Apr. 30, 1895, Sept. 9, 1896, Jan. 3, 1895, Apr. 30, 1902, Jan. 2, 1907.

16. Ibid., Jan. 1, 1882.

17. For the origins of the term *miscegenation,* see Sidney Kaplan, "The Miscegenation Issue in the Election of 1864," *Journal of Negro History* 34 (July 1949): 277–78; Roediger, *Wages,* 155–56.

Epilogue: The "American Century"

1. For more on American Protestant missionaries and U.S. foreign policy in China, see Jane Hunter, *The Gospel of Gentility: American Women Missionaries in Turn-of-the-Century China* (New Haven: Yale Univ. Press, 1984); William R. Hutchison, *Errand to the World: American Protestant Thought and Foreign Missions* (Chicago: Univ. of Chicago Press, 1987); and M. H. Hunt, *Special Relationship.*

2. Luce, "American Century," 61–65.

3. In varying efforts to establish international norms of fair and standard human conduct, the discourses of international property rights and human-rights violations are often tangled by premises of possessive individualism. For example, see Karen J. Warren, "A Philosophical Perspective on the Ethics and Resolution of Cultural Property Issues," in *The Ethics of Cultural Property: Whose Culture? Whose Property?* ed. Phyllis Mauch Messenger (Albuquerque: Univ. of New Mexico Press, 1989), 1–25.

4. *New York Times,* Jan. 20, 1997.

5. Samuel P. Huntington, *The Clash of Civilizations and the Remaking of World*

Order (New York: Simon and Schuster, 1996). See also the study of conservative British immigrant Peter Brimelow, who proposes reimposing U.S. immigration restrictions on those of non-British racial heritage. Peter Brimelow, *Alien Nation: Common Sense for America's Immigration Disaster* (New York: Random House, 1995).

6. For an elaboration of this point, see Tchen, "Pluralism and Hierarchy."

SELECTED
BIBLIOGRAPHY

Archival Sources

Barnum and Bailey Poster Collection. Bridgeport Public Library, Bridgeport, Conn.
Barnum Collection. Boston Athenaeum Library, Boston.
Barnum Collection. Bridgeport Public Library, Bridgeport, Conn.
Barnum Museum. Bridgeport, Conn.
Beekman Papers. New-York Historical Society, New York.
Billy Rose Theater Collection. New York Public Library at Lincoln Center, New York.
Broadside Collection. American Philosophical Society, Philadelphia.
Brooklyn Historical Society Library, Brooklyn, N.Y.
Bunker Collection. Surry County Historical Society, Dobson, N.C.
Bunker Files. Mount Airy County Library, Mount Airy, N.C.
Campaign Broadsides. Manuscripts Collection, New-York Historical Society, New York.
Chang and Eng Bunker Collection. North Carolina State Archives, Raleigh.
Charles Thomson Papers. Library of Congress, Washington, D.C.
Edward Harrigan Papers. Manuscripts and Archives Section, New York Public Library, New York.
Fonda Collection. New-York Historical Society, New York.
George W. Gift Collection. Southern Historical Collection, University of North Carolina, Chapel Hill.
George Washington Papers. Manuscripts Division, Library of Congress, Washington, D.C.
Harvard Theater Collection. Harvard University, Cambridge, Mass.
Heiser Papers. New-York Historical Society, New York.
Holker Papers. Manuscripts Division, Library of Congress, Washington, D.C.
John Green Papers. Philadelphia Maritime Museum, Philadelphia.
Keying File. South Street Seaport Museum Library, South Street Seaport Museum, New York.
Kishi Collection, New York.
Library Archives. Library Company of Philadelphia, Philadelphia.
Local History Collection. Belleville Public Library, Belleville, N.J.
Margaret Woodbury Strong Museum, Rochester, N.Y.
Museum of Chinese in the Americas, New York.
Mütter Museum, Philadelphia.
Newark Historical Society, Newark, N.J.

Newark Public Library, Newark, N.J.

P. T. Barnum Manuscripts. Manuscripts and Rare Books Room, New York Public Library, New York.

Papers of Albert Gallatin. New-York Historical Society, New York.

Papers of Robert Morris. Queens College, City Univ. of New York, New York.

Parker Papers. Massachusetts Historical Society, Boston.

Rare Books and Manuscripts Collection. University of North Carolina at Chapel Hill.

Rare Books Collection. New York Society Library, New York.

Ronald G. Becker Collection. Special Collections, Syracuse University Library, Syracuse, New York.

Sanders Collection. New-York Historical Society, New York.

Sheet Music Collection. Music Division, Library of Congress, Washington, D.C.

Ship Manifest Files. Library, Peabody Museum of Salem, Salem, Mass.

South Street Seaport Museum Library, New York.

Stewart Culin Papers. Library, Brooklyn Museum of Art, Brooklyn, N.Y.

Theater Collection. Museum of the City of New York, New York.

Thomas Jefferson Papers. Manuscripts Division, Library of Congress, Washington, D.C.

Will of John Jacob Astor. New-York Historical Society, New York.

William Duer Papers. New-York Historical Society, New York.

Wong Ching Foo Collection, Brooklyn, N.Y.

Government Sources

Committees of the Senate of the United States for the Second Session of the Forty-fourth Congress, 1876–77.

Crew Lists, Port of New York. National Archives.

Department of State Documents. National Archives.

Federal Census Manuscripts, New York County, 1870 and 1880. Washington, D.C.

Massachusetts Report of Bureau of Statistics of Labor.

Naturalization Records, 1792–1906. New York Superior Court, New York County Clerk's Office, New York.

New York City Municipal Archives, New York.

New York County Clerk's Office, New York.

New York State Archives, Albany, N.Y.

New York State Census Manuscripts. New York County Clerk's Office, New York.

New York Supreme Court Records. New York County Clerk's Office, New York.

State of New York—Matteawan State Hospital Records. New York State Archives, Albany, N.Y.

Additional Primary Sources

Adams, John. *Diary and Autobiography of John Adams.* 4 vols. Edited by L. H. Butterfield. Cambridge: Belknap Press of Harvard Univ. Press, 1961–66.

Alcott, Louisa May. *Eight Cousins.* Cleveland: World Publishing, 1948.

Alray, Jamily. *"Rough on Rats": The 1887 Dream Book and Almanac—A Facsimile of the Original Edition.* New York: Random House, 1971.

Baker, George M. "New Brooms Sweep Clean." In *The Social Stage: Original Dramas, Comedies, Burlesques, and Entertainments for Home Recreation, Schools, and Public Exhibitions.* New York, 1870.

Baldwin, Mrs. S. L. *Must the Chinese Go? An Examination of the Chinese Question.* New York, 1890.

Barnum, Phineas T. *Selected Letters of P. T. Barnum.* Edited by A. H. Saxon. New York: Columbia Univ. Press, 1983.

Barrett, Walter [Joseph A. Scoville]. *The Old Merchants of New York.* 5 vols. New York, 1863–66.

Caldor, M. T. *Curiosity.* In *English and American Drama of the Nineteenth Century.* Edited by Allardyce Nicoll and George Freedley. Chester, Vt.: Readex, 1965–84.

Campbell, Helen. *Darkness and Daylight, or Lights and Shadows of New York Life.* Hartford, Conn., 1892.

Conwell, Russell H. *Why and How: Why the Chinese Emigrate, and the Means They Adopt for the Purpose of Reaching America—With Sketches of Travel, Amusing Incidents, Social Customs, &c.* Boston, 1871.

de Courtin, Antoine. *The Rules of Civility, or Certain Ways of Deportment Observed in France amongst All Persons of Quality upon Several Occasions.* London, 1678.

Delano, Amasa. *A Narrative of Voyages and Travels.* Boston, 1817.

Denison's Make-up Guide for Amateur and Professional. Chicago: T. S. Denison and Co., n.d.

Destutt de Tracy, Count Antoine Louis Claude. *A Treatise on Political Economy.* Translated by Thomas Jefferson. New York: A. M. Kelley, 1970.

Doggett's New York City Directory, 1850–1856. New York, 1850–56.

Draper, John William. *Thoughts on the Future Civil Policy of America.* New York, 1865.

Drummond, William Hamilton. *The Rights of Animals, and Man's Obligation to Treat them with Humanity.* London, 1838.

Du Halde, Jean Baptiste. *Description de l'empire de la Chine.* Translated by Father Premare. Paris, 1735.

———. *The General History of China, Containing a Geographical, Historical, Chronological, Political, and Physical Description of the Empire of China.* London, 1736.

Dumont, Frank. "The Chinee Laundry Man." Sheet music. Philadelphia, 1871.

———. "The Chinee Laundryman." Sheet music. Philadelphia, 1880.

Elliot, John M. "Eng-Chang." New York, 1839.

Emerson, Ralph Waldo. *Ralph Waldo Emerson: Essays, Poems, Addresses.* Edited by Gordon H. Haight. New York: Walter J. Black, 1941.

Foster, George G. *New York by Gas-Light, with Here and There a Streak of Sunshine.* New York, 1850.

Franklin, Benjamin. *The Papers of Benjamin Franklin.* 33 vols. Edited by Leonard W. Labaree. New Haven: Yale Univ. Press, 1959–78.

———. *The Works of Benjamin Franklin.* Edited by Jared Sparks. Boston, 1836.

Girls, Don't Fool with Cupid, Songster. New York, 1871.

Goodrich, Samuel. *The Child's Second Book of History.* Boston, 1840.

Graves, Jesse Franklin. "The Siamese Twins as Told by Judge Jesse Franklin Graves, 1829–1894." Unpublished manuscript, North Carolina State Archives, n.d.

Greeley, Horace. *Essays Designed to Elucidate the Science of Political Economy....* Philadelphia, 1869.

Gutzlaff, Charles. *The Journal of Two Voyages along the Coast of China, in 1831 and 1832.* New York, 1833.

———. *Sketch of Chinese History, Ancient and Modern.* New York, 1834.

[Hale, James]. *A Few Particulars Concerning Chang-Eng, the United Siamese Brothers, Published under Their Own Direction.* New York, 1836.

Hale, James W., ed. *An Historical Account of the Siamese Twin Brothers, from Actual Observations.* New York, 1831.

Hamilton, Alexander. *Alexander Hamilton's Pay Book.* Edited by E. P. Panagopoulos. Detroit: Wayne State Univ. Press, 1961.

———. *The Papers of Alexander Hamilton.* 26 vols. Edited by Harold C. Suyrett. New York: Columbia Univ. Press, 1961–87.

Hamilton, [Dr.] Alexander. *Gentleman's Progress: Itinerarium of Dr. Alexander Hamilton.* Edited by Carl Bridenbaugh. Chapel Hill: Univ. of North Carolina Press, 1948.

Harte, Bret. *The Heathen Chinee.* Illus. Joseph Hull. Chicago, 1870.

———. *The Heathen Chinee.* Illus. S. Eytinge Jr. Boston, 1871.

———. "The Heathen Chinee." Sheet music. Music by Henry Tucker. New York, 1871.

———. "Heathen Chinee Songster." *Beadle's Dime Song Book* no. 27. New York, 1871.

———. "Two Men of Sandy Bar" (1876). In *The Writings of Bret Harte.* Boston: Houghton Mifflin, 1896–1914.

Havens, Catherine Elizabeth. *Diary of a Little Girl in Old New York.* New York: H. C. Brown, 1920.

Hobbes, Thomas. *The Leviathan.* Buffalo, N.Y.: Prometheus Books, 1988.

[Holbrook, Silas]. *Sketches by a Traveller.* Boston, 1830.

Hone, Philip. *The Diary of Philip Hone, 1828–1851.* Edited by Allan Nevins. New York: Dodd, Mead, and Co., 1936.

Hume, David. "On Luxury." In *Political Discourses.* Edinburgh, 1752.

Hunt, Freeman. *Worth and Wealth: A Collection of Maxims, Morals, and Miscellanies for Merchants and Men of Business.* New York, 1856.

James, William. *The Principles of Psychology.* New York, 1890.

Jefferson, Thomas. *The Life and Selected Writings of Thomas Jefferson.* Edited by Adrienne Koch and William Peden. New York: Random House, 1944.

———. *Thomas Jefferson Papers.* Edited by Julian Boyd. Princeton: Princeton Univ. Press, 1950–86.

Johnson, J. M., and S. C. Swan. "The Chinese Laundry Man." In *The Gint and Came to See Songster.* 1881.

Knight, Franklin. *Monuments of Washington's Patriotism Containing a Fac Simile of His Public Accounts Kept during the Revolutionary War, June 1775–June 1783.* Vol. 4. Washington, D.C., 1844.

Lanman, J. H. "The Chinese Museum in Boston." *Hunts Merchant's Magazine* 14 (1846): 347–49.

Ledyard, John. *John Ledyard's Journal of Captain Cook's Last Voyage.* Edited by James Kenneth Munford. Corvallis: Oregon State Univ., 1963.

Levy, Lester S. *Flashes of Merriment: A Century of Humorous Songs in America, 1805–1905.* Norman: Univ. of Oklahoma, 1971.

Locke, John. *An Essay Concerning Human Understanding.* Edited by Peter H. Nidditch. Oxford: Clarendon Press, 1975.

Luce, Henry R. "The American Century." *Life*, Feb. 17, 1941, 61–65.

Macaulay, Catharine. *An Address to the People of England, Scotland, and Ireland, on the Present Important Crisis of Affairs.* London, 1775.

Mackie, Milton. "The Chinaman, Domestic, Scholastic, Iconoclastic, and Imperial." *Putnam's Magazine* 9 (April 1857): 337–50.

Magoon, E. L. *Westward Empire, or the Great Drama of Human Progress.* New York, 1856.

McCabe, James Dabney. *Lights and Shadows of New York Life.* Philadelphia, 1872.

———. *New York by Sunlight and Gaslight.* Philadelphia, 1882.

Moreheid, Hon. J. N. *Lives, Adventures, Anecdotes, Amusements, and Domestic Habits of the Siamese Twins: One of the Greatest Wonders of the Present Time, Being Two Perfectly Formed Persons, Whose Bodies, by a Singular Caprice of Nature, Are United Together as One.* Raleigh, 1850.

Morris, Robert. *The Papers of Robert Morris, 1781–1784.* Vol. 8. Edited by Elizabeth M. Nuxoll and Mary A. Gallagher. Pittsburgh: Univ. of Pittsburgh Press, 1996.

Murphy, Arthur. *The Orphan of China, a Tragedy, as Performed at the Theatre-Royal, Drury-Lane.* London, 1797.

Perry, Matthew Calbraith. *The Japan Expedition, 1852–54.* Edited by Roger Pineau. Washington, D.C.: Smithsonian Institution Press, 1968.

[Peters, John R., Jr.]. *Barnum's Chinese Museum.* New York, 1850.

Peters, John R., Jr. *Guide to, or Descriptive Catalogue of the Chinese Museum.* New York, 1849.

———. *Guide to, or Descriptive Catalogue of the Chinese Museum of the Marlboro' Chapel.* Boston, 1845.

Putnam, Alfred P. *A Noble Life: A Discourse Commemorative of Abiel Abbot Low, Delivered in the Church of the Saviour, Brooklyn, N.Y.* Boston, 1893.

Riis, Jacob. *How the Other Half Lives.* New York: Dover Publications, 1984.

Robin, Abbé. *New Travels through North America: In a Series of Letters . . . in the Year 1781.* 1783; reprint New York: New York Times, 1969.

Rode's New York City Directory, 1850–1856. New York, 1850–56.

Sabine, William H. W., ed. *Historical Memoirs From 16 March 1763 to 25 July 1778 of William Smith.* New York: New York Times and Arno Press, 1969.

Saxon, A. H., ed. *Selected Letters of P. T. Barnum*. New York: Columbia Univ. Press, 1983.

Shaler, Nathaniel Southgate. *The Individual: A Study of Life and Death*. New York: D. Appleton and Co., 1900.

Shaw, Samuel. *The Journals of Major Samuel Shaw, the First American Consul at Canton*. Edited by Josiah Quincy. Boston, 1847.

Smith, Adam. *The Wealth of Nations*. London: Penguin Books, 1970.

Smith, John. "A Little Teatable Chitchat, a la Mode, or an Ancient Discovery Reduced to Modern Practice" (1781). In *Dramas from the American Theatre, 1762–1909*. Edited by Richard Moody. Cleveland: World Publishing, 1966.

Smith, Matthew Hale. *Sunshine and Shadow in New York*. Hartford, Conn., 1868.

Spofford, Harriet P. *The Servant Girl Question*. Edited by Leon Stein. Salem, N.H.: Ager, 1977.

Stokes, I. N. P. *The Iconography of Manhattan Island, 1498–1909*. 6 vols. New York: Dodd, 1915–28.

Stryker, Peter. *The Lower Depths of the Great American Metropolis*. New York, 1866.

Swinton, John. *The New Issue: The Chinese-American Question*. New York, 1870.

Thornburn, Grant. *Forty Years' Residence in America*. Boston, 1834.

Trow's New York City Directory, 1850–1856. New York, 1850–56.

Van Evrie, John H. *Negroes and Negro "Slavery": The First an Inferior Race, the Latter Its Normal Condition*. New York, 1861.

Van Norden, Warner M. *Who's Who of the Chinese in New York*. New York: Warner Van Norden, 1918.

Washington, George. *Diaries of George Washington*. 4 vols. Edited by John C. Fitzpatrick. Boston: Houghton Mifflin, 1925.

———. *The Writings of George Washington from the Original Manuscript Sources, 1745–1799*. 39 vols. Edited by John C. Fitzpatrick. Washington, D.C.: United States Government Printing Office, 1931–44.

Winner, Septimus. "The Coolie Chinee." Sheet music. Philadelphia, 1871.

Young, Jenny. *The Ceramic Art: A Compendium of the History and Manufacture of Pottery and Porcelain*. New York, 1879.

Secondary Sources

Agnew, Jean-Christophe. *Worlds Apart: The Market and the Theater in Anglo-American Thought, 1550–1750*. Cambridge: Cambridge Univ. Press, 1986.

Ahmad, Aijaz. *In Theory: Classes, Nations, Literatures*. London: Verso, 1992.

Albion, Robert Greenhalgh. *The Rise of New York Port, 1815–1860*. 1939; reprint Boston: Northeastern Univ. Press, 1984.

Aldridge, A. Owen. "China in Early American Writing." Unpublished paper presented at the Library Company of Philadelphia, fall 1989. Deposited at the American Philosophical Society.

———. *The Dragon and the Eagle: The Presence of China in the American Enlightenment*. Detroit: Wayne State Univ. Press, 1993.

Altick, Richard D. *The Shows of London.* Cambridge: Harvard Univ. Press, 1978.

Amin, Samir. *Eurocentrism.* New York: Monthly Review Press, 1989.

Anderson, Benedict. *Imagined Communities: Reflections on the Origins and Spread of Nationalism.* London: Verso, 1983.

Anderson, E. N. *The Food of China.* New Haven: Yale Univ. Press, 1988.

Andrews, Charles M. "Boston Merchants and the Non-importation Movement." *Trans. of the Colonial Society Massachusetts* 19 (1916–17): 92.

Appadurai, Arjun, ed. *The Social Life of Things: Commodities in Cultural Perspective.* Cambridge: Cambridge Univ. Press, 1986.

Appleby, Joyce. *Capitalism and a New Social Order: The Republican Vision of the 1790s.* New York: New York Univ. Press, 1984.

———. *Liberalism and Republicanism in the Historical Imagination.* Cambridge: Harvard Univ. Press, 1992.

Appleton, William W. *A Cycle of Cathay: The Chinese Vogue in England During the Seventeenth and Eighteenth Centuries.* New York: Columbia Univ. Press, 1951.

Arkush, David, and Leo O. Lee. *Land without Ghosts: Chinese Impressions of America from the Mid-Nineteenth Century to the Present.* Berkeley: Univ. of California Press, 1989.

Arneil, Barbara. *John Locke and America: The Defense of English Colonialism.* Oxford: Clarendon Press, 1996.

Ashfield, Andrew, and Peter de Bolla, eds. *The Sublime: A Reader in British Eighteenth-Century Aesthetic Theory.* Cambridge: Cambridge Univ. Press, 1996.

Auslander, Leora. *Taste and Power: Furnishing Modern France.* Berkeley: Univ. of California Press, 1996.

Baker, Jean H. *Affairs of Party: The Political Culture of Northern Democrats in the Mid-Nineteenth Century.* Ithaca: Cornell Univ. Press, 1983.

Baldwin, Frances Elizabeth. *Sumptuary Legislation and Personal Regulation in England.* Baltimore: Johns Hopkins Univ. Press, 1926.

Barth, Gunther. *Bitter Strength: A History of the Chinese in the United States, 1850–1870.* Cambridge: Harvard Univ. Press, 1969.

Basu, Dilip Kumar. "Asian Merchants and Western Trade: A Comparative Study of Calcutta and Canton, 1800–1840." Ph.D. diss., Univ. of California, Berkeley, 1975.

Beck, Louis Joseph. *New York's Chinatown: An Historical Presentation of Its People and Places.* New York, 1898.

Bender, Thomas. *Community and Social Change in America.* Baltimore: Johns Hopkins Univ. Press, 1978.

———. *New York Intellect.* Baltimore: Johns Hopkins Univ. Press, 1987.

———. "Wholes and Parts: The Need for Synthesis in American History." *Journal of American History* 73 (June 1986): 120–36.

Benjamin, Walter. *Illuminations: Walter Benjamin, Essays and Reflections.* Edited by Hannah Arendt. Translated by Harry Zorn. New York: Schocken, 1969.

Berger, Mike. "New York Chinatown." Chinese Chamber of Commerce of New York, Fiftieth Anniversary Issue. New York, 1957.

Berger, Peter L., and Thomas Luckman. *The Social Construction of Reality: A Treatise in the Sociology of Knowledge.* New York: Doubleday, 1966.

Berman, Marshall. *All That Is Solid Melts into Air: The Experience of Modernity.* New York: Simon and Schuster, 1982.

Bernstein, Iver. *The New York City Draft Riots: Their Significance for American Society and Politics in the Age of the Civil War.* New York: Oxford Univ. Press, 1990.

Berridge, Virginia, and Griffith Edwards. *Opium and the People: Opiate Use in Nineteenth-Century England.* New Haven: Yale Univ. Press, 1987.

Blackburn, Roderick H. *Cherry Hill: The History and Collections of a Van Rensselaer Family.* Albany: Historic Cherry Hill, 1976.

Blackmar, Elizabeth. *Manhattan for Rent, 1785–1850.* Ithaca: Cornell Univ. Press, 1989.

Blassingame, John W. *The Slave Community: Plantation Life in the Antebellum South.* New York: Oxford Univ. Press, 1979.

Blumer, Herbert. *Social Interactionalism: Perspective and Method.* Berkeley: Univ. of California Press, 1969.

Blussé, Leonard. *Strange Company: Chinese Settlers, Mestizo Women, and the Dutch in VOC Batavia.* Dordrecht, The Netherlands: Foris Publications Holland, 1986.

Bogdan, Robert. *Freak Show: Presenting Human Oddities for Amusement and Profit.* Chicago: Univ. of Chicago Press, 1988.

Boime, Albert. *The Art of Exclusion: Representing Blacks in the Nineteenth Century.* Washington, D.C.: Smithsonian Press, 1990.

Bolland, Nigel. "Proto-Proletarians? Slave Wages in the Americas." In *From Chattel Slaves to Wage Slaves: The Dynamics of Labour Bargaining in the Americas.* Edited by Mary Turner. London: James Currey, 1995.

Bonner, Arthur. *Alas! What Brought Thee Hither? The Chinese in New York, 1800–1950.* Madison, N.J.: Farleigh Dickinson Univ. Press, 1997.

———. "The Chinese in New York, 1800–1950" (1991). Unpublished manuscript in author's collection, New York.

Boughton, Robert Lee, Jr. "From Clipper Ship to Clipper Ship: A History of W. R. Grace and Co." Senior thesis, Princeton Univ., 1942.

Bourdieu, Pierre. *Distinction: A Social Critique of the Judgement of Taste.* Translated by Richard Nice. Cambridge: Harvard Univ. Press, 1984.

———. *Outline of a Theory of Practice.* Translated by Richard Nice. Cambridge: Cambridge Univ. Press, 1977.

Boxer, C. R. "Notes on Chinese Abroad in the Late Ming and Early Manchu Periods, Compiled from Contemporary European Sources (1500–1750)." *T'ien Hsia Monthly* 9 (Aug.–Dec. 1939).

Brah, Avtar. *Cartographies of Diaspora: Contesting Identities.* London: Routledge, 1996.

Braudel, Fernand. *Capitalism and Material Life, 1400–1800.* Translated by Miriam Koch. London: Widenfeld and Nicolson, 1973.

———. *The Mediterranean and the Mediterranean World in the Age of Philip II.* 2 vols. Translated by Sian Reynolds. New York: Harper and Row, 1972–73.

Breen, T. H. "'Baubles of Britain': The American and Consumer Revolutions of the Eighteenth Century." *Past and Present* 119 (May 1988): 73–104.

———. "An Empire of Goods: The Anglicization of Colonial America, 1690–1776." *Journal of British Studies* 25 (1986): 467–99.

Brigham, David R. *Public Culture in the Early Republic: Peale's Museum and Its Audience.* Washington, D.C.: Smithsonian Press, 1995.

Brimelow, Peter. *Alien Nation: Common Sense for America's Immigration Disaster.* New York: Random House, 1995.

Brindley, H. H. "The 'Keying.'" *Mariner's Mirror*, 1922, 305–14.

Bristowe, W. S. "Robert Hunter in Siam." *History Today*, Feb. 1974, 92.

Brouwer, Norman. "New York's Unusual Visitor: The Junk *Keying.*" *Seaport Magazine*, spring 1991, 18.

Brown, Gillian. *Domestic Individualism: Imagining Self in Nineteenth-Century America.* Berkeley: Univ. of California Press, 1990.

Buck-Morss, Susan. *The Dialectics of Seeing.* Cambridge: MIT Press, 1989.

Bushman, Richard L. *The Refinement of America: Persons, Houses, Cities.* New York: Alfred A. Knopf, 1992.

Butler, William. "New Yorkers' Taste: Chinese Export Porcelain, 1750–1865." *Antiques*, Feb. 1984, 430–37.

Campbell, Colin. *The Romantic Ethic and the Spirit of Modern Consumerism.* Oxford: Blackwell Publishers, 1987.

Caplan, Aaron. "Nathan Dunn's Chinese Museum." Paper deposited at the American Philosophical Society, 1986.

Carnes, Mark C. *Secret Ritual and Manhood in Victorian America.* New Haven: Yale Univ. Press, 1989.

Carrier, James G. *Gifts and Commodities: Exchange and Western Capitalism since 1700.* London: Routledge, 1995.

———, ed. *Occidentalism: Images of the West.* Oxford: Oxford Univ. Press, 1995.

Champagne, Roger J. *Alexander McDougall and the American Revolution in New York.* Schenectady, N.Y.: New York State American Revolution Bicentennial Commission in Conjunction with Union College Press, 1975.

Chan, Sucheng. "The Exclusion of Chinese Women, 1870–1943." In *Entry Denied: Exclusion and the Chinese Community in America, 1882–1943.* Edited by Sucheng Chan. Philadelphia: Temple Univ. Press, 1992.

Chang, K. C., ed. *Food in Chinese Culture: Anthropological and Historical Perspectives.* New Haven: Yale Univ. Press, 1977.

Chauncey, George. *Gay New York: Gender, Urban Culture, and the Making of the Gay Male World, 1890–1940.* New York: Basic Books, 1994.

Chen, Julia I. Hsuan. "The Chinese Community in New York: A Study in Their Cultural Adjustment, 1920–1940." M.A. thesis, American Univ., 1941.

Ch'en, Kuo-Tung Anthony. *The Chinese Insolvency of the Chinese Hong Merchants, 1760–1843.* Taipei: Institute of Economics Academia Sinica, 1990.

Chen Shou-yi. "The Chinese Orphan: A Yuan Play." *Tien Hsia Monthly* 3 (Sept. 1936): 89–115.

Cheng, Lucie, and Edna Bonacich, eds. *Labor Immigration under Capitalism: Asian Workers in the United States before World War II.* Berkeley: Univ. of California Press, 1984.

Chesneaux, Jean. *Pasts and Futures, or What Is History For?* London: Thames and Hudson, 1978.

———. *Secret Societies in China in the Nineteenth and Twentieth Centuries.* Translated by Gillian Nettle. Ann Arbor: Univ. of Michigan Press, 1971.

China on Our Shelves. Exhibition catalogue. Philadelphia: Library Company of Philadelphia, 1984.

Chiu, Ping. *Chinese Labor in California, 1850–1880.* Madison: Wisconsin State Historical Society, 1963.

Choy, Philip P., Lorraine Dong, and Marlon K. Hom. *The Coming Man: Nineteenth Century American Perceptions of the Chinese.* Seattle: Univ. of Washington Press, 1994.

Christ, Carol T., and John O. Jordan, eds. *Victorian Literature and the Victorian Visual Imagination.* Berkeley: Univ. of California Press, 1995.

Chu, C. Y. *Meiguo Huaqiao Gaishi* [A History of Chinese People in America]. New York: China Times, 1975.

Chu, Limin. *The Images of China and the Chinese in the Overland Monthly, 1868–1875, 1883–1935.* San Francisco: R. and E. Research Associates, 1974.

Clarke, Sidney W. "The Annals of Conjuring." *Magic Wand,* Dec. 1928.

Clayton, Lawrence A. *Grace: W. R. Grace and Co.—The Formative Years, 1850–1930.* Ottawa, Ill: Jameson Books, 1985.

Clifford, James. *The Predicament of Culture: Twentieth-Century Ethnography, Literature, and Art.* Cambridge: Harvard Univ. Press, 1988.

Clifford, James, and George E. Marcus, eds. *Writing Culture: The Poetics and Politics of Ethnography.* Berkeley: Univ. of California Press, 1986.

Cmiel, Kenneth. *Democratic Eloquence: The Fight over Popular Speech in Nineteenth-Century America.* New York: William Morrow, 1990.

Cohen, Lucy M. *Chinese in the Post–Civil War South: A People without a History.* Baton Rouge: Louisiana State Univ., 1984.

Cohen, Warren I. *East Asian Art and American Culture: A Study in International Relations.* New York: Columbia Univ. Press, 1992.

Commager, Henry Steele, ed. *Documents of American History.* Englewood Cliffs, N.J.: Prentice-Hall, 1988.

Conner, Patrick. *Oriental Architecture in the West.* London: Thames and Hudson, 1979.

Cook, Jacob Ernest. *Alexander Hamilton.* New York: Charles Scribner and Sons, 1982.

Coolidge, Mary Roberts. *Chinese Immigration.* New York: Henry Holt, 1909.

Cooper, Patricia. *Once a Cigar Maker: Men, Women, and Work Culture in American Cigar Factories, 1900–1919.* Urbana: Univ. of Illinois Press, 1987.

Cott, Nancy. "Notes toward an Interpretation of Antebellum Childrearing." *Psychohistory Review* 7, no. 4 (1973): 20.

Countrymen, Edward. *A People in Revolution: The American Revolution and Political Society in New York, 1760–1790.* Baltimore: Johns Hopkins Univ. Press, 1981.

Cranston, Sylvia. *HPB: The Extraordinary Life and Influence of Helena Blavatsky, Founder of the Modern Theosophical Movement.* New York: G. P. Putnam's Sons, 1993.

Crary, Jonathan. *Techniques of the Observer: On Vision and Modernity in the Nineteenth Century.* Cambridge: MIT Press, 1990.

Creel, Herlee. *Confucius, the Man and the Myth.* New York: John Day, 1949.

Crossman, Carl L. *The China Trade: Export Paintings, Furniture, Silver, and Other Objects.* Princeton: Pyne Press, 1972.

Croy, Homer. "The Amazing Siamese Twins." *New Yorker,* Sept. 2, 1933.

Csikszentmihalyi, Mihaly, and Eugene Rochberg-Halton. *The Meaning of Things: Domestic Symbols and the Self.* Cambridge: Cambridge Univ. Press, 1981.

Curry, Richard O., and Lawrence B. Goodheart, eds. *American Chameleon: Individualism in Trans-national Context.* Kent, Ohio: Kent State Univ. Press, 1991.

Curtin, Philip D. *Cross-Cultural Trade in World History.* Cambridge: Cambridge Univ. Press, 1984.

Curtis, Lewis Perry. *Apes and Angels: The Irishman in Victorian Caricature.* Washington, D.C.: Smithsonian Institution Press, 1971.

Davies, John D. *Phrenology, Fad and Science: A Nineteenth-Century American Crusade.* New Haven: Yale Univ. Press, 1955.

Dawley, Allan. *Class and Community: The Industrial Revolution in Lynn.* Cambridge: Harvard Univ. Press, 1976.

Dawson, Raymond. *The Chinese Chameleon: An Analysis of European Conceptions of Chinese Civilization.* London: Oxford Univ. Press, 1967.

de Beauvoir, Simone. *The Second Sex.* New York: Vintage, 1974.

Dell, Robert M., and Charles A. Huguenin. "Vermont's Royall Tyler in New York's John Street Theatre: A Theatrical Hoax Exploded." *Vermont History* 38 (spring 1970): 105.

Denker, Ellen Paul. *After the Chinese Taste: China's Influence in America, 1730–1930.* Salem, Mass.: Peabody Museum of Salem, 1985.

Dennett, Andrea Stulman. *Weird and Wonderful: The Dime Museum in America.* New York: New York Univ. Press, 1997.

Dennett, Tyler. *Americans in Eastern Asia: A Critical Study of the Policy of the United States with Reference to China, Japan, and Korea in the Nineteenth Century.* New York: Macmillan, 1922.

Detweiler, Susan Gray. *George Washington's Chinaware.* New York: Harry N. Abrams, 1982.

Dexter, Will. *The Riddle of Chung Ling Soo, Chinese Conjuror.* New York: Arco, 1976.

Dimock, Wai-chee. *Empire for Liberty: Melville and the Poetics of Individualism.* Princeton: Princeton Univ. Press, 1989.

Diner, Hasia. *Erin's Daughters in America: Irish Immigrant Women in the Nineteenth Century.* Baltimore: Johns Hopkins Univ. Press, 1983.

Doerflinger, William, ed. *The Magic Catalogue: A Guide to the Wonderful World of Magic.* New York: Dutton, 1977.

Downs, Jacques M. "American Merchants and the China Opium Trade, 1800–1840." *Business History Review* 17 (winter 1968): 418–42.

D'Souza, Dinesh. *Illiberal Education: The Politics of Race and Sex on Campus.* New York: Free Press, 1991.

DuBois, W. E. B. *The World and Africa: An Inquiry into the Part Which Africa Has Played in World History.* New York: Kraus International, 1965.

Dubs, H. H., and R. S. Smith. "The Chinese in Mexico City in 1635." *Far Eastern Quarterly* 1 (Aug. 1942): 387–89.

Dudden, Arthur Power. *The American Pacific from the Old China Trade to the Present.* New York: Oxford Univ. Press, 1992.

Duke, James A. *Ginseng: A Concise Handbook.* Algonac, Mich.: Reference Publications, 1989.

Dundes, Alan. *Cracking Jokes: Studies of Sick Humor Cycles and Stereotypes.* Berkeley: Ten Speed Press, 1987.

Dunn, John. *The Political Thought of John Locke.* Cambridge: Cambridge Univ. Press, 1969.

Durkheim, Emile, and Marcel Mauss. *Primitive Classification.* Chicago: Univ. of Chicago Press, 1963.

Ernst, Robert. *Immigrant Life in New York City, 1825–1863.* New York: Kings Crown Press, 1949.

Espina, Marina E. *Filipinos in Louisiana.* New Orleans: A. F. Laborde and Sons, 1988.

Ewen, Elizabeth. *Immigrant Women in the Land of Dollars: Life and Culture on the Lower East Side, 1890–1925.* New York: Monthly Review Press, 1985.

Eze, Emmanuel Chukwudi, ed. *Race and the Enlightenment.* Oxford: Blackwell Publishers, 1997.

Fairbanks, John King. *Trade and Diplomacy on the China Coast: The Opening of the Treaty Ports, 1842–1854.* Cambridge: Harvard Univ. Press, 1964.

Faragher, John Mack. *Daniel Boone: The Life and Legend of an American Pioneer.* New York: Holt, 1992.

Febvre, Lucien, and Henri-Jean Martin. *The Coming of the Book: The Impact of Printing, 1450–1800.* Translated by David Gerard. Edited by Geoffrey Nowell-Smith and David Wootton. London: Verso, 1984.

Federal Writer's Project. "A History of Belleville." Belleville Public Library, n.d.

Fenn, William P. *Ah Sin and His Brethren in American Literature.* Peiping: College of Chinese Studies, with California College in China, 1933.

Fessler, Loren. *Chinese in America: Stereotyped Past, Changing Present.* New York: Vantage, 1983.

Fiedler, Leslie. *Freaks: Myths and Images of the Secret Self.* New York: Simon and Schuster, 1978.

Fink, Gary M., ed. *Biographical Dictionary of American Labor Leaders.* Westport, Conn.: Greenwood Press, 1974.

Foner, Eric. *Free Soil, Free Labor, Free Men: The Ideology of the Republican Party before the Civil War.* New York: Oxford Univ. Press, 1970.

————. *Reconstruction: America's Unfinished Revolution, 1863–1877.* New York: Harper and Row, 1988.

Foster, John Burt. "China and Chinese in American Literature, 1850–1950." Ph.D. diss., Univ. of Illinois, Urbana, 1952.

Foucault, Michel. *Discipline and Punish: The Birth of the Prison.* Translated by Alan Sheridan. New York: Vintage Books, 1979.

————. *Madness and Civilization: A History of Insanity in the Age of Reason.* Translated by Richard Howard. New York: Random House, 1965.

————. *Power/Knowledge: Selected Interviews and Other Writings, 1972–1977.* Edited by Colin Gordon. Translated by Colin Gordon, Leo Marshall, John Mepham, and Kate Soper. New York: Random House, 1980.

Fowler, Orson S., and Lorenzo N. Fowler. *Phrenology: A Practical Guide to Your Head.* New York: Chelsea House, 1969.

Fox-Genovese, Elizabeth. *Within the Plantation Household: Black and White Women of the Old South.* Chapel Hill: Univ. of North Carolina Press, 1988.

Frank, Andre Gunder. *ReOrient: Global Economy in the Asian Age.* Berkeley: Univ. of California Press, 1998.

Frederickson, George M. *The Black Image in the White Mind: The Debate on Afro-American Character and Destiny, 1817–1914.* New York: Harper and Row, 1971.

Freeman, Douglas Southall. *George Washington: A Biography.* 7 vols. New York: Charles Scribner's Sons, 1948–57.

Friedman, John Block. *The Monstrous Races in Medieval Art and Thought.* Cambridge: Harvard Univ. Press, 1981.

Furber, Holden. *Rival Empires of Trade in the Orient, 1600–1800.* Minneapolis: Univ. of Minnesota Press, 1976.

Gallagher, Mary. "Charting a New Course for the China Trade: The Late Eighteenth-Century American Model" (1966). Robert Morris Papers, Queens College, City Univ. of New York.

Garlin, Sender. *Three American Radicals.* Boulder: Westview Press, 1991.

Gates, Henry Louis, Jr., ed. *"Race," Writing, and Difference.* Chicago: Univ. of Chicago Press, 1985.

Gay, Peter. *The Bourgeois Experience: Victoria to Freud.* Vol. 1, *Education of the Senses.* New York: Oxford Univ. Press, 1984.

Gebauer, Gunter, and Christoph Wulf. *Mimesis: Culture, Art, Society.* Translated by Don Reneau. Berkeley: Univ. of California Press, 1992.

Gebhard, Elizabeth L. *The Life and Ventures of the Original John Jacob Astor.* Hudson, N.Y.: Bryan Printing Company, 1915.

Gilder, Rodman. *The Battery.* Boston: Houghton Mifflin, 1936.

Gilfoyle, Timothy J. *City of Eros: New York City, Prostitution, and the Commercialization of Sex, 1790–1920.* New York: W. W. Norton, 1992.

Gilroy, Paul. *The Black Atlantic: Modernity and Double Consciousness.* Cambridge: Harvard Univ. Press, 1993.

Ginsberg, Elaine K. "The Politics of Passing." In *Passing and the Fictions of Identity.* Edited by Elaine K. Ginsberg. Durham, N.C.: Duke Univ. Press, 1996.

Glausser, Wayne. "Three Approaches to Locke and the Slave Trade." *Journal of the History of Ideas* 51 (Apr.–June 1990): 199–216.

Glenn, Evelyn Nakano. *Issei, Nisei, War Bride: Three Generations of Japanese American Women in Domestic Service.* Philadelphia: Temple Univ. Press, 1986.

Godwin, Parke. *A Biography of William Cullen Bryant, with Extracts from His Private Correspondence.* 2 vols. 1883; reprint New York: Russell and Russell, 1967.

Goldstein, Jonathan. *Philadelphia and the China Trade, 1682–1846: Commercial, Cultural, and Attitudinal Effects.* University Park: Pennsylvania State Univ. Press, 1978.

Gomez-Peña, Guillermo. *The New World Border: Prophecies, Poems, and Loqueras for the End of the Century.* San Francisco: City Lights, 1996.

Gossett, Thomas. *Race: The History of an Idea in America.* New York: Schocken, 1965.

Gould, Stephen Jay. *The Mismeasure of Man.* New York: W. W. Norton, 1981.

Greenberg, Michael. *British Trade and the Opening of China, 1800–1842.* New York: Monthly Review Press, 1979.

Greenbie, Sydney, and Marjorie Barstow Greenbie. *Gold of Ophir.* Clinton, Mass.: Colonial Press, 1937.

Greene, Jack P. *Pursuits of Happiness: The Social Development of Early Modern British Colonies and the Formation of American Culture.* Chapel Hill: Univ. of North Carolina Press, 1988.

Griggs, Veta. *Chinaman's Chance: The Story of Elmer Wok Wai.* New York: Exposition Press, 1969.

Grimstead, David. *Melodrama Unveiled: American Theater and Culture, 1800–1850.* Berkeley: Univ. of California Press, 1987.

Grosrichard, Alain. *The Sultan's Court: European Fantasies of the East.* Translated by Liz Heron. London: Verso, 1998.

Grossberg, Lawrence, Cary Nelson, and Paula Teichler, eds. *Cultural Studies.* New York: Routledge, 1992.

Gutman, Herbert. "The Missing Synthesis: Whatever Happened to History?" *Nation,* Nov. 21, 1981, 521.

Gyory, Andrew. "Rolling in the Dirt: The Origins of the Chinese Exclusion Act and the Politics of Racism, 1870–1882." Ph.D. diss., Univ. of Massachusetts, Amherst, 1991.

Halttunen, Karen. *Confidence Men and Painted Women: A Study of Middle-Class Culture in America, 1830–1870.* New Haven: Yale Univ. Press, 1982.

Hammack, David C. *Power and Society: Greater New York at the Turn of the Century.* New York: Columbia Univ. Press, 1982.

Hanyan, Craig R. "China and the Erie Canal." *Business History Review* 35 (1961): 558–66.

Hao, Yen-p'ing. *The Commercial Revolution in Nineteenth-Century China.* Berkeley: Univ. of California Press, 1986.

Harlow, Alvin F. *Old Bowery Days.* New York: D. Appleton, 1931.

Harris, Neil. *Humbug: The Art of P. T. Barnum.* Chicago: Univ. of Chicago Press, 1973.

Hatch, Nathan O. *The Democratization of American Christianity.* New Haven: Yale Univ. Press, 1989.

Hayden, Dolores. *The Power of Place.* Cambridge: MIT Press, 1995.

Henderson, Daniel. *Yankee Ships in China Seas.* New York: Hastings House, 1946.

Heyrman, Christine. *Commerce and Culture: The Maritime Communities of Colonial Massachusetts, 1690–1750.* New York: Norton, 1984.

Hibbert, Christopher. *The Dragon Wakes: China and the West, 1793–1911.* London: Longman Group, 1970.

Hill, Herbert. "Anti-Oriental Agitation and the Rise of Working-Class Racism." *Trans-Action: Social Science and Modern Society* 10 (1979): 25–44.

Hirschman, Albert O. *The Passions and the Interests: Political Arguments for Capitalism before Its Triumph.* Princeton: Princeton Univ. Press, 1977.

History of Berkshire County, Massachusetts. Vol. 1. New York, 1885.

Hobsbawm, Eric J. *The Age of Capital, 1848–1875.* New York: Vintage Books, 1996.

———. *The Age of Empire, 1875–1914.* New York: Vintage Books, 1989.

———. *The Age of Revolution, 1789–1848.* New York: Vintage Books, 1992.

Hodges, Graham. "'Desirable Companions and Lovers': Irish and African Americans in the Sixth Ward, 1830–1870." In *The New York Irish.* Edited by Ronald H. Bayor and Timothy J. Meagher. Baltimore: Johns Hopkins Univ. Press, 1996.

Hoffman, Henry B. "President Washington's Cherry Street Residence." *New-York Historical Society Quarterly Bulletin* 23 (July 1939): 95–97.

Holt, Thomas C. *The Problem of Freedom: Race, Labor, and Politics in Jamaica and Britain, 1832–1938.* Baltimore: Johns Hopkins Univ. Press, 1984.

Honour, Hugh. *Chinoiserie: The Vision of Cathay.* New York: Harper and Row, 1961.

Horsman, Reginald. *Race and Manifest Destiny: The Origins of American Racial Anglo-Saxonism.* Cambridge: Harvard Univ. Press, 1981.

Horwitz, Morton. *The Transformation of American Law.* Cambridge: Harvard Univ. Press, 1977.

Howard, David Sanctuary. *New York and the China Trade.* New York: New-York Historical Society, 1984.

Hsiong, George. *Chinatown and Her Mother Country.* New York: New China Company, 1939.

Hu-DeHart, Evelyn. "Chinese Coolie Labor in Cuba and Peru in the Nineteenth Century: Free Labor or Neoslavery?" Paper presented at the Latin American Studies Association's Fifteenth International Congress, San Juan, Puerto Rico, Sept. 21–23, 1989.

———. "Coolies, Shopkeepers, Pioneers: The Chinese of Mexico and Peru (1849–1930)." *Amerasia Journal* 15, no. 2 (1989): 91–116.

Hummel, Arthur W. "Nathan Dunn." *Quaker History* 59 (spring 1970): 34–39.

Hunt, Alan. *Governance of the Consuming Passions.* New York: St. Martin's Press, 1996.

Hunt, Michael H. *The Making of a Special Relationship: The United States and China to 1914.* New York: Columbia Univ. Press, 1983.

Hunter, Jane. *The Gospel of Gentility: American Women Missionaries in Turn-of-the-Century China.* New Haven: Yale Univ. Press, 1984.

Hunter, Kay. *Duet for a Lifetime.* New York: Coward-McCann, 1964.

Huntington, Samuel P. *The Clash of Civilizations and the Remaking of World Order.* New York: Simon and Schuster, 1996.

Husband, Charles. "Racist Humour and Racist Ideology in British Television, or I Laughed Till You Cried." In *Humour in Society: Resistance and Control.* Edited by Chris Powell and George E. C. Paton. London: Macmillan Press, 1988.

Hutchison, William R. *Errand to the World: American Protestant Thought and Foreign Missions.* Chicago: Univ. of Chicago Press, 1987.

Hyde, Stuart W. "The Chinese Stereotype in American Melodrama." *California Historical Society Quarterly* 5 (1955): 357–67.

Hymes, Dell, ed. *Pidginization and Creolization of Languages.* Cambridge: Cambridge Univ. Press, 1971.

Isaacs, Harold R. *Scratches on Our Minds: American Images of China and India.* New York: John Day, 1958.

Isani, Mukhtar A. "The Oriental Tale in America through 1865: A Study in American Fiction." Ph.D. diss., Princeton Univ., 1962.

Jackson, Carl T. *The Oriental Religions and American Thought: Nineteenth Century Explorations.* Westport, Conn.: Greenwood Press, 1981.

Jacobson, Dawn. *Chinoiserie.* London: Phaidon, 1993.

James, Marquis. *Merchant Adventurer: The Story of W. R. Grace.* Wilmington, Del.: Scholarly Resources, 1993.

Jay, Robert. *The Trade Card in Nineteenth-Century America.* Columbia: Univ. of Missouri, 1987.

Jennings, Michael W. *Dialectical Images: Walter Benjamin's Theory of Literary Criticism.* Ithaca: Cornell Univ. Press, 1987.

Jones, Jacqueline. *Labor of Love, Labor of Sorrow: Black Women, Work, and the Family, from Slavery to the Present.* New York: Vintage, 1985.

Jones, Robert F. "The Public Career of William Duer: Rebel, Federalist Politician, Entrepreneur, and Speculator, 1775–1792." Ph.D. diss., Univ. of Notre Dame, 1967.

Jordan, Winthrop. *White over Black: American Attitudes towards the Negro, 1550–1812.* New York: Penguin, 1968.

Kaplan, Sidney. "The Miscegenation Issue in the Election of 1864." *Journal of Negro History* 34 (July 1949): 277–78.

Karp, Ivan, and Steven D. Levine, eds. *Exhibiting Culture: The Poetics and Politics of Museum Display.* Washington, D.C.: Smithsonian Institution Press, 1991.

Kasson, John F. *Rudeness and Civility: Manners in Nineteenth-Century Urban America.* New York: Hill and Wang, 1990.

Katznelson, Ira, and Margaret Weir. *Schooling for All: Class, Race, and the Decline of the Democratic Ideal.* New York: Basic Books, 1985.

Keep, Austin. *History of the New York Society Library.* New York: De Vinne Press, 1908.

Keller, Morton. *The Art and Politics of Thomas Nast.* New York: Oxford Univ. Press, 1968.

Kenin, Richard. "Introduction." In *A Facsimile of Frank Leslie's Illustrated Historical Register of the Centennial Exposition, 1876.* New York: Paddington Press, 1974.

Kessner, Thomas. *The Golden Door: Italian and Jewish Immigrant Mobility in New York City, 1880–1915.* New York: Oxford Univ. Press, 1977.

Klein, Melanie. *Love, Guilt, and Reparation and Other Works, 1921–1945.* New York: Free Press, 1975.

Kooiman, William. *The Grace Ships, 1869–1969.* Point Reyes, Calif.: Komar Publishing, 1990.

Kowaleski-Wallace, Elizabeth. *Consuming Subjects: Women, Shopping, and Business in the Eighteenth Century.* New York: Columbia Univ. Press, 1997.

Kulik, Gary. "Designing the Past: History-Museum Exhibitions from Peale to the Present." In *History Museums in the United States: A Critical Assessment.* Edited by Warren Leon and Roy Rosenzweig. Urbana: Univ. of Illinois Press, 1989.

Kuo, Chia-ling. *Social and Political Change in New York's Chinatown: The Role of Voluntary Associations.* New York: Praeger, 1977.

LaFargue, Thomas. "Some Early Chinese Visitors to the United States." *T'ien Hsia Monthly* 11 (Oct.–Nov. 1949): 128–39.

Lach, Donald. *Asia in the Making of Europe.* Vol. 1. Chicago: Univ. of Chicago Press, 1965.

Lai, Him Mark, Joe Huang, and Don Wong. *The Chinese of America, 1785–1980.* San Francisco: Chinese Culture Foundation, 1980.

Lai, Walton Look. "Chinese Indentured Labor: Migrations to the British West Indies in the Nineteenth Century." *Amerasia Journal* 15, no. 2 (1989): 117–28.

———. *Indentured Labor, Caribbean Sugar: Chinese and Indian Migrants to the British West Indies, 1838–1918.* Baltimore: Johns Hopkins Univ. Press, 1993.

Latourette, Kenneth Scott. *The History of Early Relations between the United States and China, 1784–1844.* New Haven: Yale Univ. Press, 1917.

Lebovics, Herman. "The Uses of America in Locke's *Second Treatise of Government.*" *Journal of the History of Ideas* 47 (Oct.–Dec. 1986): 567–81.

Lee, Jean Gordon. *Philadelphians and the China Trade, 1784–1844.* Philadelphia: Philadelphia Museum of Art, 1984.

Lee, Rose Hum. *The Chinese in the United States of America.* Hong Kong: Hong Kong Univ. Press, 1960.

Levine, Lawrence W. *Highbrow Lowbrow: The Emergence of Cultural Hierarchy in America.* Cambridge: Harvard Univ. Press, 1988.

Lewis, Reina. *Gendering Orientalism: Race, Femininity, and Representation.* London: Routledge, 1996.

Lindfors, Bernth. "Circus Africans." *Journal of American Culture* 6 (summer 1983): 9–14.

Liu, Melinda. "Pass a Snake, Hold the Rat." *Newsweek,* July 29, 1991, 35.

Loewen, James. *The Mississippi Chinese: Between Black and White.* Cambridge: Harvard Univ. Press, 1971.

Longmore, Paul K. *The Invention of George Washington.* Berkeley: Univ. of California Press, 1988.

Lott, Eric. *Love and Theft: Blackface Minstrelsy and the American Working Class.* New York: Oxford Univ. Press, 1993.

Lovejoy, Arthur O. *The Great Chain of Being: A Study of the History of an Idea*. Cambridge: Harvard Univ. Press, 1936.

Lowe, Donald. *The History of Bourgeois Perception*. Chicago: Univ. of Chicago Press, 1982.

Lowe, Lisa. *Critical Terrain: French and British Orientalisms*. Ithaca: Cornell Univ. Press, 1991.

Lubbock, Basil. *Coolie Ships and Oil Sailers*. Glasgow: Brown, Son, and Ferguson, 1955.

———. *The Opium Clippers*. Boston: Brown, Son, and Ferguson, 1933.

Ludlum, David M. *Early American Winters, 1604–1802*. Boston: American Meteorological Society, 1966.

Lukes, Steven. *Individualism*. London: Basil Blackwell, 1973.

Lydon, Sandy. *Chinese Gold: The Chinese in the Monterey Bay Region*. Capitola, Calif.: Capitola Book Company, 1985.

MacCannell, Dean. *The Tourist: A New Theory of the Leisure Class*. New York: Schocken, 1976.

MacKenzie, John M. *Orientalism: History, Theory, and the Arts*. Manchester: Manchester Univ. Press, 1995.

MacNair, Harley Farnsworth. *The Chinese Abroad: Their Position and Protection—A Study in International Law and Relations*. Shanghai: Commercial Press, 1924.

MacPherson, C. B. *The Political Theory of Possessive Individualism: Hobbes to Locke*. Oxford: Clarendon Press, 1962.

Magnusson, Lars. *Mercantilism: The Shaping of an Economic Language*. London: Routledge, 1994.

Malone, Dumas, ed. *Dictionary of American Biography*. New York: Charles Scribner's Sons, 1936.

Marcuse, Herbert. *One Dimensional Man*. Boston: Beacon Press, 1964.

Matas, Jill T. *Unstable Bodies: Victorian Representations of Sexuality and Maternity*. Manchester: Manchester Univ. Press, 1995.

Mauss, Marcel. *The Gift: The Form and Reason for Exchange in Archaic Societies*. Translated by W. D. Halls. New York: W. W. Norton, 1990.

Maverick, Lewis A. *China a Model for Europe*. San Antonio, Tex.: Paul Anderson, 1946.

Mayhew, Henry. *London Labour and the London Poor*. New York: Dover Publications, 1968.

Mazumdar, Sucheta. *Sugar and Society in China: Peasants, Technology, and the World Market*. Cambridge: Harvard Univ. Press, 1998.

McClellan, Robert. *The Heathen Chinee: A Study of American Attitudes toward China, 1890–1905*. Athens: Ohio State Univ. Press, 1971.

McCracken, Grant. *Culture and Consumption*. Bloomington: Univ. of Indiana Press, 1988.

McCurry, Stephanie. "The Two Faces of Republicanism: Gender and Proslavery Politics in Antebellum South Carolina." *Journal of American History* 78 (Mar. 1992): 1246–47.

Meagher, Arnold Joseph. "The Introduction of Chinese Laborers to Latin America and the 'Coolie Trade,' 1847–1874." Ph.D. diss., Univ. of California, Davis, 1975.

Meinig, D. W. *The Shaping of America: A Geographical Perspective on Five Hundred Years of History.* Vol. 1, *Atlantic America, 1492–1800.* New Haven: Yale Univ. Press, 1986.

Meisel, Martin. *Realizations: Narrative, Pictorial, and Theatrical Arts in Nineteenth-Century England.* Princeton: Princeton Univ. Press, 1983.

Melder, Keith. "Becoming American: Citizenship." In *A Nation of Nations.* Edited by Peter C. Marzio. New York: Harper and Row, 1976.

Mendez, Cecilia. "Los Chinos culies en la explotacion del guano en el Peru" [The Use of Chinese Coolies in the Exploitation of Guano in Peru]. *Primer Seminario sobre Poblaciones Immigrantes.* Vol. 2. Lima: Consejo Nacionale de Ciencia y Tecnologia, 1988.

Mészáros, István. *Marx's Theory of Alienation.* London: Merlin Press, 1970.

Meteyard, Eliza. *The Life of Josiah Wedgwood.* Vol. 1. London, 1865.

Miller, Christopher L. *Blank Darkness: Africanist Discourse in French.* Chicago: Univ. of Chicago Press, 1985.

Miller, Stuart Creighton. *The Unwelcome Immigrant: The American Image of the Chinese, 1785–1882.* Berkeley: Univ. of California Press, 1969.

Mills, Charles W. *The Racial Contract.* Ithaca: Cornell Univ. Press, 1997.

Mink, Gwendolyn. *Old Labor and New Immigrants in American Political Development: Union, Party, and State, 1875–1920.* Ithaca: Cornell Univ. Press, 1986.

Mitter, Partha. *Much Maligned Monsters: A History of European Reactions to Indian Art.* Chicago: Univ. of Chicago Press, 1992.

Montgomery, David. *Beyond Equality.* Urbana: Univ. of Illinois Press, 1981.

Moody, Richard. *Ned Harrigan: From Corlear's Hook to Herald Square.* Chicago: Nelson-Hall, 1980.

Morgan, Edmund S. *American Slavery, American Freedom: The Ordeal of Colonial Virginia.* New York: Norton, 1975.

Morgan, Edmund S., and Helen M. Morgan. *The Stamp Act Crisis: Prologue to Revolution.* Chapel Hill: Univ. of North Carolina, 1953.

Morgan, Hal. *Symbols of America.* New York: Viking, 1986.

Morse, Hosea Ballou. *The Chronicles of the East India Company Trading to China.* 5 vols. Cambridge: Harvard Univ. Press, 1926–29.

Moy, James S. *Marginal Sights: Staging the Chinese in America.* Iowa City: Univ. of Iowa Press, 1993.

Nandy, Ashis. *The Intimate Enemy: Loss and Recovery of Self under Colonialism.* Delhi: Oxford Univ. Press, 1983.

Nash, Gary. *Red, White, and Black: The Peoples of Early America.* Englewood Cliffs, N.J.: Prentice-Hall, 1974.

Nash, John. *Views of the Royal Pavilion.* London: Pavilion Books, 1991.

National Cyclopaedia of American Biography. Clifton, N.J.: James T. White, 1924.

Negt, Oscar, and Alexander Kluge, *Public Sphere and Experience.* Translated by Peter Labanyi, Jamie Owen Daniel, and Assenka Oksiloff. Minneapolis: Univ. of Minnesota Press, 1993.

Neth, Mary. "Cultural Conflict and Cultural Mixing: Tap Dance and American Popular Culture." Paper presented at the Organization of American Historians' Annual Meeting, 1993.

Nichols, Frederick Doveton, and Ralph E. Griswold. *Thomas Jefferson, Landscape Architect.* Charlottesville: University Press of Virginia, 1978.

Nicoll, Allardyce. *A History of Late Eighteenth-Century Drama, 1750–1800.* Cambridge: Cambridge Univ. Press, 1927.

Niranjana, Tejaswini. *Siting Translation: History, Post-structuralism, and the Colonial Context.* Berkeley: Univ. of California Press, 1992.

Nisbet, Robert. *History of the Idea of Progress.* New Brunswick, N.J.: Transaction Publishers, 1994.

Northrup, David. *Indentured Labor in the Age of Imperialism, 1834–1922.* Cambridge: Cambridge Univ. Press, 1995.

Norton, Thomas Elliot. *The Fur Trade in Colonial New York, 1686–1776.* Madison: Univ. of Wisconsin Press, 1974.

Novick, Peter. *That Noble Dream: The "Objectivity Question" and the American Historical Profession.* Cambridge: Cambridge Univ. Press, 1988.

Noyes, Gertrude E. *Bibliography of Courtesy and Conduct Books in Seventeenth Century England.* New Haven: Tuttle, Morehouse, and Taylor, 1937.

Obeyesekere, Gananath. *The Apotheosis of Captain Cook: European Mythmaking in the Pacific.* Princeton: Princeton Univ. Press, 1997.

Odell, George C. D. *Annals of the New York Stage.* 1931; reprint New York: AMS Press, 1970.

O'Leary, Brendan. *The Asiatic Mode of Production.* London: Basil Blackwell, 1989.

Ollman, Bertell. *Alienation: Marx's Conception of Man in Capitalist Society.* Cambridge: Cambridge Univ. Press, 1971.

O'Malley, Michael. "Specie and Species: Race and the Money Question in Nineteenth-Century America." *American Historical Review* 99, no. 2 (1994): 369–95.

Omi, Michael, and Howard Winant. *Racial Formation in the United States from the 1960s to the 1980s.* New York: Routledge and Kegan Paul, 1986.

Orvell, Miles. *The Real Thing: Imitation and Authenticity in American Culture, 1880–1940.* Chapel Hill: Univ. of North Carolina Press, 1989.

Osajima, Keith. "Asian Americans as the Model Minority: An Analysis of the Popular Press Image in the 1960s and 1980s." In *Reflections on Shattered Windows: Promises and Prospects for Asian American Studies.* Edited by Gary Y. Okihiro, Shirley Hune, Arthur A. Hansen, and John M. Liu, 165–74. Pullman: Washington State Univ. Press, 1988.

Padover, Saul K. *The Mind of Alexander Hamilton.* New York: Harper and Brothers, 1958.

Paine, Albert B. *Thomas Nast.* New York: Chelsea House, 1980.

Painter, Nell Irvin. "Thinking about the Languages of Money and Race: A Response to Michael O'Malley, 'Specie and Species.'" *American Historical Review* 99, no. 2 (1994): 399.

Palissy, Bernard. *The Delectable Garden.* Translated by Helen M. Fox. Peekskill, N.Y.: Watch Hill Press, 1931.

Paolino, Ernest N. *The Foundations of the American Empire: William H. Seward and U.S. Foreign Policy.* Ithaca: Cornell Univ. Press, 1973.

Pateman, Carole. *The Disorder of Women.* Stanford: Stanford Univ. Press, 1989.

———. *The Sexual Contract.* Stanford: Stanford Univ. Press, 1988.

Patterson, Orlando. *Freedom.* Vol. 1, *Freedom in the Making of Western Culture.* New York: Basic Books, 1991.

Pearce, Roy Harvey. *Savagism and Civilization: A Study of the Indian and the American Mind.* Berkeley: Univ. of California Press, 1988.

Pernicone, Carol Groneman. "'The Bloody Ould Sixth': A Social Analysis of a New York City Working-Class Community in the Mid-Nineteenth Century." Ph.D. diss., Univ. of Rochester, 1973.

Pessen, Edward. *Jacksonian America: Society, Personality, and Politics.* Urbana: Univ. of Illinois Press, 1969.

Phillips, Clifton Jackson. *Protestant America and the Pagan World: The First Half Century of the American Board of Commissioners for Foreign Missions, 1810–1860.* Cambridge: East Asian Research Center, Harvard Univ. Press, 1969.

Pimpaneau, Jacques. *Promenade au jardin des poiriers: L'opera chinois classique.* Paris: Musée Qwok On, 1983.

Pocock, J. G. A. *The Machiavellian Moment: Florentine Political Thought and the Atlantic Republican Tradition.* Princeton: Princeton Univ. Press, 1975.

Pointer, Richard W. *Protestant Pluralism and the New York Experience: A Study of Eighteenth-Century Religious Diversity.* Bloomington: Indiana Univ. Press, 1988.

Polanyi, Karl. *The Great Transformation.* Boston: Beacon Press, 1944.

Pomerantz, Sidney. *New York: An American City, 1783–1803.* New York: Columbia Univ. Press, 1938.

Poovey, Mary. *Uneven Developments: The Ideological Work of Gender in Mid-Victorian England.* Chicago: Univ. of Chicago Press, 1988.

Porter, Kenneth Wiggins. *John Jacob Astor: Business Man.* 2 vols. Cambridge: Harvard Univ. Press, 1931.

Pratt, Mary Louise. *Imperial Eyes: Travel Writing and Transculturation.* London: Routledge, 1992.

Quigley, David. "Reconstructing Democracy: Politics and Ideas in New York City, 1865–1880." Ph.D. diss., New York Univ., 1997.

Rabibhadana, Akin. "Clientship and Class Structure in the Early Bangkok Period." In *Change and Persistence in Thai Society: Essays in Honor of Lauriston Sharp.* Edited by G. William Skinner and A. Thomas Kirsch. Ithaca: Cornell Univ. Press, 1975.

Rafael, Vincente L. *Contracting Colonialism: Translation and Christian Conversion in Tagalog Society under Early Spanish Rule.* Durham, N.C.: Duke Univ. Press, 1992.

Reddy, William M. *Money and Liberty in Modern Europe: A Critique of Historical Understanding.* Cambridge: Cambridge Univ. Press, 1987.

Retamar, Roberto Fernandez. *Caliban and Other Essays.* Minneapolis: Univ. of Minnesota Press, 1989.

Riddle, Ronald. *Flying Dragons, Flowing Streams: Music in the Life of San Francisco's Chinatown.* Westport, Conn.: Greenwood Press, 1983.

Ringer, Benjamin B. *"We the People" and Others: Duality and America's Treatment of Its Racial Minorities.* New York: Tavistock Publications, 1983.

Ritvo, Harriet. *The Animal Estate.* Cambridge: Harvard Univ. Press, 1987.

Robertson, Archie. "Chang-Eng's American Heritage." *Life,* Aug. 11, 1951, 78.

Rodecape, Lois. "Celestial Drama in the Golden Hills: The Chinese Theatre in California, 1849–1869." *California Historical Quarterly* 23 (1944): 96–116.

Rodgers, Daniel T. *The Work Ethic in Industrial America, 1850–1920.* Chicago: Univ. of Chicago Press, 1974.

Rodriguez-Pastor, Humberto. *Hijos del Celeste Imperio en el Peru (1850–1900): Migracion, agricultura, mentalidad y explotacion.* Lima: Instituto de Apoyo Agrario, 1988.

Roediger, David R. *The Wages of Whiteness: Race and the Making of the American Working Class.* New York: Verso, 1991.

Rogin, Michael Paul. *Fathers and Children: Andrew Jackson and the Subjugation of the American Indian.* New York: Alfred Knopf, 1975.

Rosenberg, Rosalind. *Beyond Separate Spheres: Intellectual Roots of Modern Feminism.* New Haven: Yale Univ. Press, 1982.

Rosenwaike, Ira. *Population History of New York City.* Syracuse: Univ. of Syracuse Press, 1972.

Ross, Marc. "John Swinton, Journalist and Reformer: The Active Years, 1857–1887." Ph.D. diss, New York Univ., 1969.

Roth, Rodris. "Tea-Drinking in Eighteenth-Century America: Its Etiquette and Equipage." In *Material Life in America, 1600–1860.* Edited by Robert Blair St. George. Boston: Northeastern Univ. Press, 1988.

Rothman, David J. *The Discovery of the Asylum: Social Order and Disorder in the New Republic.* Boston: Little, Brown, and Co., 1971.

Rudolf, Frederick. "Chinamen in Yankeedom: Anti-unionism in Massachusetts in 1870." *American Historical Review* 53 (Oct. 1947): 2–28.

Rutherford, Jonathan, ed. *Identity: Community, Culture, Difference.* London: Lawrence and Wishart, 1990.

Rydell, Robert. *All the World's a Fair: Visions of Empire at American International Expositions, 1876–1916.* Chicago: Univ. of Chicago Press, 1984.

Sahli, John A. "An Analysis of Early American Geography Textbooks, 1784–1840." Ph.D. diss., Univ. of Pittsburgh, 1941.

Sahlins, Marshall D. *How "Natives" Think: About Captain Cook, for Example.* Chicago: Univ. of Chicago Press, 1995.

Said, Edward. *Culture and Imperialism.* New York: Vintage Books, 1994.

———. *Orientalism.* New York: Pantheon, 1978.

Sandemeyer, Elmer. *The Anti-Chinese Movement in California.* Urbana: Univ. of Illinois Press, 1973.

Saxon, A. H. *P. T. Barnum: The Legend and the Man.* New York: Columbia Univ. Press, 1989.

Saxton, Alexander. *The Indispensable Enemy: Labor and the Anti-Chinese Movement in California.* Berkeley: Univ. of California Press, 1971.

————. *The Rise and Fall of the White Republic*. New York: Verso, 1990.

Schama, Simon. *The Embarrassment of Riches: An Interpretation of Dutch Culture in the Golden Age*. New York: Vintage Books, 1987.

Schechner, Richard, and Willa Appel, eds. *By Means of Performance: Intercultural Studies of Theatre and Ritual*. Cambridge: Cambridge Univ. Press, 1990.

Schiller, Dan. *Objectivity and the News: The Public and the Rise of Commercial Journalism*. Philadelphia: Univ. of Pennsylvania Press, 1981.

Schudson, Michael. *Discovering the New: A Social History of American Newspapers*. New York: Basic Books, 1978.

Schurz, William Lytle. *The Manila Galleon*. New York: Dutton, 1939.

Schwendinger, Robert J. *International Port of Call*. Woodland Hills, Calif.: Windsor Publications, 1984.

————. *Ocean of Bitter Dreams: Maritime Relations between China and the United States, 1850–1915*. Tucson, Ariz.: Westernlore Press, 1988.

Scott, Joan Wallace. *Gender and the Politics of History*. New York: Columbia Univ. Press, 1988.

Secor, Robert. "Ethnic Humor in Early American Jest Books." In *A Mixed Race: Ethnicity in Early America*. Edited by Frank Shuffelton. New York: Oxford Univ. Press, 1993.

Sekora, John. *Luxury: The Concept in Western Thought, Eden to Smollet*. Baltimore: Johns Hopkins Univ. Press, 1977.

Sellars, Charles. *The Market Revolution: Jacksonian America, 1815–1846*. New York: Oxford Univ. Press, 1991.

Sessions, Ralph. "The Image Business: Shop and Cigar Store Figures in America." *Folk Art Magazine*, winter 1996–97, 54–60.

Shain, Barry Alan. *The Myth of American Individualism: The Protestant Origins of American Political Thought*. Princeton: Princeton Univ. Press, 1994.

Showalter, Elaine. *The Female Malady: Women, Madness, and English Culture, 1830–1980*. New York: Viking Penguin, 1985.

Silverman, Kenneth. *A Cultural History of the American Revolution*. New York: Columbia Univ. Press, 1976.

Simmel, Georg. *The Philosophy of Money*. Translated by Tom Bottomore. Edited by David Frisby. London: Routledge, 1990.

Sinha, Mrinalini. *Colonial Masculinity: The "Manly Englishman" and the "Effeminate Bengali" in the Late Nineteenth Century*. Manchester: Manchester Univ. Press, 1995.

Siu, Paul C. P. *The Chinese Laundryman: A Study of Social Isolation*. Edited by John Kuo Wei Tchen. New York: New York Univ. Press, 1987.

Skinner, George W. *Chinese Society in Thailand: An Analytic History*. Ithaca: Cornell Univ. Press, 1957.

Smith, Bernard. *European Vision and the South Pacific*. New Haven: Yale Univ. Press, 1975.

Smith, P. C. F. *The Empress of China*. Philadelphia: Philadelphia Maritime Museum, 1984.

Snyder, Robert W. *The Voice of the City: Vaudeville and Popular Culture in New York.* New York: Oxford Univ. Press, 1989.

Soja, Edward J. *The Postmodern Geographies.* New York: Verso, 1989.

Sowell, Thomas. *Ethnic America.* New York: Basic Books, 1981.

Sowerby, E. Millicent. *Catalogue of the Library of Thomas Jefferson.* 5 vols. Washington, D.C.: Library of Congress, 1952–59.

Spann, Edward K. *The New Metropolis: New York City, 1840–1857.* New York: Columbia Univ. Press, 1981.

Spear, W. F. *History of North Adams, Massachusetts, 1749–1885.* North Adams, 1885.

Spears, John R. *Captain Nathaniel Brown Palmer: An Old Time Sailor of the Sea.* Stonington, Conn.: Stonington Historical Society, 1996.

Spence, Jonathan D. *The Question of Hu.* New York: Vintage, 1989.

Stafford, Barbara Maria. *Body Criticism: Imaging the Unseen in Enlightenment Art and Medicine.* Cambridge: MIT Press, 1991.

Stallybrass, Peter, and Allon White. *The Politics and Poetics of Transgression.* London: Methuen, 1986.

Stansell, Christine. *City of Women: Sex and Class in New York, 1789–1860.* New York: Knopf, 1986.

Stanton, William. *The Leopard's Spots: Scientific Attitudes toward Race in America, 1815–59.* Chicago: Univ. of Chicago Press, 1960.

Stelle, Charles C. "American Trade in Opium to China, Prior to 1820." *Pacific Historical Review* 11 (Dec. 1940): 425–44.

Stewart, Watt. *Chinese Bondage in Peru: A History of the Chinese Coolie in Peru, 1849–1874.* Durham, N.C.: Duke Univ. Press, 1951.

Still, Bayrd. *Mirror for Gotham.* New York: New York Univ. Press, 1956.

Stocking, George W., Jr. *Victorian Anthropology.* New York: Free Press, 1987.

Stone, Candace. *Dana and the Sun.* New York: Dodd, Mead, and Co., 1938.

Stradling, J. G. "American Ceramics and the Philadelphia Centennial." *Antiques,* July 1976, 150.

Susman, Warren. *Culture as History: The Transformation of American Society in the Twentieth Century.* New York: Pantheon, 1973.

Swanberg, W. A. *Luce and His Empire.* New York: Charles Scribner's Sons, 1972.

Taylor, William R. *Cavalier and Yankee: The Old South and American National Character.* Cambridge: Harvard Univ. Press, 1979.

———. *In Pursuit of Gotham: The Commerce and Culture of New York City.* New York: Oxford Univ. Press, 1992.

Tchen, John Kuo Wei. "Believing Is Seeing: Transforming Orientalism and the Occidental Gaze." In *Asia/America: Identities in Contemporary Art.* New York: New Press, 1994.

———. "Eight Pound Livelihood: A History of Chinese Laundry Workers in the United States." Exhibition, New York Chinatown History Project, 1983, Museum of Chinese in the Americas, New York.

———. *Genthe's Photographs of San Francisco's Old Chinatown, 1895–1906.* New York: Dover Publications, 1984.

———. "Modernizing White Patriarchy: Re-viewing D. W. Griffith's Film *Broken Blossoms*." In *Moving the Image: Asian Pacific Americans in the Media Arts*. Edited by Russell Leong. Los Angeles: UCLA and Visual Communications, 1991.

———. "New York Chinese: The Nineteenth-Century Pre-Chinatown Settlement." *Chinese America: History and Perspectives*, 1990, 157–92.

———. "Pluralism and Hierarchy: 'Whiz Kids,' 'The Chinese Question,' and Relations of Power in New York City." In *Beyond Pluralism: Essays on the Definition of Groups and Group Identities in American History*. Edited by Edward Landsman and Wendy Katkin. Urbana: Univ. of Illinois Press, 1998.

———. "Quimbo Appo's Fear of Fenians: Chinese-Irish-Anglo Relations in New York City." In *The New York Irish*. Edited by Ronald H. Bayor and Timothy J. Meagher. Baltimore: Johns Hopkins Univ. Press, 1996.

Thomas, Keith. *Man and the Natural World*. London: Penguin, 1984.

Thompson, E. P. *Customs in Common*. London: Merlin Press, 1991.

Tinker, Hugh. *A New System of Slavery: The Export of Indian Labor Overseas, 1830–1920*. London: Oxford Univ. Press, 1974.

Toll, Robert C. *Blacking Up: The Minstrel Show in Nineteenth-Century America*. New York: Oxford Univ. Press, 1974.

Toppin, Aubrey J. "The China Trade and Some London Chinamen." *English Ceramic Circles Transactions* 3 (1935): 36–45.

Torgovnick, Marianna. *Gone Primitive: Savage Intellects, Modern Lives*. Chicago: Univ. of Chicago Press, 1990.

Tsai, Shih-shan Henry. *China and the Overseas Chinese in the United States, 1868–1911*. Fayetteville: Univ. of Arkansas Press, 1983.

Tuan, Yi Fu. *Dominance and Affection: The Making of Pets*. New Haven: Yale Univ. Press, 1984.

———. *Topophilia: A Study of Environmental Perception, Attitudes, and Values*. Englewood Cliffs, N.J.: Prentice-Hall, 1974.

Tully, James. *A Discourse on Property: John Locke and His Adversaries*. Cambridge: Cambridge Univ. Press, 1980.

———. "Rediscovering America: The *Two Treatises* and Aboriginal Rights." In *Locke's Philosophy: Content and Context*. Edited by G. A. J. Rogers. Oxford: Clarendon Press, 1994.

Turner, Mary, ed. *From Chattel Slaves to Wage Slaves: The Dynamics of Labour Bargaining in the Americas*. London: James Currey, 1995.

Turton, Andrew. "Thai Institutions of Slavery." In *Asian and African Systems of Slavery*. Edited by James L. Watson. Berkeley: Univ. of California Press, 1980.

Ukers, William H. *All about Tea*. New York: Tea and Coffee Trade Journal Company, 1935.

Velez-Ibenez, Carlos. *Border Visions: Mexican Cultures of the Southwestern United States*. Tucson: Univ. of Arizona Press, 1996.

Venn, Couze. *Occidentalism and Its Discontents*. London: New Ethnicities Unit, Univ. of East London, 1993.

Ver Steeg, Clarence. "Financing and Outfitting the First United States Ship to China." *Pacific Historical Review* 22 (1953): 1–12.

Waldstreicher, David. "Rites of Rebellion, Rites of Assent: Celebrations, Print Culture, and the Origins of American Nationalism." *Journal of American History* 82 (June 1995): 37–61.

Waley, Arthur. *The Opium War through Chinese Eyes.* Stanford: Stanford Univ. Press, 1958.

Wall, Diana diZerega. *The Archeology of Gender: Separating the Spheres in Urban America.* New York: Plenum Press, 1994.

———. "At Home in New York: Changing Family Life among the Propertied in the Late Eighteenth and Early Nineteenth Centuries." Ph.D. diss., New York Univ., 1987.

Wallace, Irving, and Amy Wallace. *The Two: A Biography.* New York: Bantam, 1978.

Wallerstein, Immanuel. *Geopolitics and Geoculture: Essays on the Changing World System.* Cambridge: Cambridge Univ. Press, 1991.

———. *The Modern World System.* New York: Academic Press, 1974.

Ward, David. *Poverty, Ethnicity, and the American City, 1840–1925: Changing Conceptions of the Slum and the Ghetto.* Cambridge: Cambridge Univ. Press, 1989.

Ware, Norman J. *The Labor Movement in the United States, 1860–1895: A Study in Democracy.* New York: D. Appleton and Co., 1929.

Warren, Karen J. "A Philosophical Perspective on the Ethics and Resolution of Cultural Property Issues." In *The Ethics of Cultural Property: Whose Culture? Whose Property?* Edited by Phyllis Mauch Messenger. Albuquerque: Univ. of New Mexico Press, 1989.

Weber, Max. *The Protestant Ethic and the Spirit of Capitalism.* Translated by Talcott Parsons. New York: Charles Scribner's Sons, 1958.

Weiner, Annette B. *Inalienable Possessions: The Paradox of Keeping-While-Giving.* Berkeley: Univ. of California Press, 1992.

Wertenbaker, Thomas Jefferson. *Father Knickerbocker Rebels: New York City during the Revolution.* New York: Charles Scribner's Sons, 1969.

West, Richard Samuel. *Satire on Stone: The Political Cartoons of Joseph Keppler.* Urbana: Univ. of Illinois Press, 1988.

White, David Gordon. *Myths of the Dog-Man.* Chicago: Univ. of Chicago Press, 1991.

White, Richard. *The Middle Ground: Indians, Empires, and Republics in the Great Lakes Region, 1650–1815.* Cambridge: Cambridge Univ. Press, 1991.

White, Shane. *Somewhat More Independent: The End of Slavery in New York City, 1770–1810.* Athens: Univ. of Georgia Press, 1991.

Wiebe, Robert H. *The Opening of American Society.* New York: Alfred A. Knopf, 1984.

Wilentz, Sean. *Chants Democratic: New York City and the Rise of the American Working Class, 1788–1850.* Oxford: Oxford Univ. Press, 1984.

Williams, Frederick Wells. *Anson Burlingame and the First Chinese Mission to Foreign Powers.* New York: Scribner's, 1912.

Williams, Patrick, and Laura Chrisman, eds. *Colonial Discourse and Post-colonial Theory.* New York: Columbia Univ. Press, 1994.

Williams, Raymond. *The Country and the City.* Oxford: Oxford Univ. Press, 1973.

Williams, Richard. *Hierarchical Structures and Social Value: The Creation of Black and Irish Identities in the United States.* Cambridge: Cambridge Univ. Press, 1990.

Williams, William Appleman. *Empire as a Way of Life.* New York: Oxford Univ. Press, 1980.

Wills, John H., Jr. "Maritime Asia, 1500–1800: The Interactive Emergence of European Domination." *American Historical Review* 98 (Feb. 1993): 83–105.

Wilson, James Grant, and John Fiske, eds. *Appleton's Cyclopaedia of American Biography.* New York, 1889.

Wishy, Bernard. *The Child and the Republic: The Dawn of American Child Nurture.* Philadelphia: Univ. of Pennsylvania Press, 1967.

Wittke, Carl. *Tambo and Bones.* Durham, N.C.: Duke Univ. Press, 1930.

Wong, Bernard. *Chinatown: Economic Adaptation and Ethnic Identity of the Chinese.* New York: Holt, Rinehart, and Winston, 1982.

———. "Patronage, Brokerage, Entrepreneurship, and the Chinese Community of New York." Ph.D. diss., Univ. of Wisconsin, 1974.

Wood, Gordon S. *The Creation of the American Republic, 1776–1787.* New York: Norton, 1969.

———. *The Radicalism of the American Revolution.* New York: Knopf, 1992.

Wood, Neal. *The Politics of Locke's Philosophy.* Berkeley: Univ. of California Press, 1983.

Wu, William F. *The Yellow Peril: Chinese Americans in American Fiction, 1850–1940.* Hamden, Conn.: Archon Books, 1982.

Wyatt, David K. *Thailand: A Short History.* New Haven: Yale Univ. Press, 1982.

Yegenoglu, Meyda. *Colonial Fantasies: Towards a Feminist Reading of Orientalism.* Cambridge: Cambridge Univ. Press, 1998.

Young, Alfred F. *The Democratic Republicans of New York: The Origins, 1763–1797.* Chapel Hill: Univ. of North Carolina Press, 1967.

Young, Linda. *Crosstalk and Culture in Sino-American Communications.* Cambridge: Cambridge Univ. Press, 1994.

Young, Myrl. "The Impact of the Far East on the United States, 1840–1860." Ph.D. diss., Univ. of Chicago, 1951.

Yung, Judy. *Chinese Women in America: A Pictorial History.* Seattle: Univ. of Washington Press, 1986.

Zhang, Qingsong. "The Origins of the Chinese Americanization Movement: Wong Chin Foo and the Chinese Equal Rights League." In *Claiming America: Constructing Chinese American Identities during the Exclusion Era.* Philadelphia: Temple Univ. Press, 1998.

Zhu Jieqing. *Dongnaya Huaqiao Shi* [A History of Overseas Chinese in Southeast Asia]. Beijing: Gaoden Jiaoyu Chubashe, 1990.

INDEX

Abut, George, 232
Acco family, 228
Achoy, Joseph, 85
Adams, John, 11
advertisements: images of Chinese people in, 272, 273, 282
Afoo, John, 232
African Americans, 72–73, 172, 291; images of, in commercial culture, 205, 208, 219; place of, in racial hierarchy, 149, 221–22
Ahchung, Charles, 231
Ah Ken, 82–83
Ah Lee, 253
Ah Lin Wang, 252
Ah Long, 253
Ah Muk, 229
Ahoa family, 226
Ah Sin, 196, 198, 214, 222, 223, 285; origins of, 196, 198; in political cartoons, 209, 211; as stereotype in commercial culture, 198, 199, 275
Ah Sue, 81–82, 235
Ah Woh, John, 247
Ah Yee, Thomas, 247
Alconda, Taysona, 85
Alcott, Louisa May, 158
Aleet-Mong, 120, 122
Alexander, J. W., 264
"American Century," xv, 291, 292
American Fur Company, 45. *See also* Astor, John Jacob
American Magazine, 69–70
American Museum, 118–23, 133
American Revolution, xv, xvi, xix
Ammidon, Philip, 48
Amoy, John, 249
Anderson, Benedict, 190

An Ew, 77
An Fow, 77
An Ow, 77
An Son, 77
anti-Chinese agitation: in California, 170, 186, 187, 194, 203 (*see also* Kearney, Denis); national scale of, after 1869, 167–68, 175–88, 205; violent, 225, 252–53. *See also* Chinese Question
An Too, 77
Appo, George Washington, 285
Appo, Quimbo, 90–93, 96, 159–63, 229, 284–91, 294
A. Row, 77
Arthur, Chester A., 279–80
Arwo family, 226
Ar Yeep, 77, 83
Ashmore, Reverend William, 169
Asine, John, 85
Assam, John, 76
Assam, William, 76
Assing, Norman, 86
Assing, William, 226, 232, 247
Assing family, 226
Astor, John Jacob, 41–43, 44–47, 52–53, 54, 55–56
Atchen, John, 77, 82
Atchen, Louisa, 77
Auchung, John, 227
Auong, John, 233
Ava, John, 83
Aw Hone, 77
Aw Yan, 77
A. Yung, 77

Backus, Charles, 270–71
Baldwin, Esther E., 185–86
Baldwin, Reverend Stephen L., 185–86

Library of Congress
Cataloging-in-Publication Data

Tchen, John Kuo Wei.
New York before Chinatown : Orientalism
and the shaping of American culture,
1776–1882 / John Kuo Wei Tchen.
p.   cm.
Includes bibliographical references
and index.
ISBN 0-8018-6006-7 (alk. paper)
1. China—Foreign public opinion,
American—History—18th century.
2. China—Foreign public opinion,
American—History—19th century.
3. Public opinion—New York (State)—New
York—History—18th century.   4. Public
opion—New York (state)—New York—
History—19th century.   5. New York
(N.Y.)—History—1775–1865.   6. New
York (N.Y.)—History—1865–1898.
I. Title.   II. Title: Orientalism and the
shaping of American culture, 1776–1882.
DS706.T4   1999
303.48'251073—dc21   99-10665
CIP